Fear and Progress

Ordinary Lives

This series focuses on the experience of ordinary people living through times of radical upheaval and oppression in modern history. Drawing on a variety of source materials, authors explore the social, economic, and cultural interactions between different authoritarian states and their citizens. They also shed light on the importance of factors such as class, gender, age, and ethnicity in history. Above all, the books remind us of the profound, daily struggles people often faced under these regimes, and they attest to the resilience of the human spirit.

Published

Fear and Progress: Ordinary Lives in Franco's Spain, 1939–1975
Antonio Cazorla Sánchez

Forthcoming

Ordinary Lives in Nazi Germany
Jill Stephenson

Ordinary Lives in Stalin's Russia
Elena Osokina

Fear and Progress

Ordinary Lives in Franco's Spain, 1939–1975

Antonio Cazorla Sánchez

A John Wiley & Sons, Ltd., Publication

This edition first published 2010
© 2010 Antonio Cazorla Sánchez

Blackwell Publishing was acquired by John Wiley & Sons in February 2007. Blackwell's publishing program has been merged with Wiley's global Scientific, Technical, and Medical business to form Wiley-Blackwell.

Registered Office
John Wiley & Sons Ltd, The Atrium, Southern Gate, Chichester, West Sussex, PO19 8SQ, United Kingdom

Editorial Offices
350 Main Street, Malden, MA 02148-5020, USA
9600 Garsington Road, Oxford, OX4 2DQ, UK
The Atrium, Southern Gate, Chichester, West Sussex, PO19 8SQ, UK

For details of our global editorial offices, for customer services, and for information about how to apply for permission to reuse the copyright material in this book please see our website at www.wiley.com/wiley-blackwell.

The right of Antonio Cazorla Sánchez to be identified as the author of this work has been asserted in accordance with the Copyright, Designs and Patents Act 1988.

Wiley also publishes its books in a variety of electronic formats. Some content that appears in print may not be available in electronic books.

Designations used by companies to distinguish their products are often claimed as trademarks. All brand names and product names used in this book are trade names, service marks, trademarks or registered trademarks of their respective owners. The publisher is not associated with any product or vendor mentioned in this book. This publication is designed to provide accurate and authoritative information in regard to the subject matter covered. It is sold on the understanding that the publisher is not engaged in rendering professional services. If professional advice or other expert assistance is required, the services of a competent professional should be sought.

Library of Congress Cataloging-in-Publication Data

Cazorla Sánchez, Antonio, 1963–
Fear and progress : ordinary lives in Franco's Spain, 1939–1975 / Antonio Cazorla Sánchez.
    p.   cm.
  Includes bibliographical references and index.
  ISBN 978-1-4051-3315-9 (hardcover : alk. paper) – ISBN 978-1-4051-3316-6 (pbk. : alk. paper)
1. Spain–History–1939–1975. 2. Spain–Social conditions–1939–1975. 3. Spain–Politics and government–1939–1975. 4. Political violence–Spain–History–20th century. 5. Political persecution–Spain–History–20th century. 6. Francoism. 7. Franco, Francisco, 1892–1975. I. Title.
DP270.C38 2010
946.082–dc22

                                        2008055193

A catalogue record for this book is available from the British Library.

Set in 10.5/13pt Minion by SPi Publisher Services, Pondicherry, India
Printed in Singapore by Ho Printing Singapore Pte Ltd

1   2010

CONTENTS

CONTENTS

LIST OF FIGURES

Map

Figures

LIST OF PLATES

(Between pages 132 and 133)

1   Women in a sewing shop in Lugo, Galicia, 1941
2   Caves for immigrants in Sabadell, Catalonia, 1950
3   People in a food store, Lugo, Galicia, 1954
4   New homes for immigrants in Sabadell, Catalonia, 1963–5
5   Pro-Franco demonstration in Madrid, December 1970
6   Police repress a demonstration outside a church in Sabadell,
    Catalonia, mid-1970s
7   Journeymen harvesting grapes in Sanlucar de Barrameda,
    Cadiz, 1975

NOTE ON SOURCES
AND ABBREVIATIONS

Most of the original documents quoted in this book come from research conducted at the Archivo General de la Administración (AGA), located in Alcalá de Henares, in Madrid province. The different sections of this archive coincide with the names of the ministries of the Spanish government. Those most often used in this book come from the following ministries/sections: Interior (previously called Gobernación) (AGA-I or AGA-G); Presidencia (AGA-P); Cultura (AGA-C); and Sindicatos (AGA-S). There are other sources quoted from different archives, but most of them come from either the British Foreign Office (FO), located in Kew, London, or from the Spanish Socialist Party Archive at the Fundación Pablo Iglesias (AFPI), located in Madrid.

GLOSSARY OF KEY TERMS

Acción Católica   Catholic Action, an organization that became the focus of political dissent and protest during the dictatorship. It often helped other banned groups carry out their activities.

autarky   Economic policy adopted by the regime that included massive state intervention in the economy and was intended to enable the country to attain full economic independence from world markets. Abandoned in 1959, it cause havoc in Spain's economy.

cacique Local notables that from the mid-nineteenth century controlled politics in Spain. The word also implies corruption and abuse of power.

Caudillo   Title given to Franco by his supporters, roughly equivalent to Duce or Führer.

CNS Confederación Nacional de Sindicatos (National Confederation of Unions). The official name of the Francoist-imposed unions.

Comisiones Obreras   Workers' Commissions. An organization born out of autonomous groups of workers that rejected the official unions. Banned by the dictatorship, it eventually became Spain's largest union.

ETA   Euskadi Ta Askatasuna (Basque Motherland and Freedom). A terrorist group founded in 1958, it seeks independence for the Basque territories located in northern Spain and southern France. Active during the last years of the regime, its activities became more intense after the restoration of democracy in 1977.

Falange   Spanish fascist party founded in 1933, and then fused by Franco with other right-wing groups during the war. It was Spain's only political party for the whole period of the dictatorship. Falange's official name (from April 1937) was Falange Española Tradicionalista de las Juntas de Ofensivas Nacional-Sindicalistas.

hermandades   Brotherhoods, the term used for agrarian unions in the rural areas of Spain.

HOAC   Hermandades Obreras de Acción Católica, the workers' section of Catholic Action.

JOC   Juventud Obrera Cristiana (Christian Workers' Youth), the youth branch of Acción Católica (Catholic Action), which shared HOAC's pro-worker ideas.

Movimiento   The Movement – the name that the Francoists gave to the regime, the July 17, 1936, military rising, and to the post-war Falange party.

Opus Dei   Ultra-conservative Catholic organization closely associated with the dictatorship that provided the technocratic cadres for the economic modernization of the 1960s.

PCE   Partido Comunista de España – the Spanish Communist Party.

PSOE   Partido Socialista Obrero Español – the Spanish Social Democratic Party.

Stabilization Plan   The 1959 plan that ended autarky and allowed the Spanish economy to embrace orthodox, and fairly successful, policies.

STV   Solidaridad de Trabajadores Vascos (Basque Workers' Solidarity) – the name of the main Basque nationalist union.

Modern regions and provinces of Spain

INTRODUCTION

ORDINARY SPANIARDS
IN EXTRAORDINARY TIMES

When a person's name appears in a history book, and it is a name we do not recognize, it is often assumed that this individual lived an ordinary, not particularly noteworthy, life. This is especially true if the reader of the text is an authority on the period of history being discussed. This expression of prejudice implies that most people's lives are ordinary and do not play a key role in history. Yet these same "ordinary" people are the main players in everyday life, and are the ones who enjoy, suffer, or simply endure history's consequences. This book is about the experiences of ordinary Spaniards who lived between 1939 and 1975 when their country was ruled with an iron fist by Francisco Franco Bahamonde, known by his supporters as El Caudillo.[1] It will also consider some aspects of the Civil War years (July 1936 to April 1939), so a period of almost 40 years will be surveyed.

Ordinary people not only make history, they also see it differently from those in power at the time and from those who have the advantage of judging events after they have passed. When we look at their lives and times, we know where they were going, while they did not. More difficult for us is to know what they were thinking and expecting from the future. The prospects and aspirations of ordinary Spaniards during and after the Civil War were a world apart from those of other west Europeans during the "Golden Age" after World War II, and from those of today.[2]

Today Europe is a free continent where people are culturally very close. Europeans see each other on television, they connect instantly through the internet, they meet in various forums, they consume each other's cultural products, they do and expect the same things every day. Half a century ago, in the middle of the "Golden Age," it was not like that. In 1957, for example, countries such as the United Kingdom and Spain, that now are separated by a two-hour flight on a discount airline, and that you can visit for a weekend of leisure, were very far apart, even remote. That year there were elections in the United Kingdom, and Prime Minister Harold Macmillan could claim that most Britons had "never had it so good." He was right. Britons were enjoying freedom and prosperity, and that prosperity was being distributed more fairly than ever before. This feel-good sensation was a product of the post-war "social pact": the cooperation between capital, labor, and government which implied not only moderating labor demands but also sharing the benefits of the economic boom. Politicians could claim the same in many other countries across the Channel, such as Germany, the Netherlands, and even politically troubled France. There was, however, no contemporary "social pact" in Spain. Ruled by Franco since he won the Civil War in 1939, with the help of Hitler and Mussolini (and the indifference of Western democracies), things were very different. There was no freedom, no "Golden Age," and certainly life, at least for the majority of Spaniards, was not so good.

This was the case for a family of nine who, with their eldest daughter's fiancé, on an unremarkable day in the winter of 1957 in the poor Mediterranean city of Almeria, were finishing supper. As usual, the mother distributed dessert; it consisted of just two oranges for 10 people. Males had preference over females, older people over younger ones. Three segments were served to the father, two to the son-in-law, and one was divided between the rest of the family (the mother, three boys, and four girls). They were poor. Both the parents and the son-in-law were illiterate. The children all had some schooling, but only the youngest boy would complete his training as a mechanic. The rest were destined to have unskilled jobs. The father, a former farm worker, was a doorman at a government office; his wife helped him and did the cleaning after the office closed. The son-in-law was a fisherman. His young fiancée would be a servant most of her life, but would also work in a factory, and as a cook, a cleaning lady, and a janitor. Her brother, the next eldest, became a chauffeur, then a taxi driver, and he once attempted to become a bullfighter. The second eldest sister would sew and the other girls would be servants most of their adult lives, while another brother would always work as a waiter.

Since her marriage in the early 1930s, the mother had been pregnant almost continuously. Some of the children were born before the Civil War, others during the war, and most of them in the daunting post-war years. Other siblings had died in infancy and there had been multiple miscarriages. For her daughters and future daughters-in-law, however, this was not to be the case. Of the siblings seated at the table only the eldest daughter would have more than two children: she had four. The fourth child, a boy, was born after the loss of the family's second child, a girl, who had died of a brain hemorrhage while still a baby, and had left them in deep mourning. That fourth child today teaches history at a Canadian university and is the author of this book.[3]

Like the lives of millions of other ordinary Spaniards, the harshness of life for the people seated at this table was the product not just of their poverty but of politics as well. However, these people did not protest, at least in public, and certainly they did not talk politics. In fact they chose to forget things that were "inconvenient" and painful to remember. It was not only that the father and the son-in-law's father had been republican soldiers. Almeria was republican for the duration of the war. Notwithstanding the fact that they had voted regularly for the left and even joined the socialist union, they had been forcibly recruited into the republican forces. They were simple men and they had done nothing noteworthy or exceptionally brave as soldiers, and had survived the war sometimes by *avoiding* their duties, not unlike Jaroslav Hašek's *Good Soldier Švejk*. They did not talk about my maternal grandfather's brief participation in post-war clandestine socialist meetings – my grandmother waiting in the house, full of terror, for his return – or about the son-in-law's uncle who lived exiled in Oran, then French Algeria, after having helped republican guerrillas escape Spain in a boat a few years before. Their biggest secret, a secret they were all careful never to talk about, was a different one.

On the wall of the room where they were finishing supper there was the photograph of a handsome young man in a strange uniform. Aunts and uncles from their extended family had the same picture on the walls of their houses as well. He was cousin Rafael, a republican medical officer who had been shot in prison after the war. The family also knew that Maria, my mother, the young fiancée at the table, a child of 8 at the time (1940), was the first who had learned, after a rude remark by a prison officer, that cousin Rafael had been executed. Nobody talked about where his body had been laid, although they had learned its exact location, in an unmarked mass grave in the city's cemetery. The family had come to accept their secret, and silence helped them to reconcile their experiences with their present reality. They did not dream of revenge. More surprising perhaps for today's readers, neither did they did dream of freedom. They even thought that Franco was a good man who knew nothing of the crimes, injustices, and miseries committed against people like themselves. When Franco came to Almeria they went to cheer him. They had no money to buy flags so they hung a shawl from their window. "Our eyes were closed back then" they would say when remembering those years; because once democracy was restored in Spain they "discovered" or "remembered" what they had earlier chosen not to see.

***

What happened to my family's memories and old loyalties was not unusual. Millions of other families in Spain, formerly left-wing, had been forced during the first two decades of the dictatorship to accommodate their ideas, their vocabulary, and their expectations to the harsh reality. Unlike most west Europeans, who lived and prospered in democracy, for ordinary Spaniards post-war meant being forced to abandon any hope of freedom in exchange for some peace in their private lives and, just as importantly, in the streets. Franco claimed that his was a normal European regime with a specific Spanish nature. In fact, in the rest of western Europe (Portugal and Greece were the exceptions), people could vote their politicians in and out of office. In Spain, to confront the dictatorship meant automatic state violence, and people feared that responding to that violence would risk restarting the Civil War with all its horrors. Unlike most west Europeans, Spaniards sacrificed personal and collective freedom in exchange for peace, even if that peace was that of an oppressive and criminal regime.

The exchange of freedom for some form of peace would be harrowing enough if it had not also carried the second anomaly of economic stagnation. While freedom and democracy brought prosperous peace to the continent, the Francoist dictatorship and its peculiar peace brought unspeakable material suffering to ordinary Spaniards. Moreover, while in most of Europe the state and other public institutions worked effectively for the common good, in Franco's Spain they were inefficient and often both hostile and repressive. This affected Spaniards' values, making them pessimistic in social and collective matters. They became individualistic, because the only institution that they could always count on was a very private one: family. This collective pessimism helped poor Spaniards cope with the ruthless post-war years and, at the same time, it all but completely eroded the values that support civil society. Government repression did the rest, and this resulted in a society that grudgingly but passively accepted the unbearable social conditions that persisted into the early 1960s, while the rest of free Europe experienced the post-war economic boom. The Francoist dictate of peace over freedom carried the never officially recognized burden of peace over prosperity.

For all the above reasons, in 1957, if my family or millions of others like it had read or heard the news, they still would have known next to nothing of the dilemmas facing the regime. Official censorship prevented ordinary people from knowing of the government's disturbing internal reports in the late 1950s regarding the need for drastic changes in the nation's economic policies as inflation spiraled out of control and currency reserves quickly disappeared.[4] Common people knew nothing of the fact that Franco, the "good man," resisted changing economic policies. Neither were they told that the sycophants of the Falange – the leaders of Franco's corrupt, pseudo-fascist party – were still dreaming of the re-fascistization of the dictatorship as if the defeat of the Axis powers in 1945 had not taken place.[5] Nor that, on the other hand, Opus Dei, the "modernizing" wing of Franco's government, wanted to open up the Spanish economy to Western capitalism.[6]

Opus Dei was (and still is) an ultra-conservative social and religious Catholic organization created shortly before the Civil War. It became increasingly powerful in the post-war years thanks to both its contacts with Francoist politicians and its focus on recruiting and training young technocrats. In spite of its reactionary political agenda it was remarkably open to modern technical ideas, which made it popular among some sectors of the Francoist elites. Its proposals for economic reform were finally (and grudgingly) accepted by Franco in 1957. The old Falangist guard lost out. That year a cabinet reshuffle tilted power to Opus Dei technocrats and to their program for economic liberalization which was to make Spain wealthier, but, at the same time, leave it politically and socially repressive.[7] Shortly after, in 1958, this major policy shift led Spain to join the International Monetary Fund and the Organization for Economic Cooperation and Development. After two decades of economic mismanagement, Francoism embraced modern capitalism. It was a political and economic watershed for the regime that changed the lives of most Spaniards. It also guaranteed the dictatorship's survival for two more decades.

Dictatorships, by their very nature, are based on repression and lies. Yet the ideas and actions of the people who have lived under dictatorial rule cannot be interpreted solely through their experience of repression. This is particularly valid for Francoism because of the regime's longevity. Between 1939 and 1975, during and long after the strong repression of the early 1940s, many complex social changes occurred which decisively affected people's lives. To explain Spaniards' lives during the dictatorship while only taking into account which side they stood on regarding this violence would be a simplistic representation of reality. Conversely, to explain Francoism, from the first to the last day of its existence, without taking into account the repression and fear it unleashed would be a distortion of the past, and a mockery of people's suffering.

The long duration of authoritarian rule in Spain, and its place in the context of events elsewhere on the continent at this time, have presented historians and other academics with the problem of establishing periods or stages of the dictatorship.[8] There is an overall consensus that, in *political* terms, we can talk of two periods. The first is the semi-fascist period up to 1945. The defeat of his friends the Axis powers in World War II forced Franco to inaugurate a second phase. The Spanish dictator discarded the most strident external aspects of his regime and embraced a Christian, anti-communist outlook. By then, the worst of the repression against the defeated republicans was over. This period was to last, in general terms, until the regime's end. It included active support of the Vatican and a formal alliance with the United States, established in 1953, which saw the US give financial help to the dictatorship in exchange for the establishment of American military bases in Spain.

The social and economic history of Francoism is more complex because it includes the transformation of Spain from an essentially agrarian country in 1939 to a modern, urban one when the dictator died in 1975.[9] However, most scholars agree that in *socio-economic* terms there are three main periods. The first period, which lasted until 1952, was dominated by a policy of autarky or economic self-reliance, and was characterized by serious food shortages which caused widespread famine among the poor.[10] Under autarky, the regime, copying fascist Italian and Nazi polices, tried to make the country independent of the world's economy. In the first years of World War II, when both the USA and the UK offered economic help, the pro-Axis dictatorship dismissively rejected it.[11] The Francoist state massively intervened in the economy, regulating both trade and the supply system. It also manipulated markets, imposed import substitution, and forced industrialization. The result was an unmitigated economic and human disaster. The second period, which lasted from 1952 until 1959, has been called a transitional or semi-normal period. Responding hesitantly to the catastrophe, in 1952 the government semi-liberalized the economy and dropped some of its most dysfunctional and irrational policies. Finally, the third period started in 1959 as the government adopted a stabilization plan – the brainchild of the Opus Dei's technocrats – that restored order after the economic chaos of the previous two decades and opened the door to the Spanish economic "boom" or "miracle" of the 1960s and early 1970s.[12]

The story of "ordinary people" and the changes in their lives through those 40 years would be complicated enough if Spain was a culturally, economically, and demographically homogenous country, but it wasn't in 1939 and it isn't today. Spain is a "little continent," a diverse country with deep economic, social, and cultural differences between and within its various regions and nationalities. In 1939 the majority of the population was rural, but the large cosmopolitan cities of Madrid and Barcelona, along with secondary centers such as Seville, Valencia, Bilbao, and Saragossa, were already well established. Some regions were fairly industrialized. Coalmining and iron mills dominated the landscape of extensive areas in Asturias and the Basque country, while in Catalonia, especially around Barcelona, there was a concentration of textile production. Madrid provided services, both through private interests such as banking and through a highly centralized state. Other parts of the country had less concentrated and weaker industries connected with food-processing and a variety of exports. In all regions, including the richest ones, backward and poverty-stricken villages could be found no more than a few kilometers from cities and industrial centers. Major agricultural production was divided between the traditional wheat regions in Castile and parts of Andalusia. Other parts of Andalusia were covered with olive groves, while there were important fruit- and wine-exporting areas on the Mediterranean coast. North of Madrid in the eastern part of the peninsula small farms were the norm, whereas further south and west, large landed estates dominated and provided temporary, ill-paid work for hundreds of thousands of landless peasants.[13]

Culturally and politically there were significant regional and local differences in 1939. Across Spain most people spoke Castilian, but the use of native languages was extensive in Catalonia, Galicia, and, to a lesser extent, the Basque country, particularly in rural areas. Until their banning by the dictatorship there existed strong nationalist political parties in both Catalonia and the Basque country. In these regions, as in the rest of Spain, farmers and people living in rural areas generally voted for the right, whereas landless peasants and people living in urban and industrial centers were either left-wing or at least republican.

During the war, Basque, Galician, and Castilian peasants formed the bulk of the soldiers in Franco's armies, often as volunteers, while many landless peasants were forcibly conscripted from western Andalusia, a traditionally anarchist stronghold that fell to the Francoist rebels. The republican troops came from both urban centers and the east of Spain. These ideological divisions mirrored religious attitudes in Spain, such that in regions where a rural, property-owning peasant population dominated, particularly in the north, attendance at mass and religious observance were high. In contrast, workers, both rural and urban, predominantly practiced religious indifference when not exercising outright anti-clericalism.[14] These old divisions and diversity will be crucial to understanding political and social movements in the last years of the dictatorship, because in the regions and cities with an old, well-established working class the level of protest against the regime was far more intense than in agrarian and conservative Catholic areas.

These material and cultural differences within Spain only made the Civil War more complex. It would be both simplistic and misleading to summarize the conflict as having been between the rich Francoists and the poor republicans. There were many poor people who volunteered for Franco's side and many middle-class citizens among his opponents.[15] Furthermore, the cultural, regional, and identity differences all over the country were too numerous and complex to allow such categorization. It would, however, be fair to describe the outcome of the war as a crushing defeat for the poor, both immediately, in the case of workers and landless peasants, and later in the life of the dictatorship, in the case of small, landowning farmers. In the end, both groups suffered from the imposition of policies that ran against their interests. In the 1940s and 1950s Franco's policies caused unspeakable hardship for the landless peasants. The demise of the small landowners among the peasantry largely took place in the 1960s.[16]

**

At the end of the war all Spaniards, whatever their political ideas, witnessed (what they felt is a different matter) the suffering of millions of people during the terrible "Hunger Years," which lasted from 1939 to 1945.[17] Two sinister developments mark this period. First, Franco's extremely harsh and ruthless political repression was practiced against the vanquished republicans as hundreds of thousands of people were imprisoned. At one point in 1941 the jails had 280,000 political inmates. Some 50,000 of them were shot between 1939 and 1945, while hundreds of thousands suffered legal and extralegal persecution.[18] Francoist claims that it was a normal European government, just another Western Christian regime, were opportunistic lies. Two factors negate such spurious claims. First Franco's repression far surpassed the repression of political enemies (fascists, collaborators, etc.) that took place in France and Italy during and immediately after the liberation of those countries at the end of World War II. The total number of people killed in these two countries – which witnessed by far the most significant crimes of this nature in western Europe between 1943 and 1946 – was about 25,000, roughly half the number of those executed in Spain (50,000) after the end of the Civil War in 1939.[19] Spain had at that time a population that was three times smaller than France and Italy combined. Moreover, most of those murdered in France and Italy were killed by anti-fascist gangs and guerrillas in the chaos during liberation. In Spain, most of those shot were sentenced by military courts.

The second extraordinary aspect of Francoist policies was starvation. Historians have frequently analyzed the mechanisms and the breadth of political repression in Spain, but the scale of the suffering caused by hunger, which has been largely neglected until relatively recent studies, cannot be exaggerated. Not since the last pre-modern famine in the south in the 1880s had so many died of hunger in Spain. Numbers can give only a cold indication of the harrowing reality. It has been estimated that between 1939 and 1945, that is *after* the Civil War had ended, 200,000 Spaniards starved to death.[20] This compares very badly not only with the efforts of post-1945 liberation governments all over western Europe to feed their people, but even with the effects of Nazi food policy in occupied France during the years 1940–4, which caused very serious shortages and a sharp increase in mortality rates but not mass starvation. It is difficult to find a similar outcome to Franco's Spain food policy elsewhere in western Europe. The situation is closer to that created by the then desperate Nazis in the Netherlands in the winter of 1944, when up to 30,000 people died of starvation-related causes. Since the Dutch population was a third of the Spanish, this notorious famine, although imposed by a ruthless foreign power, was less than half as lethal, given the relative sizes of the populations, than the famine unleashed by Franco on his own people.[21]

Post-war suffering was intense and affected the majority of the population. War and autarky caused real incomes to drop by 66 percent between 1935 and 1945 (figure 1). Furthermore, during the period of economic decline in the early 1940s, the agrarian workforce increased – it had been 45.5 percent of the total working population in 1930, but rose to 55.5 percent in 1940. This was a phenomenon without parallel in modern Europe, with the exception of Russia during the Soviet revolution and its subsequent civil war. This shift had deadly consequences, because it helped to depress wages even further. The reduction of wages was not just the product of "neutral" macro-economic adjustments: new, lower wages were imposed by the winners of the war, who had resented the Republic's pro-worker labor laws and policies. It was social revenge at its crudest, and the result was that even employed adults went hungry and their children starved.

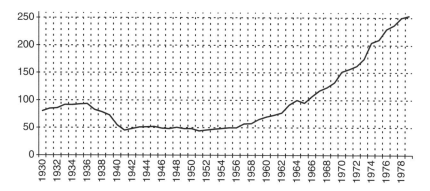

Figure 1 Inflation-adjusted salaries for male agrarian workers, 1930–1979 (1964 = 100)

Source: Carreras and Tafunell, *Estadísticas históricas de España: siglos XIX y XX.*

The worst years for hunger, and for illness for those weakened by it, came between the end of the Civil War and 1942. During this period, numerous epidemics, particularly typhus, ravaged the country. The advance of the dreadful pellagra – an illness caused by a poor diet – became common. In 1940 and 1941 there were thousands of, until then, healthy young adults who lost their sight, developed painful cracks in their skin, and died from hunger or from eating poisonous plants while trying to fill their stomachs in despair.[22] Tuberculosis, another product of misery, returned and became a symbol of this desperate period. Young children (figure 2) and the elderly were the main victims of hunger and its related illness.

In spite of this horror, and usually indifferent to its resulting suffering, Franco and his generals remained enthusiastic about autarky. They thought that if it had made their admired Nazi Germany so strong, it would certainly work for Spain.[23] The Caudillo, so they reasoned, would soon be able to have 2 million men in arms, thousands of airplanes, and dozens of battle cruisers at his disposal.[24] In 1939 he spoke with characteristic dismissiveness of the "liberal economy" as being part of "foreign Jewish capitalism."[25] These racist ideological views, class prejudices, and sheer ignorance are key to understanding why there was more hunger in Spain after, rather than during, the war.

The conflict itself did not greatly affect agriculture, but post-war misery came from the adoption of the twin polices of economic autarky – when the Spanish economy became isolated from the world, especially from its

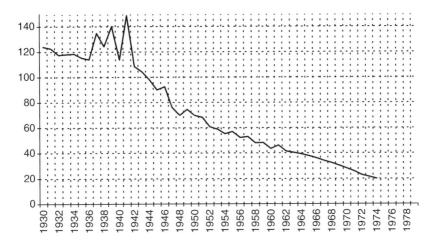

Figure 2   Child mortality, 1930–1979 (per thousand)
Source: Carreras and Tafunell, *Estadísticas históricas de España: siglos XIX y XX*.

traditional British and French commercial partners – and massive but inefficient state intervention in the marketplace. These policies demonstrated the callousness of the leaders of the dictatorship towards ordinary people's suffering.[26] For consumers, the combination of these two policies meant that not enough food was being distributed through the rationing system while there was plenty of it on the unaffordable, for the majority, black market. Food often failed to appear at distribution points because of corruption. In a country where hundreds of people were shot every day, only one single Francoist official was ever executed because of corruption. In this particular case his dissenting political activities, not the fact that he stole food and caused other people's deaths, was the real motive behind his killing.[27]

During the 1940s, and even into the 1950s, basic staples such as wheat and olive oil were sold on the black market at an average of two to three times the official prices, and often much more than that. Profits were exorbitant, particularly for big landowners and those with the political connections that allowed them to act with impunity. Participation in the black market was widespread, and millions of small producers reaped their share as well.[28] This period left a deep imprint on the collective memory of Spaniards, which is marked by an obsession and worry about food that survives today.

The years of hunger and repression – preceded by the years of civil war rife with horrific killings between republicans and Francoists, bombing of major cities, and displacement of a large portion of the population – fundamentally shaped the lives and values of the generations that experienced these events. To this day, many of Spain's intrinsic sociological and political patterns can be traced to the traumatic war and oppressive realities of the post-conflict period. However, memories about that period can be very different because the dictatorship's pursuit of autarky and political repression meant one thing for those closely associated with the regime and quite another for other Spaniards. A minority made fortunes out of everybody else's pain. Those who owned a business or had a farm did not always suffer the period's miseries. For most people, however, autarky meant imposed policies that they had neither chosen nor could protest against, and for which they paid heavily. For example, in 1930 Spanish disposable income per inhabitant was 13 percent below that in Italy; in 1950 it was 40 percent lower, and the Italian "economic miracle" was still to come. In that year, Spain was the only Western country that had yet to recover its 1929 production levels.[29]

In spite of the 1952 economic reforms, the economy stumbled from crisis to crisis during the rest of the 1950s as it was besieged by bottlenecks in the procurement and distribution of materials and products, inflation, trade deficits, currency emergencies, and, most worryingly for the government, a wave of strikes. Not even the arrival of American economic assistance ($487.8 million between 1954 and 1957) erased the possibility of a complete economic collapse.[30] It was only after the implementation of the Opus Dei technocrats' 1959 Stabilization Plan, and after a sharp contraction of the economy, that a spectacular period of economic growth occurred and industrialization gained a safe footing (figure 3).

Between 1960 and 1975 Spanish national income doubled, an increase that surpassed the figures for all other industrialized countries in the West with the exception of Japan. For this period, the average annual growth of GDP was an impressive 7 percent (figure 4). Foreign investment increased dramatically, from just $40 million in 1960 to $697 million in 1970. Sunny, friendly Spain now became a popular country for vacationing: numbers jumped from barely 6 million tourists in 1960, to more than 30 million visitors in 1975, and these visitors left behind more than $3 billion that year. Tourists were not the only ones on the move.[31]

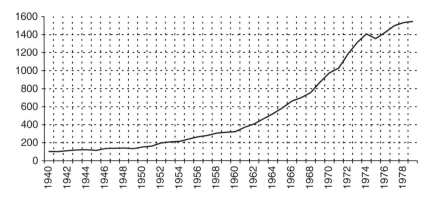

Figure 3 Industrial production levels, 1940–1979 (1929 = 100)
Source: Carreras and Tafunell, *Estadísticas históricas de España: siglos XIX y XX*.

Between 1950 and 1975, about 6 million Spaniards, a full 20 percent of the population, relocated. Most of them were peasants who fled the countryside to cities. More than 2.3 million people migrated to Europe, temporarily or permanently. A modern economy in Spain demanded that people moved where capital was invested, a rational option, perhaps, from an economic point of view, but a harsh one in social or personal terms. This migration due to need can be considered as another form of human suffering for the Spanish during this period; it represented another toll that the poor had to pay. The massive migrations of the 1950–75 period meant the end of rural Spain as it had been for centuries and an accelerated process of social and cultural change in both rural and urban settings. It was progress, but one achieved through a suffering that cannot be separated from the reign of fear that Francoism imposed on Spaniards.

At the moment of Franco's death in 1975, Spain was a modern, industrial, and mostly urban country, yet not all sectors had moved at the same pace. The rewards of economic and social development were very unevenly distributed both geographically and between classes. Between 1964 and 1967 income disparities grew, and only after 1970 were those disparities between the rich and the poor to be slightly reduced. In 1974, half of the country's population received only 20.9 percent of the disposable national income, while the other half collected nearly 80 percent (of those, the richest 10 percent took home almost 40 percent of income).[32] In geographic terms, more than half of the national income was concentrated in an area of just 11 percent of Spain, while 53 percent of the territory shared only

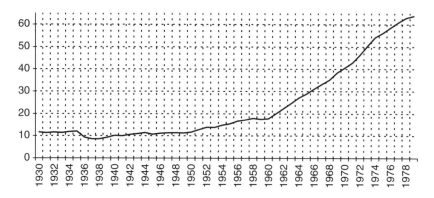

Figure 4 Spain's GDP, 1930–1979 (1995 = 100)
Source: Carreras and Tafunell, *Estadísticas históricas de España: siglos XIX y XX.*

14 percent of the nation's wealth. In the early 1970s Spain was divided into five regions according to the pre-eminence of economic activity, their social profiles, and the concentration of wealth. The industrial areas of the Basque country, Barcelona (and other parts of Catalonia), and Asturias ranked first; Madrid was second, as its economy included a very active service sector in addition to industry; the third area, dominated by urban middle classes and small businesses, included regional capital cities such as Corunna, Santander, Saragossa, and Valencia; the agrarian areas of rural small farming of the interior and the north of Castile, Leon, and Galicia were fourth; and fifth stood the rural areas of the large agricultural estates and the impoverished urban centers of Andalusia, Extremadura, and La Mancha. In addition, the last group of regions suffered a demographic hemorrhage during the dictatorship, and the south in particular was left with many areas where abject poverty and illiteracy were rampant and social services scarce.

✳✳✳

The social and economic changes that took place in the latter years of the dictatorship have led many people, academics included, both inside and outside Spain, to believe that Francoism was the basis for the country's successful transition into a modern nation.[33] The central thesis of this book argues that exactly the opposite is true. If we were to ignore the brutally harsh 1940s and the miserable 1950s, one can say that Spain's development was indeed facilitated by the regime's economic liberalization in 1959. But Franco's apologists also forget that the "economic miracle" was made possible only by the extraordinary exploitation and sacrifice of ordinary Spaniards, particularly landless peasants and workers, and their families. Throughout the Franco years, the poorest members of Spanish society bore the brunt of both economic mismanagement and change, and they were the last to profit from the economic "boom."

The regime can be credited with two main achievements in the process of Spain's development that some may call "merits," but these were obtained at great cost and both were socially selective. The first merit was, after 20 years of failure, to change economic policies in 1959 from autarky to orthodox capitalism, which had proved successful in the rest of the continent since the late 1940s. The second "merit" was that Francoism created an afford-able, disciplined workforce which was achieved by the killing of union lead-ers, by the destruction of genuine, representative organizations, and by instilling fear and pessimism in the general population. The combination of these factors made possible the optimum exploitation of employees by both the state and capital interests. The state guaranteed employers a "business-friendly environment" with a docile and cheap workforce.

Hence capital, both local and international, had "never had it so good" as it did in Spain. This can be seen not just in terms of the poor salaries ordi-nary Spaniards received or the expensive consumer products they were forced to buy in a protectionist market, but also, and probably most impor-tantly, in terms of the deficient services that the indolent state offered Spanish workers. It is an irony that, not unlike the Chinese "economic mir-acle" of today under communism, this controlling and repressive state even-tually adopted policies very close to a laissez-faire liberal economist's wildest dreams. It offered an excellent package to capital investment, comprising low taxes, a disciplined and inexpensive workforce, and a captive consumer market.[34] Spain did not have a modern, progressive income tax system until 1977. This was a boon for the wealthy, but it also meant the state had very little money to spend. In 1965 income tax represented only 14.3 percent of the total amount the state collected from taxes (the OECD average was 26 percent), and public expenditure was only 15 percent of GDP (the OECD average was 31 percent). As late as 1970, public sector expenditure was barely 20.1 percent of the country's GDP, while Germany's was 36.8 percent, France's 51 percent, Italy's 43.3 percent, and the UK's 53.2 percent.[35] The price of Spain's "miracle" was mostly paid by those who went hungry, those who did not receive adequate social or educational services, those who had to migrate to survive, those who worked hard and consumed little, and those who were forced to buy whatever the protected economy put in front of them. They were the poor, and they were the majority of Spain's population; they were, by definition, the "ordinary" Spaniards.

Behind these policies, numbers, and dates stand the lives of ordinary people. A history using either a traditional political or socio-economic framework would tell us relatively little about how they lived throughout the different stages of the Franco dictatorship. This book wants to tell their story according to their own memories, which throughout the text are frequently contrasted with the official version of events. It begins by illustrating how political violence and repression were experienced, creating an atmosphere of widespread, but often unspoken, fear, and how this fear was manipulated by the regime. Next, it describes the social cost that Spaniards had to pay for political decisions taken by the government on socio-economic matters, and how the interests of the majority often came last when the dividends of progress were distributed. Thirdly, the book examines the phenomenon of massive migration that ended the traditional, rural Spanish way of life, as people looked for better opportunities in distant places, and looks at how the process of migration changed them. The fourth chapter describes how social, demographic, and economic forces contributed to accelerating the process of changing values. Finally, the book explores the diversity of perspectives and socio-political opinions in the last years of the dictatorship, as the regime's mounting problems and Franco's physical decay opened up the possibility of political change. This last chapter is an interpretation of how Spaniards slowly liberated themselves from the fears of the past and thus planted the roots of their country's rapid and relatively peaceful transition to democracy between 1975 and 1977.

1

THE POLITICS OF FEAR

The beautiful Barranco de Viznar is located in an area a few kilometers north of the Andalusian city of Granada. Between Viznar and the neighboring town of Alfacar there is a spring called La Fuente Grande (the Big Fountain). It is a refreshing area, popular for picnicking in the sweltering summer months of southern Spain, and ideal for picking mushrooms in the fall. It is set high in the mountains where pine trees, planted by the government to combat soil erosion in the 1950s and 1960s, provide shade. This bucolic setting was also, from 1936 to the restoration of democracy in 1977, a huge, unmarked grave containing the remains of the internationally celebrated poet Federico García Lorca.[1] That Lorca was buried there made the site quietly famous during the Franco years and legendary today, but also served (and still does) partly to obscure the fact that this is also the grave of thousands of other people who were executed in the area by the Francoist rebels during the Civil War. The Barranco de Viznar is in no way exceptional. Until very recently even less was known about the existence of hundreds of similar unmarked mass graves all over Spain. These graves contain the remains of at least 30,000 people who were summarily executed by the Francoists during the conflict, hastily buried, and then officially deemed not to exist by the dictatorship.

In spite of this and too many other places of sorrow, and just as in other countries with a dictatorial and murderous past such as Russia, Italy, Germany, or Austria, in post-Franco Spain many people express nostalgia for the supposedly good old days of no crime, no political crisis, no terrorism, and plenty of morality.[2] This idea coincides with the dictatorship's pretension, propagated for 40 years, that it brought peace to Spain. If pressed, the same people who look back at the time of the dictatorship with nostalgia would admit that life was hard in the 1940s, and that perhaps there was too much harshness both in public and in private life, but they would also add that the times were a product of a past that had been far worse, and that life had actually improved under Franco.

This nostalgia, like all kinds of nostalgia, selects from the past what is convenient and ignores what is not. It focuses, for example, on the hard but honest lives of men and women who made the best of the post-war period and worked until Spain became what it is now: a prosperous and wealthy country. It likes to highlight that under Franco people did not care about politics, and that made life simpler and happier. This recollection is compelling because it uses real stories, real lives of ordinary and decent people. A problem surfaces when one begins to question *what* events those memories leave aside, and *which* people, those with different memories, they do not include. It fails to remember the terror the dictatorship imposed on society. It ignores the lives and fates of those who did not agree with the regime's policies, who were murdered, injured, or silenced, or those who, because of they were poor, were condemned to starve.

Manipulating Fear

The pro-Francoist narrative forgets, or does not consider it important, that the regime forced Spaniards to renounce their basic civil and social rights. This discourse does not recognize that, by blocking any negotiation over the country's future, Francoism left open only a single and unacceptable door for opposition politics: to take up arms and start a second round of the Civil War. This was not a real option, at least not one that the absolute majority of ordinary Spaniards would ever accept. In this way, peace was nothing but the regime's manipulation of Spaniards' fear of more violence. To be fair, the dictatorship was not solely responsible for all this fear. It had started before the war. During the Second Republic (1931–6), the left, mainly the anarchists, had often resorted to violence. However, as the Republic became more moderate after 1933, the Socialist Party (PSOE) became more enchanted with the idea of revolution. In October 1934 the socialists embarked on a rebellion in Asturias against the legal right-wing government that resulted in close to 2,000 victims being killed and led to at least 15,000 people (other sources say 30,000) being arrested. Some of those who perished were killed in combat, but others were victims of both left-wing crimes and the government's repression. After Asturias, Spanish politics became radicalized and murderous. In the following months, Falangists, communists, socialists and anarchists committed numerous crimes against each other.[3] In July 1936 the Civil War broke out – now as a rebellion of the right against the legal left-wing government – and gave way, particularly during its first months, to massive killings. However, it is important to point out that the republican government strove to reduce repression. By the end of 1936 they had done this to a great extent, but it was never completely achieved.[4] The Francoist forces, on the contrary, continued to practice massive repression during and after the war.

The dictatorship did not try to bring reconciliation among Spaniards. On the contrary, it fueled and used fear opportunistically to achieve its own objectives. The result of this cycle of fear was that some Spaniards feared the authorities, others not, but, overall, Spanish society was insecure and afraid of itself: it had been "convinced" by the recent past, and constantly reminded by the regime's propaganda, that Spaniards did not know how to live in peace; that they needed to be ruled with iron discipline to avoid falling again into fratricidal killing.[5] Because of this fear, Spain was not a normal west European post-war society as the regime, its supporters, and anti-communists' foreign friends claimed. This was a society in the hands of a ruthless man who used collective pain to preserve his ill-gotten power, and in the process manipulated the past, erasing or tarnishing the memory of its own victims. Only this type of regime could have declared July 18 a national holiday (it remained an official holiday until the restoration of democracy in 1977).[6] To this day, national laws state that Spaniards will receive double pay checks from their employers in the month of July, just as they do in December in celebration of Christmas. Most ordinary Spaniards celebrated the day off, used the extra money, and spent time with their families relaxing at the beach or enjoying a picnic. However, the Franco regime and its hard-core supporters celebrated something else on this day: the official date of the beginning of the war in 1936 (it actually started on July 17). The official reason for so much rejoicing on that day was that Spain had been saved by a national movement that fought against a godless republic led by criminal leaders and supported by murderous hordes.

For many pro-Franco people, July 18 was also a day on which to remember loved ones who had fought for the rebels (they called themselves the Nationals) and who had died in the war, either fighting at the front or murdered in the republican zone. Within the regime's selective memory, these were the only people that were recognized as having been killed during the conflict. This discourse conveniently ignored that for every "good Spaniard" murdered by the hordes approximately four "reds" had been assassinated: over 38,000 nationalists murdered against perhaps 100,000 republicans during the war, and another 50,000 people executed after the war. It also "forgot" that there were neither survivor pensions for republican widows, orphans, or amputees nor consolation.

Most adult Spaniards knew that there was much hatred behind the July 18 celebrations and knew that many things were not to be discussed on that day. They also were aware that the wounds of the war were still open and feared that a second round of war might await them, but the authorities did not talk openly about these fears or the hatred on that day. Rather, they celebrated by delivering official speeches that praised Franco's Peace and the country's purported prosperity while they inaugurated new buildings, projects, or tributes to the triumph of the regime. It was the day when the keys to new social housing projects were given to their new owners, or irrigation systems were unveiled. For the civil governors, who were also the heads of the local Falange and represented the regime in each province, it was a day to start to relax. The months leading up to these events were often difficult for these authorities. Because of the poor performance of the economy in the 1940s and early 1950s, quite often there was little, and sometimes nothing at all, for officials to inaugurate or to give away.[7]

With these and other ceremonies, the dictatorship tried to convince Spaniards that El Caudillo was on the side of right, and that he had brought peace and progress to the country. This claim was made more credible by the fact that people had no taste for politics. The majority concentrated on surviving hunger, rationing, and other daily miseries. The actively dissident minority was cowed. The efforts by the opposition to resist and to reorganize always ended in more killings, ruthless repression, and new political defeats. In the second half of the 1940s, confronted with this systematic failure to maintain their clandestine organizations, opposition militants started to abandon politics and to join the mass of Spaniards who lay low. Those who knew what had happened did not dare to challenge the official truth in public, or even within their families. By not talking about things and people long gone, about freedoms and hopes dashed in blood, society started to forget. This led people, especially the young, to accept Francoism's version of events. In this way, Spain became a society where amnesia and half-truths connived, and where the very same people who had lost so much because of the dictatorship quite often turned to Franco as the only hope that something would improve in the hopeless post-war decades. It was a relatively rapid process, and by the early 1950s Spanish society had become mostly Francoist, and at least until the 1970s continued to be so, even if this widespread Francoism carried in its belly the contradictions, stories, and identities that would one day re-emerge.[8]

The regime constructed its portrayal of the past (today we would call this a "historical memory project") not just with words but also with monuments. The most significant monument built by the Francoists to symbolize their view of the war was the "Valley of the Fallen" (Valle de los Caidos). Located just north of Madrid, this grandiose architectonic complex was built over a 20-year period (1940–59), in part by political prisoners. There, presided over by a cross 150 meters high, a huge basilica was built into a granite mountain and more than 40,000 (perhaps as many as 70,000) fallen soldiers, mostly Francoists, were buried. A few hundred, perhaps even a few thousand, republican soldiers are there too (the process of collecting the bodies was chaotic). The intended meaning of including the burial of some "enemy" soldiers at the valley was that Franco's Christian Spain had forgiven these people for having been lured into fighting for the republicans by their criminal political leaders. According to the 1959 tourist guide to the valley, the first in English, the monument

> should be regarded by all Spaniards as a just tribute to the memory of all those who gave their lives for their ideals. [That] there cannot be more lasting reminder of this than the Holy Cross […] Therefore the monument is religious in character, because it is thus more in keeping with the simple piety of the Spanish people, who have remained outside the current of agnosticism which has secularized Europe in this century.[9]

Franco himself was buried in the valley in November 1975, not far from the founder of the Falange party, José Antonio Primo de Rivera, elevated by the regime's propaganda to the post of foremost Fallen One among the 1936 rebels and, by extension, the symbol of Spain's suffering. For decades, many of the regime's most solemn ceremonies were held in the valley.

There were other Francoist monuments in almost every town in Spain, where the officially recognized victims were also remembered with plaques and crosses with the names of those "fallen for God and Spain." At the same time, the official memory of the executed republicans was either completely erased or, when it was recalled, was defamed.[10] This was not accidental. The regime's propaganda continually repeated stories about the crimes committed against its supporters by hordes of individuals little better than beasts in the years of "red" terror behind republican lines. The following two excerpts show how those massacres were explained, and how those explanations justified "forgetting" about the republicans' fate. The first was published in 1939, and it is not very different from hundreds of other books and pamphlets published after the war. It explains the moral and social meaning of Franco's Peace, as compared with the days of "red" domination in Madrid:

> In the theatres [...] there will no longer be found, dressed like ladies and adorned with jewelry [...] the vengeful cook and the unfaithful maid, who after causing the killing of their masters now wear magnificent furs over their prostituted bodies, taken for a drive by the bandit of a chauffeur in the master's car [...] the shameless doorman and concierge, inducers of the most horrendous crimes [...] the most smelly human garbage from the outskirts of the city living in palaces.[11]

The Francoists explained class and ideology as a result of biological differences. According to them, "red" Spaniards were not only socially inferior but also degenerate, resentful individuals. This biological degeneration was what made poor people embrace left-wing ideas. The quotation below is an explanation of the *natural* difference between pro-Franco prisoners during the war and their republican guards. It was written long after the war, in 1956, when passions should have cooled down:

> Our captives, for God and for Spain, behaved in accordance with what they were: perfect gentlemen. Equally, their guards, usually, demonstrated and confirmed their low-born nature if not the worst instincts of lack of respect, to the point of reaching the subhuman level of crime and murder [...] Perfect gentlemen, the aristocracy of blood and of Spanish *hidalgos* [...] they proved that if [...] the rich knew how to be poor, the poor did not know how to be rich. All of this proved that their dignity and greatness of soul were kept intact, while the villains, given their abject nature, could not hide what they were even when disguised as gentlemen.[12]

Never did the Francoists publicly recognize the pain among the defeated, much less among the general population, that their repression had caused. However, a few times, and only among themselves, they made more or less implicit remarks about their repression. One of these acknowledgments appeared in a February 1956 internal report. The news that the long-standing, hardline Falangist José Luis Arrese had been reappointed to the cabinet as minister for the party was received with high expectations by die-hard fascists, who now believed the pre-1945 golden days would return forever.

Arrese's short-lived 1956 neo-fascist project led him to reorganize and expand the party's spy service with the opening of new provincial branches. Upon learning of the idea another long-standing Falangist, himself a member of the spy service, wrote to the head of the service to advise him against the idea because it would increase party unpopularity by reopening old wounds. As he put it, during the war years, in the areas controlled by the Francoist forces, ordinary people "associated" the spy service with "repression, detentions and executions, even if the reality was different." And in the areas "liberated" from the republicans "many [of our] comrades, with a desire for revenge or because of a police-minded spirit [...] have left unpleasant memories in the streets [...] and animosity, if not [outright] hatred and contempt towards us by our enemies and by many who could be our friends."[13]

That was for internal consumption only. All through its existence, the dictatorship contrasted images of the "peaceful" present with a violent past, trying to hammer home that only Franco's government prevented Spaniards from relapsing into social strife and war. The continually reinforced message was that Franco and his regime meant peace, while liberal democracy meant chaos and death. It followed therefore that for Spaniards to enjoy peace, they had to give up freedom, to which they were unsuited. In this message, liberal democracy was un-Spanish and served only as a back door for communism. The fact that the Communist Party presented itself as the only real anti-Francoist alternative helped the dictatorship confirm this tenet.

The regime's propagandist claims were assisted by international events early in the dictatorship that reinforced Franco's image as a man of peace.[14] Franco was never a pacifist, and for years he dreamed about wars of conquest. However, his real plans were frustrated by the events of World War II and, paradoxically, this accidental circumstance allowed people's anxieties to identify with the dictatorship's propaganda. Because his plans were never publicly revealed, it became most Spaniards' perception that Franco wished to remain neutral in order to save his people from further horrors.[15] It all started with the outbreak of World War II. After the fall of France in June 1940, Franco toyed with the idea of imitating Mussolini and joining the conflict on Hitler's side. Victory was supposedly at hand for the Axis powers, and the Spanish dictator had his own ambitious plans, which were mostly centered on carving out a new empire in the north of Africa at France's expense. He had even made plans for attacking and annexing Portugal.[16] Luckily for him, he did not reach an agreement with Hitler when they met in Hendaye in October of 1940. Franco asked for a lot, but had little to offer to the then confident German dictator. Spaniards knew nothing of what was being discussed, but feared the worst. After the meeting, upon realizing that the specter of war had disappeared for the time being, the majority, regardless of ideology, breathed a sigh of relief.

The fact that Franco was not going to get his share of the war spoils did not prevent him from helping the Germans with both material and logistics. He went even further after the invasion of the Soviet Union in June 1941, when he was imprudent enough to send a division of "volunteers," the Blue Division, to fight alongside the Nazis. He was lucky that Stalin did not bother to declare war on Spain because it might have forced the rest of the Allies to follow suit, plunging Spain into the heart of the conflict. At that time, the regime's propaganda machine was blasting not only the Soviets but also what it referred to as decadent, Jewish-controlled, liberal, plutocratic democracies.

Another critical moment arrived in November 1942, when Anglo-American forces landed in northern Africa. The regime and most Spaniards again held their breath, fearing that the Allies would continue to advance first through Spanish Morocco and on to the Iberian peninsula itself. The advance did not happen, but this particular threat of war, brought on by the close proximity of foreign troops, helped to generate a sentiment of gratitude to the dictator for preserving Spain's supposed neutrality.

This convoluted relationship between people's opinion, war, and the dictator's image was far from unique to Franco's Spain. It could be found elsewhere. Mussolini's popularity in 1939 was linked to the Italians' public perception that he did not want war. His decline after June 1940 happened because he entered the conflict and, furthermore, by this move brought defeat and suffering to Italians.[17] Ordinary Germans did not want war in 1939, but while the initial victories increased Hitler's prestige, after Stalingrad and subsequent defeats, popular opinion started a process of disenchantment with the Nazi dictator.[18] Perhaps the dictator whose fate was most similar to that of Franco was Stalin, a contemporary murderer of his own people, a victorious war leader, and a man who ended up described in both propaganda and nostalgic recollection as a bearer of peace and prosperity. Of course, the Georgian was a far crueler and more damaging man than the Galician, but both eventually buried their crimes and presented themselves, with remarkable success, as gentle grandfathers looking after their respective peoples' wellbeing, even if they had been the main cause of their suffering. Finally, both, in spite of being rather incompetent commanders, used victory to appoint themselves as generalissimos; surrounded by courtiers who lauded them as military geniuses (the third generalissimo of the century, the Chinese nationalist dictator Chiang Kai-shek, was no better a commander).[19]

After 1945, the regime's propaganda machine quickly made the best of the dictator's newfound role as the nation's peacemaker. Peace for Spain and Franco's rule became increasingly identified with one another in the tightly controlled media and therefore in popular opinion (public opinion only exists in free societies; in dictatorships people have to guess the truth from propaganda, rumors, and personal deductions). Nationalism and dictatorship were used interchangeably in official language. Foreign intervention or demands for a political transition toward democracy were seen as their antithesis. Any effort to bring freedom to Spain was presented as an attempt to impose slavery on the country by its eternal enemies, who were also the enemies of religion. Whatever people's feelings about freedom or religion, almost everybody understood that, while Franco was alive, change likely meant war. When, in December 1946, the newly created United Nations made a declaration asking for the diplomatic boycott of the Spanish dictatorship while condemning the regime as "fascist," many ordinary Spaniards perceived this as a dangerous and unacceptable intrusion into the internal affairs of their country, an attempt to impose change by foreign people who knew nothing of the cost of change. There were huge demonstrations of support for the regime in the country's main cities. These were officially sanctioned and organized, but popular support was, for the most part, genuine.

In later years the regime would bask many more times in the rays of this type of mass demonstration, denouncing international interference in Spain's peace and its national concerns. The dictatorship always reminded Spaniards that any foreign declarations against Franco were the design of communists or other hostile politicians in exile who wanted to restart the war. Spaniards may or may not have completely believed these assertions, but the mere possibility of again falling into civil strife drove ordinary people to support the notion that peace could only be preserved by Franco. Many of the ambiguities of Franco's Spain can be explained in this way; underlying contradictions reached back to a civil war that had never really ended.

The Cold War, and particularly the USA's interest in having strategically placed Spain as an ally, ended any doubts about the regime's future. The regime claimed victory in 1950 when Spain was readmitted to the international theater as the UN reversed its sanctions against the dictatorship, including the 1946 diplomatic boycott. Foreign ambassadors returned to

Madrid. They had already begun to see Franco, or so they pretended, as a sort of misunderstood anti-communist champion. Among the great powers, the Americans led the adoption of the pro-Francoist view of the past. In 1949 the US attaché in Madrid wrote to Washington:

> Stable democracy in Spain is a possibility only in the indefinite future. Past efforts at democracy had produced instability and chaos. These people, high or low, do not know the difference between liberty and license. [...] Franco is not to blame for all the things that are wrong here in Spain and, while he himself is a devout Catholic, there is no indication that he or his regime members support that old Inquisition spirit found in the Spanish Catholic Church and among the people.[20]

Spaniards knew nothing about what the free world thought of them. They did not know, for example, why they were different from Germans or Italians who, having embraced Nazism or fascism until very recently, now had the right to live in peace and freedom. In any case, they surely were relieved by the end of international sanctions. But ordinary Spaniards' main concern had nothing to do with politics or international matters. They had long since become concerned about something else altogether: they simply wanted to live better lives. As a confidential 1950 Falangist report from Malaga explained, while it was understood that the ambassadors' return represented a personal victory for Franco, people also expected this to begin a period of normalization of the country's economy, a reduction of useless bureaucracy, and the inauguration of a new period of political "austerity."[21] Similarly a report from Valencia said much the same thing: Spaniards did not want more involvement in politics, they just wanted lower prices, better salaries, food, and access to a greater number of goods and services.[22]

Franco's pundits claimed at the time that Spain was leaving the problems of the past behind. This was "confirmed" when in 1953 the United States and the dictatorship signed a number of agreements for military and economic cooperation. American dollars and new economic ideas began to flow into the previously isolated, impoverished country. The dictatorship was definitely safe. A more generous ruler would have seized the opportunity that his regime's stability provided to seek real reconciliation among Spaniards. He did not, among other things because there were too many lies and victims behind his power; this is why his regime continued to present a vision of the past that excluded millions of Spaniards and made a mockery of the history of the whole nation. The survivors were left with two options: to forget or to keep the memories of the past until one day they could speak freely again. Those who decided not to forget had too many terrible stories to preserve, but also too many interests against them.

The Fruits of Terror

The Francoist manipulation of Spain's recent history only included, for example, a selection of the events that took place in the small town of Camargo, located in rural Santander. This area remained in republican hands until the summer of 1937. It is situated in the heart of northern Spain, and it was here that, in the early months of the war, a pocket of doomed republican fighters found themselves surrounded by Franco's armies and their Italian fascist allies. Not far from Camargo, on one side of a road, there is a deserted area called Peñas Negras (Black Cliffs). It was, and still is, a place of haunted memories. This was a place used by both "red" and "blue" assassins for night-time extra-judicial killings. During the first months of the war, republicans sometimes burned the bodies of their victims here. In an interview given in the early 1990s, Isidro R., a priest, who spent the first year of the war in hiding, admonished the republicans, saying that red "persecution was asocial, not a social revenge against capital. It was against religion, only against religion." He "proved" this by explaining that people with money, factory directors for example, remained unharmed while five young workers from his parish were killed because they regularly attended mass and were Catholic Action members. At the same time, this priest, like most of the people of the town, also remembered Silvio Fombellida, the republican mayor, who was later killed by the Francoists even though he was described as "be[ing] a good and decent man" who saved many people, including Isidro himself.[23]

Even though he was a man who had clearly declared himself pro-Franco, Isidro's nuanced recollection was not included in its entirety in the *General Cause*, the official Francoist account of the republican (and only republican) crimes committed during the war. This document ignored the "good" deeds of Mayor Fombellida and accused him instead of being the mastermind behind 56 killings.[24] Father Isidro was more forgiving and pardoned Mayor Fombellida when he stated, "I would not have killed him. Perhaps if he had gone into hiding and wait[ed] for the moments of rage to pass …"[25]

The killing of the teacher of Escobedo in the republican town of Saturnino in the Peñas Negras region was another story that did not fit neatly into Franco's official history. The day rebel troops entered the town, the teacher was knifed to death and his body was hastily buried. Three days later, his father came asking for him, but "the whole town went mute, afraid that he would start shooting." The teacher's father was an officer in the Civil Guard. He was fighting for Franco and for the side that had just murdered his son.[26]

Situations as complex as those described above never fitted into the simplistic, one-sided version of events that Francoism always propagated, which characterized *all* republicans as degenerate monsters. Its moral ally, the Catholic Church, agreed with this and added to this campaign. From the then recently elected Pope Pius XII (1939–58), who rushed to congratulate Franco on his victory in April 1939, to the cardinals and bishops who almost unanimously supported the rebellion through a joint letter to the Catholic world in July 1937, the Church's leaders wholeheartedly embraced the unyielding repudiation of the republican side. Though there were many exceptions to this, such as local priests who at times protected members of their communities, there were also numerous cases of clerical indifference and even incitement to murder.

A local example of the Church's pro-Franco, but at times confused, activities during the war, happened in rural Galicia, a region that had been controlled by the Francoists in the summer of 1936. There was no armed resistance there at the time.[27] The only reason behind the killing of republicans was to exterminate and to terrorize the local population. Only this can explain what J. A. Dacoba saw in rural Orense in the summer of 1936:

> when they detained Castor [Sánchez, local socialist mayor], don Francisco, the Montefria priest, he told those workers who were asking him to save them [the mayor and the other men]: I am not going to, because if I do, they will kill him sooner. [Eventually] it was the priest of Parada who ordered Castor to be killed, telling the Falangists: He has many children and is a good person. [But] he is too smart [...] if you want to control the town, he will bother you.[28]

Afterwards, the priest of Parada registered this man's death in the parish book (in thousands of cases such deaths went unrecorded), even describing it as a killing and including the details of where, why, and by whom (the Falangists) this man and another two had been murdered. He also wrote that the victims had lived apart from the Church. Nevertheless he asked God to "forgive them." Other religious people were not as cautious as this priest. In the early days of the rebellion, the parish priest of neighboring

Palmes personally led a Falangist squad into the local socialist clubhouse and helped to destroy it. In subsequent days, many of the local Socialist Party and union leaders were killed. Among those killed was a respected local president of the agrarian society. He had seven children.[29]

The Church was both victim and perpetrator. During the war, nearly 8,000 members of the clergy were assassinated. They were killed by republican militias and committees, mostly in the summer months of 1936, and their murders were often horrific. Many of these victims were later beatified in the last years of the pontificates of John Paul II (1978–2005) and Benedict XVI.[30] However, during and after the war, the Church failed to preach or to practice forgiveness. In the midst of the unfolding violence, only the Church could have spoken out against repression and murder, but she remained mostly silent. This silence gave impunity, and perhaps peace of mind, to those who during the war dumped bodies at roadsides and in cemeteries every morning. The Church's silence meant moral endorsement for the military courts which, after the war, legally murdered tens of thousands of Spaniards. These court sessions were open to the public; priests were often seem seated there, either as spectators or because they went to testify.

These legal executions were not the only, nor even the last, killings to take place in post-war Spain. The war did not completely end when the republican armies surrendered and were made prisoners in late March 1939. Many republicans, refusing to accept defeat, headed for the mountains. The price for those who tried to wage a guerrilla war (very active between 1944 and 1949) was high, and weighed heavily on their relatives. In their fight against the communist-dominated guerrillas, the Francoist forces habitually used family members as hostages, knowing that fugitives would feel responsible for the fate of their loved ones. Mothers, wives, sisters, and even children – anybody could be forced to betray or used to convince the guerrillas to surrender. The Asturian Marcelo García, then a child, later remembered how his uncles sought protection in the hills from the Francoists. Falangists and the Civil Guard beat Marcelo. Then they took his grandmother and tortured her by placing her upside down. His aunt Araceli was also tortured and became gravely ill, finally losing a lung as the result of her mistreatment. Finally, he related, "my father's brothers when they learned what was happening, surrendered, and both of them were shot in Oviedo." His experience was far from unique.

Manuel Gil was a guerrilla fighter who escaped from Spain in 1948. His wife was only 18 when the police started to routinely torture her because "they wanted to learn the truth by beating [...] they put her in prison, then released her, and so on, every two days she had to go to the Civil Guard, then to the Civil Government, another day to the Military Government [...] she lived like that for eleven years."[31] During the 40 years of dictatorship, people like Araceli or Manuel and his wife did not officially exist and their experiences, no matter how traumatic, went unrecorded.

Conversely, much publicized and recorded in post-war Spain were the crimes carried out by the guerrillas, who were routinely (and sometimes justifiably) described as "bandits." Many people, particularly in small rural communities, were caught up in the vicious guerrilla war of the late 1940s. On the one hand, the guerrillas proclaimed that they were rescuing "the people" from the dictatorship, thus justifying the murder of local Francoists and the extortion of rich, and not so rich, peasants. On the authorities' side, the victims of the guerrillas were martyrs, and those killed or tortured in counter-insurgency operations, guilty or not, were simply dismissed as criminals or accomplices.[32] Rural Spain lived in terror well into the early 1950s.

Francoist repression reached everywhere. It could affect almost anybody, adults and children, not just because of what they did but also because of what they thought or what the authorities suspected they might have done or thought.[33] G.L., for example, was a Basque child who returned to post-war Spain from abroad, where his parents had sent him during the conflict. As an adult, he remembered the fear of having failed to stop when passing near a school and the Falangist anthem, *Cara al Sol* (Facing the Sun), had suddenly played. "I didn't know, and the first time my aunt told me: Stop! You must salute! I was so afraid and trembling; I thought they were going to throw us in jail!"[34] Not to stop and adopt a martial position when the national anthem or any of the regime's other anthems were played was an unwritten crime in the early 1940s. What might happen if a policeman or a Falangist discovered that he had been in exile? What about an adult who fought for the Republic?

Having been, or just the possibility of being perceived to have been, on the wrong side in the past made people of all ages afraid. This terror of the unknown was even present during leisure activities. At the cinema, before a film started, a newsreel called NODO would play. It would, without fail, include the activities of El Caudillo, and failing to clap when Franco appeared on the screen was considered an act of sedition.[35] At the end of a movie the national anthem would play, and everyone was expected to greet it with the fascist salute.

Fear ran through people's veins because punishment for dissent was merciless. Everybody knew that there was a more or less secret world in which bad things happened, and that a wrong turn could put you there. These were Franco's prisons. By the end of 1940 there were 240,916 political prisoners in Spain, 7,762 of them on death row, awaiting execution. These prisons were deadly, not just because of the executions and the frequent beatings that took place in them but also because illness and starvation were rampant. Nothing of this officially existed and yet the relatives and friends of those who struggled to survive behind bars knew of their plight. People heard rumors and whispered stories. Perhaps someone knew of Antonio Morales, a socialist teacher, who left Spain in 1953, after 14 years in prison. His first years there read like a list of horrors: bodies full of lice, bed bugs, and skin diseases, hunger, cold nights, sleeping in the rain, eating rotten food, and several mock-executions. Antonio remembered comrades "who died poisoned because they ate what they found in the garbage and devoured grasses to mitigate their hunger."[36]

Executions were only supposed to come at the end of a legal process, but quite often they were the culmination of a tragic parody of justice. J.C. remembered how one day, in the provincial prison of Murcia, the director of the jail and his guards pointed randomly at five men as the inmates marched past them. All five were shot soon afterwards. Other horrors also took place. Concha Fuentes, a woman prisoner in Murcia, remembers how, along with a fellow inmate, she was repeatedly gang-raped by guards, sometimes six or seven at a time. On one occasion, a fellow prisoner who was pregnant was gang-raped in the same prison. She later miscarried and was then shot at dawn.[37]

For Concha Fuentes, a former militia woman and a member of the Communist Youth, prison, albeit a harrowing experience, cemented her faith in her comrades, who demonstrated constant solidarity.[38] When two of them were shot, she breastfed their babies along with her own: "I nursed three babies in prison." The source of this miracle was that other prisoners always saw to it that she received a large portion of the little food that they gathered from outside or inside the prison walls, including the nauseating broths full of black worms that they were served. Her plight did not end when she left the prison at the end of 1941. She could find no work, but was resolute in her commitment to the cause. She was among the communists who established vigils at the local cemetery. When they heard that someone had been shot, they would go to identify the victim and tell their relatives what had happened.[39]

The experience of Concha was that of a committed militant, but prison for the politically lukewarm José Aldomar was essentially a place where he met all kinds of people, mostly simple individuals who struggled to keep their moral strength intact. Until 1939, Aldomar had been a liberal-minded railway inspector. Immediately after Madrid surrendered he was arrested, and was quickly condemned to death after a hastily prepared military trial. A loyal Francoist's denunciation was the main evidence against him. Like tens of thousands of others, he met his defense lawyer for the first time in court. He was not executed, just condemned to death and then pardoned, but not before suffering a series of prison transfers before being released in 1941.

Aldomar was a compulsive writer who kept a secret, almost daily, record of life behind bars. There, he observed political prisoners making the best of their situation. They had an orchestra, and produced theater shows, once losing a leading actor to a firing squad on the eve of the first performance. Mostly, the people he met dreamed of freedom, food, and family. He also met and wrote about cruel prison officials and vengeful nuns and priests, while at other times he observed other members of the clergy and guards who tried to help the inmates. For Aldomar, prison became an archive of the stories of the very different people he encountered, oral histories of what had happened in Spanish towns before, during, and after the war, accounts of prisoners' relatives, their lost jobs and properties, their personal tragedies. He promised himself to preserve as many of these stories as he could, stories he knew were otherwise bound for extinction. He kept notes, smuggled letters, and, during the long decades of the dictatorship, he reconstructed these records and painstakingly typed them up.[40] Even though he was officially "pardoned," throughout the dictatorship he had to fight to have his right to a pension recognized. He died in 1978, a few months after democratic Spain had been established and he had finally reinstated his pension rights as a former employee of the railway company (RENFE).[41]

The effects of terror did not stop at people's doors. They could be felt within families, and turn their members against each other. For example, the agrarian region of Santander had a reputation for being conservative and staunchly Catholic. Here, as in the rest of Spain, defeated republicans living under Franco could expect official persecution and social rejection for having fought on the wrong side in the war, even from their own families. Two former republicans, Román V. and Antonio G., suffered their relatives' bitter criticisms for the "disgrace" that their political ideas had brought the families during the dictatorship. If they had not had those "ideals, they [their families] would not have suffered their consequences such as prison, being fired from jobs, hunger, and begging." Even in the early 1990s, when democracy was on a safe footing, they preferred not to talk too much about their activities during the Civil War.[42]

Other people managed to hide their past, not only from the general public but from their own relatives in order to protect them, to maintain their innocence in the face of an unforgiving present, thus creating an invisible intergenerational wall. In neighboring Asturias another former republican, Nazario Lozano, explained to the young person who interviewed him in the 1980s that during the dictatorship "it was more important to forget than to remember." Only once democracy had been restored, and legislation had been passed to compensate veterans of the republican army, did Nazario finally disclose to his own children that he had been a loyalist (republican) captain in the war.[43]

Francoism used terror not only to eliminate its enemies but also to remind people of what their place in society was; to reverse any progress towards social equality and fairness at work achieved in the previous decades. Poor people soon learned that silence and outward submission were essential to survive.[44] This mechanism of self-defense took on many forms, and these forms were never entirely linear in nature. For example, the province of Cordoba was known as a "godless" region with a rich revolutionary tradition where, from the nineteenth century on, agrarian workers had revolted many times against their misery and against deep social inequalities. From the early days of the Civil War most of the province, including the capital city, had been controlled by the Francoist forces and repression there was extremely harsh. Historians have so far been able to name 9,579 republicans who were killed.[45] Worse still, the killing continued well beyond the end of the conflict because left-wing guerrillas remained very active until the end of the 1940s.[46]

When a researcher conducted a study of Cordoba's economy and its people's attitudes in the late 1960s, he found that the memory of the repression, during and after the war, and the historical defeat of the local landless peasants, had left a deep imprint. He also found that these seasonal laborers knew how best to defend themselves against a present that they felt they could not control. After a time, the researcher gained their trust and they explained to him that to have political ideas when you were poor was a dangerous thing. It was risky to even mention politics, just as it was risky to be publicly associated with anyone who dared discuss them. People who took the risk were called men and women of "ideas": individuals who expressed their political dissent against Franco's regime as openly as they dared while trying to keep banned unions and political parties alive.[47]

Most peasants and workers felt a mixture of fear, contempt, and a degree of hidden admiration toward these people who, in spite of all the odds, remained "political."[48] Those who viewed them mostly with contempt identified political "ideas" with the possibility of a revival of the horrors of the war. Some, assuming the official propaganda line, even insinuated that those "politicals" were just the remains of the defeated "killers" (republican militiamen). Those who admired them saw in these men and women of "ideas" the remnants of the honesty and courage of a bygone era and of things that might have gone well, but, in the end, had turned out very badly. Perhaps the most common view was that, although these dissenters belonged to the same social group as "we the poor," their tenacity was considered both extremely foolish and something that only brought disgrace upon themselves and their families.[49] For those peasants, the rules were clear: while politics were not for them, at work, both they and their employers had to respect agreements and customs. If either of the two sides failed to do so, then they could protest but only in the name of "custom" and "honor," never using words or carrying out actions that could be identified as political.

Those peasants' attitude was in no way exceptional. Most Spaniards shared their view. There were many historical reasons for this distrust of politics. Obviously, at the outbreak of the war in 1936 Spanish society had been politically mobilized as never before. What is in question is simply the extent of this mobilization and the degree of enthusiasm among the general population for political discourse.[50] In this sense, it is tempting, but inaccurate, to confuse the images of militant fervor on both sides of the Civil War, as displayed in newsreels and other graphic or literary-historical accounts, with the mindset of ordinary people during the conflict. The most common feeling in 1936 among Spaniards was neither of revolutionary nor counter-revolutionary fervor, but rather of horror. This expression of horror also includes a condemnation of the fact that political confrontation had led the country to civil war.[51]

The limited data available on the opinions of ordinary people during the war also reveal that the commitment to either side was in great measure accidental and/or imposed (by both sides) and that most people wanted first and foremost for the war to end.[52] This included the combatants. When, for example, in the summer of 1937 the Francoist forces took over 106,000 military prisoners in the just eliminated northern front, they proceeded to conduct a careful political screening of their captives. They were on the lookout for committed republicans, and they had a well-earned reputation for using the slightest excuse to declare anyone an enemy. However, they found that only 10 percent of those prisoner soldiers were "criminals" (militant republicans) and another 20 percent of dubious political allegiance; the rest, for the most part, could be immediately enlisted in their own forces.[53] If asked, the majority of soldiers would have preferred to go home and forget about the war.

This disgust regarding politics can be detected in oral histories. There, a recurrent theme, which can be seen as symbolic attempt to re-establish peace in the local communities, is that most killings were carried out by strangers from other, larger and more problematic, places. For example, N.G. from Beniel (Murcia), when remembering an anarchist column of militiamen that came to her town in 1936, said that "they were thieves [...] they went to Beniel and took them [right-wing people] out to the Port, they killed them. I do not agree with that, because a left-wing person, an honest one, doesn't do that, those are not real ideals."[54] The implicit message in this type of recollection is that strangers killed each other *only* because of their different ideologies. However, studies of the repression conducted by historians show otherwise: killers and victims often knew each other; they were neighbors, and politics was only one of the motivating factors behind the crimes.[55]

Most people, regardless of their political sympathies, if they had any at all, remained physically untouched by the violence of either side during the war and afterwards, and preferred to lie low during the war and the dictatorship. Their rejection of politics was caused by a desire to avoid any more suffering. They adopted new anti-political values, which included forgetting, at least the side of the story that the regime wanted Spaniards to forget.[56] This double process of accommodation and amnesia was assisted by the fact that, after 1943, direct repression became the problem of a small minority. After 1945, only a few thousand political prisoners (about 16,000), people of "ideas," would remain in prison.[57]

Terror gave the regime a second victory over the republicans: it not only physically destroyed the opposition but also destroyed hope for the return of democracy. However, it would be a mistake to conclude that this triumph and the hegemony that Francoist propaganda's distortions of the past exercised over society were the product of repression alone. Terror may have damaged millions of lives and cowed millions more but, for millions of other people, it secured property rights and the protection of their Catholic values. This is well known; less known is the fact that terror also brought material rewards and privileges for those who took part in repressive activities or took advantage of the opportunities that a regime based on terror provided. In sum, it is forgotten that terror was also a profitable business.

Silence about the fate of the republicans often served the material interests of those who observed it. A strategy critical to the dictatorship's aim of keeping the results, both political and social, of the war alive in the minds of Spaniards was the practice of rewarding its supporters, often by commandeering the jobs and properties of enemies of the regime. For example, when Aldomar was arrested in April 1939 someone else took his job, held it, and eventually received a pension. His case was very common. At the end of the war, the ranks of civil servants and public employees were subjected to a purge that resulted in sanctions and mass expulsions. Conversely, 80 percent of all new positions in public administration were reserved for former Francoist combatants, for those who had been held prisoner by republicans, or for direct survivors of Francoists who had been killed in the war. Widows of fallen soldiers received small pensions, and their children obtained preferential treatment in the award of scholarships and with regard to placement in schools and welfare institutions.[58] These were small rewards, but in starving, post-war Spain they made a huge material and psychological difference. For example, the widows of Franco's army were not to suffer the same fate as the women in the formerly republican city of Badajoz, a city infamous for the summer of 1936 when Francoist forces shot thousands of republican militiamen. It is not surprising that, in 1943, a local police officer explained that numerous "young war widows that, either because of vice or because of not having any other income, must resort to prostitution."[59] The irony of this statement was that these "morally fallen" women were trying to feed the children of the mortally fallen men who now neither officially existed nor, according to the state, were ever killed. To this day, some pro-Franco historians deny that the Badajoz massacre ever happened.

The combination of fear and greed also prevented any public discussion about the fate of the property of thousands of murdered or imprisoned republicans. During and after the war, homes, machinery, trucks, and other property were either confiscated by Francoist supporters on the spot or awarded by courts and official commissions after the war as "reparations" for supposed damages. This means that, while some of the expropriations were achieved "legally," quite often they were just gunpoint transactions, completed with the murder of the victim: they were war's loot.[60] So far, historians have been able to discover just the tip of the iceberg and only in some provinces. For example, in 1938 in the province of Asturias alone there were 6,692 files aimed at appropriating property from "red" owners. In Biscay in the same year, the Francoist authorities opened up to 25,000 expropriation files.[61] How much of this project was carried out or expanded in those two provinces and in the other 48 provinces of Spain remains unknown. Furthermore, expropriations did continue long after the war, now as a result of the fines imposed on republicans (sometimes on dead republicans) by the so-called Political Responsibilities courts, which by 1945 had started proceedings against between 500,000 and 700,000 Spaniards.[62]

Perhaps nowhere was terror more profitable than in the countryside, and not only because of the expropriations. Here tens of thousands of sharecroppers and renters had their contracts unilaterally broken or altered by newly empowered landlords. Almost nobody, in public or on paper, dared to challenge this. An exception was the case of Antonio Castillo. In 1939 he was 68 years old, illiterate, of very modest means, and had been sharecropping in Paterna del Rio (Almeria) since 1929. He either had too much courage (which proved to be futile in the end), or was naive enough to state that within days of the end of the war, the landlord's administrator had come and "fired me, confiscating the harvest […] and forbade me from ever returning to this land. He also said that if I reported on him, I would be sent to prison, and if I wanted to earn a living I should hit the road and look for work elsewhere."[63]

Antonio lived the war in "red" territory, but this was not the cause of his eviction. It was revenge and a spoil of victory conceded by the regime to the social victors of the war. However, the problem of evictions from the land was particularly acute in Extremadura, which had either been with Franco since the beginning of the war or came to be controlled by him soon afterwards. In 1957, in the province of Caceres alone, which before and after the war had terrible social problems, the Francoist authorities estimated that "20,000 families of sharecroppers [were] expelled in recent years." These sharecroppers became drifting laborers, often unemployed, and were joined by "close to five thousand war veterans, their children or the unemployed children of fallen soldiers, [and] more than three thousand had had to emigrate in recent years."[64] The Francoist hold on society was not just anchored in fear and propaganda; it was firmly supported by interest, including a pact of silence and complicity in the oppression of the defeated and the weakest, even if, as in this case, they had fought for Franco.

The Lost People and the New Country

Prisoners, dead people, and stolen property and rights were not the only things missing from Franco's Spain. Also erased from the official record were the approximately 300,000 Spaniards who managed to escape into exile. Most of them went to France, others to Latin America, mostly to Mexico. Like the dead, when they were recalled in the official propaganda time and distance did not spare them from being insulted. One of those exiled was Fernando Pradal. He was 9 years old when he left Spain in March 1939, and he eventually became a respected scientist in France. In some ways, he can be considered lucky. His father was a republican MP whose friends managed to send Fernando and other members of their family to Oran, then part of French Algeria. Fernando's temporary refugee camp was called El Asnan, in a town called Carnot, near Orléansville.[65] Other refugees who followed suit in the last days of the war from the ports of Alicante and Almeria suffered, after being prevented from disembarking in Oran, desperation and squalor on board the ship as they sat in the North African harbor. They were forced to meet their physical needs over the broadside of their cramped boats anchored a few hundred meters from port, and were observed and mocked, as a sort of pastime, by people strolling by the sea.

Most refugees who ended up in France, or in French-controlled territories, were interned in hastily built, inadequately equipped camps where no sanitation, no barracks, and insufficient food were the rule. Often the authorities managing these camps could barely conceal their contempt for them. In general, the attitudes of the French population were far more generous than those of their government. While many kind people tried to help, the language of the right-wing French press was replete with ideological prejudices and racist adjectives when describing the refugees.

Not only were there Spanish civilians living in these refugee camps, but soldiers from the defeated republican army landed there as well. Joan Martorell crossed the French border from Catalonia in February 1939. He was only 19 at the time and spent 11 months in four camps of the Midi (Saint-Cyprien, Adge, Barcarès, Argelès). In January 1940 the French army recruited him to work in a factory that manufactured components for defense. After the French were defeated by the Nazis in June of that year, he again found himself a prisoner. When the Francoist government was asked about him, or other republicans, the answer that came back was that they were no longer considered Spaniards. Franco and his powerful brother-in-law and right-hand man, Ramón Serrano Súñer, left them in the hands of the Nazis. Thousands of Spaniards paid for this with their lives. Joan escaped again and contacted other republicans and former members of the International Brigades who had fought in Spain, and joined the French Resistance. He was arrested again in 1943, this time by the Vichy police, which promptly delivered him to the Germans, who sent him to Dachau in a railway cattle car along with 120 other anti-fascists. He was among the minority of Spaniards who survived the camps. Just before his liberation, Joan witnessed the arrival of the so-called "death train" from Le Vernet that carried mutilated republican soldiers. Half of them died en route, the rest died while interned. When American soldiers arrived at Dachau in April 1945 the surprised troops were greeted by ragged men hoisting a Spanish republican flag over the main door. Joan was among them.[66]

The list of exiles who fled the dictatorship is full of famous names, including those of the winner of the Nobel Prize in Literature, Juan Ramón Jiménez, the great jurist Luis Jiménez de Asúa, and the scholars who founded the prestigious Colegio de México. Highly educated, with international reputations, most of these women and men found opportunities in their adopted homes; but nearly all refugees were either ordinary civilians or young defeated soldiers. For these people life was much harder. Moreover, regardless of their personal situation, all exiles shared the painful experience of adapting to a foreign country while at the same time struggling to preserve their identity and to retain the memory of what their country had been. Their memories kept them close to, but at the same time very distant from, their beloved but changing Spain.

When those in exile were able to return, often for a brief visit, their experiences were often almost as painful and alienating as they had been when they fled. The country that they found had changed after many years: it was neither the land of their youth nor the Spain depicted by anti-Francoist critics. For Josep Muriá, who went back to Spain in the late 1960s, the shock was finding out how "materialistic" and "rude" people had become.[67] Carmen Roure cried when the plane which brought her back began to fly over Spain, but then, while visiting her native Lerida, she was shocked to see how narrow-minded her former friends were. "Either I had changed a lot or they had," she thought. But when Manuel Martínez returned for the first time in 1957, he had "a bad impression [...] because things were better than our propaganda said [...] they were many needs in Spain but people now ate ... and the country was rising [from] its ashes."[68]

Those who returned often found that the Spanish consuls who processed their documents and the policemen who greeted them on their arrival were less hostile than they had feared. Sometimes these officials were overly courteous. Unlike the dictatorship they served, it seemed that many civil servants wanted to put the war and the hatred behind them. Furthermore, not unlike many intellectuals and former pro-Franco politicians, many ordinary right-wing people now conceded some validity to their former enemy's cause. Shortly after returning from Mexico for a visit in the 1960s, while strolling in the streets of the small town of Vendrell in Tarragona province, Pascual Casanova met the town's mayor, a Falangist and former Francoist soldier. They had been friends before the war and now the mayor crossed the street to embrace him. "Neither of us said anything. We just left it there."[69]

The exceptions to these more humanitarian feelings were both the Falangists and the regime's propaganda apparatus. They used the return of exiles as a proof of Spain's "peace" and Franco's triumph. In 1957, for example, a number of Spanish exiles, most of whom had been children when they left the country, returned from the Soviet Union. To "confirm" the success of the dictatorship and its superiority over communism (and to prove how misguided was criticism by democratic public opinion worldwide) a number of confidential directives were issued by the government to facilitate the refugees' reintegration into Spanish society (such as jobs, validating academic titles, and housing allowances). These people were given unofficial preference ("without showing apparent favor") for the disposal of the state's meager social services. This caused deep resentment among the Falangists who, ironically, were then given the job of spying and informing on the opinions and movements of the refugees.[70]

The Spain these exiles returned to was a country where, for most people, Francoism was a fact of life they simply had to deal with, whatever feelings they harbored. The main strategy for achieving the goal of a normal life was to concentrate on personal and family matters and to avoid politics. Not surprisingly, intellectual life, from universities to coffee shops, was dormant, stiff, and pretentious.[71] Spain had become, in the middle of democratic post-war Europe, a country without public opinion, one based on propaganda and rumors. This implied that people had only a few, censored newspapers to choose from. In many provinces where it had been normal before the war to have several daily newspapers, readers were now forced to buy the local Falangist mouthpiece because it was the only publication allowed. More committed readers were able to secure the single national newspaper that would arrive from Madrid one day late. Not surprisingly, newspaper readership declined throughout the 1940s, when Spain had one of the lowest rates of newspaper readership in the West. In 1948, Italy's newspapers published three times as many copies as their Spanish counterparts (5 million versus 1.6 million), despite the fact that Italy's population was only a third larger than Spain's.[72]

Franco ruled over a disengaged and individualistic society. This was probably the opposite of what those people abroad who accused him of being a rabid fascist imagined. The regime could be deadly murderous, but Franco's Spain was not Hitler's Germany, and the Falange never had a portion of the power and mobilization capability that the Nazi party displayed. Unlike Germans under the Third Reich, throughout the dictatorship Spaniards had few incentives to participate in voluntary or community associations. The state's main function was to control rather than to mobilize community activity, and there were very few publicly sponsored opportunities for volunteer engagement apart from those connected to the ruling party and its women's and youth organizations.[73] However, despite the attention that has been devoted to them by historians because of their fascist affiliation, these official organizations were poor, ill-funded copies of their Italian and Nazi models, and only engaged a small minority of the population. At their peak, they enrolled less than a third of all young Spanish males, and never more than 15 percent of their female counterparts. Furthermore, Franco's youth organizations were primarily urban-focused, only superficially reaching rural areas late in the regime's existence.

Most of the activities of the remaining community-based organizations revolved around the Catholic Church through its parish structure and private schools, through the youth sections of Catholic Action, or through involvement in the Church's mass processions and pilgrimages. However, the Church's power of penetration was very limited in many parts of the country, because religious attendance was very low in urban industrial areas and in the traditionally "pagan" southeast, where in the 1940s only 20 percent of the population was believed to attend Sunday mass.[74] The Church's influence was further diffused because its youth organizations always retained an elitist and urban profile that deterred poor and rural families.

With the exception of the school system, interaction between regime and population was basically a matter of public order. The only period in which ordinary Spaniards were mobilized by the dictatorship was, for young males, the mandatory two- or three-year period of military service. Franco's army was not a people's army, not even of the SS type. Social prejudice, favoritism, and corruption were rife, reflecting the political nature and daily practices of the dictatorship. Being drafted meant very different things to different people depending on what social class they belonged to, and the connections they did or did not have. Families of recruits from the middle and upper classes could use influence to get comfortable postings for their sons, while poor families did not have this option. Having influence also meant that some recruits could opt to be reserve officers where they would be treated like gentlemen during their time of service.

For poorer people the post-war (and in this case until the 1970s) experience of military service was usually far more difficult and painful. It usually began with the boarding of a third-class coach on a train to begin a lengthy, uncomfortable trip (given the poor quality of the rail service) to their barracks. Once there, recruits would spend an average of three months (illiterate men spent twice that time), being poorly fed, poorly housed, and often mistreated by NCOs (even though these officers themselves often came from a humble background). The recruits received ill-fitting uniforms and coarsely executed haircuts that often caused injuries to their scalps. Because they received next to no pay their time in service meant a significant loss of income to their families, with whom they were to have only limited contact as they were often posted as far away as Spain's African possessions. Many recruits and their relatives were illiterate, so contact by mail was difficult at best. Corporal punishment, particularly face-slapping, was common.

Franco's was not an "egalitarian" fascist state – if there ever was one – but an unusually cruel, traditional, reactionary, personal dictatorship based on privilege, corruption, and social prejudices. Poor people had nothing to add but their labor to the process of building the New Spain. For the average Spaniard, obeying was far more important than understanding or believing. Ordinary people did things because the authorities said so, and because protesting brought trouble. The less they knew and the fewer their contacts with authority, the better for them. Not surprisingly, when the army conducted a survey on its draftees in 1950 it exposed two important facts: (a) the general fear of and opposition to mandatory military service on the part of soldiers and their families, and (b) the extremely low level of knowledge of, and active engagement with, the regime, as only 5 percent of recruits were found to understand basic Francoist political principles.[75] This lack of knowledge about politics was not solely the product of intellectual failure but also, or rather, the first lesson that poor Spaniards had learned in 1939 – to avoid thinking about politics – which helped them to survive 40 years of dictatorship.

Imposing Consent

The low level of political knowledge and community activity among the population did not dissuade the regime from *pretending* that Spaniards willingly and enthusiastically supported the dictatorship. Throughout its existence, Francoism maintained that the regime had restored harmony to society by being fair, and by convincing former enemies, particularly landless peasants and the working class, to embrace the cause. The strategy was based on distinguishing between two kinds of enemies: the perverse, defeated republican leaders, and the good, ordinary Spaniards who had been led astray by foreign ideologies and perverse politicians. "Good" was the code word for workers, a term that was avoided and replaced by "producers." The name change only reflected the barely hidden anxieties of the dictatorship. For the regime, the working class was the real problem, because workers were potential revolutionaries. Workers were also one of the main problems for the regime's most important ally, the Catholic Church, which saw them as potentially dangerously anti-clerical (the Church called this the "apostasy of the masses"). Recollections of the Civil War invoked in memoirs published well into the 1960s always contain references to, and often shocking images of, workers and their lustful, bloodthirsty wives, committing morally repulsive crimes against good, respectable people (for example, representatives of the Church as well as the upper and middle classes). The regime would have preferred to erase the proletarians from the Earth's surface but, since modern Spain could not, regrettably, go back to the guild system of medieval times, it was stuck with a population that had to be controlled by force, and if possible convinced of the regime's goodness; or at least appear to have been convinced.[76] The dictatorship and the Church had their plans to impose or to pretend conformity, and they often worked closely together to implement them.

The charade of achieving a new social and national harmony by "persuading" workers to embrace the dictatorship was carried out mainly by an organization which supposedly represented their labor and social concerns. This was the National Confederation of Unions (CNS), a copy of the Italian corporate-fascist model in which workers and employers were brought together by the paternalistic state to share one institution, itself divided in two sections: social (employees) and economic (employers). As in Italy, the "Confederation" was a sham. It barely concealed the fact that its main role was to discipline workers and impose upon them the policies dictated by a government with a decidedly pro-business agenda (even if autarky, regulations, and restrictions annoyed many businesspeople).[77] Despite claims to the contrary by the Falangists who were put in charge of running them, the unions remained at all times instruments of the government. "Producers," along with everyone else concerned, including the unions' Falangist bosses, knew this.[78]

The regime, which ironically called itself National Syndicalist, was never interested in creating powerful unions. This was reflected by a chronic shortage of funding and by the slow process of building the CNS. The organization of the unions was not completed in the main cities until well into the 1950s, while in the countryside the process lasted another decade. A 1953 report from the province of Salamanca, in the Francoist Castilian heartland (its capital had at one point been Franco's provisional seat of government during the war), typifies this situation. CNS's provincial head-quarters in the capital were located in an old and decrepit building, while its offices in the province's second-largest city, Bejar, were in the old socialist "People's House" which was also in a "deplorable" condition. The level of activity demonstrated by the elected presidents of the union's branches was worse still. The man in charge of the cereal branch (the key product in the region) did not "bother at all" with his job, and neither did the presidents of the other main union branches of construction, entertainment, cattle (another key product of the area), chemicals, olive oil, or paper. The fruit and insurance branches had not yet been organized, and nor had several of the social ("workers") sections of each of the previous branches.

The lack of funding for the CNS was not restricted to Salamanca; it was acute in many other regions as well. In the conservative province of Zamora, a local Falangist complained in 1954 that they had to run the union's admin-istrative function on a voluntary basis because they were severely under-staffed.[79] Four years later, in 1958, the unions from the important steel-milling town of Sagunto, near Valencia, requested action "to make [it] possible to develop our work with decency and efficiency," a need com-pounded by a lack of space for social functions or recreation for the grow-ing working population.[80]

The Falangists did recognize their failure to "convince" workers of the benefits of the unions, but only in private. An internal union report from Barcelona complained in 1954 that "We had had in our hands the easiest biggest masses for [the] molding of Spain and we did not know how to [channel] and capture them [...] Perhaps the Falange was not ready for this mission." The reason cited for this failure was that, when Barcelona was conquered in early 1939, the Falange forced workers to join by using "orders and commands," "coercion and threats." The Falangists also said that the unions "lacked social content." Accordingly, "the unions are today in a situ-ation of [being viewed with] deep disrespect among workers" and even employers.[81] There were nice words in favor of a more socially responsible state, but every time that strikes had occurred, like the ones in Barcelona and Madrid three years before, in 1951, armed Falangists had been ready to jump into cars "with secret plates […] to [suppress] the distribution" of clandestine propaganda or to intimidate people in order to force them back to work. These actions did not prevent the Falangists from later musing about the need to rethink strategies for "the political conquest of the much-neglected proletariat."[82]

Workers saw no reason to identify with these unions or with their Falangist bosses. The older generations missed the old, class-structured unions, while young workers were extremely skeptical of what politics might offer them, at least until the late 1950s, if not later. Nevertheless, unable to change or to challenge the stringent structures Franco had imposed on them, workers used these unions pragmatically, especially when they knew that the law was on their side.[83] Workers from Huesca, for example, complained in 1949 to the minister in charge of the Falange that "the disparity between the real income of workers and prices [was] becoming more acute" and asked for an end to "the useless intervention in food and price controls." In the same letter, they complained about the reduced amount that workers received for sick leave from social security.[84] The unions were at least a channel to voice specific demands and to try to influence the authorities.

Nevertheless, workers had to be careful. In March 1953, the heads of the social section of the Biscay metal union, "representing 70,000 producers," sent a report to the national head of the unions explaining their demands for wage increases. These "producers" were very careful to use Falangist language, and tried to be as respectful as possible towards the authorities, often praising Franco's efforts. In this case they complained, and proved, that inflation had eroded their purchasing power. However, prices kept rising while salaries did not. Respect for the regime's imposed channels led nowhere and workers became impatient. They broke the rules when a group of 13 "producers" abandoned work in November 1953. Then the Falangist Genaro Riestra, the sinister governor of Biscay, and his henchmen flexed their muscles to repress this "act of rebellion, to describe it in good Castilian," as the governor wrote. The act of "rebellion" was made worse when the strikers, bypassing the union, used the chaplain of one of the major companies, Babcock and Wilcox, to convey their demands directly to the managers. It all ended quickly as the strikers were identified, arrested, and probably beaten.[85] In any case, whatever happened behind bars stayed there.

In the countryside things were simpler. There landowners and local political bosses imposed their will more easily and did not rush to build the organization's structures. At least until the 1960s, in many towns the farmers' brotherhoods (*hermandades*), as the rural unions were called (the name implying that generally pro-Franco landowners and starving landless peasants were "brothers"), when they existed, had a phantom presence. Again in Salamanca in 1953, of the 404 *hermandades* that in theory existed, at least 150 "had no activity at all" and existed only "on paper," while another approximately 150 were very "deficient" in their functioning. In addition to this, corruption and unorthodox accounting and administrative practices were rife among the provincial organization's nearly 140 civil bureaucrats. The auctioning procedures exercised by union officials, which dictated the use of public meadows and forests in this region, so crucial to the local cattle economy, became particularly notorious for their corruption.[86] The situation in Salamanca was no worse than that in other places. In Ciudad Real in 1955, the local unions reported that only "three or four *hermandades* in big towns and another six or seven in smaller ones" were actually working while "the rest of the *hermandades* [had] no activity whatsoever." Moreover, the local heads and the secretaries were in "many cases men without spirit and badly prepared." The conditions of other branches of the union were very similar and their presidents often did their work "only on paper."[87] With unusual frankness, a leading member of the regime at the time wrote that "in practice, in both local and provincial spheres, farmers are not interested in [participating in] the unions."[88]

Old power structures and tyrannical social conditions were entrenched in the post-war countryside. Unions barely made a difference for the simple reason that the bigger landowners had no interest at all in changing the situation, and cared less about populist and demagogic poses.[89] However, the limited penetration of the official agrarian unions into the rural workforce was not only the result of the lack of official interest, poor budgets, ill-trained civil servants or local notables' interests. It also came from below, being a consequence of farmers' objections to the interference of the state in their lives. They perceived that very little came back to them in return for the taxes and fees that were taken from them. In the mid-1950s union leaders in the Galician province of Orense, a region that had provided tens of thousands of soldiers for the Francoist armies during the war, complained of the "resistance by small farmers" to paying union dues and fees for the "services" provided. Only direct pressure by the Civil Guard caused them to comply.[90]

Unions were supposed to be representative and to have a voice in the country's political decisions. That was the theory, but in reality neither was the case. Union elections were cautiously introduced by the regime in 1944. At first workers voted timidly, but by the late 1940s electoral participation for union representatives increased to an average of 80 percent of potential voters nationwide. By then workers had concluded that some representation was better than none. Union voices could be raised from their social sections to denounce unfair situations and to promote specific changes, providing they used orthodox Falangist language. It was precisely in the late 1940s when many former left-wing militants began to infiltrate the system to work against it from inside. The authorities' efforts to detect subversives were incessant, particularly during periods of conflict, such as the Barcelona general strike of 1951, when many union delegates played a fundamental role. They were identified and then subjected to dismissal, beatings, and imprisonment.[91]

Having learned their lesson, the authorities developed a preventive screening system.[92] This system, as described in an internal report for the 1961 elections, tried to ensure that no "red" would again be elected.[93] Their technique consisted of a complex system of first taking a census of all worker representatives and then assigning them to one of three main groups (loyal, indifferent, and opposed) and then further subdividing them into 15 more groups, ranging from "old shirt Falangist" (Falangist since before the war) to "dangerously hostile." This was done with the help of the police, the Civil Guard, and the Falange's own information service. All of this surveillance was carried out secretly, carefully following instructions to maintain the façade of legality because of the "certainly delicate nature of the service."[94] No sooner were they elected than the ideologically dubious elements were dispossessed of their positions as workers' representatives.[95] The system proved faulty, however, and in the 1960s the penetration of Franco's union by opposition workers and the election of independent representatives intensified (see chapter 5).

On paper, unions had their own representation in the rubber-stamp Francoist parliament (the Cortes) created in 1942. They were represented directly by the presidents and directors of the unions' sections, and this constituted 58 seats. These seats were, by their nature, held by the regime's supporters. Another 88 union members were technically meant to have been elected and were to be equally divided between representatives of employers, technicians, and workers. In fact, no one took this egalitarian pretense seriously and, so, with a good deal of overlapping of functions and a variety of ad hoc arrangements, the unions were left short of official representation in parliament and, to all intents and purposes, devoid of any real means of representing for workers. Worker representation was further controlled by the state by the fact that candidates for *procurador*, or MP, had to be vetted by the National Voting Committee (Junta Nacional de Elecciones). In 1971, of the 561 members of the Francoist parliament, only seven described themselves as "workers." Of those, only two were agrarian workers (one was president of the board of the official agrarian union), while two other "workers" sat on the boards of two important banks.[96]

The Catholic Church actively cooperated in this process of socializing the masses, to try to convince them to support the regime. Its main effort was originally focused on displaying its newly acquired power in very theatrical and public ways. During the war, after a town had been "liberated" by rebel troops, one of the Church's first public acts would be to initiate a solemn procession through the main streets in order to praise God and to thank the local saint or patron for his intercession on their behalf. Similarly, post-war Spain was full of huge public masses, pilgrimages, and political-religious demonstrations. However, both the Church and Franco understood that the problem was not that of attracting committed Catholics, but of reaching the people who refused to attend these public demonstrations or, if they did attend, had their minds and hearts elsewhere. Knowing that whole sectors of society had rejected Catholicism, at least Catholicism in its role as a powerful associate of the state, both the dictatorship and the Church wanted to impose a religiosity whose main feature was a patronizing, demeaning attitude that dictated that the main obligation of ordinary people was to obey authority and believe that it was God who had sent Franco to save their country. He was, after all, Caudillo "by the grace of God" ("por la gracia de Dios"). This subservient "National Catholicism" became the main staple of Spain's school system. But children were only part of the problem. More immediate, and difficult, was the issue of the adults who had lived through different times and had been exposed to very different values. It was decided that they were to be brought back to the Church through what became known as "missions."

As soon as the numbers of clerics had recovered from the losses of the Civil War, and the first waves of new priests and monks from the seminaries were ready, the missions were sent to regions of Spain with low levels of Catholic obedience. This meant conquering most working-class areas of the country and the rural communities that had been traditionally indifferent or openly anti-clerical.[97] These missions were planned well ahead of time and carefully orchestrated with the help of the government. They implied storming the designated localities. Bars, cinemas, and other distractions were closed to the public for the day as local and out-of-town clerics, with the help of lay Catholic militants, organized processions, mass confessions, sermons, and other public forms of piety in the streets of their target town.

The first wave of missions started in 1949 and lasted until 1953. The second wave started in 1958. Priests, monks, and Catholic activists worked hand in hand with the state, the official unions, and, in particular, the Ministry of the Interior (though according to union sources some priests "manifested reticence in apostolically cooperating with the state's political and union organizations").[98] In 1949, for example, the missions were concentrated in the "difficult" provinces of Leon, Palencia, Teruel, Murcia, and Saragossa. In total, 120,000 souls from 70 different towns were "cured" that year by 40 Capuchin monks and 20 Jesuits. The next year Caceres, Cuenca, Teruel, Murcia, Almeria, Asturias, Leon, and even Navarre had their turn. In these regions it was claimed, that exactly 26,857 souls were "treated" by 41 Capuchins.[99]

Missions pretended to be about morals and religion, but the organizers knew that they were also about politics. In 1961, well into the regime's tenure, a typical mission was held in the mining town of Puertollano (Ciudad Real). Several dozen priests and monks took part, and received, first in Madrid and then in the local headquarters of the union, careful instructions on how to proceed. They were instructed to concentrate their efforts neighborhood by neighborhood (a brief analysis of the socio-religious outlook of each neighborhood was provided); they were told what topics to address and what not to address ("abstain from talking about social matters" because this is a "workers' town"); they were given a list of activities ("in the morning rosary and mass"), and so on.[100] In public at least, nobody talked politics, but the shadow of politics, especially for the regime and its allies, was always present.

Faking Politics

Francoism pretended to represent the will of all good Spaniards. To achieve this, the regime proceeded to construct an alternative political system to the despised liberal-democratic one. The problem was that Francoism rejected party politics. Furthermore, the regime rejected the word "party," referring to the "dictatorship," the July 18, 1936 rebellion, and even its single party system as a "movement" (El Movimiento). This term was another copy from Mussolini's times. For the Francoists, politics meant division, confrontation, and, ultimately, civil war. Politics, they claimed, were not well suited to the Spanish temperament. Many people, and not only conservatives, came to share this idea in the wake of the bitter and bloody experiences of 1936–9. The irony of the situation was that the regime created a "political" party, FET-JONS (the impossibly named Falange Española Tradicionalista de las Juntas de Ofensivas Nacional-Sindicalistas), which everybody called the Falange, and that Franco appointed himself its lifelong leader in April 1937.[101] Franco, however, never spent a great deal of time running the Falange. He left this relatively minor task to party notables with political experience from the pre-war period. In 1945 he was on the brink of dissolving the party, and left it without a secretary general for over three years. That happened when fascism was not fashionable any more.

The Falange was always a very unpopular organization, even among many of the regime's supporters and particularly with the army. Party members knew that most ordinary people relished the idea of being rid of them. With great self-pity, Falangists attributed their poor public standing to the fact that they were being used by the "far right" (i.e. conservatives, Catholics, the army, and so on) to impose "difficult" policies on "the people," while claiming that in reality they had almost no power. As they put it as early as 1942, "this discredit and unpopularity which Falange has earned [is] because of political naivety [because] all the power, all the strength, all the neuralgic institutions and all strategic points are in the hands of people who are not Falangists."[102] This was a typical lament, heard from the beginning to the end of the dictatorship, which did not prevent those unsatisfied fascists from flocking to be appointed to the best jobs and sinecures or from striking hard at the "people" when they were asked to do so. Falangist self-pity was inseparable from corruption, pettiness, and political "gangsterism."[103]

The Falange was born of a small, failed, pre-war fascist organization, but most of its members under Francoism did not have a fascist past. Some were new to politics, others were experienced conservative politicians, while many, at the local level in particular, were members of the networks of patronage and corruption (referred to as *caciquismo*) that had controlled public life in Spain since the 1870s.[104] These people brought their old interests and habits with them to the new party, and they fought hard and dirty to impose them on others, rewarding friends and punishing enemies. In this way, local *caciques* (or political bosses) controlled not only the local branches of the party but, more importantly, the different levels of local public administration such as city councils and local sections of the unions. The result was widespread corruption in public life in the 1940s. Public jobs, concessions, and even administrative proceedings were riddled with favors, recommendations, and endorsements from the locally powerful. Public administration under Franco embodied the Spanish adage: "To the friend the favor, to the enemy the law." The destruction by Francoism of civil society and representative government was immediately translated into widespread corruption and arbitrary power. This, not fascist fervor and mobilization, was the true, daily face of "Franco's Peace" for most Spaniards.

Many of the *caciques*, local Falangists, and other powerful people reinforced their role in their community by acting as a parallel judiciary. They used their connections either to ensure that their local enemies were punished or to help their clients.[105] A typical example of this was recalled by M.M., from Murcia, who many years afterwards told the story of how her brother was imprisoned after the war in the Valencia region and had been condemned to death. Her mother went to see a local businessman who had been appointed judge after the war, and for whom her mother had worked as a nanny, raising his only daughter, who later married a Civil Guard colonel. They were friends with "Martínez Moya, and Gaspar de la Peña, those big *caciques* that we had in Murcia, they were the masters of Murcia in those times, and they saved my brother."[106] People's lives depended on their relationship to power, their place in the vast patronage system that Francoism re-created, in which friends and protectors, or enemies, were far more important than truth or justice.

This is how the regime worked at the local level. Ignoring this, the dictatorship's propaganda machine declared that the New Spain was ruled by a unique form of "organic" democracy. This meant that instead of being based on disruptive, fatal party politics, the Spanish system relied on a far superior and more harmonious model in which people were "naturally" represented through the places in which they lived (municipalities), in which they worked (unions), or through their family (heads of household). Accordingly, both city councils and the parliament of the New Spain were composed of people who were "organically elected" from these three areas. And male Spaniards were allowed to vote, in a sense.

The first municipal elections after the war were held in 1948. There were to be three tiers of city councilors "elected" by family heads, unions, and other public entities. However, institutional "candidates" (from unions and public entities) were proposed by the civil governor, rendering the "campaign" for the candidates for positions in these two groups little more than an award ceremony. The candidates for the family tier of counselors were vetted, spied on, and threatened to allow only good, pre-selected Francoists to put their candidacy forward. As a safeguard, the presidents of all polling stations were forced to sign blank result documents that would be completed later by state officials in favor of their pre-selected winners. This balloting technique was first successfully employed in the 1947 referendum, in which Franco had been "confirmed" regent for life. Organic democracy was no ordinary democracy. For example, before the 1948 municipal "elections," the governor of Barcelona reminded his collaborators that "This election will be held in my office, because I do not believe in democracy." Nevertheless, this governor took no chances and used all his influence to prevent any surprises; of the 44 people who declared their candidacy, only 26 were accepted. Party members who announced their candidacy without the permission of the governor were "persuaded" to withdraw. Some were threatened with professional or economic sanctions. In at least one case a candidate who "withdrew" only learned about his "decision" when he arrived to pick up his electoral credentials. When he protested, he was forcibly removed from the civil government building. When the official results of the Barcelona elections were made public, it was announced that between 70 and 80 percent of eligible voters had participated. Newspapers were prevented from listing detailed results by district in order to avoid the discovery of any discrepancies there might be between these numbers and voters' personal observations. The reality in Barcelona that year was that three out of four voters stayed home.[107]

Low voter turnout was the result of genuine popular political apathy. For once these feelings coincided with those of Falangists and many authorities who found elections distasteful, unnecessary, or at best a propaganda stunt staged for foreign liberal democracies and the United States in particular.[108] Falangists preferred to be appointed and to make back-door deals rather than to run in liberal-type elections. In Pontevedra, "party militants" first had to overcome their "initial disagreement only to obey the Caudillo's orders" before preparing for the 1948 municipal elections.[109] In Valladolid, during the pre-election period, the governor spoke of the "general impression" everybody shared that holding an election was "a desire by the

Generalissimo to have a card to play against European and American democracies." Furthermore, the call for elections only opened up dormant political appetite for in-fighting among local elites, a process the governor felt he was able to control, but the net result of which was that he found it difficult "to mobilize voters, [in order to] create an ambiance of interest."[110]

Repressive tactics, combined with widespread passive acceptance that Francoism was there to stay, almost always made the electoral process in Spain straightforward for the Falangists. The two most difficult tasks were to make sure that all candidates were loyal to the dictatorship and to encourage Spaniards to show up to vote. The careful selection of candidates made the results completely predictable. As the governor of Valencia explained, if the 1948 elections were really free they would "break the political continuity which has taken so much to achieve."[111] His colleague from Cuenca guaranteed, without any sense of irony, that the elections held in his province would "take place in an environment of orderly enthusiasm." He also said it was to be taken for granted that there would be a "careful selection of candidates." For him it would be a simple task made even easier because no opposition candidates dared to step forward. These two and many other governors made much of their ability to repress enemies and to bring together right-wing personalities in order to create unified, Falangist-led candidacies.[112] Seville's governor made it very clear that he was ready to falsify results if voters either decided not to vote or if there was any discussion of accepting "real polling" as opposed to the "official" results. This gentleman stated, in no uncertain terms, that the official, hand-picked candidates would be the ones elected. In this socially complex province, where misery and hunger existed on the doorstep of aristocratic glamour, the governor was proven to be successful, as the newly elected candidates, "representing" the families of the province, were, among others, colonel in the airforce, an army lawyer, a marquis, and the son of a marquis.[113]

Political repression, fear, hunger, and political apathy were inextricably linked, and those connections were used by the authorities in perverse ways during election times. In 1948 the governor of Ciudad Real reminded voters that they were required to show up at polling stations carrying their ration cards. These cards would only be valid if they had been stamped "vote" after they had participated in the election. The vital need to have the stamp validated on one's ration card explained the seemingly popular fervor for the elections that the local newspaper photos conveyed.[114] As the governor of Orense stated, "we have adopted the necessary steps to avoid abstention among voters."[115]

The regime would always claim that its elected officials came from a cross-section of Spanish society, but a closer look at the results tells a different story. The 1951 election results indicated that, of the 9,005 mayors "elected" or appointed, only 478 were described as working-class, while farmers (landowners) numbered 5,195 and industrialists (this term usually meant owners of small businesses) 812. In ideological terms, only 136 elected officials were said to have a left-wing or a republican past of any description, while 7,307 were Falange party members; 2,630 had been combatants in the Civil War on Franco's side, 401 had been captives of the republicans, and a further 60 were war amputees. Of the 54,089 city councilors only 4,868 were said to be workers, compared to 33,316 farmers and 5,212 industrialists; 14,157, or one-fifth of these councilors, had formerly been Francoist soldiers. This vast majority of the elected representatives, made up of small landholding farmers and veterans, constituted the true political backbone of the dictatorship in rural Spain.[116] Franco was not alone during his harsh rule. The dictatorship represented the interests and cultural values of wide segments of society which identified with the regime's policies and found acceptable the suffering of millions of other Spaniards.[117]

Civil governors made sure that politics and debates ended as soon as the "elections" were over. Normalcy, or rather apathy, was quickly reimposed. Ordinary citizens were encouraged to go about their business, and so they did, to the dictatorship's satisfaction. For example, even in the traditionally combative province of Guipuzcoa and its capital city San Sebastian, where Basque nationalism and worker mobilization had dovetailed in the past, the local Falange reported full "normalcy" in the summer of 1950. The banned and harshly repressed opposition groups had tried but found themselves unable to summon organized protest. In Guipuzcoa, also in 1950, when communist leaflets opposing the Korean War were distributed, most people ignored them because "without any doubt," the governor proudly reported, locals were more interested in the performance of Spain's national soccer team at the world championship in Rio de Janeiro than in faraway wars.[118] The same year in Barcelona, the governor explained that "politics seemed to have disappeared in all social sectors" as people became primarily concerned with their personal standard of living, either "criticizing or praising [events in Spain] that they believe are negative or positive" for themselves, and were not as concerned about the "greater good."[119] The governor had highlighted one of the pillars of the regime he served: the destruction of the idea that the common good depended on the common will.

Electoral incidents, when they happened, were most often the result of personal differences between the regime's own supporters. For example, during the 1954 municipal elections in the Balearic Islands, the lack of cooperation between old Falangists and the governor allowed a small number of trade unionists to be elected to municipal councils which went against common Francoist practices; but these incidents were infrequent.[120] More common were the behind-the-scenes pressures and maneuverings of the regime's supporters as they worked their political networks of patronage.[121] Hopefuls with the wrong connections or wrong approach were easily rejected. In Ceuta a local doctor, well known in the city for his charitable work with the poor, had managed to be elected to the city council in 1952. Despite his excellent work in the field of public health, which was even recognized by his enemies, he was still considered suspect because his father had been a member of a local Masonic lodge. In 1957, when this councilor's brother, who was also a doctor, was rumored to be preparing his candidacy, the local Falange boss ensured that there was not another "mistake."[122] As the governor of Soria explained in preparation for that year's elections, candidates suspected of harboring "bastard intentions" should be legally eliminated from the race to avoid "surprises."[123]

In spite of the above, it would be incorrect to portray all elections under Francoism as staged rituals with no real political meaning. This was the case until the late 1960s but, as the future of the dictatorship became cloudier, elections in some sectors became an escape valve for the tensions arising from uncertainty. This was particularly true of elections for the parliament's third tier of "family representatives," where voter turnout sometimes became as high as it would later be once democracy was established. In 1971, for example, participation by eligible voters in Huesca in the September elections was over 69 percent, while in the province's capital almost 75 percent exercised their franchise. At the same time, in the far more controlled election for National Counselor of the Movement, tensions ran high. The rivalry here was between a local notable who had held the position for several years and who was now attempting to steer a more liberal course and an orthodox Falangist, a woman, who with the not-so-veiled help of state authorities finally won the "election" (the total number of voters was only 556, all of whom were members of the Falange or of local state institutions).[124]

Late Francoism's elections were also an indirect indicator of the regime's standing among the population, and they would give a cross-section of support for the dictatorship. In general, it could be argued that in regions where anti-regime activities were strongest, participation in the elections was lowest (in Madrid in 1971, for example, voter turnout was barely 31 percent, and in Seville it was only 30 percent). The extreme case was Biscay, where electoral participation in the 1971 elections in this Basque province was less than 27 percent.[125] When local populations were convinced that nothing was at stake in these elections and the usual candidates would inevitably be elected, participation was as low in backward regions of Spain as it was in the more "political" and "modern" parts of the country (in 1971 in three poor provinces participation was: 35 percent (Las Palmas), 35 percent (Guadalajara), and 32 percent (Leon)).[126]

***

Terror allowed Franco to impose his political and social agenda. To cover the damage done, his propaganda machine ignored or vilified the dictatorship's victims. Terror created a society that was never quite capable of putting behind it the trauma of the Civil War. While many Spaniards suffered because of these policies, others profited from them and supported Franco, whom they considered to be the best guarantor that the outcome of the war would not be reversed. One of the results of these policies was that in the 1970s, as had happened in the early 1940s, the dictatorship and its servile Falangists were busy at faking the will of the Spanish people, and denying them a voice in the name of preserving Spain's peace. That was grave enough, but the exchange of peace for freedom had appalling consequences for wide segments of the population and for the country's economy. The trade-off carried a heavy, but unequally distributed, price: starvation, exploitation, personal and collective humiliation, and, finally, the negation of the right to education. This is explained further in the next chapter.

2

THE SOCIAL COST OF
THE DICTATORSHIP

A common though superficial impression formed by casual observers, and an argument continually repeated by the regime's propaganda machine, is that, compared to most post-war European countries, Spain was an oasis of peace during the 40 years of Franco's rule. For those living in the upper echelons of Spain's social structure this was true. The interventions of Franco's government in the national economy and in the daily lives of ordinary Spaniards were obtrusive but cost little, and were therefore very popular with those who had property. Even if services were poor and the country's infrastructure was abysmal, it was well worth the inconvenience for the wealthy since there were plenty of low-paid domestic workers at home and a docile workforce to help run their businesses, and there was security in the streets.

Franco's Peace, however, meant misery for millions of Spaniards. They lacked a political voice and representation, and this resulted in their exploitation, starvation, or death. No one felt Franco's lack of political responsibility more harshly than those who could not produce their own food, owned no property, or who were only temporarily employed or out of work. These were the majority of ordinary Spaniards, such as workers and landless peasants and their families; and, below them, poor widows, orphans, and those with physical or mental disabilities. These were the people who suffered one of Europe's little-known tragedies of the past century: Franco's quiet famine in the early 1940s. They were also the people who suffered most the imposition of a completely irrational economic doctrine: autarky. Nowhere was these people's suffering more acute than in the peripheries of industrial cities and in the southern part of the country, the land of the landless. It was there that Civil War and the repression that followed broke the back of the organized working-class movement and of the dispossessed peasantry. Defeated and terrorized, they paid a heavy price for losing the war and living in Franco's Spain.[1]

From Famine to Misery

Many terrible things happened in World War II, when tens of millions were killed or allowed to die. One of the main atrocities was mass starvation, which the Nazis practiced at different stages and with varying intensity in Poland, the Jewish ghettoes, the Soviet Union, and Greece. Spain also had its famine, but it was not imposed by ruthless foreign invaders but caused rather by Franco's disregard for the fate of the poor, with the complicity of those, from top bureaucrats to small farmers, who turned a blind eye or who profited from it. Mass killings need mass complicity. In a sense, Franco and his accomplices had been lucky. The scale of the famine passed almost unnoticed by foreign observers during and after World War II because it happened at the same time as the terrible events of that conflict, and in a relatively remote and uninteresting country. The regime's propaganda machine certainly hid the harrowing reality from those who did not want to see it, and the history books that children studied at school did not mention it. The result is that, even in today's Spain, this tragedy is little known or is downplayed as a brief, regrettable aspect of the dictatorship. Yet those who suffered the famine know how terrible it was to be poor in the early 1940s, and how many relatives died, and how many nights they went to bed thinking, or rather dreaming, about food.

V.Z. remembers this. He was a Basque child. To keep him out of harm's way, his parents sent him abroad during the Civil War. He was among the Spanish children who were sent to Belgium, while others went to the United Kingdom and still others to France and the Soviet Union. When the conflict was over, V.Z. was able to return to "liberated" Spain. He was among the losers of the war, both politically and socially. Like so many Spaniards who found themselves on the wrong side in Franco's Spain, he mostly remembers two things from those years: "Misery, misery, misery and hunger … hunger and misery. What can I tell you? Hunger … hunger all the time, I dreamed of food went I went to bed … hunger all the time."[2] His experience was far from unique. A 1941 study of levels of nutrition among Spaniards showed that there was a national average deficit of 61.5 percent in fats, 66.2 percent in carbohydrates and 66 percent in calories. This was an average, which means that millions ate better than this, but also that millions ate less well. Worse still, it was not a passing problem soon to be solved: in 1955, average calorie consumption was still 10 percent lower than it had been in 1935.[3]

At the end of the war, hunger did not go from bad to better. On the contrary, before it eventually got better it became far worse. There was scarcity during the war, especially in the more urban republican zone, that had no access to the grain-producing regions of Spain, controlled by the Francoist forces. Hunger arrived with the "liberation" troops, when the new regime put into practice its rationing policies and built the autarkic system. Economic crisis and scarcity first, and hunger and famine next, spread to the areas where they had not been before. In the Balearic Islands, for example, which (with the exception of Minorca) had been loyal to Franco's side from 1936 on, the war years had been relatively normal. In fact, the textile and shoe industries had prospered by selling products to the rebel army. The islands even exported food, but the 1940s were a very different story as the local economy collapsed. In 1941 the shoe industry produced about 3 million pairs, but in 1946 the figure was 10,000, and in 1947 cereal production was at 60 percent of the pre-war average, mainly because there were no fertilizers. The consequences manifested themselves very quickly. As early as January 1941, before the full crisis exploded, the local chief of the Falange reported that there was practically no food in the markets and prices were so high that most workers could not afford them. Many families ate only oranges, and 40 percent of children showed signs of tuberculosis. He also added:

> People favored by fortune have an easy life with no privation because with money they can buy everything [while] misery is plainly visible in factories, shops and construction sites: frequently workers suddenly stop working, and fall to the floor because of lack of food.[4]

In 1946 the situation in the islands was so bad that people said that "they were worse than if they were living in an [African] colony."[5]

While hunger and misery were common in industrial areas like the Basque country or in the still backward Balearic Islands, conditions were even more harrowing in the south, where unemployment, the dominance of large estates, and a declining mining industry created social landscapes of horror. In 1940 and 1941 there were reports from several places that people experienced an illness that first made walking painful, then caused them to suffer from unstoppable trembling in their limbs, and then led to complete immobility. Quite often they also lost their sight. It seems that this new condition was caused by the combination of lack of vitamins (something similar would happen in Cuba in the 1990s during the "special period") and the consumption of indigestible, poisonous grasses.[6] In 1941 Dr. Janney of the Rockefeller Mission, an organization that sought to alleviate Spain's desperate sanitary and food conditions, reported that the hunger problem "had to be studied on the ground to [be] believe[d]," and that in the south and on the Mediterranean coast adults from poor families "ate only a third of the necessary calories to survive, and children merely a fifth."[7]

This sad reality stands in sharp contrast to the self-congratulatory rhetoric of the Francoist tyranny. In 1941, for example, one of the regime's propagandists had written, without any apparent sense of irony, that "Spain is clearly on its way, in spite of the fact that the international conflict opposes its progress."[8] While those words were being written British diplomats in Spain, and especially those posted to Andalusia, reported that workers were unable to perform normally for lack of food, many of them even collapsing while at work. The British consul in Seville observed that the food situation was worsening and a great number of deaths were taking place in the hospitals "because of starvation."[9] He was not exaggerating. According an official confidential 1941 government report compiled on the basis of research carried out by several medical commissions, in both Caceres and Badajoz provinces there were tens of thousands of people who had eaten nothing for months but grasses boiled in salted water. This same report predicted that up to 2 million Spaniards would starve to death in the following months.[10] In the olive oil-producing province of Jaen, an area dominated by large estates, one in three newborns died in 1942.[11] All over the south, bands of desperate children and adults, often dressed in rags and with no shoes, roamed the fields looking for anything – figs, corn, melons – to eat, only to be chased away by farmers and armed guards, who beat them with impunity. Current estimates of deaths directly related to hunger vary, but it has been estimated that between 1939 and 1945 as many as 200,000 people died during Franco's quiet famine.[12] This is only a rough calculation; perhaps the real number is much, much higher.

Unlike the suffering caused by the Nazis in eastern Europe, this famine was not a deliberate attempt to kill an undesirable or potentially hostile population. However, the results were practically and morally similar. The suffering could have been avoided: there was enough food in Spain at the time. People could see that the shelves of grocery stores were full of items that they could not afford, but official rationing failed to feed them. The problem was not rationing itself but how it was executed and the socio-economic context in which this happened. In both the wartime United

Kingdom and Nazi Germany rationing actually helped to reduce diet imbalances and infant malnutrition among the poor, because the British poor could vote, and the Nazis believed in the health of their "racial community."[13] In Franco's Spain neither of these things was true. Food was in short supply, but its distribution was riddled with incompetence and massive corruption. This was compounded by wages that were kept low by a regime that sought to curb workers' demands.

Famine was the by-product both of a decision to favor the interests of money and of badly conceived policies regarding poor people's needs. While millions of people were starving employers profited handsomely because they paid very low salaries. Others, including farmers, and particularly large landowners, profited by dealing in the extensive black market. Falangists and bureaucrats took their cut. Finally banks, which enjoyed a monopoly themselves, administered the savings earned through both legal and illegal activities related to food-hoarding and black-marketeering. When, for example, in 1945 a kilo of wheat was sold (if it was available) at 0.84 pesetas in the official market, it would typically be resold on the black market at between 2.75 and 10.75 pesetas. Oil was sold for 5.19 pesetas per liter on the official market, and for 16 pesetas and even up to 35 pesetas on the black market. Evidently someone was making money from this. This someone could be a modest small farmer or a desperate housewife trying to feed her children, always afraid of being caught by the police; but quite often it was a large landowner, who colluded with civil servants, junior and senior, and even with the provincial civil governor (who was responsible for suppressing the black market) to make a killing, literally. And if by any chance some unwise person reported them, he or she would end up accused of defaming the authorities.[14]

While many people profited, those who suffered – who were represented by nobody, and who often happened to be the defeated "reds" – were condemned to starve. It was a scandal, and even some of the most staunchly conservative minds realized that it was also a massive catastrophe. When, in 1944, the Bilbao Chamber of Commerce report stated in rather sanitized language that "the available food does not allow [...] the distribution of what is indispensable to reconstitute the muscular force exhausted or unnerved by work," it was expressing its unease at the consequences of the policies (albeit not of the principles) of the regime that most employers supported.[15] In fact, what was done to correct the policies which led to hunger was done badly and belatedly. As late as 1950, for example, the governor of Almeria reported that in the previous years, on top of deaths caused by epidemics (mainly typhus), there had been frequent cases of "people starving to death."[16]

Hunger and misery were the twin products of corruption, but they were also caused by economic inefficiency rooted in Franco's cherished policy of autarky. Even when it became obvious that this policy was a disaster in economic and social terms, the dictator repeatedly refused to acknowledge his mistakes and to change course. In macro-economic terms, this meant that Spain missed more than a decade of economic growth – growth seen by other European nations, including those countries with dictatorships such as Portugal and Greece. Spain's pre-war (1936) production levels were not regained until the early 1950s, while most of Europe had recovered its pre-war (1939) levels by 1947–8.[17]

The regime tried to hide its home-made socio-economic disaster behind lies. In 1953, for the first time, the government carried out a study, later made public, of salaries by collecting data directly from companies. The results were compared to salary levels in 1936, and then to the growth of prices during the same period. The data were mildly but falsely reassuring: the purchasing power of employees in 1953 was supposed to be between 82 and 85 percent of that in 1936. In some sectors, such as railways and state monopolies for example, it was stated that salaries had surpassed the 100 percent level. These figures seemed even more positive when the value of the services provided by social security were taken into consideration, as workers were now, in overall terms, supposedly receiving more "invisible" income than before the war (110 percent).[18]

Confidential sources said otherwise. According to these, in 1948–9 the purchasing power of salaries was only 50 percent of what it had been in 1936.[19] Moreover, a 1950 union report indicated not only that workers' salaries were far lower than during the Republic, but that "the distribution of national income was less favorable for the working class" than it had been before.[20] According to a recent study of wages and prices in Madrid, between 1947 and 1951 the latter increased 100 percent while the paycheck of, for example, a construction foreman grew only slightly more than 25 percent.[21] This is confirmed by other sources. For example, in 1956 the official Chemistry Branch of the unions stated that the average worker in this sector made 26.18 pesetas per day (plus the 1.16 pesetas paid to social security), while the cost of basic needs for a family of four was 50.44 pesetas.[22] This depreciation in salary levels was even felt by those who held traditionally well-paid jobs, like those in the mining and metalworking sectors. According to another 1958 union report, a metalworker with a wife and a child (families were normally in those days much larger than that) had to work 15.20 hours every day at current wages to meet his family's needs "with dignity."[23]

This was for the elite of the working class. For unskilled workers, and especially, seasonal, landless agrarian workers, things were much worse. For these people, wages were abysmally low, and many were, in any event, out of work. In 1949 there were 400,000 people unemployed in the country, most in the agrarian sector and in construction. Rural unemployment was concentrated in the south, while most unemployed construction workers lived in Madrid and Barcelona.[24] Unemployment meant not just poverty, but extreme misery and often death. In 1952, when reporting on the problem of unemployment in the province of Jaen, the governor recognized that there were 20,000 people in the province who were permanently unemployed and that, during certain months, especially between August and December, a further 58,000 people went without work. As terrible as these numbers appear in isolation, the effect of this scale of destitution was even more daunting:

> This situation of [the] lack of jobs kills the life [*sic*] of the working population in years of bad harvests and is not solved either by unemployment subsidies or [by] the cantinas opened by different municipalities to distribute free meals, etc., etc. This is what happened in the deadly year of 1946, in which just Jaen province [alone], represented more than 25 percent of all deaths in Spain because of starvation [...] Children cannot go to school because they have to spend their time begging to avoid succumbing.[25]

That children did not go to school was rather easy to understand, according to Jaen's Falange in 1951, at least in the case of the estimated 60,000 families whose maximum aspiration "for five to six months every year, [was] to have the minimum olive oil and bread not to perish" of hunger. Those children, if they could move, had to find food. They lived in abject misery but still there were other human beings below them: one step lower were the approximately 20,000 families, sheltering in shacks or caves, whose children had no shoes, were dressed in rags, and who were, according to the same source, "living in conditions that we thought to have left behind us in the Paleolithic period."[26]

This was for families headed by men, even if employed only temporarily or completely unemployed; because hunger was not only a question of politics but also of gender. Another step down the scale of horror was the situation of the even lower-paid and badly treated single-parent mothers, and their children. Hunger and misery had led many women to a job market that paid next to nothing, or to prostitution. The husbands of many of these women were "missing": that is to say, many were buried in unmarked mass graves, had left behind young widows because they had been killed as republican soldiers, or were in prison. Unlike those of the Francoist soldiers and murdered supporters, these widows had no right to a pension. Since these women were considered to be on the losing side of the war, Franco's new Catholic state decided that, along with their children, they deserved nothing.

Women with children or on their own had few options, and they all were very difficult. A woman working 10 to 14 hours a day as a domestic servant might earn between 2 and 5 pesetas in the early 1940s. This was insufficient to maintain a family. A woman working as a prostitute would be paid between 5 and 25 pesetas, or even as much as 75 pesetas a day if she worked in a luxurious brothel. Thousands of women became full-time or part-time prostitutes. Despite the new code of morality propagated by the dictatorship, prostitution and venereal disease increased after the Civil War. According the Patronato de Protección de la Mujer (the Francoist foundation for the re-education of "fallen" women) in 1941 there were close to 65,000 cases of syphilis across the country, while six years later the number leapt to nearly 268,000 cases. Since the number of officially registered prostitutes remained below 10,000 during this period (prostitution was still legal), the increase in venereal diseases can probably be explained by the rise in the clandestine sex trade practiced by ordinary women trying to keep their families from starvation.[27] The number of registered prostitutes began to decline only in the mid-1950s as economic conditions, or at least the availability of food, improved. We can safely assume that the number of irregular or occasional prostitutes also declined.[28]

Hunger meant misery, death, and humiliation for the poor, but it was also a political opportunity for the regime's demagogues who nursed ambitions for greater power. No one played this card more shamelessly, or more often, than the Falangists as they resorted to their familiar social justice rhetoric, arguing for a change in direction in the country's policies in order to make them yet more "Falangist." Their recipes were vague, but were presented with the full theatrical passion and demagogy that the Falangists were so good at. In the context of the 1955 series of provincial meetings of the Falange party in poverty-stricken Ciudad Real, the provincial Falange chief (and governor) of the province said that it would be necessary to lower food prices, especially of "those products key to workers' diets" because "we must pay more attention to economic matters if we do not want to ruin our politics." The head of health services demanded that "more vitamins" should be included in the products distributed through rationing. The head of the unions said that "this bad situation has to be resolved as soon as possible" or a situation like Barcelona's, where a major strike had taken place in 1951, could arise. He also suggested the closing of exclusive shops that were reserved for public employees "because they may be the object of disapproval by the needy classes." The provincial Falange head then denounced the role of middlemen and merchants. He added that before, or at least at the same time as, lowering prices, the main priority should be to "solve the problem of unemployment" because regardless of prices "a portion of the working class can buy nothing." The meeting concluded that black marketeers and middlemen had an anti-patriotic attitude and that the "Falange raises the flag of lowering prices and calls on all Falangists [...] to cooperate in this patriotic campaign" and to show their repugnance for the present levels of scarcity, a situation that ran against "the desires of our national leader, Generalissimo Franco." The governor, who was also a member of the National Council of the party, closed the meeting by stating that the "Falange must become more sympathetic to the public by helping in services and places wherever necessary." They all then sang the Falange anthem and the provincial chief "gave the usual hurrahs which those in the meeting seconded."[29]

The Almeria Falangists demonstrated their priorities during one of their own meetings in 1951, which, according to the official record, was mostly concerned with organizing the diverse activities of the party and, in particular, with helping to organize the "Canonical Coronation of the Very Holy Virgin of the Sea [Virgen del Mar]" for which money from the social funds of the party were used. They closed their meeting by recommending a study on "the present economic and food situation of the middle and lower class in order to palliate, in whatever way possible, the situation they are going through." As part of this last item, they included the finalization of two apartments in the fishermen's neighborhood, where thousands of people lived in caves and shacks. The apartments were to be given soon to "two comrades."[30]

Surviving

After first serving its supporters' interests and, within its meager means and narrow ideological horizons, the dictatorship tried to help. The Falange opened a wide network of communal kitchens run by the women of its female branch working for the Auxilio Social, in imitation of their Nazis counterparts' Winter Relief.[31] And feed the poor they did (when they had food in their storage rooms), but obviously not enough, because people kept dying. Another strategy, erratic and confused, was the beginning of a social safety net. The Francoist version of a welfare state was a painfully slow process. A "mandatory" health insurance was created in 1942 to provide benefits and free medical attention to workers and their families. It developed at what could best be termed a very modest pace. In 1953 only 530,000 workers were insured, which meant that, including family members, a total of only 1.6 million people were covered. Since Spain's population at the time was 28 million, it also meant that less than 6 percent of the total population was protected. What is worse, mandatory public insurance progressed at a very slow pace, and sometimes it went backwards. For example, the total number of people insured in 1953 was less than the number who had been covered in 1949 (1.62 million).[32] Furthermore, both workers and employers resented an insurance plan that, on the surface, seemed to be a good idea, but, in times of rampant inflation, ate away a good portion of their salaries. Workers were forced to allocate a significant amount of their paychecks to the plan in exchange for poor services; medical attention was often cursory, riddled with bureaucratic indolence, and delivered with notorious rudeness.

One of the main contradictions of the regime's approach to social policy was that while its economic strategies, and particularly its economic interventionism, were causing starvation among the poorest, it continued and augmented originally republican programs to improve the health of children and their mothers. The maternity insurance introduced by the Republic in 1931 was included by the dictatorship in 1944 in its newly implemented health insurance. Like other contemporary dictatorships, Francoism was obsessed with population increase and controlling women by putting them back into the home. The twin pillars of this program were the regime's women's organization, the Sección Femenina (Women's Section) of the Falange, and the developing social security program. By 1947, the Auxilio Social of Falange was managing 160 centers in 39 provinces that, along with several other institutions for nursing mothers, nurseries, and orphanages, were dedicated to monitoring children's nutrition. Its rural volunteer health educators, *visitadoras rurales*, usually young women who taught practical and scientific methods of nursing and rearing children, helped reduce child mortality in the short term, and instilled new knowledge and practices that would make a great contribution to reducing the problem in the coming decades. That same year, 1947, the health insurance program had a network of a further 250 health centers and nine hospitals with about 4,500 mid-wives working for the state.[33] Midwives and nurses performed a crucial task because, by the end of the 1940s, about nine out of ten births were taking place at home. This was by far the regime's biggest and most successful achievement in health care for a government with a record that rarely attained even the mediocre.

These were steps in the right direction, but they were taken for the wrong reasons, and in conjunction with badly misconceived economic policies, particularly in the food-supply system. Moreover, the division of responsibilities between the Falange, the official unions and social security was never clear, causing confusion and unnecessary bureaucracy. Despite the many merits and the honest, hard-working, selfless dedication of the people who participated in these programs, volunteers and professionals, these efforts were unable to compensate for the famine and the related health catastrophe caused by autarky. In any case, the embryonic social security system developed too slowly to combat the misery that ravaged the 1940s.

Since survival depended on adapting to forces that they could not control, ordinary people had to take matters into their own hands. Tragically, in order to live, poor people had to participate in some of the same criminal activities that were making their lives so miserable, and in particular in black marketeering.[34] Women in particular became black marketeers and smugglers. Often moving in small groups, they went from countryside to city and from the borders of France through the Pyrenees, from Portugal or from the territories of Gibraltar and northern Morocco to clandestine markets in their home towns. Luxury items, like coffee and sugar, were very profitable and they were easy to find and reasonably priced in post-war Portugal, which took these products from its rich colonial empire. Such activities, however, posed a real risk, because while those who ran big operations acted with impunity, it was the ordinary people who got caught and punished.

Paula, for example, was barely a teenager in post-war Huelva, the Andalusian province bordering the Portuguese Algarve. "During the hunger years" she frequently crossed the border into Portugal because "there was nothing here," avoiding both the Spanish Civil Guard patrols and their Portuguese counterparts, the Guardinha. She would travel at night with relatives and neighbors in small groups through ravines and creek beds, sometimes hiding between rocks or in caves while carrying a heavy bag or a backpack. They would go to a known Portuguese home or farm and buy 3 or 4 kilos of flour, coffee, sugar, or chickpeas and then swiftly return to Spain with their modest stock of contraband. If caught, she said, their meager treasure would be confiscated and they might be beaten, fined, or put in jail.[35] They had no protectors.

Paula's experience contrasts with that of D.J. and his group, who were nearly caught by the Murcian Civil Guard while moving three carts of wheat. This was a well-organized, important smuggling operation that required good contacts. What saved them was the protection of a *cacique*, a black marketeer himself, from the hamlet of El Raal. D.J. said that this local notable told them: "do not be afraid, even if you hear their steps [of the guards]." D.J. explained why those words were comforting: "He knew the Civil Guards and furthermore they owed him many favors because he fed them on several occasions. He trafficked with mules and was very rich. Pepe Luis, that was his name, and he behaved very well towards us."[36]

The local boss of El Raal, the *cacique* Pepe Luis, was becoming richer during the hunger years, but at least he was kind to the poor. Not everybody was the same. A certain Paradela, mayor of Amoeiro (Orense), was a man of a different, and more common, stripe. This is how another survivor, Juan Dacoba, remembers him:

> When he was the mayor, Paradela black-marketed our allocations of sugar, oil, and flour given by the state, but he did not give them to the shops. We went five months without having any rations. He prepared a truck with wood and under it he carried away sacks of flour and cans of oil to sell them in Vigo. And people waited with their mouths wide open! [Later] he used to threaten old people [saying he would] take away their pensions if they did not give him sixty *duros* [300 pesetas] under the counter and he became rich with that![37]

The different standards for the poor and the powerful were felt everywhere. The Canary Islands were under military control for most of World War II as their strategic location in the Atlantic left them at great risk of invasion. Franco's pro-Axis policy had led the British to draw up contingency plans for their occupation. This military control extended to the economy, and its results were devastating for business and for the general population. The so-called Economic Command (1941–6) ruined the local exporting sector and greatly reduced all shipping activity, the two traditional cornerstones of the islands' economy. At the same time, it caused a boom in the black market and the smuggling trade. The latter activity was not new; but what was new was the disproportionate amount of repression of small-scale smugglers, known as the *cambulloneros*, who traditionally traded with the crews of foreign vessels. New also was the lack of control over the local elites who, through their connections with the regime, controlled the majority of smuggling activities.[38] This was denounced in 1950, in Santa Cruz de Tenerife, by a local Francoist, who said that large-scale local black marketeers amassed "colossal fortunes that represent[ed] an offense to the honest citizens who have to deal daily with difficulties as they observed never-ending price increases or the difficulties of acquiring food."[39]

Small grocery shops were crucial components of the black market structure. Every neighborhood or small town had at least one shop, and municipal authorities channeled the food rations through them. Grocers picked up rations from the city council, and these were then distributed according to what was available and what people were entitled to, depending on the type of ration card they had. That was the theory. The practice varied widely. To start with, what was supposed to be distributed very often did not arrive or arrived only in insufficient quantities. Secondly, corruption among the local authorities was rampant and the city councilors in charge of rationing and their accomplices appropriated considerable quantities of the rations, filling their own pantries before lining their pockets with the profits from selling the remaining products. Grocers, too, took their cut or exchanged better products for lower-quality ones. What was left then appeared on the stores' shelves.

It would, however, be completely unfair to dismiss small shop owners simply as parasites who only took advantage of their neighbors' plight. They were one of poor people's limited tools of survival. In small towns and working-class neighborhoods in particular, grocers sold on credit all kind of items, from food to shoes. Small grocery stores doubled as food banks or micro-credit institutions. People with a reputation for honesty who had fallen on hard times frequently received food on credit from shop owners who meticulously recorded this activity in the store ledger. These notebooks often had two columns, one with the items and prices recorded by the grocers and the other with an acknowledgment of the debt by the customer.[40] These debts were supposed to be repaid when things improved, and people who did not do so, or who first spent money on non-essential items, were the target of criticism by their neighbors. This criticism was not only a matter of censoring morally "ugly" conduct, but was also recognition that if these debts were not repaid this crucial mechanism of social welfare would be put at risk.

There were other mechanisms employed to avoid starvation. If sickness, unemployment, or any other disaster struck, and family or friends could not provide funds, poor people often resorted to pawn shops. These were usually run by branches of the savings and loans institutions, themselves controlled by the Church (Montes de Piedad y Cajas de Ahorros). Blankets, sheets, cutlery, an odd jewel or bicycle, and many other items could be pawned and recovered with interest.

At other times when a small loan was needed, people resorted to independent middlemen referred to as *teleros* in some regions. These middlemen worked with specific shops where they would send potential buyers. If, for example, someone wanted to buy a pair of shoes or a coat they had a limit, set by the middleman, on how much they could spend. Buyers did not pay the shop, the intermediary did, at a discounted price. He would then receive monthly installments, at a high interest, from the buyer. This system continued to be used until the early 1970s, and the last consumer item poor Spaniards bought through this type of middleman was probably their first television set.

However, the main, most decisive tool to survive autarky and famine was the family. While other European societies were constructing welfare states to meet the demands of the modern world and allowing people to feel free and to exercise their influence through political involvement, in impoverished Spain attachment to the family, especially among those in the lower social strata, became the social and economic pillar. Protecting this pillar was more important to ordinary Spaniards than asking for societal change because, during the dark days of autarky and long afterwards, family was the only choice for homes for the elderly when parents or grandparents grew infirm; for day care when mothers and older children went to work and left infants to be minded; or for credit for anything from a down payment for a modest home to a sewing machine or a bicycle. Family also meant communal kitchens when uncles or aunts could not pay for food for their branch of the family; they were the source of unemployment insurance when no money was coming into the home; and they were overcrowded hostels for newly married couples who could not afford their own home. As a result it was normal that several generations would live under the same roof, eat at the same table, take care of one another, and, of course, argue, while trying to preserve some sense of independence, intimacy, and individual dignity. These arrangements were neither ideal nor easy for most, but for the poor, besieged by their abysmal standard of living, they were the only solution available.

Women played the main role in the family-based survival system. The relationship between mother and daughter was crucial, but it often functioned within a wider framework of relationships that included aunts, cousins, and nieces, sometimes even needy neighbors who for whatever reason had no relatives. Through this network, resources were distributed and, when necessary, conflicts resolved. In traditional households, men were supposed to know nothing about how their homes were run. They were supposed to give their salary to their wives and, keeping a small portion for their own expenses, ignore what it was done with it. At the end of the day, women were ultimately responsible for food appearing on the table and for clothes being ready to wear.

The only other option, reliance on Catholic charities, was considered a humiliation because it always came with conditions attached, or, worse, because it was a sign of being a bad son, daughter, or sibling. For example, it was thought to be socially and morally preferable to have senile parents remain in the home rather than to have them cared for in Church facilities (the dreaded *asilos para viejos*). Similarly, it was preferable to take care of an orphaned nephew rather than sending him to a religious institution.

The Humiliations of Misery

The regime, once its abysmal economic failures became evident, argued that misery in Spain was a result of the Civil War, and the difficulties caused by World War II, drought, and international boycotts.[41] The Francoists tried to draw a thick veil over what was the truth: that misery was mainly the product of autarky and a cruel socio-economic structure which the dictatorship not only failed to change, but fully endorsed. And this is why those who survived the deadly 1940s were still living miserable, harrowing lives in the 1950s and even the early 1960s, long after international wars and boycotts were over. This long-lasting misery was particularly intense in the south. Here the main factor was the appallingly unequal distribution of land and the lack of employment opportunities for hundreds of thousands of people who could find work for a few months of the year at most. The war may explain why, for example, in 1940, 112,303 landless peasant men and 376,187 women officially qualified to be recorded as permanently "inactive" by the authorities there; but it does not explain why in 1950 these numbers were 132,682 and 373,705 respectively.[42] Autarky and the *latifundia* (large estates) system, however, do: because they perpetuated abysmal rural poverty in the best years and catastrophe, even famine, in the bad ones, when, for example, drought prevailed.

The years 1945, 1946, and 1949, were very bad, but just as terrible was 1954, 15 years after Franco's troops marched victorious on the streets of Madrid, when drought hit the wheat, olive oil, and wine-growing areas of Andalusia.[43] In Cordoba, in the fall of that year, unemployment levels, already alarming during the summer months, became "anguishing." The local authorities predictably resorted to, and only to, a request for an increase in public works.[44] In neighboring Jaen there were at least 35,000 unemployed peasant laborers in September 1954. It was estimated that another 10,000 had emigrated in the previous weeks.[45]

Perversely, this sort of tragedy periodically offered a good opportunity for Falangist populism. Two years later, those peasants' sufferings were employed in defense of the landowners' interests. In February 1956, when there was a circumstantial labor shortage in the province, representatives of the agrarian unions reported to the government that they were satisfied with the present social situation, suggesting, even though salaries continued to lag far behind prices, that the official prohibition on Sunday work be lifted "in the interest of our economy" and because "the difficult situation of our journeymen [would] improve with one payday more per week."[46]

Everybody who wanted to know knew that an extra day's wage would change nothing. A study published by Catholic Action in 1953, based on data provided by a Falange-controlled institution, the Seville Socio-Economic Council, concluded that, after reviewing the growth of salaries for 22 different professions from 1936 to 1953, the purchasing power of agrarian workers' wages had been cut in half. This implosion of living standards was particularly catastrophic for landless peasants, since it was estimated that up to 15 percent of them were permanently unemployed. While the average daily wage for these peasants was about 70 pesetas (which was really 40 pesetas once idle days were included), it was estimated that in order for those even with small families to meet their basic needs their daily pay should have been closer to 200 pesetas, that is to say three to four times what they were earning. In other words, in 1953, hundreds of thousands of southern families were trying to live on one-third of the amount they actually needed to survive. It is not surprising that, because of his "deficient nutrition," the average productivity of a daily wage laborer in 1953 was 20 to 25 percent lower than it had been during "the worst and most anarchic years of the Republic."[47] The "reformist" Falangist and Catholic authors of the report did not forget to include among the causes of this productivity decrease "the lack of moral formation and concept of duty" of these laborers.[48]

While those in the regime worried about moral deficiencies, the fact remained that, a decade and a half after the end of the Civil War, the dispossessed Andalusian peasantry was often starving and was always insufficiently fed. In the rich, cereal-producing lands of the Guadalquivir valley of Cordoba and Seville, before 14 hours of field labor, a laborer's breakfast consisted – when working, of course – of bread with olive oil or fried flour (*migas*), sometimes coffee, and only rarely milk. Lunch was a salad of diced oranges, onions, olives, bread, and occasionally some fried eggs or potatoes with lard. A stew of chickpeas with potatoes or just beans and bread was supper; to which sometimes they could add dried figs or lettuce. A rare feast for these workers and their families was a meal of rice or potatoes with either clams or fish. It was a diet high in carbohydrates but poor in vitamins, fats, calcium, and protein. What protein there was came primarily from vegetables due to the scarcity of meat, fish, or milk. This diet was supposed to sustain the daily need of 4,000 calories for an average adult male, but it did not. The effect on the local rural population was devastating. According to the 1953 report, there was widespread malnutrition and chronic illnesses; frequent cases of underdevelopment among children; and signs of precocious senility among adults.[49]

This misery was not limited to the interior of Andalusia. In 1950 Malaga, the future glamorous tourist destination that would be known as Costa del Sol, could more accurately have been called the Costa del Hambre (hunger).[50] Had a traveler dared to navigate the national highway to Cadiz – it was in many parts "impassable" – and visited the towns along the way, he or she would have discovered the humiliations and the unspeakable living conditions of people caught between semi-feudal conditions and rampant capitalist greed, with a fascist bent.

The province of Granada is located east of Malaga. In 1955 the largest local landowner in the town of Moreda, the marquis of Motilla, wanted to convert his 190 tenants' contracts from rental agreements to the more profitable system of sharecropping, something that his tenants resisted fiercely. The marquis' manager (*administrador*) was pulling strings for him in Madrid, "constantly making a display of his real or fictitious friendships" with the authorities and party leaders. To achieve his ends, the manager harassed the tenants, denouncing them to the local Civil Guard for purported infractions, making them sign blank documents, requesting more payments, and curtailing their customary rights. The chief agronomist of the province suggested to the government that expropriation of the estate, with compensation, by the National Institute for Colonization would be the best solution. This was the option preferred by the tenants, who went so far as to request the local bishop's help to mediate with the marquis. The provincial governor and the head of the union pushed for a new agreement between the two sides, even though they were well aware of the proprietor's lack of good faith and the tenants' "natural reaction, and self-defense, against abuses." In the end, incapable of contravening one of the main tenets of the regime – that of the sacred nature of private property – the union's authorities simply made a vague request that a solution should be sought from the "public powers" (and were they not precisely the public powers they referred to?) to this "grave social problem."[51] Then they washed their hands, and nothing was done.

There were worse places than Moreda, where people had some land, even if they did not own it. The province of Cadiz is located west of Malaga. In 1960, Castellar de la Frontera had 2,491 inhabitants, most of them landless peasants, distributed across three small villages. The land in this municipality, 17,722 hectares in total, was divided up among the following owners: Corchera Almoraima, a cork-producing company linked to the duke of Medinaceli's estate, 16,078 hectares (91 percent of the total); the estate of the duchess of Medinaceli, 1,139 hectares (6.5 percent); and another 40 proprietors, 505 hectares (2.5 percent). The vast majority of the land was used for producing cork and for recreational hunting, activities that offered very few, and only temporary, jobs. In this idyllic, immaculately preserved, natural setting, social conditions were so horrific, according to a Falangist confidential report, that they did not bear detailed description. A simple glance left a "deep impression" of grinding poverty, with people living in shacks while earning "completely inadequate" salaries when work was available, in the worst possible working conditions, 10 to 12 hours a day. On top of this, the cork company had begun to evict the few tenants who lived in the area without compensating them in any way. Asking for protection from this assault, the locals requested that the authorities help them: "God will thank you, for all of this is not more than Christian charity."[52]

If conditions in this pseudo-medieval region of the Cadiz countryside were horrendous, not far from there but still in the same province, in the strongly capitalist, world-renowned sherry-producing area whose axis follows the Guadalquivir river from Jerez de la Frontera to Sanlucar de Barrameda, the situation was nearly as bad. In early 1961 the lack of rain meant that work started late, causing unemployment to be even higher. In Sanlucar (where the delicious Manzanilla sherry is produced) the city council (*ayuntamiento*) tried to help by offering 200 temporary public construction jobs at the miserable rate of 40 pesetas a day. That was better than nothing and more than 1,000 people gathered looking for work. This created a "tense, but peaceful situation." The authorities recognized "that [the workers] were in despair, due to long-lasting unemployment and the situation of utter penury that they were living [in] at home." Finally, they managed to get some cooperation from employers in the area and 470 positions were offered.[53]

Structural unemployment and misery went beyond the large estates of west Andalusia, even reaching zones where large landed properties were the exception rather than the rule, and stretching all over southern and southeastern Spain. In Toledo, just over an hour's drive from Madrid, there were more than 25,000 unemployed workers in December 1954 with no relief in sight.[54] In the town of Cieza (Murcia), with a population of 23,000, the esparto (a fibrous grass with applications in textile and paper production) industry collapsed in the late 1950s. In April 1957 there were 1,000 workers permanently unemployed there, with another 5,000 soon to join them.[55] In the heart of Malaga province, 23,000 people were unemployed in 1960 and wages there were falling "because of a recent increase [in the number] of available hands."[56] By then, the Stabilization Plan was hitting the poor hard. The following year, in 1961, the number of unemployed in Malaga climbed to more than 27,000 even though the hemorrhage of emigration to Europe had already begun. More than two decades after the end of the war, the situation in the south was well described by the following lines written in 1962 by Almeria's official unions:

> Even if we can always discuss the relationship that exists between welfare and economic progress, it seems indubitable that the level of this latter factor in Almeria renders impossible the development of a complete human existence, at least as we understand this in the Western world.[57]

In the rest of the country to have a job, even a stable one in what used to be elite employment, did not guarantee escape from misery and humiliation. Rail workers, who had a strong tradition of left-wing union militancy, were notoriously ill treated by the state-owned company RENFE. They were subjected to military-style discipline and harsh punishment if they stepped out of line. Since RENFE employees were often working while exhausted and used old machinery, deadly accidents became commonplace. So ruthless, however, was company discipline that, as a matter of course, workers were assumed to have caused these accidents. They were imprisoned as soon as the accident happened and for the period of the investigation, which could take years to complete. Suicide was not uncommon among those fearing arrest.[58]

Railway workers' salaries were kept very low, even by the standards of the period of autarky. In early 1950 a railway worker's starting salary was barely 10.5 pesetas a day, while a barber easily made twice this amount. In April of that year, when their daily wages were raised to 15.75 pesetas, or 450 pesetas a month, this was still not enough to sustain a family. The price of a kilo of bread was between 12 and 17 pesetas, a dozen eggs cost 29 pesetas, and a liter of olive oil 30 pesetas. Married men were paid so-called "points" every two or three months for having a family, and it was this "bonus" money that was used for purchasing extras such as replacing a pair of old sandals or repaying debts at the local grocery shop. Most railway workers needed to have a second job, or to cultivate a piece of land, to complement their salaries, while their wives worked as hard or harder by taking on odd jobs in addition to their domestic duties. To supplement their salaries, many railway workers also used their position to make extra money on the black market while others, including ticket collectors, turned a blind eye to black marketeers in exchange for small bribes.[59]

The situation of the much-castigated railway workers was such that, in 1950, even the governor of Valladolid himself felt it necessary to report directly to the government. He stated that the company's behavior was discriminatory and unfair. The previous year, he stated, engineers and managers had received substantial wage increases while the salaries of the lower ranks, or most of the company's 12,000 employees, remained horribly inadequate and inflation was forcing workers into destitution. As an example, the governor explained how the wife of a maintenance worker had to put one of their children in a sanatorium because they could not feed him.[60]

In fact, the company treated its own workforce badly, and when it took on temporary workers it acted with the utmost contempt. Men working at publicly sponsored jobs repairing the railway track around the town of Barcenas de Reinosa (Santander) during the spring of 1954 found their living quarters had no beds or blankets. They were forced to sleep with each other in cots to combat the cold. They were ill fed, having a breakfast of just soup and noodles, a dish of potatoes or beans for lunch, and the same with some bread for supper. They lacked toilets and showers.[61] At times, living and toiling next to these temporary workers were political prisoners serving their sentences.[62]

Miners, who had formerly been at the vanguard of the union movement, were another group of workers who now toiled and lived in the most appalling conditions. Some of the last surviving lead mines of Spain were located in the area of Linares-La Carolina, in Jaen. The region was among the most neglected in the country. For example, as late as 1955 no new public housing had been built in Linares, with a population of 60,000, since the end of the Civil War. Silicosis was rampant among the roughly 5,000 miners because of the lack of basic work safety measures. This explains why some workers became chronically ill as early as five years after starting in the mines. However, when a miner was declared to be suffering from grade 1 silicosis he was taken out of the pit and fired. After receiving 18 months of paltry unemployment payments, he and his family were left to fend for themselves. Moreover, because of the stigma that their illness brought and because of their reduced capacity for work, their opportunities for employment elsewhere were very limited, as companies were reluctant to hire "sick workers who contracted their illness working for someone else."[63]

Mining was on the decline in Spain, but the Falange's demagogy was not. Although foreign capital had been in retreat in this sector for decades, Falangists pointed to foreign ownership of some important mines as the cause of their downturn and of their workers' oppression. An example was the Rio Tinto mine in Huelva, the jewel of British nineteenth-century economic colonialism in Spain, where "the company control[led] everything." According to a Falangist report of 1955, miners lived in narrow, disease-infected, one-room houses into which up to a dozen people were crammed. Excrement was taken out in buckets to be thrown into a cesspit.[64] There were, however, more than a few cracks in this passionately patriotic National Syndicalist report. One was that the British company's CEO in Spain was not a foreigner but rather a former government minister and a large landowner, Joaquín Benjumea, a man "of good faith and great political qualities." Secondly, notwithstanding the appalling work conditions, the Falangists had to admit that miners had easier access to medical care through the company than the state's new social security plan was able to offer.

Miners' salaries were low and their working conditions were horrendous, with their employers valuing their lives cheaply. In 1953 a blast killed 11 workers at the Calvo Sotelo coalpit in Puertollano, Ciudad Real. The company belonged to the state. In 1958 another gas explosion killed 12 more at the same mine. This time, however, the bitter complaints of the survivors grew louder (the previous catastrophe had been quietly blamed on a careless deceased worker) because no real security measures had been taken since the 1953 accident. Miners were not prepared to accept that "another name of those registered as working" in the pit (that is, the name of a worker who was now dead) would be found guilty while, as with the previous accident, no manager would ever be blamed. In their complaint, the miners explained to the official union that the safety measures that should have been taken to detect gas had, first, barely been implemented after the previous accident and, later, had been completely abandoned. This happened despite complaints by the miners that another accident could happen at any time.[65]

Not far away at the state-owned Almaden mine, notorious for its poisonous mercury, miners were being consistently subjected to arbitrary rules set by the company directors. In 1958 the company fired 72 workers and punished another 72 because their productivity had decreased. The workers' lack of motivation, however, was not a product of laziness. According to a confidential union report, the "by-laws regulating safety, shifts, salaries and working conditions were unfair, outdated and often illegal." Workers toiled using obsolete technology and, when new machinery arrived, the report stated, hinting at corruption or incompetence, it often proved to be "less effective" than the equipment it was intended to replace. When the official union established the "company jury" (an advisory council in which workers were to be represented), as mandated by law, the company illegally dissolved it. In addition it ignored the collective agreement and usurped land that had been set aside for workers to use as vegetable plots, a privilege they had enjoyed since the eighteenth century. Meanwhile, the local union offered no services and no recreational or health facilities to help compensate for these privations. Nor did the union build social housing for the miners. Was it any surprise that miners "did not need us [the official union] or barely believe in us?" the Falangists asked themselves, or perhaps their masters.[66]

Autarky's Long Agony

The post-war misery exhausted Spaniards, not only physically but also in terms of their capacity to believe in real progress. They had long realized that promises of improvements were just acts of propaganda. In April 1950, for example, a "general confusion on economic matters and growing discontent because of living conditions" was reported by the authorities in the conservative agrarian province of Orense.[67] A similar situation existed in the far more diverse and socially polarized southern province of Seville.[68] By 1950, even in the relatively well-off province of Alava, the Basque province that had so wholeheartedly supported the anti-republican rebellion in 1936, economic concerns about scarcity and high prices consumed people's lives.[69] The same concerns were reported in Tenerife in the Canary Islands, as was widespread disgust at the extensive corruption that existed there.[70] Life was very harsh, and autarky was widely condemned.[71]

In the early 1950s there were voices within the regime itself that had recognized the failure of the policy of economic autarky and the catastrophic impact it had had on society. Complaints would not always take issue with state intervention but rather with how autarky was implemented. For example, on the one hand, Falangists felt that intervention should be put under their unions' control; on the other, they complained that the social situation put them in an increasingly difficult position in the great urban and industrial centers. There, they said, they did the dirty work for someone else's policies, thwarting the legitimate complaints of the population while being left alone to "discipline" workers. Worse, the Falangists knew that there was no relief in sight. As an internal 1951 report from Biscay stated, all economic policies had "failed," creating a growing disparity between wages and prices, and it was "fear[ed] that this abyss [would] grow deeper tomorrow" as it was made worse by corruption and the black market.[72]

Perhaps the sector that best exemplified autarky's never-ending damaging effects was the textile industry, largely centered in Catalonia. "Chaos" was the word used by union officials in 1949 when explaining that, while industrialists still believed in and cherished Franco, the autarkic system had created "violent feelings" among them.[73] The same union officials acknowledged in a 1950 report that large companies and well-connected individuals had easier access to materials than smaller ones. They also said that Catalonian industrialists had greater advantages than the rest of the country. In any case, the results of these erratic policies were under-production, bankruptcy, and unemployment, which mostly affected small companies and, of course, their employees. In the cotton-manufacturing sector in 1950 alone, there were 171 factories which completely ceased production, while a further 295, lacking materials, operated on only a few days per week. The net result was between 50,000 and 67,000 workers being either temporarily or permanently unemployed in the Barcelona area.[74]

The Catalan textile industry had endured an ever-deepening crisis since the mid-1940s. On top of having to fight through corruption to acquire the necessary materials, industrialists in the region found themselves at the mercy of constant power shortages. These were officially blamed on the lack of rain. In reality, the problem was misallocation of resources and lack of planning by the government. This did not prevent the regime from constantly making claims in propaganda exercises about great public works that were either completed or about to be completed. However, given the persistent electricity shortages in Barcelona, these claims soon turned against them.[75] This problem extended throughout the region, affecting all aspects of daily life. In Gerona, local authorities reported, in December 1954, that the lack of electricity had been the root cause of "the paralysis of industrial production" resulting in a 20 percent reduction in production from the previous year. Officials responded with the ludicrous measure of banning "the installation of small machines such as coffee makers in cafeterias and motors in wells."[76]

Again, the Falangists saw crisis and poverty as a political opportunity. On several occasions they tried to present themselves as having the only true alternatives to existing policies in order to position themselves to gain political influence. Their demagogic appropriation of ordinary citizens' pain reached an apex during the early 1950s, as rampant inflation and stagnant salaries caused deep, widespread discontent. In the Canary Islands, for example, the Falangists were so open in 1950 in their criticism of the government's economic policies that the governor was forced to arrest several of Tenerife's Camisas Viejas ("Old Shirts") and to demote the leader of the "Old Guard" organization.[77]

Nowhere did this cheap populism cause more alarm than in Barcelona in February and March 1951. It began there as a political vendetta by the local Falangists against a hated governor. They printed leaflets inciting people to protest a hike in streetcar fares. However, this demagogic gesture turned into an uncontrolled civic revolt and a mass strike. People, and not only anti-Francoists, seized the opportunity to voice their anger at the intolerable living conditions. Eventually this resulted in a general strike and streetcar boycott that completely paralyzed Barcelona for two days (March 12 and 13). The government responded by sending in troops and by rallying the deeply worried Falangists, who now understood that they had played with fire. Not surprisingly, the Falangists reverted to their old loyalties and they were soon assaulting the strikers and patrolling the deserted streets in their cars, armed with guns. The 1951 Barcelona "streetcar strike" was the largest civil action in Spain since the end of the Civil War and brought together activists from different ideological backgrounds and a cross-section of the population that included Catholics and communists alike. In fact, it was a strike of protest, with no political agenda and no party directing events, and this is precisely what guaranteed its popular appeal. Two months later, when the banned political opposition groups called for a mass strike on May 1 (Labor Day), most people, workers included, either remained at home or went to work.[78]

In spite of occasional and sometimes massive protests, workers felt that survival, rather than ideology, was their main concern. Their pain worked to the regime's advantage. While people thought of food and bills they had no time for political alternatives. There was, however, only an uneasy solace in this for the dictatorship, as a collective reaction to so much suffering could surface at any time. The risks were most obvious in regions where there had been strong evidence of working-class mobilization in the past, such as in Barcelona, in the Basque country, in Asturias, and in Madrid.[79]

On the other hand, even if they were discontented with autarky most employers still supported the regime, especially at critical moments of strikes or boycotts. There are nationalist myths about Basque and Catalan employers having been sympathetic to their workers' plight during the Franco years, protecting them as much as they could from the evils of fascist Spain in the name of their common national interests. Nothing could be further from the truth. For example, workers in the huge Euskalduna and Constructora Naval metalworks in Biscay walked out on a peaceful strike in December 1953. Workers at other companies followed suit. Everyone involved knew that these men had tried for months to have their complaints heard by the company and their unions, but to no avail, and that their salaries were being rapidly eaten up by inflation. The companies did not seek a compromise; instead they fired the strikers: 1,900 of the 2,000 workforce in Euskalduna alone. The result for these workers was the loss of their seniority rights (which then amounted to at least 20 percent of their paychecks) and of their salaries for the period "between their dismissal and the resolution of their request." It was the company, not the fascist unions that acted so ruthlessly against their exhausted, underfed employees and then "demanded" that the strikers reapply for their jobs. The civil governor and his police actually helped the employers to destroy further resistance. The leaders of the strike and those unfortunate enough to have been arrested were badly beaten by the police. Anyone deemed to have "bad political antecedents" was permanently fired.[80]

The police were not alone in helping both unions and employers to control workers. As happened in Barcelona in 1951, the Falange frequently collaborated in the repression of labor unrest. In 1954, when the Seville Tramway Company was allowed to increase its tariffs, the main protesters were students, who had the support of the tram workers, who had been lobbying for a pay hike at the time, and of the general public, who had seen too many accidents. The Falange, as was their habit, solved the situation by dispatching 150 of their members to act as informers. They were disguised as "ordinary passengers [and listened to] conversations and [the] public mood to prevent new incidents." Spies were also sent to the city's main factories.[81]

Repression was one tool of control; lies were another. These reached new lows in 1957 when the dictatorship was accused by the International Labour Organization in Geneva of oppressing Spanish workers and of violating their right to freedom of association. Of course, Franco's representatives claimed, this was not true. They steadfastly maintained that their official unions were pluralist and that their role was "to mediate and to conciliate," but never to impose policies. Membership in the official unions was just a "consequence of being a member of [the] social security" plan. The government "never intervenes in the [work of] unions." Furthermore, the regime retorted, the cause of most labor conflicts since 1950 had been that "continually improving standards of living created a movement among workers against working extra time because they believed that their normal salaries were enough for their needs and [they] preferred to spend more time resting and amusing themselves."[82] This is how Franco's sycophants tried to portray the New Spain to the world, but their internal communications told a different story.

With reference to "improving standards of living," a confidential report from Santander, dated October 1957, explained "continuous rising prices, very sharp in the northern provinces [...] have decreased salaries' purchasing power, making the last raise ineffective." When discussing government intervention, the report clarified the matter of the recent union elections stating that among the new representatives there were Falangists, apolitical members, Catholic activists, and "individuals from the old organizations; and we are making detailed inquiries about them to gain a clear understanding of their intentions."[83] The system by which the regime came to know the intentions of the newly elected representatives was simple.

In November 1957 the Falange spying service in Valencia noted that either the police or they themselves would go to the factories or, in order "to finish quickly, [we would go] to their houses" to interrogate the recently elected workers' representatives; "sometimes it was difficult for them [the workers] to answer many of the questions because most of them had cooperated in one way of another with the Red [Republican] Army."[84] In a report in traditionally convoluted Falangist language of May 1957 the Political Secretariat of the party explained:

> Even if it is admissible and advisable [to have] a generous and forgiving attitude towards all the political mistakes committed in labor matters and [towards] the reinstatement at work of all those who represent elements opposed to Spain, it is completely unacceptable, because it is dangerous, [to have] a neutral attitude when the positions of representatives in city councils or in unions are at stake.[85]

Repression left workers little room to take direct measures to improve their situation. This was particularly so where they were in a minority, such in the sleepy provincial capitals, where collective protest was all but impossible because troublemakers could be easily identified. Instead of risking beatings, dismissals, or imprisonment, spreading news and cynical remarks became an alternative safe way to convey their opinions to the regime's elites. The Falangists were always listening. The local unions in Orense reported in March 1956 that people were certain they had been deceived since their recent salary raises were far lower than they had expected. They were afraid that prices would soon climb again.[86] In rural, backward Guadalajara, the unions recognized that salaries were not enough to have a "dignified" life.[87] When the long-awaited salary increase of 20 percent arrived in April 1956, the word "deception" was in widespread use after workers realized their new salaries "could [only] buy the same things that they had [purchased] with the previous ones."[88] In October 1956 in Granada, workers adopted an attitude of "wait and see" after authorities had made explicit promises for wage increases over the previous months. According to official data, these months had witnessed price increases of 30 percent on basic items, but employees were fearful that whatever raise they might receive would be offset by inflation.[89] This is exactly what had happened the previous spring when their wage increase had not kept up with rising prices, causing deep and widespread "discontent."[90] In October 1956 Salamanca's unions notified the central authorities about the dangerous situation in their province. This was a province where the majority of the population was supportive of the regime and of Franco in particular, but workers were now fearful of the future. The union's report stated that workers entirely distrusted official announcements.[91]

People had good reason to distrust the authorities' promises. There was galloping inflation in the late 1950s, reaching annual averages of almost 12 percent between 1956 and 1958. When, in May 1956, there had been strikes in the neighboring Basque country and Navarre, even in faraway Salamanca's union officials had to spend a great deal of time visiting factories and consulting with workers' representatives in places "that presented the most danger" of striking.[92] Discontent was reaching even people who should have been unquestionably loyal. In Navarre, the province most loyal to the rebels' cause in 1936, even priests were criticizing the government in sermons. Here, workers had abandoned any "caution" and were talking openly about "striking as the most natural of things."[93] If this was happening in conservative Navarre, it was not surprising that in June 1957, in traditionally more radical Biscay, the unions were predicting an "absolute disorientation and a black future," among other things, because in "September salaries will be worth less than in August of last year and in this way we will start over again."[94] What these workers did not know yet was that autarky had already run its miserable course. In February, Franco had changed his government, and included in the cabinet the men who would eventually design and implement the Stabilization Plan.

Looking back at the two decades of autarky, it is fair to ask why, if misery and resentment had been running so high, workers didn't revolt? Was it just because of fear? Certainly both fear and ever-present repression are crucial to understanding this relative passivity; but we also need to understand how this fear operated in the historical context. It is important to keep in mind what employees relied on for support on a day-to-day basis, what limited the scope of their protests. A modern, post-industrial society offers many possibilities for protest because people have both the material and legal resources to do so: the support of individual wealth, a social safety network, public and private education, freedom of movement and reliance on family and relations, among other things. A modern democratic society also offers open dissent, protected by laws which are based on fundamental human rights. In many ways, we have come to take these things for granted. However, most post-war Spaniards had none or next to none of the above-mentioned items, except one: the support of their families.

The preservation of the family influenced the approach most people took to surviving and even resisting the material and social despair caused by Franco's autarkic experiment. This in part explains why the forms of protest that workers most frequently employed were non-confrontational, such as refusing to enter the workplace, or reducing the pace of work. In this way, workers fought to save the security of their homes while recognizing that the basic, moral covenant of work in exchange for a minimum living wage had been broken by both the state and employers. Union officials were not unaware of this, but what really mattered to them was the preservation of their jobs and their positions of authority.

Knowing the limitations that labor protest faced, Falangists always encouraged workers to demonstrate good behavior when complaining. This meant showing respect to authority, not disrupting public order, and following official union administrative channels. Union leaders wanted to see "their" workers as children and themselves as stern but caring fathers who would sometimes be their advocates but who ultimately knew what was best. For example, when reporting on the 1961 strike at the mining company Cruz Chiquita SL in La Union, the leader of Murcia's official unions stated, "neither in terms of the way workers acted, and I was in permanent contact as soon as I learned of the incidents, nor in terms of the size of the company [it was a very small company] did events have, in our opinion, any significance [...] Workers acted without knowing the significance of their acts."[95] On this occasion it was convenient for all those implicated to close the matter in this fashion.

If the "protégés" (workers) stepped out of this subservient role, then the stern stepfather put on the blue Falangist shirt, and acted. For example, in May 1958 construction workers went on strike in Madrid. The head of their official union addressed the workers of the company Taller del Temple de Ballesta and admonished them for their "clumsiness and very grave responsibility" for playing a game initiated "by the enemies of workers' tranquility and prosperity." Many of these workers had just arrived from the famished south, and the same official explained to them "the possibility of returning to their places of origin." The threat was clear: accept what is given to you or go back to your miserable villages. In this case the employer vouched for his workers, out of goodwill or perhaps because labor was scarce in the capital's construction sector, explaining to the union official that "they were good people, without grand ideas."[96] Confrontation here was taken a bit further than in the previous case, but it was eventually avoided by the third party, the employer, again arguing in a way that was in tune with the Falangists' views.

The "convenient misunderstandings" of the Falangist–worker relationship were exposed, when workers decided that compromise was less effective than open protest and decided to behave like independent, free adults. This happened more frequently in the areas of strong, decades-old, working-class identity. In Asturias, for example, there were massive strikes and protests among coalminers during 1957 and 1958. Reductions in real wages, devoured by rapid price increases, had created widespread resentment.[97] The government had confronted events with its usual mix of warm words, demagogic declarations and actions, threats, and, eventually, the usual harsh reprisals (beatings, detentions, sackings, etc.). However, when touring the region in 1958, the Minister of Labor and former head of the official unions, Fermín Sanz Orrio, tried to use the old populist trick and allow "simple workers" to vent their complaints in public in tightly controlled town-hall meetings (plainclothes and fully uniformed policemen were present). Things were certainly not helped by the fact that the visit coincided with the latest accident in which several miners had died. While the touring party was met in the streets with "total public coldness," meetings with the minister soon became heated as brave individuals refused to play the role of pliant good folk limited to talking about improving things and listening to new and certainly empty promises. These people put hard questions to the authorities about things such as the arrest and deportation of workers, demotion of representatives, militarization of workplaces, and freedom to form independent unions. It was then that the paternalistic Falangist gave way to the thug, as the minister publicly accused the more daring miners of being "stupid and idiotic," and of being manipulated by subversive forces.[98]

Most labor conflicts under Francoism, and particularly during autarky, followed a similar pattern. After increasing tension the Falangists went from paternalism to threats, and then, if these did not suffice, to repression. At the end of the conflict, workers were "forgiven." The objective was to sustain the fiction of union–worker harmony. This was a system in which workers tried to obtain as much as they could while minimizing risk, and Falangists gave the impression that they had workers' loyalty. However, in spite of the regime's pretensions this system was not static: in this suffocating atmosphere something was slowly moving. During the last years of autarky, workers' political culture evolved, transforming itself into a force that the Falangists would feel increasingly unable to pretend that they controlled. In spite of the Falangists' illusions that they knew better than simple people, many workers, did indeed have "grand ideas," and in the 1950s they were in the process of developing them further. The first step had been to learn from past mistakes, abandoning the rigid organizational structures of the pre-war unions and the more overtly political strikes of the 1940s. Both had led nowhere except to more defeat and suffering.[99] Since the late 1940s many old militants had realized that one way to act against the regime from the inside and under cover of legality was to infiltrate the official unions by presenting their candidacies to union representatives. This infiltration was done by workers on their own, with no guidance from any illegal party or union.

A consequence of this infiltrating strategy was that old left-wing militants started to interact with younger generations of workers who, like them, had also become representatives in the official unions. The process brought together idealists from different traditions and generations. A surprise among the old left-wing militants was to find young people associated with a Catholic organization called HOAC (see chapter 4) who shared their criticism of the regime. HOAC was a small Catholic Action workers' group that by the early 1950s had become increasingly disenchanted with Francoism's social policies and repressive methods. This new phenomenon led to further change in the old militancy's political culture, with the gradual discarding of crude, left-wing, anti-clerical and anti-Catholic attitudes.[100] Workers also learned to use the official unions' language, the Falangist rhetoric of social justice, to promote their interests and to call for change. In sum, the new generations of labor militants took from the unions what was useful to them and rejected, openly or otherwise, the rest.[101] Repression did not lead workers to nihilism but, rather, to pragmatism.

The practicality of the newly emerging labor movement was both cause and consequence of the fact that worker protests under autarky were essentially defensive and non-confrontational. Poor people knew how weak their position was and how far they could go with their demands. This was particularly evident in periods of deep economic crisis (or rather of crisis within the permanent crisis), when workers' main bargaining power, the possibility of quitting and taking their skills elsewhere, all but disappeared. For example, one of the immediate effects of the 1959 Stabilization Plan and the dismantling of the autarkic system was a sharp economic recession that further took away from workers any possibility of striking successfully. Their situation deteriorated as salaries were severely reduced and overtime, incentives, and other extra income were banned. Furthermore, unemployment increased as many companies began to close their doors and lay off their employees.[102] This resulted in a sudden reduction of workers' purchasing power of between 20 and 50 percent (official data reported 4 percent, but secret memos from the official Falangist unions stated otherwise).[103] Yet in spite of this extra oppression the number of strikes *declined* during the plan's implementation. They only increased, and in fact became a wave of massive strikes, when the economic recovery became a "boom" in 1962, because now the first labor shortages for skilled workers started to occur. In spite of what the Falangist godfathers wanted to think, "simple folk" knew when and how to act.

Failure to Educate

Today it is all but ignored how Francoist prejudice and callousness left behind a catastrophic educational legacy, which except for Salazar's Portugal has no parallel in contemporary western Europe.[104] The dictatorship's dedication to a low tax base and its disregard for the poor meant that, in terms of education and training, for 40 years Spain lagged well behind most of Europe. In the anemic budgets of the long post-war period, defense, not education, was the regime's number one priority. In 1935, the republican state had devoted 2.3 times more funding to defense than to education. In 1941, the dictatorship spent close to 8.4 times more on defense than education, and still over 4.5 times more in 1955. By reversing the liberal education policies they had despised in the previous republican years, Francoists ensured that Spain went backwards in educational policy precisely when European societies were expanding their education systems as part of the post-war "social pact"; but no such thing existed in Spain. In fact, the opposite, social revenge, occurred.

The country's education deficit was not new; it long pre-dated Francoism. While central and north European countries were establishing their universal education programs in the mid-1800s, successive Spanish governments did relatively little for public education and offloaded the responsibility to municipalities, which were chronically underfunded and often corrupt. The result was that, for the poorer provinces, especially those of the south, the level of illiteracy remained astonishingly high. In 1900 it was estimated that almost 64 percent of the Spanish population (56 percent of men and 71 percent of women) could neither read nor write. This situation began to change with the arrival of mass politics and with new attitudes among some sectors of the elite and the emerging middle classes, which rejected the country's weak and backward socio-economic structure. In fact, education was not seriously addressed until the Second Republic instituted a vast program for the construction of schools, training of teachers, and raising their salaries, during its short tenure (1931–6). This financial effort, it must be remembered, happened in the aftermath of the Great Depression. This program was, in turn, completely halted during the first decade and a half of the dictatorship.

The Francoists boasted that they had brought back real education to Spain, only to offer data in their internal reports that contradicted these claims. For example, in a study conducted for the 1956–7 state budget, the Minister of Education, the Catholic (and later Christian Democrat) Joaquín Ruiz-Giménez, criticized the liberal governments of the past for "having small budgets" and not spending enough on education. However, in the statistical table that accompanied his proposal it was clear that, in 1935, the republican government (then formed by a center-right coalition) had devoted 1.39 percent of its national budget to education, while between 1940 and 1954 Franco's regime allocated an average of well below 1 percent of national expenditure to education. In addition, it was an erratic effort. The regime spent a high of 1.1 percent of the budget in 1949, but in 1951 it fell as low as 0.64 percent. In 1954, according to UNESCO, Spain allocated 0.9 percent of its national budget to education, while Ireland spent 3 percent, Sweden 2.71 percent, Italy 2.68 percent, and West Germany 2.5 percent. In strict dollar terms, Spain's spending on education was a third less than Venezuela's, less than half of Argentina's, and less than Egypt's, South Africa's, or Portugal's.[105]

There were some exceptions, or at least some better news, in terms of national illiteracy levels, which stood at over 44 percent in 1930, but had improved to just above 15 percent in 1950. These data, however, do not reflect the enormous disparities that still existed between rich and poor provinces and between cities and the countryside. In 1950 the number of people who remained illiterate in rural areas was proportionally at least a third higher than in urban centers. Illiteracy remained a huge problem in the southern provinces and the Canary Islands. Cordoba, Malaga, Granada, Huelva, Jaen, Almeria, and Cadiz had illiteracy rates of over 35 percent well into the 1950s. In a very practical sense, the problem of education for people living in the poorer southern provinces remained because they simply had far fewer public schools than the northern provinces.

The "good news" on illiteracy was not quite so good because it included another statistical mirage. Post-war poverty resulted in a very high proportion of children who either went to school only occasionally or did not go to school at all. According to the state organization responsible for eradication of illiteracy, Junta Nacional Contra el Analfabetismo, the number of children effectively attending classes in the academic year 1950–1 was only 35.7 percent of those of school age, down from 46.9 percent in 1940–1.[106] This situation was in part a product of autarky's catastrophe, in which children were forced to skip school to survive hunger, because they were sent to work, to beg, or to forage for food. In addition, many of those not working could not attend school as there were not enough available spaces for them. In 1950 the total deficit of classrooms in the country was estimated at 55,000. Given this deficit, it seems obvious that the national decline in the number of illiterate people was not an achievement of Franco's; rather, it was primarily the result of the school programs instigated by the defeated Republic, and of the new attitudes of parents who saw the need for their children to learn the basics of reading, writing, and arithmetic. In fact, because of widespread poverty, this new attitude translated into very short periods of schooling, usually two or three years, for millions of children, as we can see from the decline of school registration and attendance. Those pupils, though not technically illiterate, were so in practice; a nuance that the official data fail to reflect.[107]

Spain compared very badly to other European countries in almost every aspect related to education. In 1955 the duration of mandatory education in Spain was only six years while in Germany it ranged between eight and nine years, in Belgium it was eight years, and in Norway and the United Kingdom it was seven years.[108] The average teacher-to-student ratio was 1:35 in Spain, 1:30 in the UK, 1:26 in Italy, 1:23 in Austria and Belgium, and 1:21 in Sweden. "Even less satisfactory," according to the Minister of Education, was the proportion of school-age children actually registered in, much less attending, schools: 67 percent in Spain, 98 percent in Austria, 97 percent in Germany, 90 percent in Norway, 86 percent in Sweden, and 72 percent in Italy. Approximately 1,400,000 children, or 30 percent of all those who were of school age, did not have "appropriate school access" in Spain. Not surprisingly, teachers were among the worst paid in Europe. Their purchasing power was officially estimated to be 20 percent of what it had been in 1936 (a popular saying of the times was "to go hungrier than a school teacher"). School materials were "in an intolerable condition," prompting government officials to state that "we propose a modest increase of 1,000 pesetas per school." It was reported that there were deficiencies in 80 percent of the "buildings and installations" of public libraries and that the same number of librarians as "fifty years ago" supported these. The report added, "This honorable body is among the worst paid [...] but they must limit themselves to a role of conservation."[109]

The key to understanding the under-investment in public education during Franco's rule is that education was seen by the dictatorship as essentially a tool to maintain the existing social and political inequalities. Until the late 1960s, quality education was the preserve of the rich, the growing middle classes, and of males. Upper- and middle-class families could, and often did, send their children to private, faith-based schools and frequently made this choice for their children's secondary years. Private Catholic high schools flourished in the 1940s, while enrolment in state high schools declined. Each year until 1957, public high schools had fewer students enrolled in them than they had had in 1940. The result is that, by 1957, private Catholic centers were graduating nearly four times more pupils than the public system (205,974 and 62,422 respectively). The vast majority of the high-school graduates were boys. While in 1950 slightly more than half of elementary students were girls, in high schools and universities the situation was very different. Girls made up only a third of all secondary students in 1950 and only reached 45.6 percent in 1970, and young women constituted barely 15 percent of all university students in 1951, and only 27 percent in 1970.[110]

Predictably, the total number of people reaching intermediate or tertiary education was very low. As late as 1965, only 18.6 percent of children aged 11 to 16 were enrolled in high school. This was one of the lowest proportions among industrial countries (even in India a third more high-school students per capita were enrolled at the time). What is more, high schools were concentrated in those places where the richest families lived. In Madrid, for example, wealthy neighborhoods such as Chamartín, Argüelles, or Salamanca had four to five times more students enrolled per capita than the poorer Madrid neighborhoods such as Moratalaz or Vallecas. Moreover, most high schools in affluent areas were private.[111]

Reactionary ideology not only affected the means and resources for the delivery of education but also paid close attention to its content. For the dictatorship, the school system was a means by which it could implement its ultra-conservative social values of Catholicism, chauvinist nationalism, sexism, and class prejudice. Franco's approach to education was one that sought the submission of its students. It strove to have children blindly obey rather than think. The base for this was a crusade against "rationalism," considered by both the state and the Church one of the greatest illnesses of modernity. One of the first measures introduced by the dictatorship was to have co-education banned, and physical punishment restored ("Letters go down better with blood"). In both the private and public systems, students were told that not only were women and men different but that women had to obey their fathers and husbands, and could never aspire to be equal to their brothers.[112] The then ultra-conservative Church not only strongly supported this project but directed it through the frequent appointment of a Catholic Minister of Education and, thanks to the flourishing private Church schools, enjoyed an increased social and economic role. This was the other side of an educational landscape that included millions of school-age children who either did not attend class or did so in half-ruined school buildings staffed by teachers who were paid abysmally low salaries.[113]

A crucial element in this project was control of the history curriculum. Students were told that power and history came from God. The history of Spain was represented by a tall pyramid with the Creator at the top, with the different stages of civilization following below. In this model, the first key moment was the supposed arrival of St. James to evangelize Spain in Roman times. The rest was a struggle between eternal, Catholic Spain and the alien forces that sought its destruction. The last assault against true Spain was carried out by foreign ideas and movements such as the Enlightenment, liberalism, and socialist revolution – until saved by Franco, a providential man who, accordingly, answered only to God and history.[114] This was taught under the crucifix that presided over all of Spain's classrooms, flanked on both sides by pictures of Franco and of José Antonio, the Falange's founder. In those classrooms, children learned, or rather deduced, on which side their fathers had fought in the war: for God or for the Devil. And in this way the portrayal of their parents' or grandparents' lives and experiences was manipulated to suit the dictatorship's purposes.

Francoism's educational tragedy was in full flow during the years of the "economic boom" in the 1960s and, at least in the most backward regions of the country, it did not fully abate until well into the 1970s. In 1960, for example, when the regional education inspector visited a school in the little town of Villamanrique in the province of Seville, she was told that of the 240 girls officially registered in the school, only 170 regularly attended class and only 157 were present on the day of her visit. She was also told that of the 138 boys registered an average of 120 attended regularly, but, again, the number present that day was lower: only 103.[115] Like many places in Spain, real change only came to this village in the early 1970s, and in this case it came at the hand of a new mayor, Antonio, a conservative, strictly Catholic farmer. A pivotal moment arrived when someone "discovered" that about 45 children in the town were employed tending pigs and did not attend school at all. The mayor called the parents to a meeting and invited the sergeant of the Civil Guard to be present. At this meeting, Antonio threatened the parents. The children subsequently went to school. Later, the mayor would say: "Today, even the Gypsies' kids go to school, even though some manage to escape."[116]

This was a representative, not an isolated, case. When, in 1972, the Spanish Ministry of Education published a study of regional levels of school enrolment during the previous decade, it depicted a situation that can only be described as catastrophic.[117] The report revealed that the regions with the lowest levels of enrolment were all in the south, the Canary Islands, on the Mediterranean coast, and in Madrid, Biscay, and Pontevedra. The most notorious among these provinces were Malaga, where in 1968 only 55.5 percent of children attended school, followed by Tenerife (59.6 percent). Modern, developed provinces such as Madrid (only 73 percent attendance), Biscay (78.6 percent), and other industrial areas were included on this list because the rapid rate of immigration had outpaced school construction.[118] The overall balance for the whole country revealed that, around 1970, only 75 percent of Spanish children were considered to be fully attending school. It was then estimated that the school system lacked over 400,000 spaces (even allowing for 40 children per class, this amounts to 10,000 classrooms), while another 721,000 spaces were in institutions whose buildings and infrastructure were considered inadequate for proper education. In absolute numbers, the deficit of pupil positions in Barcelona was estimated at almost 250,000, in Madrid at 155,000, in Corunna at 90,000, in Valencia at 87,000, and in Seville at 74,000.[119] Almost as astonishingly, the male illiteracy rate was still higher than 25 percent in the country's poorest regions (Extremadura, La Mancha, Levant, Andalusia, the Balearic Islands, and the Canary Islands). Even more appallingly, in these same regions the female illiteracy rate was, on average, another 5 percent higher.

Francoism's educational elitism and reactionary policies extended to the small and inefficient university system. In 1970 only 9.2 percent of 20- to 24-year-olds attended university.[120] The country had one of the lowest proportions of university students in Europe: 653 for every 100,000 people, while poorer Greece had 856, and Italy, traditionally the closest nation to compare with Spain's performance in any field, had 1,280 per 100,000 (in the USA the number was 4,137). Failure to complete post-secondary studies was a frequent occurrence in Spain. Moreover, when enrolment in universities did begin to expand rapidly in the last decade and a half of the dictatorship (from 76,458 in 1960 to 213,069 in 1970) the resources devoted to university buildings and the recruitment of professors lagged far behind the needs of the institutions. Of the 8,500 university instructors teaching in 1972, roughly 2,000 had a permanent position, while the rest worked in precarious situations. This naturally provided fertile ground for them to join protests against the university system and the dictatorship.[121]

***

Francoism's damage to society has no equivalent in any post-war west European society. It could be said without exaggeration that only the most callous of dictators could have maintained for so long such absurd economic and social policies. Only a political regime that did not answer to its people could have survived the social disaster that these policies caused. Francoism offered Spaniards peace in exchange for freedom, only to deliver suffering and humiliation. Yet, in spite of the regime's policies, poor people adapted and survived, and many even thrived. The main keys to this were their own sacrifice, their hard work, and, for millions, their decision to escape misery by migrating. How this happened is explained in the next chapter.

3

MIGRATION

Migration is another of those hard-to-quantify taxes that the weakest pay almost exclusively so that the system can function, and those who profit from it can prosper even more. Not only do poor people pay the tax of migration, poor regions do as well, losing the human resources that make economic progress possible. That said, governments can help to relieve this pain, this extra contribution of the humble. Post-war migrations happened with a different intensity and a different rhythm all over Europe. In Spain, however, the dictatorship had an impact, because it was one of the very few Western governments that had no need to answer to public scrutiny, or placate angry voters. To migrate within or from a country as a full citizen was quite different from doing so as the subject of a tyrannical regime. For this reason, migration and its cycles in Franco's Spain cannot be separated from the dictatorship's policies and the heavy toll that they imposed on the poor. When we compare empirical data from Spain and from any democratic European country, the numbers tell us that millions of people moved, but they say nothing of what people experienced, what they thought, what they discovered, and what they achieved through migration.

Migrations and regional disparities were not new in Spain. They existed long before the dictatorship seized power and they were part of the century-long process of Spain's industrialization. Historians and geographers have pointed out the vastness of the phenomenon and the related territorial effects. In 1900, Barcelona was the most densely populated province in the country, 10 times more so than the least densely populated, Soria. In 1975, both provinces continued to represent the extremes of provincial population density but by this time Barcelona was 56 times more densely populated. The key periods for the acceleration of this process of demographic transfer were the years of the huge migrations of the 1950s and the 1960s when the populations of Madrid, Barcelona, Valencia, and the three Basque provinces of Biscay, Guipuzcoa, and Alava grew at a spectacular rate. The big "winners" were Madrid and Barcelona; each gained nearly 1.4 million people, while Valencia received a net immigration of 275,000 people and Biscay 264,000. In the meantime, the population of the interior of the peninsula and the south – 21 of the country's 50 provinces in total – declined in absolute numbers. In total, 34 provinces were net exporters of population. The southern provinces were the big losers. In those two decades the province of Jaen alone lost more than 400,000 people, Granada lost 334,000, Badajoz 332,000, and Cordoba 321,000.[1] The result was that in 1975 one out of four Spaniards was living in a municipality different from that of his or her birth.[2]

The End of the Peasantry

Arguably, the main social phenomenon in the history of Europe in the twentieth century was the end of the peasantry.[3] In 1950, for example, peasants formed 23 percent of West Germany's labor force; in 1971, they barely amounted to 9.7 percent. During the same two decades, in the rich lands of Italy's Emilia Romagna region, the proportion of peasants in the labor force declined from 52 percent to 20 percent. Most of those who left agriculture also abandoned the countryside and migrated to cities. Between 1955 and 1971, 9 million Italians migrated.[4] Spanish peasants too, like tens of millions of others in post-war Europe, moved from the countryside to cities, from one country to another, and from tilling the land to working in factories or in service industries. This was part of a process of accelerated urbanization.[5] In 1940, the number of people living in towns with fewer than 2,000 inhabitants was very similar to the number of people living in towns with more than 100,000. In 1970 this ratio became one to three.

The end of the peasantry and the urbanization process changed the economy. In 1950, the agricultural sector represented 46 percent of working people, the same proportion it had represented in 1930. By 1970, agriculture had lost 2.3 million active workers to other sectors, leaving only 22.2 percent of the working population tilling the land (this number further declined to 4.75 percent by the year 2000). In the process peasants became waiters and janitors, cleaning ladies, and even minor civil servants, but the majority became workers in the secondary sector, which increased from 27.4 percent of the total workforce in 1950 to a record 48.4 percent in 1970.

This created a new and unique situation in Spanish history, because never before or since had workers been so numerous and never before had their values, efforts, or fate had a greater impact on the character of Spain and its expectations of the future.[6]

Who emigrated from the countryside and why? In the 1940s and 1950s migrants were mostly seasonal and landless agrarian workers, but between 1960 and 1968 more than 1 million people, mostly small landowners, simply abandoned agriculture for good. Not all farmers left the land, however. Those who were better off and those who were elderly generally stayed, while younger peasants or those in precarious situations tended to move. A study of Extremadura showed that in the 1960s peasants with more than 50 hectares tended not to emigrate, while the same could be said about people who were 45 or older. What becomes clear in most studies of emigrants is that they did not want to work in agriculture ever again. In addition, not only did children refuse to take the agrarian jobs of their parents, but their parents did not want their children to follow in their footsteps. Cities and their comforts, steady salaries, and access to education became the ideal, while rural life was increasingly considered undesirable.[7]

Long before small farmers left the land in search of a better life, the southern landscapes of misery were the first regions of Spain that people migrated from. For these people migration was not a lifestyle choice but their last hope for survival, of escaping starvation. This was particularly true for the agrarian laborers on the big estates of Andalusia and Extremadura; the people who worked in the breadbaskets of the country and were dying of hunger during the endless post-war period because of their miserable salaries. The plight of olive pickers serves as an example. Olive oil is, no doubt, an exquisite and a healthy product, but for the laborers, women as well as men, who lived on the olive-growing estates of the southern regions, it represented a bitter way of life filled with temporary jobs at best, meager wages, and suffering. Not being passive people, they did not always accept these conditions with resignation. Long before Franco's rule, they had fought for their rights and had tried taking the land for themselves, but they had always met defeat. During the Civil War many killed their masters or turned them out; they then redistributed the land and often formed collectives. This agrarian revolution, in which at least 6 million hectares were taken, left deeply divided memories in the countryside.[8]

When the Republic lost the war, landless peasants, and not only those who had participated in the revolution, were repaid in kind. They became the main victims of the dictatorship's direct repression, and their starving families bore the brunt of autarky. It was a political and social defeat that permanently broke the back of the militant, landless peasantry. It was no accident that the regions of Andalusia with the highest rates of migration were the olive-producing areas of Jaen and Cordoba, the land celebrated by poets because of its olive trees and poor yet proud people. By 1975, one-third of the 1945 population of Jaen had left.[9]

Just as in Jaen, in the immediate post-war years landless peasants in the neighboring province of Cordoba left their miserable existence in the region of La Campiña, the fertile area irrigated by the Guadalquivir river, en masse. The town of Bujalance had a long tradition of peasant protest and struggle and, accordingly, Francoist repression was very harsh. In 1940 Bujalance had nearly 16,000 inhabitants; by 1970, barely 9,000. People there remember the summer of 1945, one of the most horrible years of that terrible decade. "There were no cereals and olives, almost none," recounted one of the elderly people of the town. They had begun leaving for Barcelona, Madrid, Saragossa, and Valencia, and "they wrote or sent money, because there was work, life was better […] it became a chain […] you had no option but to leave. Many unlucky ones had no time to go and died of hunger […] some days they buried 14, 12, 10 […] and you saw people out there, eating grass like animals … while the granaries were full."[10] Many years afterwards in democratic, affluent Spain, survivors had trouble convincing their grandchildren of what they had gone through. Grandparents, for the most part, were not insulted by their innocent disbelief. Their concern was that these youngsters "don't have to experience what I endured."[11] In 1945, the year that Europe was liberated from fascism, the peasants of La Campiña had started their own great liberation: it was called migration.[12]

The peasants with smallholdings in Castile and other regions of northern Spain joined the migration in the early 1960s. They had been the backbone of agrarian conservatism, and were known for their loyalty to the Francoist regime. However, pro-industrial policies and the 1959 Stabilization Plan meant the dismantling of most of the more damaging economic controls of autarky that, in part, had sustained the old agricultural structures of Castile's countryside. The double phenomenon of migration and agrarian mechanization made these peasants less dependent on daily laborers, but mechanization was expensive and not affordable for all the farms. Many peasants were forced to abandon their land and move to the cities. Franco's state did nothing to palliate the effects of this huge, crucial, social and economic transformation. Priorities were elsewhere and economic liberalization was not paired with a reversal of the state's chicanery regarding social spending. At best, the dictatorship encouraged peasants to enroll in cooperatives and to rationalize the use of their land. The results were often disappointing in economic terms, and in any case insufficient to stop the demographic hemorrhage.

Just as the province of Jaen serves as an example of the post-war misery of the south, Zamora serves as a typical case of how Franco's economic miracle left behind, or rather emptied, the agrarian, conservative heartland of Spain. In the early 1960s, 60 percent of the employed population in Zamora province tilled the land. Most properties were small and their farming activities did not require large amounts of capital. Harvests were primarily of cereal but, since only 10 percent of the land's surface was irrigated, yields were poor. With no significant industry at hand the main exports of the province were hydroelectricity and people. In the 1950s the province lost more than 46,000 inhabitants through emigration (more than in the previous three decades combined). The process accelerated between 1961 and 1965 as another 41,000 people left, primarily to go to Germany and the Basque country. In 1970, the province had 64,000 fewer people than in 1950. More than one in three people born in Zamora left in the 20 so-called "Golden Years" of the Spanish economy.[13]

There were other "victors" of the war, Galicia's seasonal worker peasants, who also saw their traditional way of life disappear in the late 1950s and early 1960s. They were far poorer than Castilians, having had to migrate for centuries to harvest wheat from May to August each year in central Spain. They traveled in work gangs (*cuadrillas*) of various sizes that were made up of men of all ages and that also included children. They came from places like A Terra Chá in the rural heartland of Lugo province. Most among them owned some land, but their plots were too small to support their needs, prompting the men to find temporary work elsewhere. Women remained at home to take care of the farm. They spent little, saving almost their entire income, consuming a simple diet consisting of chickpeas with lard or, less often, meat to help replenish their strength. They worked hard to finish their working trip as quickly as possible because it was important to them to return home by the Day of the Virgin, August 15, a religious holiday and a day of dancing and drinking in most towns in rural Spain. However, in the late 1950s mechanization rendered them redundant: they were expensive and thus increasingly unattractive to landowners. Young people preferred to go to the cities, to the Basque country, or to Madrid, and increasingly they also started to go to Germany. Life, they had come to learn, could be better.[14]

During the 1960s peasants of all conditions, full of pessimism, could see that their villages were losing more and more young people every day. Fields were increasingly left untilled and the value of the harvest plunged in relation to the cost of consumer products, machinery, and other inputs. They looked at their perpetually bankrupt municipalities, unpaved streets, and lack of services, compared these to what they saw in the media or in the movies, and drew their own conclusions. On long winter nights, peasants intently watched on their first television set all the fantasies promised by consumerism and big cities. They became aware that they were increasingly perceived as people of the past, if they were thought of at all. Adding further pessimism to their condition was the fact that their own children were moving to the cities, either to work or to study, and adopting the very values and, often, ideologies that their parents had opposed all their lives. It was a brutal and accelerated change.[15]

The historic betrayal of Francoism of its former peasant soldiers did not, however, make the rural victims of modernization hostile to the regime. These small farmers knew that they were losing the battle against new values and industrialization, and they were well aware that Madrid was a far-away capital which catered to other, more important, groups. What they did resent, however, was what they perceived (mistakenly) as government support for employees, including their historical enemies, agrarian laborers. Common suffering did not make these two groups allies: they had considerably different historical trajectories and there were too many conflicts and cultural differences between them. Furthermore, as one perceptive observer has noted, for Castilian villagers, politics were viewed with hostility or indifference and this was, effectively, a demonstration of their support for the regime and for Franco in particular. At most, they blamed the times or the government, almost never their wartime leader, the man who restored their property rights in the war, their Caudillo.[16]

History, however, had not completely forgotten the Franco-supporting Spanish peasantry; it had just arranged an ironic, if sad, rendezvous. In the cities they and their children ended up being neighbors of the people who had fought the war, and suffered after it, on the other side. These people found themselves living next to each other in the poorly equipped suburbs, or working together in the factories of Spain or elsewhere in Europe. Up until this time, agrarian laborers and small landholders had seen each other as class enemies, but now they were both just alienated peasants in the cities, and seen as urbanites in their former villages.

Migration accelerated cultural change in the Spanish countryside. In the cities, former peasants were poor, anonymous people living at or near the bottom of society. But they were also consumers, and were close to modernity. They learned, for example, that it was necessary to use something called deodorant, or to brush their teeth. In the villages they had left they were often seen as the bearers of novelties from the city.[17] Here, perhaps the first transistor radio or Italian liquor anyone had ever touched or tasted arrived in their suitcases. The first German car to appear (if not driven by a tourist who had lost his way) was theirs. Perhaps more important, their sons were the first to show up for the summer festivities with long hair, listening to a maddening music with English lyrics, and their daughters were probably the first girls to smoke in public or to wear a mini-skirt.[18]

To the City

Since the beginning of the twentieth century, as industrialization began to take off in Spain, each region that became a beneficiary of migration had a primary source of immigrants. Southerners, Aragonese, and Levantines moved mainly to Catalonia; northern Castilians and Galicians migrated to the Basque country; and Madrid was the main destination of central Spaniards. As cities grew rapidly during the post-war years, so did their peripheral neighborhoods and industrial belts, upon which fell a disproportionate demand for housing and services, a demand the regime failed to address. Poor suburban neighborhoods became problematic as they grew overcrowded and more culturally diverse, developing in stark contrast to the more "native" city centers, which were richer and provided with far better services.

The institution that made it possible to settle in these new suburbs was not the callous state but (as we saw in chapter 2) the family. It was the best, and often the only, social security system, savings and loans, childcare, and housing scheme for poor people. The cohesion, sense of duty, sacrifice, and hierarchical, authoritarian values that underlay it made it possible for people to endure separation, misery, and exploitation. The harshness of the experiences of an anonymous but typical family of new immigrants is described in a classic book on migrants in Catalonia. The family was from Granada, where the father had been a construction worker, walking 14 kilometers every day to work for a miserly wage. He decided to migrate, and went to Catalonia in 1949 after a brother-in-law talked to him about Barcelona, telling him "there, there is plenty of work." In Barcelona he earned 140 pesetas a week and sent his wife and five children everything he could save. He lived meagerly, eating just once a day, a stew at night. Then he found a job that paid 225 pesetas a week. His wife and two eldest daughters moved to Barcelona, leaving the three smaller children "with the family" in the village. They had a shack under the Montjuic mountain that a friend from Granada lent them for free.[19] His wife found a job that paid 125 pesetas weekly while the daughters stayed home in the shack with the friend's wife. To save money, the couple walked to work. For four years they did not take a single bus or tram. Progress for them meant self-exploitation: the eldest daughter got a job as an apprentice.

After a year of living in the shack, with the help of a modest loan from another acquaintance from Granada and with a small amount they had won in the lottery, they had saved 3,000 pesetas, enough to buy their own shack. Still their situation was far from secure: they lived under the threat of having it demolished by the authorities until 1957, when their home was finally made legal. This was no small achievement for, in that year, there were nearly 13,000 shacks housing about 66,000 people in Barcelona alone.

The family welfare system kept working. The rest of the children came from the village that year; other relatives followed. At one point, a total of 14 people lived in the shack (two more children were born in Barcelona). The family's finances improved because, with the exception of the infants, all the children were soon working. The father also "progressed" further: he was now toiling eight hours a day in a factory and another eight as a night-time security guard. This is how they were able to save more, sell the shack, and buy a small apartment in nearby L'Hospitalet. When he was interviewed in the mid-1960s the father was satisfied with his achievements and was chiefly proud of having put the misery of Andalusia behind his family: "Here, for the first time in my life, I am wearing white underwear."[20]

Migration was less of a solitary experience than we might think. Chain migration, the pattern of following a relative or friend, a "pioneer" who migrated first, was very common, and it often led to a concentration of people from the same town of origin settling in the same area. The village of Matian in the municipality of Cullar (Granada) provides an example of communal migration. What follows is the brief story of a small town that became almost completely depopulated in the 1960s as most people moved together to Ibi (Alicante).

People in Matian were very poor. For the most part, they farmed land they did not own, being sharecroppers who had to pay just over a fifth of their meager harvest of cereals to absentee landlords, from whom they also rented the dirt-floor homes in which they lived. Commercial exchanges were scarce, and took place every Monday at Cullar's market. Women ran this market and worked in the fields and at home. Bread was baked in a communal oven; they never drank real coffee and only occasionally ate the cheapest of fish. Men, but never women, drank in the local tavern and played cards. After turning 8 children started to take care of the animals and so either never attended school at all or received only the most basic education delivered by itinerant teachers who taught in exchange for food. The prestige of the local teacher, a woman, was very low. Among other things, she regularly left the classroom in order to make lunch for her family. There was no doctor in the village. Their holidays were marked by the Church. St. Anthony was the town's patron. Courtship was tightly regulated, but eloping was common as it was a cheap and easy way of getting married while avoiding family objections and fuss. For centuries, people had lived, courted, married, and died like this in Matian until one day, in 1963, one of the villagers settled in Ibi. Toy manufacturers and other types of factories were expanding there, and on hearing of the wonders of the "pioneer's" new life, his relatives began to move there. Others followed soon after, forming a human river. By 1975 Matian had all but disappeared while Ibi, between 1960 and 1975, had tripled its population, from 6,000 to close to 19,000.[21]

As people left, they changed the places where they settled, and, in doing so, themselves. For the first time in their lives they lived among thousands of other people, most of whom were socially very similar, and all of whom were living without the social and political constraints of their former villages. As people populated and created new areas, a neighborhood or *barrio* identity was born and then reinforced. A single reference to the neighborhood in which a person lived revealed that this person or his or her parents were immigrants, what kind of house they had, their family income, and their level of education. There was an element of pride when declaring which neighborhood a person belonged to, and to some extent this replaced the pride of declaring which small village a family was from. Neighborhood identity and image developed: particular characteristics were ascribed to the inhabitants, purportedly to differentiate one neighborhood from another. *Barrios*, and even whole towns, were as much a sign of identity as of exclusion: to be from Tarrassa in Barcelona, Mostoles in Madrid, or

Llodio in Alava implied that a person was almost certainly a poor, working-class immigrant, and sometimes served to identify their original native town and mother tongue. This also helped the construction of new collective identities. People trusted their siblings and extended family first, but, secondly, they felt they could trust others from their village, province, and even region. The result was that people who may never have met before migrating, and never have identified themselves with anything or anyone beyond the borders of their own village, became acquaintances and members of a much larger community by virtue of the simple fact that they were from the same region. They began, for example, to identify themselves as Andalusians in Catalonia or Galicians in the Basque country.

Migration implied new identities but also potential cultural and even political conflicts. Some sense of security was preserved when people from the same town or region moved and settled en masse, but isolation from other communities, and particularly from the native population, often followed. Certain communities "took" whole towns, creating distinctive, isolated enclaves. This pattern was widespread throughout Barcelona's industrial belt where, for example, in Tarrassa in 1965 non-natives made up 49 percent of the population. In Sabadell in 1967 this reached 43 percent, and in L'Hospitalet in 1970, 56 percent of the population had been born elsewhere. Half of this immigrant population was from Andalusia. Although it was not officially acknowledged the challenges of inter-community coexistence and interaction became worrisome during the dictatorship. Integration was further complicated by the fact that the native and the local communities not only had different perceptions of reality, but even different traditions and maternal languages (in Catalonia and the Basque country) and the pressure for the newcomers to conform to the ways of their new communities often created a backlash. The usual stereotypes about "the other," especially the "philistine" (*ignorante*) label, appeared. Immigrants were considered "different" for many reasons: they did not speak the native languages, they used different gestures, their dress, food, and drinking customs differed from those of the natives, and they appeared obsessed with remaining in their own communities. Unlike the locals (in the Basque country), immigrants did not go to mass. Along with this, immigrants were marginalized, in part for political reasons, because they represented another "Spanish" invasion of these regions. This is why, in the last years of the regime and afterwards, Spain and Francoism would be identified as the same thing among radical (and some "moderate") nationalist circles, forgetting the contribution of their own people to the Francoist side during the Civil War.[22]

However, it must be said that integration, or rather accommodation, eventually became the norm and many people, like the man who came to Catalonia from Jaen in 1941, would say with pride, "My children are Catalonian."[23] Migration became an element of pride in, especially, Catalan identity. Three out of every four Catalans are descendants of immigrants or are immigrants themselves. They know that without their immigrant ancestors, the second, post-war, industrialization of Catalonia (and of the Basque country) would not have been possible.

The Basque case was more difficult. The tensions linked to post-war migration were particularly evident because, unlike in both Madrid and Barcelona, immigration dramatically affected many small towns that until then had been almost self-sufficient, rural communities. As they had in Catalonia, new immigrants posed serious problems for both Basque identity and services in the receiving communities. One example of this was Llodio, in the province of Alava, an important center for metallurgy. Up until 1940, the population growth of this mostly agrarian municipality had depended almost exclusively on natural cycles. In that year, the town's population amounted to barely 3,000 people, but in the next three decades it increased five fold. Every year in that span several hundred new immigrants arrived to settle into what, until then, had been a highly cohesive agrarian, Catholic town. Apart from the cultural shock felt by both sides, the main problem created by the arrival of these immigrants was a sudden competition for scarce housing and social services, neither of which would be satisfied during the tenure of the dictatorship.[24]

A similar situation transpired in Barakaldo, not far from Bilbao, even though this was an area that had a longer tradition of immigration. With immigrants arriving primarily from Galicia and northern Castile, this heavy industrial town saw its population grow by 84 percent in the 1950s, and "only" 40 percent in the 1960s.[25] The influx created several practical problems, including a shortage of housing and a lack of schools, but there were also less tangible issues. Among the challenges facing the local community was the large number of non-practicing Catholics among the immigrants. Barakaldo's long-standing post-war mayor, a staunchly Catholic Francoist, denounced this several times. One of his "remedies" was to limit the construction of public schools to force children to attend the flourishing private Catholic schools. This resulted in a chronic deficit of school places that primarily affected the families of the newly arrived, leaving thousands of children with no schooling.[26]

It was not only industrialized areas that became magnets for people. Regions that were soon to become known worldwide as tourist destinations began to attract immigrants as well. This was true of the Costa del Sol (Malaga) and of Costa Brava (Barcelona), but nowhere was it felt so intensely as on the island of Majorca, which was transformed very quickly from a traditionally poor land of emigration, as it had been until 1960, to a region with a surplus of immigration in that decade.[27] In the next two decades, sunny, pleasant Majorca would become a magnet for the poor of Andalusia and Extremadura. These people brought with them the scars of their suffering: a third of them arrived with no basic "mandatory" education, seeking permanent or temporary employment in hotels and restaurants. Among these migrants were many young women. Their educational level was generally even lower than that of their male counterparts and as a result their options for employment were generally limited to the domestic tasks of cooking or cleaning.

There was an important, permanent, exclusively female wave of migration during the 40-year dictatorship: the thousands of women who moved each year to the cities to work as maids. Although many servants worked in their own provinces, the middle classes in the capital cities tended to demand servants from specific areas that had a reputation for providing honest, hardworking, and obedient employees. Bilbao, for example, imported women from nearby northern Castilian areas.[28] These young women performed all kinds of work in the homes where they were employed, and the majority were "internees," which meant they lived with their employers. Many middle- and upper-class houses had small rooms off the kitchen for the purpose of boarding a domestic servant. Servants generally had virtually no free time in the day, and enjoyed one or, less often, two free days each week, but many were only allowed a day off once every two weeks. Well into the 1970s it was very cheap to have a maid, even for a modest middle-class family.

Not all migrants went to cities and big towns. During the last two decades of the dictatorship there were some streams of migration to rural areas triggered by the regime's much-publicized agrarian reform or, in Francoist language, colonization. The scale of this migration was, in general, very modest.[29] Obtaining land through the National Institute for Colonization was no bargain, for the conditions imposed upon the new *colonos* were harsh. The state-created town of Llanos del Caudillo in the province of Ciudad Real (located on the plateau south of Madrid where Cervantes had imagined Don Quixote's adventures) serves as an example of such colonization. The first *colonos*, most of them former agrarian laborers, arrived there in 1955. By the next year there were more than 500 people living in the town. They had passed a selection process that declared them fit to work and which, at the same time, was designed as a political screening. Those who had been condemned for previous political activities or who were considered to be subversives were excluded. The ideal new farmer was deemed to be apolitical and supportive of the regime. The lucky ones came to live in the new "model" town. The first to arrive found themselves surrounded by a construction site with houses that had "no doors, no windows installed." They would be without electricity for the next three years.[30]

By far the most dramatic process of inter-rural migration took place in the southeast of Spain, in the area around the town of El Ejido (Almeria). An irrigation project on what had been a semi-desert plain in the 1950s exploded during the late 1960s and early 1970s into a unique prototype of the small family farms that used greenhouses to produce three harvests of out-of-season vegetables a year, which became very profitable products to sell to the emerging national and European markets. Families moved mostly from the neighboring Alpujarras mountains nestled between Almeria and Granada to settle and work in this transformed area. All members of the family worked extremely hard, from the parents to the smallest child, initially living in atrocious conditions, lacking proper housing or, of course, any basic sanitation. The majority of young people only partially attended school or missed it entirely. Nevertheless, this phenomenon was deemed a success, at least in economic terms – a new El Dorado – and wealthy "agrotowns" emerged on sites where only sleepy hamlets had previously existed. The municipality of Dalias-El Ejido alone went from having 11,386 inhabitants in 1950 to 32,929 in 1980 – a 289 percent increase. Also between 1950 and 1980, neighboring Roquetas de Mar went from 3,761 people to 19,006, an increase of 505 percent. In total, the whole new agricultural area grew by 259 percent in the same period, a change that resulted in social and cultural tensions of a different nature to but as intense as those experienced by many Basque towns a few years before.[31]

To Europe

At the same as time people were moving to the large cities and new industrial towns of Spain, millions migrated abroad. The first post-war massive migrations went to Latin America. It was a brief mirage of past times. The end of World War II again opened the door to trans-oceanic migration, primarily to Argentina and Venezuela, two countries that experienced economic booms as a result of commodity exports, and, in the case of Argentina, because of industrialization. From 1946 onwards the number of Spaniards settling in these two countries rapidly increased, although the total number of people involved in this migration was relatively modest: 1955 was the busiest year in terms of numbers, with 62,000 migrants. It was, however, a chaotic, badly regulated phenomenon given the frequency of fraud, other procedural irregularities, and exploitation suffered by these new immigrants. Some of their crossings were terrifying and not dissimilar to the stories of the experiences of illegal African and Asian migrants and refugees today in Europe. There are accounts of fake tickets sold at exorbitant prices by traffickers of human cargo, of immigrants being rejected when they thought their visas were valid, of harrowing trips on boats that arrived after a month at sea with virtually no drinking water or food, of scurvy, and finally tales of the clandestine loading and unloading of passengers on remote beaches.[32] While the Venezuelan and Argentinian newspapers regularly carried these tales of horror, the heavily censored Spanish press barely reported any of this.[33]

Emigration to Europe surpassed trans-oceanic patterns for the first time in 1961. This new phenomenon was linked both to new opportunities on the continent and to the recession caused by the dictatorship's economic reforms of the late 1950s. The reforms caused a temporary but drastic contraction in the industrial sector between 1958 and 1960, leading to a sudden decrease in the number of people emigrating from the countryside to the big cities, where jobs became temporarily scarce. Looking for new opportunities, emigrants went instead to booming Germany, France, or Switzerland. The official annual average number of migrants to Europe in the decade following 1961 was 84,000, but the trend declined after 1970 and would come to a complete halt after 1973. These are the officially recorded numbers, for this migration was supposed to be legally channeled through the proper authorities. Spanish migrants to Europe were, in theory, officially recruited, documented, informed, assisted, and protected by the Spanish authorities, principally by delegates from the Ministry of Labor and by diplomats at Spanish embassies. This was the theory behind printed guides designed by the regime that explained to migrants how to behave and what to expect in their host country. These pamphlets were patronizing in nature, and their tone was all too predictable. For example, a guide made for Switzerland in

1966 gave brief, general descriptions of the country's weather, population, history, politics, religion, and habits, and included the statement that "the Swiss are silent and reflective and dislike any kind of noisy demonstrations ..." Even more pointedly, it explained the rights and duties of workers and how they could defend their interests according to the laws of the country. And, as if the immigrants were not used to this and worse in Spain, the guide said that, in Switzerland, it was common for people employed in the hospitality sector to work 60 hours a week and 12 hours a day.[34]

Like so many things in Franco's Spain, what was stated on paper – international agreements and official guidelines – was a different thing altogether from reality. To the average person who was seeking a better life, the irregular and uncontrolled migration routes became more important than the legal venues. In spite of the existence of an official recruitment process, the majority of the over 2 million emigrants to Europe did not bother with official channels or advice. Their experiences with bureaucracy in Spain were not likely to have been particularly encouraging. They knew that relatives, friends, and other contacts were more direct and helpful than civil servants. This explains why hundreds of thousands of Spaniards left as nominal "tourists" for Europe where, in fact, they became illegal immigrants. Researchers have shown that in only four years of the whole of the 1960s was the number of legal workers greater than the number of illegal ones.[35] The country in Europe with the worst reputation for the exploitation of illegal immigrants was the United Kingdom, where well-connected networks of human traffickers made large profits and kept the flow coming.[36]

Practical reasons and practical hopes forced people to put up with the humiliations of being a non-citizen in a continent not yet accustomed to ethnic diversity, before the advent of the concept of political correctness and the notion of a common European identity. It was not all that difficult after all: they came from a country where humiliation was commonplace if you were poor or stood on the wrong side of the political fence. The first possible, and probable, humiliation for prospective legal immigrants was a compulsory medical examination at home. Of the roughly 53,000 people examined by the German authorities in 1969, 7,800 were rejected. This number included pregnant women. Next, if they had passed their medical, emigrants left Spain on crowded trains or buses, sometimes in convoys, carrying thousands of people, and the long journey began. It was a long, uncomfortable, and smelly trip. The first encounter most Spaniards had with people from "the other" country were with suspicious customs agents who, after checking their documents, proceeded to confiscate "for sanitary reasons" the valued sausages, hams, and brandy emigrants carried in their cardboard suitcases.

Upon arrival, foremen from different companies herded them by using loudspeakers, sometimes mixing instructions with, perceived or real, barked threats. After being divided into groups according to their work destinations they were conducted to the dormitories or apartment blocks that were to house them. Here conditions varied, and while many immigrants have said only positive things about their lodgings, others encountered situations that were just slightly better than of those suffered by black workers in hostels in apartheid South Africa. They were often separated from the local population, sometimes by fences or walls. In some places, the dormitories were also separated by gender, so married couples were kept apart. This was also seen as a way of ensuring that women did not become pregnant and decrease productivity. This last experience was most frequent in Germany where there were cases of men locked in camps who were allowed to leave only to work. If they lived in flats, their accommodation was usually worse than inadequate.[37]

In several countries, it was not uncommon in taverns or parks for signs to be hung that barred entrance to dogs, Spaniards, Italians, or Portuguese. Local unions, however, frequently helped foreign workers.[38] Contact with the native population was limited, although mixed marriages and liaisons were not uncommon. For the most part, however, each community remained insular during their free time, and indications of xenophobia, reciprocal or otherwise, were common. Even among the immigrants, people from different provinces or regions formed more or less closed communities.

Like most immigrants in history, Spaniards in Europe worked at the most basic and undesirable jobs while enjoying only limited rights. In the 1960s, 65 percent of male Spaniards in France worked in construction, 25 percent in industry, and the rest in metalwork and in mines; 60 percent of Spanish women worked as domestic servants. Three out of four of these women worked illegally and had no social security at all. Because Spain was not part of the European Common Market, immigrant workers, whether in the country legally or illegally, had no right to bring their family with them (France was a notable exception in this regard). Neither did they have any other of the basic rights (for example, choice of jobs) that citizens of the host countries could take for granted.

If they put up with all of this it was because they had no choice. According to a poll conducted in 1966 by the Ministry of Labor, over 90 percent of emigrants declared three main reasons for going to Europe: to help their families, to improve their income, and to save money. Other reasons were frequently given and some overlapped with these first three. People said they were moving because their salary in Spain was bad, they wanted to improve their children's living conditions, they wanted to pay off debts, they hoped to buy a house one day, and because they were either unemployed or only temporarily employed.[39] Working for a time abroad, spending as little money as possible while saving as much as possible made sense to many Spaniards when they weighed this against the money they were making in their home town. In 1963, according to the United Nations, a non-specialized worker in the agrarian sector, the least remunerative of occupations, made 2.9 times more money per hour in Holland, 2.6 times more in Germany, 2.5 times more in Switzerland, and 2.4 times more in Belgium than they did in Spain. And these figures were recorded after the huge increases, in relative terms, of agrarian salaries in the early 1960s, when pre-war purchasing power was finally surpassed. This latter feat was achieved only because migration, and the labor scarcity that resulted, made cheap labor a thing of the recent past.[40] To gain decent wages, poor people had first paid the tax of migration.

In spite of all the blatant oppression at home, most emigrants, like most ordinary Spaniards, were apolitical. An oral history project of Galician peasants in Germany has shown that not only was the main preoccupation of these people to save money and to return to their home town, but they also had an overwhelming distaste for any discussion of politics, particularly when the question of Franco's Spain arose.[41] Nationalism mixed here with the well-learned notion that poor people did not gain anything by talking about or engaging in politics. Politics meant problems, while money meant solutions. Coming from an area in the northwest of the peninsula where small farms were predominant, the majority of them kept their property and maintained strong family links in their native villages. They made no effort whatsoever to integrate themselves into their local host community. These Galicians did not want to change the world at large, only to improve their own world. For these people, and for most migrants, the objective was to preserve their family ties and improve, not radically change, their lives. Migration, in sum, was just part of a family strategy to preserve the fading peasant way of life.

Migration, however, did not only produce wealth and reproduce the socio-economic system at home. Even if the protagonists were not aware of it, migration also transformed them, "opening their eyes" to new realities and possibilities. It changed the way they perceived the world. In Spain, Franco's Peace had disarmed workers and landless peasants politically and ideologically; potential migrants had seen themselves first and foremost as poor people, as indeed most of them were. This meant that, even in their new countries, they believed that their interests, values, and opportunities must be different from those of people with more money and power; that they had many duties and few rights, and these did not include criticism or equality. They came from a land where connections and favors were more important than laws, and social callousness was an undeclared policy. What they saw in Europe was different. After breathing freedom for a few months or years, emigrants, or at least a minority amongst them, started to acquire new points of reference. The experience gave them (and they passed to others) new parameters for comparison and judgment. The emigrant in Europe was second-class, but he or she saw a freer world of greater equality and realized that freedom had brought more prosperity to Europeans than had dictatorship to Spaniards. As a 1972 study of Spanish migrants in France stated, rather convolutedly:

> Once there, the freedom to join a union or political party of any tendency allowed Spaniards to say in public what they thought. Our research shows that there exists a certain opening up of the emigrants' spirits and it is not unusual to see them reading, perhaps for the first time in their lives, newspapers of all tendencies [...] Their immigrant situation developed in them an evolution of their feelings and opinions in general [and they] are those of their social class [...] Since most of them are going to return to Spain [...] we should realize that there are a mass of workers who have succeeded economically thanks to migration, under other political and social laws that [...] they will consider more to their advantage.[42]

The "opening" of the spirit also led many women (and men, too) to reconsider their own social and gender roles because, as the same 1972 study concluded, "after a certain time [living] in another socio-economic context, women find themselves more inclined to be influenced by certain more realistic norms and [to make decisions] independent from traditional ethic principles."[43]

The story of Cristóbal Ruiz is one of hundreds of thousands of stories of Spaniards changed, both politically and in matters related to gender, by migration. He had worked since 1966 as a miner in the notorious coalfields of Leon.[44] The pits there were old, narrow, and dangerous. His elder brother contracted silicosis. Twice Cristóbal had practically been interred and twice he had miraculously avoided death. The last time, he had been trapped for two days. Three and a half years and two accidents were enough. He decided to emigrate: "It didn't matter where. The only thing that mattered was to make money to send to my parents. I was the only one of five siblings who could help them." He signed a contract to go to Germany. He spent 36 hours en route to Hanover on a special train of 30 cars loaded with migrants from all over Spain.

They all received envelopes with directions to their final destination. On arriving, a German foreman used gestures to tell them which train to take. Cristóbal's destination was Soltau. Three men were waiting for him there and took him to a residence; none of these three spoke Spanish. The next morning he received his contract and some money. Needing food, he entered a supermarket for the first time in his life and was amazed to see not only the amount of everything there, but that that people picked things up directly from the shelves: "I was afraid to do that, I did not want them to think I was stealing." He eventually bought food, but he had never cooked before as women had always cooked for him. He was ashamed to cook, "but [realized that] all men did it there. Now it did not matter any more if they saw me cleaning or washing." On the one hand, he was sad, lonely and without friends in a factory of 600 other workers; on the other hand, he was happy. They treated him well and even paid him more than the contract had originally stated. Living expenses were similar to those in Spain and he was able to save a lot of money, which he sent to his parents. People were nice, they invited him for a beer and took him to dances and "they tried hard." Cristóbal smelled freedom. Later, in the early 1970s, he said to an interviewer, "I liked the sensation of equality between people. That place is freer than this one [Spain]. I joined a union there. They raised our salary [...] here the union is only if you have a problem [...] Furthermore, there was solidarity among workers [...] I liked that."[45]

In spite of the overwhelming political indifference of the majority of migrants, the regime always feared their ideological contamination. This could come from the atmosphere of freedom in the host country or, more worryingly, from republican exiles.[46] The network of labor offices opened by the Spanish government in several countries had two functions. One was, ostensibly, to protect Spanish workers' rights against the abuses they were subjected to by employers in their adopted country; the other was to monitor the political ramifications of having so many Spaniards working abroad. Arguably, France was by far the most dangerous country because of the force of the Spanish republican community there, which in addition had gained prestige because of its work with the Resistance.[47] In 1955, before the massive economic migration began, there were at least 366,160 Spaniards in France, although the number was surely higher, for many people had lost their citizenship as they were not recognized as citizens by the dictatorship. Of these Spaniards, 48 percent had arrived between 1936 and 1946 and at least half of them were republican exiles. Approximately three-quarters of them were manual laborers. They were primarily concentrated in and around Paris, in what was then referred to as its "Red Belt," and in the south of the country.[48] They were also the regime's worst nightmare: red workers who could interact with naive migrants and explain to them things that were never publicly discussed in Franco's Spain.

Migration has been referred to as Spain's Marshall Plan. Emigrants to Europe were wiped off Spain's unemployment ledgers, their absence forced salaries up inside Spain, and their remittances gave the Spanish economy one of its main boosts. The state paid back their contributions and sacrifices, and those of their families, with the usual meanness and greed wrapped up in cheap nationalist discourse and intermittent, but much-publicized, charity work. The hard currency that migrants sent back home was used by Franco's government for the dictatorship's ambitious development plans, but it was not invested to help these returning workers, their families, or their communities. The regime, which in the 1960s had become enchanted with economic planning, never prepared for their return, and this was sadly evident after the 1973 economic crisis. In 1972, just before the last million hardworking emigrants, who had been sending home nearly 30 billion pesetas (181 million euros) annually, returned home, they were receiving just 171 million pesetas in services from the state budget through the Spanish Institute for Migration. This translated into an average of 13 pesetas per emigrant in social assistance, 101 pesetas in legal assistance and 15.5 pesetas for education. In total, these expenses amounted to less than 1 euro per emigrant per year.[49]

The state was not the only institution that profited from and exploited emigrants. Large private institutions also took their share from their remittances and gave back very little in return. The Bank of Spain and the banks that converted the migrants' foreign currency into pesetas turned an excellent profit. In addition, the migrants' deposits had a powerful impact on the provincial savings and loans institutions, *cajas de ahorros*, which were usually controlled by the Church. The *cajas* of, for example, Orense, Vigo, Corunna, Ronda, Granada, and other provinces of mass emigration, became among the strongest in the country, but they failed to invest in their own provinces. Rather, they sent capital to the highly profitable industrial sectors of Madrid, the Basque country, or Catalonia, contributing to the perpetuation of regional and social disparities.

Finally, there was an even harsher form of migration to Europe, and one that once again highlighted the particularly miserable lives of southerners: seasonal migration to France. In the 1960s and 1970s more than 150,000 people went there every year to pick fruit, particularly grapes. It was back-breaking work that might last six weeks or six months. Whole families, including young children, traveled and worked in vineyards and orchards, sleeping and eating anywhere their employers deemed appropriate. The father was usually the only one with a contract while the rest of the family traveled as "tourists." It was a strategy for survival that came at a heavy cost, not just for the present, but for the future as well. A 1978 study of 20,000 Andalusians working in the fields of Agen found that there were 3,000 children of school age among them, but only 400 had any form of educational instruction.[50]

Housing

Migrants who moved to the cities were looking for jobs but what they needed first was a roof over their heads. People flooded Madrid, Barcelona, and Spain's other major industrial cities in search of a better life, but there was not enough housing for them. This became such an enormous problem that in the summer of 1957 the Spanish government, the self-proclaimed champion of Christian freedom and human dignity, was considering the adoption of a more typically communist piece of legislation: a law restricting the establishment of new "unregulated" workers in Madrid. The official explanations for the housing shortage were the destruction of working-class neighborhoods during the war (which had ended 18 years previously), a failure to conserve older buildings, and, of course, the attraction to workers of the economic take-off in the industrial sector in the capital.[51] The housing crisis was real, but this reasoning reflected the usual mix of lies and self-congratulatory misrepresentations of Francoism. While it was true that the industrial sector was booming, the economy as a whole was in trouble, and the regime's authorities had mishandled housing construction for the previous two decades. The results were painful. In Madrid alone, the housing deficit for 1957 was officially set at 60,000–70,000 dwellings, yet until then the authorities had not had a coherent plan to address the situation. Not surprisingly, illegal shacks were being constructed, while overcrowding and disease were common on the periphery of the city and in the depressed areas at its center.

The ultimate and sad irony in this situation was that, while there were hundreds of thousands of hardworking Spaniards without a decent roof over their heads, the housing market was saturated with expensive homes. Conversely, the construction of cheap homes was hindered by both procurement bottlenecks and corruption. In 1952, for example, a housing construction project in Santander was all but halted by lack of basic materials such as cement, iron, and zinc due to the fact that these products were being diverted to the black market where cement was "fetching about 8 pesetas per bag more than the official price."[52] Limited budgets, rampant corruption, cronyism, delays, and social prejudice were rampant in the housing business. In Guadalix de la Sierra, located in the mountains north of Madrid, it was noted, also in 1952, that the houses built for locals were in fact being occupied by other people who "improved them, they looked [like] little hotels and they enjoyed them as summer houses, they are people who live in Madrid." This information was contained in a much wider-ranging report that denounced the escalating cost of housing projects in the province that had originally been tendered for 135.57 million pesetas and whose completion cost stood at 211.43 million pesetas.[53]

This sensitive information was for internal consumption only. According to the newspapers and newsreels, there was progress being made to abate the housing crisis; and whole neighborhoods were built and new homes inaugurated by either the local or national leaders of the regime. These inaugurations provided occasions for self-congratulation and propaganda and were most often reserved for important visits or for the July 18 holiday. The message was that the regime cared for the common folk.[54] Once the pomp and ceremony of the authorities and the press had departed, problems began to appear. Those scarce humble dwellings were often of dubious quality, and always too small. The buildings that had been celebrated and photographed for the regime's glory were so shoddily constructed that many were often soon in need of repair, some even before they could be occupied. For example, difficulties found in several just-completed housing projects in different towns in Cordoba province were listed in confidential inspection reports in 1954 and read as follows: the group of "economic" houses at Hernán Cortés, a development in Castro del Rio – "unacceptable foundations," "bad roofs which cause leaks," "roofs collapsing leaving rooms completely exposed," "useless kitchens," "lamentable carpentry"; the Padre Jesús Nazareno development in Priego de Cordoba – "bad foundations," "collapsing walls," "deficient roofs," "cracking floors," "leaking w.c." The local teacher in Montilla denounced the low quality of the Gran Capitán project, stating that the "foundations were made with no cement." There were also "blocked sewers," "unusable kitchens," and "completely unusable" sanitation systems, while the streets of the development were "true rivers of pestilence." The same reports note similar conditions for three other social housing developments.[55] Quality did seem to improve over the next few years as the government exercised better control over new construction, but the bottlenecks caused by autarky constantly frustrated or delayed building projects.[56]

The failure of these public housing projects carried out by a dictatorship that considered itself efficient and all-embracing is even starker if we compare it with the post-war United Kingdom. There housing was also an enormous problem, not only because of the destruction caused by the war, but because a good proportion of existing dwellings were originally of poor quality and inadequate (at the outset of the war a quarter of them had no lavatory and nearly half lacked a fixed bath). However, despite the country's state of near-bankruptcy, both the 1945 Labour government and the local authorities managed to build a million new dwellings by 1951. Later, the Tories followed up these policies by aiming to create 300,000 new dwellings every year. As a result, by 1970 nearly a third of all homes in Britain were publicly owned.[57] The UK built more than twice as many dwellings *every year*, from 1939 to 1960, as the *entire total* of public houses built by Franco's regime in this same period.[58]

British probity had certainly not been matched in Spain. According to the chief architect of the National Housing Institute, the housing deficit in 1945 was about 400,000 dwellings while new houses were not affordable for families earning less than 1,200 pesetas per month. Very few workers, if any, in Spain earned this amount. Even for the relatively more affluent Asturian miners it had become commonplace for single individuals to rent beds for eight hours a day, with each bed serving three miners working and resting in consecutive shifts.[59] Instead of improving, the housing problem worsened in the following years. A national survey in 1950 showed that only 6 percent of buildings had been erected after the Civil War, while 74 percent dated back to the previous century. Generally, houses were of poor quality and lacked basic services: only 20 percent had running water, 20 percent were connected to sewers, and just 1 percent had heating. The absence of public investment was just one cause of the problem. Older buildings deteriorated due to a lack of maintenance as standards of living remained so extremely low that people did not have extra income to devote to house restoration. This is why, in 1950, the national deficit was estimated at more than 680,000 dwellings. In several towns and villages the number of families without their own home and therefore living with other families was more than 30 percent of the total number of households. In the city of Salamanca, for example, nearly 35 percent of families had to share a home. This dilemma of scarcity and misery, of government inaction and bad policies, was made all the more striking by the fact that, in the same year, at least 150,000 flats, most of them recently built, remained unoccupied in Spain, and close to 178,000 were only occasionally used.[60] Those flats, however, were highly priced ones; they were not just for anybody.

Impossible as it might seem, in the following years the problem grew still worse before it got better.[61] When the Ministry of Housing was created in 1957, José Luis Arrese became its titular head. He was one of Franco's "yes men" from the old Falange. Arrese, who always had a weakness for cheap populism, not only recognized the growing deficit of affordable housing but also the recent explosion of shanty towns in the big cities. Speaking in 1958, 19 years after the war had ended, he blamed the situation on the liberal and republican governments of the past and, of course, the bombing of cities during the Civil War. This last explanation was especially true of Madrid, but he failed to mention that the bombings were relentlessly carried out by his side for two and half years and that their bombs had targeted working-class districts as extra punishment for the "reds," while avoiding shelling the city's wealthier neighborhoods. Arrese repeated the claim that the situation was dire precisely because life was improving: the housing shortage was a sign of the success of industrialization.[62] Always a man of brave ideas, he launched a shock plan to build "protected homes" under the auspices of his department. These homes were to be built cheaply, with no frills and of the smallest dimensions (between 59 and 72 square meters), but given the huge demand for housing, even these tiny flats were quickly taken up. Furthermore, corruption and influence meant that quite often it was the middle class and not the poorest people who gained access to the better homes.[63]

The 1958 Ministry of Housing plan built many homes but not enough of them. In 1968, the official unions calculated the deficit of new housing. In Barcelona alone it amounted to 60,900 dwellings *annually*.[64] According to a report by the Barcelona Official College of Real Estate Agents published in that year, the main features of the housing laws were their short-term nature and their limited effects. The report went on to state that, in spite of this, the housing deficit in Spain was not merely a product of a lack of dwellings. The situation was as it had been two decades earlier; there were homes for those who could afford to buy them. In Madrid, for example, there were 50,000 unoccupied flats, but they were too expensive and in the wrong neighborhoods, at least for the poor.[65] The other main problem continued to be the lack of purchasing power among those who needed a roof over their head.[66] In Franco's Spain, the same problems and their solutions were rehearsed for decades, often, and most remarkably, by the same authorities that had "solved" them in the past.

Since the authorities were prone to solving housing and other problems with words rather than with deeds, people took independent action. This meant they were forced to act illegally or at least in parallel to the law. In working-class neighborhoods on the peripheries of the large cities whole streets of newly built shacks appeared overnight, constructed with the immigrants' own hands. This was the case in the Madrid neighborhood of Palomeras. When remembering this time for a 1990 oral history project, the "pioneers" of this neighborhood described their continual struggles, the negotiations with municipal policemen and ward politicians, and the influence-peddling needed to avoid having their hastily built homes demolished.[67] Rosario Olegario, who moved there in 1953, explained that the houses had to be built in one night and occupied immediately because, if the shack wasn't completed by morning, guards would order its demolition and the people who had built it would be fined. She also remembers the "solidarity" among people: "when we had something good we both shared it and enjoyed it because that did not happen very often and we appreciated the good things more."[68]

In a country where friends were more useful than laws, Palomeras's resident Paula García had an advantage over her neighbors. One day, her illegal shack was almost razed to the ground by the authorities. But her brother had spent a few years in a seminary, and now had well-placed friends in the municipality. He contacted these friends and they quickly deterred the policemen who had brought along trucks full of political prisoners to demolish their shack. Two of Paula's neighbors who were not so well "connected" had the houses they had built overnight completely destroyed.[69]

The "lucky," successful squatters of Palomeras in the 1950s contended with the "minor" fact that their homes had neither water nor sanitation.

Carmen Villar remembered throwing out the night's excrement from pots each morning. "In summer, flies ate you alive, because of the detritus in the street." Little by little Palomeras improved; some streets were paved and people slowly upgraded their homes. Taxi drivers, who had previously refused to enter the area because their cars got stuck in the mud, began to serve it. Electricity arrived one Christmas Eve and those who could afford them bought radio sets. Spouses could now sit together in the evening after work and listen to the soap operas.[70]

While people progressed modestly and their families grew, social services and basic infrastructure did not arrive at the same pace. Land speculation and corruption got there sooner. One day, Lucía Ribote remembered, excavators arrived and made a big hole in the ground in an area officially designated as "green," a place where it was understood by all the local inhabitants that no one should build. People wondered if this hole was for the much-demanded sewers, a park, or a new school for children so they would not have to walk kilometers every day. Sadly, they were to be hugely disappointed. The hole marked the beginning of the construction of a new colony of cheap, privately built houses to be erected by a company called Hermanos Santos. "These gentlemen, people say, were very good friends of Mr. Esteras, the district warden, and they got all the permits they needed." It was not until the arrival of a priest named Fernando in 1967, "who started to move things," that Palomeras got its first social worker. Later, the priest and this social worker managed to get the authorities to build the much-needed school.[71]

Palomeras was part of Madrid's enormous urban and social problems. In 1965 the city had more than 18,000 families living in shacks; and there were "new" neighborhoods, like Moratalaz, where only 43 percent of the houses had running water and only 55 percent had a WC. While infant mortality was roughly half of what it had been in 1940 (7.6 per thousand and 16.6 per thousand, respectively), it was nonetheless devastating among poor families. In some poorer areas more than 30 of each 1,000 children died before their first birthday. There were other problems. In 1965, nearly 17 percent of school-age children in the city did not attend school at all, while close to 50 percent of children of working-class parents left school before they were 13 years old. Two out of three of those questioned stated that the main reason for this was "the lack of economic resources" of the family. It was estimated that "only 16 percent of male and 6 percent of female children from poor families would escape poverty because they have studied beyond elementary level."[72]

Finally, at the end of the 1960s, the Ministry of Housing showed some capacity for eradicating many of the self-made houses and shanty towns, although it continued to cast the blame on the migrants themselves. Years of neglect and incompetence had left behind an enormous social problem. The challenges were now doubled: the government needed to provide services to improve the already existing neighborhoods and to build an adequate number of low-priced apartments for people without a decent home. Improvements were desperately needed to neighborhoods such as Corralejos, a place that grew up next to Madrid's Barajas airport. Corralejos's rudimentary, self-made sanitation system featured a cesspit and an open well in a small cluster of houses built by some families a few years before, but that shortly thereafter served hundreds.

New apartments were needed here and elsewhere in the capital's many Rio de Janeiro- or Caracas-style shanty towns that, with shacks built of zinc, wood, and cardboard, had never even met a minimum standard for sanitation or running water. These were the conditions in neighborhoods such as the one at the end of Enrique Velasco Street, a slum called Cerro del Tío Pío, or the notorious El Pozo del Tío Raimundo. The Pozo was a world in itself. Most of the people living there were unskilled, semi-employed construction workers who, consequently, had no rights to social security.[73] More than 900 adults regularly worked picking up garbage from the city streets (here images from today's Cairo come to mind), using horse-drawn carts as well as motorized vehicles. This community had a high concentration of Gypsies, which in Spain almost immediately meant an additional degree of misery. As elsewhere, Gypsies consistently ranked lowest in terms of access to housing, health, and education. In 1967, it was estimated there were 1,200 families and a total of 10,000 Gypsies in Madrid, although most were not registered at the record office. Most Gypsies lived outside the mainstream of society; they were not drafted for military service and did not attend school, resulting in an illiteracy level of 95 percent. There are no data for their health and mortality levels but it can be assumed that they were far worse than the rest of Spain's population.[74]

The regime's eventual solution to the problem of shanty towns proved to be dubious at best. As in other countries where social housing exploded in the post-war years, many of the initially lucky poor families moved into dwellings in newly built neighborhoods only to find themselves in authentic ghettoes, which, incidentally, had been built both to house them and to keep them apart from "normal" people. These types of projects originated in the late 1950s during Mr. Arrese's tenure. The new neighborhoods were called *poblados de absorción* (absorption settlements). The buildings featured small, ugly apartments where overcrowding was the norm. In addition, they were located on the outskirts of cities and, like the other "spontaneous" communities, there was poor access to public transport, schools, and medical services. Often streets were not paved, public lighting was deficient, and there were insufficient numbers of public telephones if there were any at all. People who lived in these dwellings were all very poor and were both socially and physically segregated from the mainstream of the urban fabric. This state of affairs only concentrated and intensified social problems such as domestic violence, alcoholism, school absenteeism, petty criminality, and loitering.[75]

From Immigrants to Neighbors

Immigration quickly and dramatically transformed urban landscapes but it also, if more slowly, transformed peasants into neighbors. The people who moved to the cities often came from clearly stratified communities in which social oppression was both direct and ruthless. In their new neighborhoods they found there was a greater sense of equality because everyone began on more or less the same footing, and they often also shared a common social and political past. Even if they did not discuss politics directly, in the casual conversations of their daily lives, on the street, in bars, or at soccer matches, they shared opinions on the common problems of work, housing, and schooling. This reinforced their belief that the state was inept and indifferent at best towards their needs. From this milieu would emerge a minority among the children of the immigrants who would study and or get involved in youth groups, initially almost exclusively Catholic ones such as the JOC (Juventud Obrera Cristiana, or Christian Workers' Youth).[76] They would start, and perhaps help their parents, to reinterpret the collective past and present realities with increasingly political language. These discussions with peers and intergenerational exchanges created a new flow of information and thinking that would be crucial to understanding the new political attitudes that emerged in the 1970s, when previously politically disarmed parents would start to follow their children's oppositional activism and become increasingly able to express their own experiences in terms of oppression by the dictatorship instead of suffering caused by "neutral" post-war circumstances. In this process, poor people adopted political terms and even ideologies to define themselves and explain the world that surrounded them. This was, of course, far in the future for people in the 1950s and 1960s.

This growing political awareness in the new neighborhoods was not so evident in many areas inhabited by the poorest of the poor. Their need to ensure material survival left no room for communal or personal development. A case in point can be found in some immigrant neighborhoods in Granollers (Barcelona) in the mid-1960s, where even a minimal level of cooperative social activity and integration in the broader community was lacking. The parish of Our Lady of Fatima in Granollers included two neighborhoods: the Barrio Norte and Barrio Xarlet.[77] In both *barrios*, more than half of the immigrant population had been born in Andalusia.

In Barrio Norte alone, 30 percent of the immigrants were from the very poor province of Almeria. There, 91 percent of residents lived in very simple one-story, humble dwellings. These neighborhoods featured young, relatively fertile populations and, like many first-generation immigrants, they tended to marry within their own communities. As a result, only 10.5 percent of all marriages were "mixed," meaning marriages involving people from different regions, including the local Catalans. Needless to say, Castilian, not Catalan, was the lingua franca of these communities. These immigrants had very hard lives and had no resources to spare. They were isolated from the local Catalan culture and their illiteracy levels were shockingly high, running at 37.2 percent for men and 62.8 percent for women. Working males toiled long hours at distant construction sites or factories; 58 percent were foremen or skilled laborers and 41 percent were unskilled.

Like Barrio Norte, Barrio Xarlet had no sewers, and both communities had unpaved, unlit streets. Many people hauled water from unregulated wells, and 30 percent of homes had no toilet. People's diets were poor, both in quantity and quality, and the foods they consumed lacked the necessary minerals, fats, and vitamins. This was the result not of choice or poor judgment but of poverty. In 1965 it was estimated that 20 percent of families living in this neighborhood lacked an income sufficient to provide an adequate diet. The lack of sanitation and poor nutrition were reflected in high mortality rates even though Barrio Xarlet had a very young population. Although they were not shacks, their houses were crowded, and 20 percent of the population lacked a roof of their own. The Catholic charity organization Cáritas reported that eight couples, with at least five children each, shared one unlit basement dwelling. Not surprisingly, there was an outbreak of typhus in the neighborhood. Nearly half of their school-age children attended class outside the district because there weren't enough local schools. Worse still, hundreds of children attended school for only a few years, or did not attend at all. As the Cáritas report stated, some children did not go to school "because they were working and others [did not attend because they had] to take care of young siblings while the mother works outside the home." Another problem that caught the attention of the Catholic volunteers attempting to help people was the lack of any communal, socially or culturally oriented associations save for a few football clubs.[78]

There were many similar immigrant communities surrounding the large industrial cities of Spain, but not all of them so completely lacked a voice or were as dispossessed. There were many *barrios* in transition towards more liberal social values and community activism, where cultural associations were increasingly created and a growing number of residents became involved. This was true of Can Oriach in Plana del Pintor and of Torrent del Capella in Sabadell, two other communities located in Barcelona's industrial belt.[79] In 1967 about 20,000 people lived in these places, of whom a third had been born in Catalonia while half were natives of Andalusia. The population was young and growing rapidly. Most workers, skilled and unskilled, were employed in textile and metallurgy factories, or in construction. Illiteracy levels ran at "only" 12.55 percent, and this primarily reflected the levels of the elderly who could not read (though 2.23 percent of school-age children were illiterate).[80]

Even in those relatively well-off neighborhoods conditions were harsh. Although there were more apartment buildings available, three out of four people still lived in overcrowded, tiny, shabbily constructed, one-story houses. These dwellings were unhealthy; only 22 percent had a shower and 25 percent a sink, and 45 percent had no sanitation whatsoever. When people contemplated improving these conditions they often found it impossible to do so since there were no water pipes in 23 percent of the streets. Services were scarce and this affected schooling in particular. There were not enough public schools, and to fill the gap five private, unregulated schools existed to "service" 460 children. Cáritas described these private schools as "a single room containing all students, without enough space or the minimum conditions for their functioning." The school deficit was estimated at 23 classrooms and 805 student places. There were no day-care centers. There were 12 public phones and a single mailbox.[81]

Nonetheless, things were changing in Can Oriach and Torrent. People were organizing and diversifying their leisure time, and also channeling their inequities and problems into organizations. The main sports activity, of course, was football. The two existing clubs played their matches on an unpaved piece of land in front of a newly built area. A novelty, a handball club, operated, and even a small chess club was active. As in most *barrios*, the main leisure-time activity was listening to radio, watching television, and frequenting bars: there were 67 of these in the area. Trophies, photos of events, and other memorabilia decorated these establishments, competing with calendars of either religious paintings or young women in bikinis. Some bars were, however, more than mere drinking places, doubling as informal community and even cultural centers. Others served as the head-quarters of soccer teams, and one hosted a dove-training club while another featured live music. There was also a hunger for entertainment, with people frequently going en masse to the movies. Every weekend they packed all three movie theaters in the neighborhood. The total capacity of these theaters was estimated at 1,500 seats, which meant that, every weekend almost 15 percent of the neighborhood was seated together, enjoying themselves. The absolute majority of people did not go to church: only 2.2 percent of adult men and 5.8 percent of women attended. However, there were 64 individuals who were members of Catholic organizations. This slow social and cultural mobilization eventually gave birth to a neighborhood association in 1964 (very early in the context of Franco's Spain), as soon as it was permitted by law. The association immediately began to publish a news bulletin. Community activism here had made inroads into historical pessimism.[82]

This progressive break with both historical pessimism and individualism was easier for younger people than for their elders. Unlike their children, the latter had many of their own historical prejudices (or defeats) to over-come, as well as cultural and gender barriers to break through. They brought their fear to the city, together with values and expectations shaped by their experiences of poverty and the harshness of their upbringing. They had been raised in a culture disconnected from the idea of the common good. They had concentrated on private matters, on family and work. They were also brought up with the concepts of submission, obedience, and duty (to family, the authorities, etc.) rather than with the notion of the freedom to choose for themselves. Yet, in spite of all their obstacles, it is remarkable that these same people could later, in a democracy, reinterpret their lives and find new and dignified identities. They did this by processing and extract-ing wisdom from their suffering, and they came enjoy their lives in a more affluent and tolerant Spain. The older generation would sometimes surprise their "modern" children by expressing, perhaps for the first time in their lives, their repressed frustrations and dreams from the past, revealing humans behind the mask of duty they had always worn. After 1975, millions of seniors began to remember and talk about their past once the deep-rooted fear and misery of Franco's regime had come to an end. This was as true for people with left-wing as for those with right-wing political sympathies. They would say, for example, how much they had always wanted to travel, to read, or to go to the theater or to music shows. This discovery of the pleasures of life would be particularly strong among women, those who had not only suffered "bad times" but who had also had the added curse of being born female in a macho society that further discriminated against them. The following stories come from the early 1990s, from women living in the working-class neighborhood of Palomeras in Madrid described above.[83]

Rosario Olegario brought her fear and double oppression (because she was poor and a woman) to Madrid. She was from a farming family in La Alcarria in the province of Guadalajara. In the early 1940s, when she was a teenager, her mother told her "not to talk to anybody." They had nothing to gain from talking too much. Their lives were hard and they knew many people who were in prison in those years. The area had been republican during the war. The whole family worked in the fields, and she had done so since she was 8 years old. She always resented her very poor education and the fact that she had left school at the age of 12. She remembered her teacher being a conservative Francoist who did not care about poor children like herself. She did not talk back then, but when she began talking in the early 1990s she expressed her belief in how important education is: Rosario had enrolled in an adult education program for seniors.[84]

Encarnación del Campo was also born in a rural community, but in the Francoist heartland of Burgos. She had begun working the land and caring for her younger siblings before she was 10, having by then stopped attending school. With her mother and her aunt, and like hundreds of thousands of other women, she was involved in the post-war black market and was caught twice. As a teenager she started to work in a local bakery. She also witnessed fear. Her employer used to say to her "we shall be quiet despite what we hear because here we have all kinds of people coming [in]." She concluded: "[There was] a lot of fear." In 1947, at the age of 17, she went to work as a maid in Madrid. From then on she never stopped working as a servant or cleaning lady. When interviewed in 1990 for the oral history project, she too was registered on adult education courses "because I wanted to learn."[85]

Puri García came to Madrid from a village in Caceres, Extremadura, in 1952. She was 5 years old, and after her arrival in Madrid she went to school for only a few years. Her parents, a construction worker and a domestic servant, were illiterate. She became a dressmaker. She was married in 1959 and moved to the neighborhood of Palomeras. She remembered her first years of work as a dressmaker: "my training was real exploitation. No social security, no limits to working hours, no food and, when the older employees were finished, I had to clean the workshop." In 1963, now working for a different employer, she went with other women to complain to the official union about their situation. "All of us with a horrible fear inside [...] It seemed we had committed a crime." One year afterwards, they finally received social security, but "I do not ever remember signing a payslip." In 1990 she was attending adult education courses with her husband.[86]

With democracy and relative prosperity, people like Rosario, Encarnación, Puri, and millions of other senior citizens finally started to talk about hunger, fear, the hard life in the fields, taking care of small children in large families with stern fathers and long-suffering, perennially pregnant, overworked mothers, and the awful neighborhoods where they settled. Now, when they were older, they were making it very clear that they did not want their children, particularly their daughters, to go through anything similar. They would say how much they enjoyed their present lives, their independence, their small pensions, their urban families, and their freedom. Their lives represent the evolution of ordinary Spaniards from 1939 until the end of the century: from peasant and poor to urban and modestly affluent, from subjects of a ruthless dictatorship to responsible, proud citizens.

The stories of these women have relatively happy endings, but not everybody succeeded in preserving their dignity, improving their lot, or even keeping their family together in their new life in the *barrio*. Peasant immigrants had to face, often for the first time in their lives, the risks and social problems associated with cities, and the perils of slums in particular. Many failed to become neighbors and were unable to find dignity.

Left Behind

The chaotic growth of marginal neighborhoods created problems that wrecked the lives of people left to their own devices to cope with these new challenges. Signs of this social distress were obvious to many observers.

They wrote about how the children of semi-literate people who had moved to large cities did not have the social and communal constraints that their parents had had. Excluded from the school system, too many children had no skills or education to help them successfully integrate into urban life. While their parents worked hard to earn a meager living, children and youngsters often roamed the streets unsupervised. Domestic violence, alcoholism, and overcrowding meant that the streets, and not their non-existent family living rooms, became the preferred turf of young people.[87] Confronted with their very different children, immigrant parents did not know how to respond or where to find help, especially when they started along the path from marginality towards crime.[88]

The phenomenon of rising levels of youth crime was already noticeable in Barcelona in the late 1960s. Here, the most common crimes committed by young people were robbery, car theft, and sexual crimes, the latter connected to female prostitution. Hard drugs had yet to arrive but hashish, often introduced by former members of the Spanish army posted in Africa, was already widely known. Alcohol seemed less alarming to social commentators in a country where young children could routinely be seen drinking in bars. The greatest concern for the authorities was the spread of prostitution. Officially forbidden since the previous decade, it primarily affected young, marginalized, immigrant women, many of whom had first worked as domestic servants while others were recruited directly from among the people coming from the fields. A quarter of the women working as prostitutes declared that they had been rejected by their fiancés after having sex with them. Many were single mothers disowned by their families. The same authoritarian and restrictive family and social values that had helped poor people to survive the post-war misery and migrations condemned tens of thousands of young females to prostitution.[89]

Marginalization during the economic and social miracle of the 1960s was not only limited to individuals. Whole occupations and geographical areas remained clearly behind or sank even further into misery. Migration was a heavy tax imposed on the poor, but emigrants' remittances were not enough to lift up millions of them from poverty or change for better the regions from which they came.

Poverty, admittedly, is a notoriously slippery concept and can extend from utter misery to a simple inability to save money having satisfied one's minimum needs (another slippery concept) for food, shelter, and clothing. However, something very important was amiss in the "boom years" when, for example, a 1968 study revealed that 71 percent of unskilled workers and

64 percent of service-sector employees considered their incomes insufficient to cover their needs.[90] These poor working people were defined by one author as the "bearers of development": those who had next to no education, lived in impossibly small and uncomfortable homes, worked long hours, had almost no holidays, whose children were likely to drop out of school, and who could rarely reach the end of the month on the family's combined earnings. In the lower strata of the working poor were a million unskilled workers in agriculture, half a million in construction, and 80,000 in fishing and service industries. Also included here should be the close to 400,000 women officially recognized as being employed as domestic servants (the real number, including part-time workers, was much higher). Finally, the nearly 200,000 people who were officially unemployed must also be added. If we add to all the previous numbers roughly 1 million homes headed by an illiterate person, the hundreds of thousands of people living on meager pensions, the semi-employed or seasonally unemployed, it has been estimated that, by 1970, between 9 and 10 million people (once their families are included) in Spain lived below the poverty line.[91] This represented at least a quarter of the total population (then almost 34 million).[92] These were the people for whom the illusions of the "economic boom" remained just that, illusions, because they were supposed to be next in line to access the comforts of Spain's modern consumer society (see chapter 4) and yet they were the hardest hit by the deep socio-economic crisis that arrived in 1974.[93]

Poverty was also unevenly distributed across the country. There were many reasons for these regional disparities and they can be enveloped in generic and perhaps empty expressions such as "underdevelopment," but there are more tangible explanations. From the mid-1960s on, hundreds of reports were written on regional poverty in Spain, most of them prepared by official institutions. They were wrapped in suitable moral language and avoided any negative overtones. Quite often, these reports clearly demonstrated how the economic and social policies of the government were not going to change the situation of backwardness any time soon. From the point of view of the local authorities, the main function of these reports was to place a region in a long, imaginary queue of have-not areas for the next time that Madrid decided to implement a new development plan or to instigate a particular project. For example, in 1969 the head of a Galician chamber of commerce wrote a report explaining how the economic boom, with the exception of some coastal industrial areas, was bypassing the region, especially the rural areas and the interior. It stated, among other things, how in the previous two decades Galicia had lost almost 25 percent of its inhabitants. Most of the 665,000 people who left came from the rural and semi-rural areas and, as a result, salaried workers had all but disappeared. The report explained what could be done to stop the demographic hemorrhage, but could not blame the obvious culprit: the government. Instead, the region was described as "sleeping" and needing to awaken.[94]

Like Galicia, another region hit hard by poverty was Extremadura. In 1969 the Commissariat for the Development Plan, the same agency that was neglecting investment in the region, produced a long, detailed study of Extremadura's economic and social structure. Its pages reveal that 75 percent of houses in the region had no running water. In rural areas, 97.7 percent of houses in Caceres province and 99.05 percent of those in the province of Badajoz had no water. There was also cultural poverty: two-thirds of the people of Extremadura had no access to printed news, only 3 percent had a television set, and only 60 percent owned a radio.[95]

There were many regions waiting to be "awakened." A 1973 study showed that 31 percent of the population of the south-central Spain and almost 30 percent of that of Galicia lived in poverty, while in Catalonia this problem affected 10 percent of the population and, in the coastal regions of the northeast, 11.5 percent.[96] Neither state investment nor its transfers of services and payments contributed to reducing these regional disparities. In 1973 a resident of Madrid or Barcelona received three to four times more services from social security than someone living in Orense or Cuenca. The result of these and other inequalities was that, at the end of the dictatorship, the living standards of the 10 richest provinces of Spain were twice as high as those of the poorer provinces. By the same indicators, residents of large cities were far better off than those in the countryside.[97]

Unsettling as they may be, the above-mentioned numbers are cold and even misleading, because they hide situations in some parts of Spain which can only be described as harrowing. Official data and reports failed to convey specific situations of abject poverty that was entrenched, and in some cases growing, in many parts of the country, such as Andalusia, Extremadura, and Galicia. It was an awful reality that had, for example, between 1961 and 1970, forced more than 100,000 poor people from Seville to be temporarily lodged in massive public dormitories because their homes were unfit for human habitation. It was a silent catastrophe that included a parish of Cadiz where in the early 1970s around 3,160 families had a single room for the entire family, while another 4,475 families "enjoyed" two rooms.[98]

Seville and Cadiz were part of the southern landscapes of misery of the post-war period and they continued to be so in the last days of the regime. Another dreadful place was the municipality of Baza, in the province of Granada. An area of poor agriculture and, at best, seasonal employment and no industry, emigration had decimated the population since the end of the war. In 1960, despite a high birth rate and declining infant mortality rates, the population was almost the same as it had been in 1940 (about 20,000 people). What particularly struck researchers about the area though, apart from the state of education there, was people's extremely poor living and sanitary conditions: as late as 1969, some 10,000 of its 25,000 inhabitants lived in about 2,000 caves. They had no running water, no toilets, no paved roads, and no obvious future.[99]

There was no future, or so it seemed, for many parts of Andalusia. In 1970, a book titled *Noticia de Andalucía* (News from Andalusia), became well known. It was written by the Catholic Marxist, Alfonso Carlos Comín, a kind man from the rich part of the country who traveled to witness the misery of the "other" Spain. He saw many terrible things when, for example, he visited the mining town of La Carolina, Jaen. He entered the home of a woman named Margarita "a widow with five children, two others died of malnutrition." One of her children told him, "I did not experience more hunger because the day is only twenty-four hours long." He also went to Almeria to a neighborhood called La Chanca and witnessed "16,000 people living in misery."[100] The neighborhood was inhabited by a mixture of fishermen, construction workers, Gypsies, and marginal types. It was already a notorious place, because it had been the subject of a book in 1962, another harrowing testimony, by the Catalan writer Juan Goytisolo.[101] It had been published in France, and immediately censored in Spain, becoming the object of an official media campaign that denied its charges.

While the regime deployed its well-tested capability for censorship, what the Francoist press could not do, and the authorities did not do, in 1962 or in 1970, was to stop and reverse the course of abject poverty. In 1974, despite much-publicized plans conceived to reverse the fate of La Chanca's people, an internal report by the official union stated that, of the 17,000 people inhabiting its 4,000 dwellings, as many as 35 percent still lived in caves. Cases of leprosy were reported.[102] Moreover, the misery that had been primarily concentrated in this neighborhood had spilled into new ones because of the local municipal policy of settling poor and marginal workers into newly created segregated social housing projects. These new slums were to become notorious, and their reputations soon competed with

La Chanca's own. 2,500 marginal people, 1,800 of them Gypsies, were sent to a place with a beautiful name, Los Almendros (The Almond Trees), located in the outskirts, next to the city's cemetery. The 1974 official report on the new ghetto stated: "we have doubts about including them among the category of workers' neighborhoods [...] given their very low economic indicators." According to official data, the illiteracy rate there ran at 80 percent.[103]

***

Migration changed both Spain and Spaniards. In the process of moving to survive or to escape poverty, migrants established new relations, confronted new problems, and found (or failed to find) new solutions and values. Migration contributed to changing social values but it was not the only, and probably not the main, source of change. There were other cultural and social movements and developments happening at the same time that contributed to the evolution of Spaniards and to their increasing alienation from the core political values of the dictatorship. The next chapter explores these.

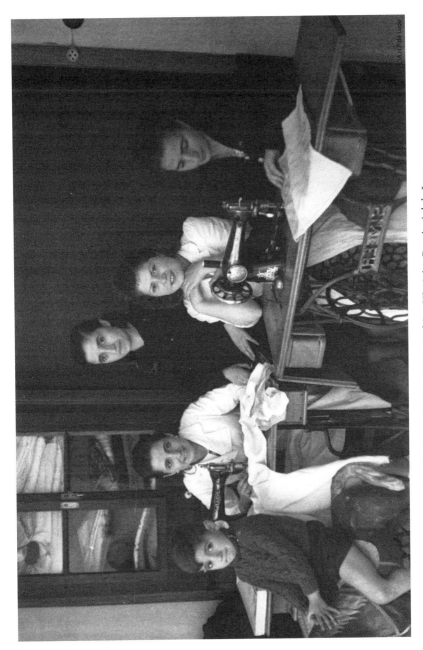

Plate 1   Women in a sewing shop in Lugo, Galicia, 1941. *Archivo Histórico Provincial de Lugo*

Plate 2　Caves for immigrants in Sabadell, Catalonia, 1950. *Archivo Histórico de Sabadell*

Plate 3 People in a food store, Lugo, Galicia, 1954. *Archivo Historico Provincial de Lugo*

Plate 4   New homes for immigrants in Sabadell, Catalonia, 1963–5. *Archivo Histórico de Sabadell*

Plate 5 Pro-Franco demonstration in Madrid, December 1970. *Archivo General de la Administración (Madrid)*

Plate 6   Police repress a demonstration outside a church in Sabadell, Catalonia, mid-1970s. *Archivo Comisiones Obreras de Sabadell*

Plate 7 Journeymen harvesting grapes in Sanlucar de Barrameda, Cadiz, Andalusia, 1975. *Archivo Histórico Comisiones Obreras de Andalucía*

4

A CHANGING SOCIETY

Despite all the nostalgia that some people may still experience for the old days of "peace" and certainty, the last decade and a half of Francoism was marked by a growing confusion that could be found even in the most remote corners of Spain. Not even the Catholic Church, the Franco regime's pre-eminent ally during the 1940s and 1950s, could be taken for granted any longer. For example, in 1971 the civil governor of Huesca complained about the sermons and other activities of several local priests. During the Good Friday sermon, the parish priest of the villages of Laluenga and Laperdiguera declared that the "land must be for those who work it." This was not an isolated incident. During the Corpus Christi sermon that year, priests from Tardienta and the Cartuja de los Monegros, in the same province, denounced the new minimum wage of 136 pesetas as being woefully inadequate. One of them stated that if it were up to him, "those who made that decision [would be asked to] live two or three years on that amount of money" to discover how it would feel. Another priest went so far as to bar local representatives of Franco's regime from leading the Corpus Christi procession, arguing that "that tradition is over" and the task was now "for real Catholics." On a separate occasion, the auxiliary bishop of the diocese spoke out publicly against the repression of Catholics who had joined workers to demand better wages and working conditions; he also stated that many priests feared reprisals from the state when workers asked them for help. All of this, the governor said, caused "confusion" and "division" both in the Church and in society as a whole.[1]

The evolution of broad sectors of the Church from a pro-Franco position to open political dissent had taken decades to occur. In many ways it mirrors the evolution of Spanish society as a whole from widespread political apathy to increased dissatisfaction with the ossified political regime. Nor had this social confusion arrived suddenly. It was the product of a society that in the last years of the dictatorship was more sophisticated than the one that had emerged from the Civil War. It was wealthier, more complex, and its values were changing; mostly because Spanish society had ceased to be primarily agrarian in nature, and new ideas, relationships, and circumstances had replaced old ones.

The Altar and the Street

One of the outstanding characteristics of post-war Spanish official Catholicism was its lack of reflection on the complexities and root causes of the Civil War and on the ensuing social problems resulting from Franco's regime. Significantly, for the first 20 years following the war no true Catholic intellectual or thinker dared to challenge the authoritarian and triumphal discourses of the Church hierarchy or of the dictatorship. During that time, Spanish Catholicism had nothing new to say to the world. The Catholic Church's harsh and callous approach to social problems was reduced, more often than not, to general comments on moral issues, while those who suffered most were routinely blamed for being the main cause of their own plight. For example, in the famine-stricken Spain of 1943, Catholic Action in Saragossa organized a conference on charity. A priest there presented a paper explaining his experiences with miners in Asturias before the war.[2] He said he had observed there that the miners enjoyed huge salaries and had no real reason to complain, but that they became revolutionaries because "they lacked morality." He added that, while their wives and children cried from hunger at home, the miners would complete their shifts and immediately rent taxis to take them to the cities of Oviedo and Gijon, where they stayed at the best hotels and ordered champagne. When asked which champagne, they said "the best you have," and when asked if they wanted just one bottle, "no – they replied – two cases." Having described the miners sipping French champagne, the good priest then asked the public: "What does it matter, gentlemen, a new distribution of wealth, while consciences remain deformed? The solution to economic problems is, before anything else, the solution to moral problems and this is only possible in the name of God and through Christian religious education." "Very well," the public unanimously assented.[3]

Behind this sort of nonsense stood class prejudice of the worst kind. Unfortunately, it was rather common at the time. For both the regime and the majority of "learned" Catholics, the people who should profit from the "peace" of the New Spain were not the starving, landless peasants and ungrateful proletarians, but the middle classes. As a 1951 Catholic Action book reasoned, the middle classes were "characterized by their cultural and economic conditions, hard work, spiritual quest and desire to improve their social standing," while the lower or working classes, on top of their "economic weakness, had a limited culture, a tendency towards material pleasures and chimerical ideas on social issues."[4] To reinforce this point of view, Catholic Action stated that the middle classes were in dire need of assistance because they had to spend nearly 70 percent of their income on food while their British counterparts spent only 40 percent. This placed the Spanish middle classes in an intolerable situation in which they resembled the "most modest proletarians of some foreign countries." Though where Spanish proletarians stood at this time and on this scale the report did not say.[5]

The most prominent Catholics not only supported the regime that brought so much suffering to the poor; they were openly proud of it. Church representatives and Francoist authorities literally walked hand in hand.[6] Nowhere was this more evident than at the Easter processions led by prominent representatives of both parties. It was an annual ritual: while somber religious music mingled with military marches, bishops, priests, military officers of the garrison, mayors, civil governors, Falangists, and other prominent authorities were escorted by troops and civil guards, these sometimes on horseback, as they headed this display of power and uncompromising, theatrical Catholicism. Hooded penitents followed the powerful, while ordinary devotees, who often carried candles while walking shoeless as a sign of either atonement or of thanks for a "small" miracle, came last in the procession. Placed physically and symbolically at the rear of the parade, both the poor and popular devotion were visually put at the service of the regime; sometimes with a grim twist. For example, Seville's famous spectacular Easter processions were for years notorious for the presence of General Gonzalo Queipo de Llano. This was the same brutal individual who had controlled the city for the rebels in 1936 and inflicted bloody repression on workers' neighborhoods. Approximately 8,000 republicans were shot under his orders during the war. When he died in 1951, he was buried in the much-revered Virgen de la Macarena basilica, the city's main church.[7]

These processions were huge symbolic events for a few days during the year. But the same messages were delivered on a weekly basis to those who attended mass. On these occasions, ordinary Spaniards heard explicit messages of support for the dictatorship like the one delivered by the bishop of Lerida (Catalonia) in his 1955 address to his flock:

> You should be grateful to Franco and his government and must ask God to illuminate them and give them comfort so they can continue with their work of enthroning social justice [...] I ask you to look at poverty and all trouble from the perspective of the divine, because, if you look at them in this way, they will seem smoother to you and you will extract from them all the treasures of eternal life they contain.[8]

At the same time that the bishop was delivering this homily, however, something had already begun to change inside the Church, albeit slowly. By the early 1950s, the persistent misery in Spain finally caught the attention of a new generation of Catholics, some of them too young to have witnessed the war, and a movement – away from a purely moral view of the plight of the poor and toward a more humanistic social approach – began to take shape. Small groups, particularly within the redoubtable HOAC, the workers' section of Catholic Action, were already crossing the line to join the growing criticism of the regime and its policies.[9] Founded in 1946, HOAC and the juvenile branch of Catholic Action, the JOC, were becoming platforms for effective political discourse and Catholic social analysis that served to counteract the regime's political and ideological monopoly.[10] The best indication that a crucial line was being crossed was that their meetings were, on occasion, visited by Falangist thugs and plainclothes policemen who either eavesdropped on what was being discussed or disturbed and even assaulted those present.[11] It must be said, however, that these dissenters were in a clear minority until the early 1970s. The bulk of Catholics within the institutions of the Church still shaped their condemnation of injustice to fall within the boundaries of "constructive" criticism and support for the dictatorship.[12]

However, much to the regime's chagrin, change was unstoppable. In the early 1960s some of the best minds of the Catholic Church began to embrace "subversive" ideologies and made it difficult, at times, to distinguish Catholic enterprises from the initiatives of illegal opposition groups. Significantly, this new approach to social Catholicism began even before the effects of the Second Vatican Council of 1962–5 had been felt.[13] There was a paradox inherent in this because, as the economy improved and the regime appeared to be on more solid ground than ever, it became normal practice in some Catholic circles to discuss social problems, particularly the plight of workers, and to question the political role of the Church. In 1964, for example, two priests who authored a book using the testimonies of their fellow clerics summed up these sentiments thus: "I am not ashamed to say that, like most of my generation, I was wrong when I believed that Spanish workers were little more than a bunch of savages, full of vice and hatred, lazy people who wanted to live without having to work." One of these priests, who lived among the working poor and proselytized in the politically troubled Asturias region for 15 years, explained (or rather "revealed") to the more conservative Catholic elements that miners worked extremely hard and that their complaints were rooted in having been abandoned by their social betters and by the Church.[14]

Self-criticism of this nature was certainly new and it helped initiate a venue for more open discussion of the direction of the Church. It also created a level of disenchantment that helped fuel a crisis that shook the Spanish Catholic Church in the late 1960s. One of the consequences of this crisis was a clear split between a conservative majority and an increasingly active anti-Francoist minority. Another consequence was that after the mid-1960s it was no longer possible to simply discuss social problems in the abstract, moral terms that the Church and the government had employed in the two previous decades. This new attitude reflected a sense of shame held by the clergy regarding Spain's social inequality and repressive political system. It was now possible for a cleric-turned-journalist to write in 1965, "All theft is a sin. And if a rich man steals from a poor one, we all should tremble."[15]

The figure of the worker priest played a fundamental role in this political and religious crisis. This new priestly role had been initiated in France and Belgium in the late 1940s, and its aim was the evangelization of the working masses by priests who became workers themselves and lived among proletarians. While the success of the Church in converting non-practicing workers into good Catholics was limited at best, many priests became worker militants in the process, joined the opposition, and quite often became laicized. This was the case of a young Jesuit priest named Luis Anoro. The Company of Jesus had traditionally been seen by militant workers as an ally of the rich and powerful, and as an enemy of freedom. The Jesuits, however, who had been working all over the world, witnessing too many injustices and dreadful political regimes, changed in the 1960s. That change also reached Spain. In 1968, Luis and many of his colleagues began to move to working-class neighborhoods and to work in factories to be closer to the experiences of ordinary people. Luis went to live in Saragossa and found a job working for a company that employed 150 men. Middle-class by origin, he learned about workers' lives and their values while toiling in the factory. He used his education to organize his new co-workers, and helped to create the factory union committee; he then took a leading role in more than one labor conflict. Eventually he was fired. Over the next few months he was fired twice more from other jobs, partly because the police kept informing his new employers of his history as a troublemaker. Many years later, Luis recounted what he had learned from his experiences as a worker priest: the reality of physical exhaustion, the meaning of real hardship, the importance of rest and enjoying life, the consequences of doing rather than talking, the significance of closeness and cooperation among workers. Using classic Marxist terminology, he also referred to his new point of view as "class consciousness." Luis found that he had broken with his past and he clearly stated that he had found out more about Jesus.[16]

Luis's experience is emblematic of the global crisis in the Catholic Church in the 1960s, experienced from Spain to the province of Quebec in Canada – a crisis that saw the traditional roles of the priesthood and the sisterhood evolve in new directions. Some were searching for a purer, simpler spirituality, while others, demanding social reforms, demonstrated an increased concern for the poor. A massive decline in the number of people working in religious vocations was felt and was reflected by both the significantly lower number of young men entering seminaries and the laicization, and often, marriage, of priests.[17] It is striking how many of those priests' personal itineraries reflect the process and even the timing of the end of the traditional small peasantry of Spain and the transition, both physical and mental, from an agrarian society to an urban one. José Manuel González López became a laicized priest (in the mid-1970s he owned a bookstore).[18] He was born in Burgos into a traditional agrarian family in 1938. Of the eight children in his family, four became nuns and two chose the priesthood. José joined the Jesuits and traveled to Madrid, where he encountered a "different reality from what I knew." His colleague, Gonzalo González Álvarez, was born in 1943 into a modest, conservative family from Leon and went to the seminary because "they took me there." However, soon after being ordained a Dominican priest in 1968 he went to work in an oil refinery in Cartagena (Murcia). The next year he moved to Valladolid, lived in an apartment instead of the order's house, and worked in construction. In 1972 he was detained for his role as a leading labor activist.[19] By this time he had broken his wows of celibacy and joined a group called Christians for Socialism. Eventually, he would abandon his ministry altogether.

José Manuel and Gonzalo's trajectory, from conservative peasant origins to labor activists, was not uncommon. Up to the 1960s, young children were often sent to the seminary either to escape poverty or to fulfill their parents' wishes, or both. They were sent before they were mature enough to understand what it meant to be a priest or to realize what they really wanted in life. Many, if not most, priests in Spain had traditionally followed this path, often for the same reasons, only to remain in the ministry for their whole lives. What was new now, and what led many of these young men to abandon the priesthood in order to engage in other activities, was the opening up of intellectual horizons and the new socio-cultural expectations developing in the country. This meant, among other things, an affirmation of individuality. It also led to a new theological message asking priests to be engaged in transforming and bettering the material world rather than only preparing souls for the next life. These new horizons and expectations were very similar to those the laity was experiencing in Spain at the same time: a growing affirmation of the desires of the individual coupled with a growing concern about, and urge to identify and act upon, the country's social and political problems.

At a higher level, the Vatican Council and Pope Paul VI (1963–78) promoted change. As a result, in the early 1970s the Spanish Church seemed to be on the verge of abandoning its moralizing approach to social problems and breaking away from the dictatorship. However, that never fully happened. A proposal demanding that the Church ask forgiveness for its one-sided role in the Civil War, brought forth in 1971 by a joint assembly of bishops and priests, failed to gather enough votes to be carried. This missed opportunity meant that, until the very end of the dictatorship, the Catholic Church failed to condemn the regime or to fully revise its political position, or even express regret over its role in the tragic events and shameful social policies of the past.[20] As a consequence, the Church and millions of practicing Catholics faced the arrival of democracy in 1977 in an even more confused and disoriented state than the rest of Spanish society.

Morals

Francoism was, in moral terms, a fundamentalist regime that left public morality in the hands of the Catholic Church. This morality was tainted by class prejudice in which workers were damned for being poor, while moral concerns for the elite were specific, and very different. The official moral message preached to the majority of the population was not about justice, and of course did not question dictatorial power. This matter was not open to discussion because power, belonging to Franco, was blessed by the bishops several times during and after the war. The messages from the pulpit were chiefly, if not only, about sex and gender relations, and their main subject was the group considered to be most at risk from potential breaches of morality: women. Here too, from the most basic pamphlet addressed to young girls to the more elaborate discourse for adult women, class distinction was always present. In the 1943 pamphlet *Do You Want to be a Good Girl?* it was explained that, to be good, one had to "love the Lord a lot because he has done very good things for you [like creating] the beautiful flowers when you look for them in the fields or in a garden."[21] This message was obviously applicable to good girls who had gardens, who dealt with plants visually, and who did not spend long, hard hours tilling the land while taking care of their siblings and their animals, and running away from civil guards with modest quantities of contraband.

Class distinctions appeared again when the Church discussed another important issue in the 1940s: dancing – that extremely dangerous interaction between sexes that was any confessor's worst nightmare. The polemics about dancing were endless, and so were the books, pamphlets, and sermons that priests and other moral authorities devoted to this vital question. One of the leading authorities on the matter, the presbyter Rufino Villalobos, entered the fray about this "passionate question" and in 1948 explained, from misery-ravaged town of Don Benito (Extremadura), that "God is not here to satisfy our desire" to move our legs and that "dancing normally, and almost always, is a sin and a cardinal sin." His mind surely gazed into a dark abyss when he imagined a married person dancing with someone other than his or her spouse, an action he automatically placed into the category of "adultery."[22] A man sensitive to the unavoidable burdens of power and ruling, Father Villalobos admitted that, at official government receptions, the spouses of important people were allowed to exchange partners while dancing. It has to be said that his views were fairly extreme: other clerics allowed a liberal inch, cautiously sanctioning the possibility of executing regional folkloric dances with strangers so long as no physical contact was involved.

For the Church, the twin succubus to "the evils of dancing" was public bathing, either at beaches or in swimming pools. This crucial moral dilemma caught the attention of both political and religious authorities every summer. Luckily, the Catalan presbyter Dr. Carlos Salicrú was an authority on this "burning matter." A progressive man, he understood the health benefits of bathing, but was definitely against "promiscuity among sexes" and the "cynical and sensual attitude of shameless voyeurs." In 1944 he recommended both the complete separation of the sexes at beaches by using physical barriers and the complete covering of the skin during the exercise of the morally dangerous activity of refreshing the body.[23]

The post-war Church, attached as it was to outdated ritual and its dogmatic understanding of its function, was ill prepared to confront the new social and moral challenges posed by an increasingly urbanized society. At the 1959 national conference on "Family and Public Morality," for example, the following reflections on the moral circumstance of the country were offered. Delegates from Alicante explained that "without deep religious education we will not resolve the possible defects our society may have"; those from Avila said that "The reigning immorality is a consequence of the cracking of Christian principles"; from the Balearics, predictably: "Tourism, on top of being a moral danger, is an ideological one because of the danger of infiltration of ideas about materialism (divorce), family (children), religion, morals, liberal thinking, etc."; and from misery-ravaged Seville: "In many households there is a real domestic Atheism [...] with no moral idea [with] parents who got together just to satisfy their bestial appetites [and with] children who never heard the word of God." Clear signs of moral decay were everywhere: "abortion" in Albacete and San Sebastian; "Malthusian virus" in Cuenca; "excessive spending" in Madrid; "increasing numbers of homosexuals" in Palencia; and, of course, "dancing [that] torture of confessors and virus of pious associations, favorite fare for the Devil," again in sinful Cuenca.[24]

It took the Church more than two decades to start moving beyond this ultra-simplistic analysis and begin to address modernity. The new attitudes came from a new generation of younger, enlightened Catholic thinkers who deemed it necessary to prepare men and women from the middle and upper classes for the new challenges faced by society.[25] The role of the modern woman, in particular, was being taken seriously by Catholic Action, which insisted on the need for women to be educated in order for them to become worthy companions for their husbands and to improve the quality of life of their families.[26] In this process, the most strident sexist and misogynist aspects of the moral discourse were being dropped. Instead of post-war demands that women remain pious, passive, and simple, mere transmitters of their husband's will, the new Catholic middle-class woman was expected to be an educated marriage partner.[27]

By the early 1960s a wife's main functions were seen to go beyond the traditional roles of reproductive vessel and servant to her husband, lord, and God. The objectives of marriage were rearranged, and "mutual help and love" between spouses now preceded reproduction as a priority; while taking care of the education of children, "the second aim of marriage," was not far behind.[28] There was now a new demand for her to be more sexually active as well, even if "her desires do not match men's rhythms." In spite of this "fact," the new Catholic woman was expected to put in "a bit of grace and tenderness, which is the salt that women have to add to this condiment often too strong for [their] sensibility." The reasoning behind the encouragement of these efforts, these sexual sacrifices, was to help her husband – who, unlike his wife, was moved by his instincts – to never "feel defrauded and vanquished" from "not having [the] physical conquest of his wife. And here is the danger."[29] Sex, at least in some contexts, was no longer an outright sin. Even if these opinions are a far cry from the recognition of women's rights and freedoms as they are understood in post-feminist societies, it is obvious that the asexual, post-war Spanish wife and mother was being replaced by a more intelligent, moderately carnal "modern" woman.

This was official morality. Popular morality was significantly different and featured far greater nuances as well as social and regional differences. Overall, gender relations remained much the same as they had been long before Francoism, and were based on discrimination against women. The same sayings and "old truths" were used and the same socially constrained expectations applied. These values clearly had rural roots – they were "traditional."[30] This tradition meant that most families were very authoritarian, with the father expected to be at the top of the pecking order while mothers were to be in charge of daily discipline through mediation with the father. Fathers were most often feared and distant. The formal *usted* for "you" instead of the familiar form, *tú*, was frequently employed by children when addressing their parents. At the table, the patriarch was served first and often received the best food.[31] Physical punishment was considered normal. This "traditional" family was remarkably similar on all sides of the political and geographic spectrum. As many female left-wing militants recalled, their fathers and their own politicized husbands were little dictators at home while they were often revolutionaries or progressive individuals in the streets.[32]

Gender discrimination started in childhood and was consolidated at puberty. In general terms, the poorer the family the more children it had (children were the social security of the poor) and as a rule only girls were obliged to work in the house at an early age and to take care of younger siblings. Boys garnered their "manhood" when they returned from military service. It was often said that only then were they allowed to grow a moustache or smoke in front of their fathers. Girls remained under constant supervision until they were married; even when they became engaged, they were still chaperoned by a family member. When married, they became second to their husbands, a discrimination that did not end in the event of widowhood. It was accepted that a widower needed a new wife, but for a widow to remarry, especially if she had children, was much less acceptable. Widowed women, far more frequently than men, were often the object of gossip. Since emotional contact between parents and children was limited, and the stronger ties were usually between the mother and the children, it is not surprising that the possibility of ending up with a stepmother or a stepfather was dreaded.[33]

The evolution of family values, practices, and structures in Franco's Spain moved toward homogeneity and the suppression of non-Catholic customs. Certainly this was true of the attitudes toward the frequent cohabitation of unmarried couples that occurred in the rural areas of Galicia, Murcia, and Andalusia, and in marginal urban areas.[34] Before the war, it was not uncommon among the poor in these areas to elope and or to marry months or years after a couple already had several children. This tradition explains why close to 8 percent of all children born in Malaga province in 1931 were born out of wedlock. As the province came under the control of Francoist troops in February 1937, the Church and the state worked quickly and closely to impose their common moral values on those who exhibited "anti-Catholic lives." The following year, Church authorities reported marrying 712 couples who had been living together; they also baptized 417 adults and 579 children.

Parish priests helped, providing government authorities with lists and addresses of people who failed to act in a proper manner. This eventually changed people's behavior. Eloping, for example, continued, but a proper church wedding soon followed and was strictly enforced by the regime's authorities. Another survey conducted in Malaga in 1942 revealed that 254 of 832 newly married couples already had children before marriage. Thirty years later, however, a study carried out by a sociological institute associated with the Catholic Church demonstrated that, even though most people in the province did not regularly attend mass, the sexual mores of the majority, particularly regarding marriage, were now more conservative than they had been in the post-war period.[35] State pressure, migration, and modernization led to the growing tendency toward formal marriage and toward people living in smaller, nuclear family arrangements. This was also true for the rest of Spain, where couples now tended to have "normal" religious weddings before cohabiting, and it became increasingly common for the firstborn to arrive no sooner than nine months after a marriage. It must be stressed, however, that this was not only the case in Spain but was also reflected in trans-continental changes of attitude. As has been observed for the United Kingdom, "so many people have never married so elaborately and as conventionally as they did in the 1950s and 1960s."[36] These changes affected rural families too, as they were adopting new familial mores as well and tended to have similar numbers of children to their urban counterparts.[37]

State-imposed morality clearly had an impact in working-class and immigrant neighborhoods where, for example, the pre-war anarchist tradition of living as faithful but unmarried partners (*compañeros*) was eradicated and substituted by the Catholic formula. A 1958 study in Madrid of the Barrio de Nuestra Señora de la Paz, also known as Pacífico, demonstrated that the forced moral and sexual normalization of the neighborhood that followed the Civil War resulted in a decline in the number of children born out of wedlock from nearly 11.2 percent in 1940 to a mere 0.4 percent in 1950. At the same time, the number of people baptized increased and the average age of baptism was reduced. In 1940, 23.3 percent of all those baptized were more than a year old, while in 1950 barely 3.5 percent of those initiated were older than 1.[38] Catholic morality, rituals and festivities, at least in their public manifestations, had been restored among the faithful and imposed on the rest.

One important rite of passage for any Spanish child was his or her first communion. Poor people made enormous financial sacrifices to make sure their child shone on that day, and dress was crucial for both girls and boys. Children were commonly dressed in traditional costumes: that of a nun or a princess/bride in the case of girls and that of a sailor or a navy officer with plenty of insignia for boys. Most families bought or had the costumes made because having the clothes on loan would have been seen as a form of charity and thus demeaning. First communions took place in May. After the ceremony, the children visited relatives and friends to collect money and to receive compliments on their attire, attire they were forced to wear all day.

In poor neighborhoods, lunch often took place in a tavern – houses were too small to accommodate guests – a habit scorned by priests but widely practiced by parents.[39]

The penetration of the official moral message and practices was, however, not as uniform or as deep as it was claimed at the time. The priests and missionaries who ministered to working-class neighborhoods recognized that these areas were small worlds unto themselves, with their own codes and traditions that did not necessarily fit the official Catholic vision. Furthermore, anti-clericalism often ran high. Most people's values were encapsulated by the common language and "wisdom" of their community. Sayings and the use of particular expressions conveyed their highly restrictive, unequal, harsh, and often cruel sense of morality, and this usually pointed to the repression of women and the punishment of unusual behavior. For example, contrary to Catholic teachings, male dalliance was by and large tolerated while female promiscuity resulted in the label of "slut" with all the stigma this tag implied. Spain was a "macho" society in which women who had too much power or freedom were said to have "put their feet outside the dish"; a woman was not supposed to go to marriage "already started," while a man "once washed" was "like new."[40] Against Christian teachings of forgiveness, homosexuals were routinely ridiculed and, until very recently, it was considered fully acceptable and amusing, even on Spanish television, to mock and ill-treat anyone who was attracted to the same sex.[41]

Discrepancies between official morals and people's beliefs were not limited to words. As only religious marriages were now recognized (the Francoists declared republican civil marriages and divorces void, a policy that created thousands of illegitimate children overnight), everybody who married did so in a church but, of course, when things went wrong, many people arranged to live their lives outside official norms, more by force of circumstance than by design. For example, in Nuestra Señora de la Paz in 1958, a poll of 2,000 people showed that 55 couples were living in an "irregular" situation, 28 people were de facto divorcees, 31 were single mothers, 49 had been involved in "dubious" moral or sexual behavior, and 14 lived a life of "free" conduct.[42]

The city and countryside shared the evolution of sexual mores. Peasants may have been taking their moral and gender values to the cities, but these were not very different from those that already existed there. In both rural and urban areas, the primary rule was the prohibition of sexual relations before or outside of marriage, a norm severely imposed on women. The preservation of female virginity was crucial for two reasons: first, in case the engagement was broken and second, as a proof of a woman's capacity for sexual restraint. A woman who gave herself to her fiancé risked abandonment and a reputation for "looseness" which would seriously restrict her prospects of marriage. If a woman got this reputation she may have to settle for a less desirable partner, a widower with children or a man with social or physical disabilities.[43]

The issues around marriage were in part connected to a broader problem: the relationship between social norms and desire. In courtship, nothing was more complicated than the continual tension between both partners' desire for sexual fulfillment and their fear of being cheated at the game. The male's role was to probe the character of his wife-to-be; the woman's role was to restrain her potential mate without being indifferent, cold, or cruel for fear he might break his vows.[44] This dynamic was further complicated by the sexual and emotional outlets men had available to them, either by resorting to prostitutes or by seeking a second fiancée. These fiancées were referred to as "girlfriends to have fun with," *novia para divertirse*, as opposite to the formal fiancée, or *novia para casarse* (to marry). These were tangled emotions and relations and, if a woman became pregnant, the crucial question became how to resolve the situation without loss of honor to any of the families involved. When it was understood that the woman's moral standing was salvageable the man most often married her, whether he wished to or not. It is telling that when a marriage transpired in this fashion it was commonly known as "paying her," obviously referring to what the man had taken, a woman's virginity and reputation. For women, especially poor ones, a good reputation was their main asset, and losing it meant ruining their lives. As A.D.G., a woman who grew up in Basauri (Basque country) recalled, her mother used to tell her during the post-war period, "If something happens to you, I chase you from the house!" "Something" meant a pregnancy or a sexual scandal. A.D.G. remembered a very young neighbor "perhaps 14 or 15" who was thrown out of her home by her parents and forced to live in distant Valladolid. The father of her child refused to marry her. "This was very common back then."[45]

The law contemplated punitive measures for a man who obtained sexual favors from a woman of good reputation by misleading her regarding his civil status or intentions. But these provisions were exceedingly difficult to enforce as it was up to the woman to prove the transgression, putting the man at an advantage. In any case, a denunciation could backfire and have terrible consequences for her. Class also played a crucial role here. Illiterate and poor women were most at risk of becoming abandoned, marginalized single mothers. The social discrimination practiced against single mothers was extended to their offspring. A man's refusal to recognize his paternity – or as people used to say "give the child his family name" – rendered these children illegitimate and discriminated against when it came to inheritance rights. In this aspect, and in other matters regarding sexual mores and legal discrimination against women, Franco's Spain was not very different from most European countries.

The tension between duty and desire was painful and its outcomes were too often tragic. What each wanted and what they expected were very often in conflict, and this was certainly true of sexual expectations. While men wanted to have sex with women, and to be a ladies' man was more a cause for jealousy than for shame, they expected their fiancées and wives to be chaste until the moment (not before and not afterwards) they went to bed with them, when suddenly they should transform themselves into sexual beings and adopt their man's fantasies.[46] It was both an unrealistic and a perturbing game, and many men, frustrated by it, had recourse to prostitutes. For women, of course, no similar activities were acceptable.

In many respects, the attitude of men towards prostitutes reflected the misery and sexual repression of both sexes during the Franco years.[47] Prostitution became technically illegal in 1956, but it was widely tolerated.[48] In a few instances, the realities of the lives of prostitutes and how they were perceived by men were studied, but most often from a strictly moral point of view.[49] It was only in the 1970s that the issue was studied in a more systematic and objective way. In a 1974 book based on interviews with Spanish prostitutes and their customers, many of the women working in the profession said that prior to becoming prostitutes they had been made pregnant by either an employer or a fiancé and were then unceremoniously abandoned. Poor, uneducated, and alone in a large city, often with a baby to care for, prostitution became their means of survival. On the other hand, most of their customers saw prostitutes as objects to be used as "physical relief" until marriage. More disturbingly, many men who were interviewed stated that they saw prostitution as a way to "get even" with women.[50]

It could safely be argued that the evolution of both social mores and family values lagged well behind economic progress, and that the burden of those traditional values continued to rest primarily on the shoulders of women. But there were clear signs of change. Already in 1959, a report on the sociology of Spanish families indicated that there was an ongoing evolution of Spanish morality. As examples, the report cited the erosion of the role of the family in matters of education, an increase in instances of "romantic" love, greater parity between spouses regarding their role in their children's education, the lowered birth rates for families, an increase in the presence of women in the labor market, and finally, a progression toward equality in the level of education between spouses.[51] The previously explained attempts to create a new Catholic, middle-class woman and a new dynamic in married couples were also a manifestation of those changes. Eventually, this slow-paced evolution was reflected in law.[52] However, any legal reform, especially the incorporation of women into officially recognized jobs, had to run against previous legislation passed by the regime in 1938 and again in 1956 that had curtailed women's legal labor rights by withholding family allowances when a mother worked.[53] Needless to say, for peasant women, who *always* had worked in the fields, regardless what the law said, the whole debate was completely alien.

These cultural changes also manifested themselves in unforeseen areas. Some themes, previously ignored in Spain, started to be publicly discussed. For example, probably the first article published on domestic violence against women was a report that appeared in the monarchist (and pro-Franco) newspaper *ABC* on November 9, 1953. Most tellingly, the regime's official censor had retained the article for several months. The author, a female lawyer, Mercedes Formica, was well connected to the regime. She denounced the frequent ill-treatment of married women and the legal discrimination they suffered. She did not say so, but this situation was in part a result of the derogation of republican laws. The article created a maelstrom of response, and hundreds of letters were sent to the newspaper, becoming the focus of the closest thing to a public debate on the family yet witnessed in Franco's Spain. As a result, lawyers, all of them men, participated in a sort of informal poll organized by *ABC* on what and how to reform. Not surprisingly, the interventions were generally patronizing. Nevertheless, the women's branch of the Falange, Sección Femenina, supported Formica, and she obtained a meeting with a seemingly sympathetic dictator.[54]

The workings of Francoism, however, when reforms were at issue, were always slow, and notorious for a half-hearted approach. In a 1958 reform of the Civil Code the property rights of women were extended, as were their judicial rights, such as the right to witness wills. Women's labor rights were extended in 1961. That year, the notorious article of the Penal Code that excluded men from severe punishment in honor killings was finally abolished. This article, reintroduced into Spanish law by the regime in 1944, had condoned the murder of a wife or daughter if they were surprised in an act of "flagrant adultery." In 1961 as well, the crime of adultery was extended to include men, albeit punishment was less severe for men than for women. In 1972 single, adult women finally gained the right to leave their home without their parents' consent before the age of 25. Previously, they had only been allowed to leave in order to marry or to become a nun.[55] Adultery wasn't finally decriminalized until 1978, once democracy had been restored. Full legal equality between sexes was not achieved until 1981, six years after the dictator's death.

Becoming Consumers

After the dreadful years of autarky, Spaniards lagged behind other European countries in three essential aspects of life: what they ate, what they owned, and what they bought. It was not until the early 1960s that all three facets took a decisively modern turn when Spain's consumer patterns followed the path that west European societies had begun to pursue some 15 years earlier. Having enough to eat was the first indicator of progress, but once this basic need was better satisfied, Spaniards came to spend less on food and more on their homes and other non-essential personal items. The portion of the country's GDP dedicated to food consumption declined from 35.25 percent in 1954 to 28.76 percent in 1962, and to 24.14 percent in 1975.[56] At the beginning of the 1960s, notwithstanding significant regional and local disparities in diet and income, residents of most villages and neighborhoods in Spain consumed daily meals that were far superior to the nutritional regimes they or their parents experienced in the years after the war. At the same time, however, their meals were strikingly similar to those their grandparents had shared at the beginning of the century, featuring a reliance on heavy fats and legumes, and a meager supply of fresh produce and high-quality proteins. Matters of food, eating well, and making sure that children and guests received ample food at home were a near-obsession at many family tables, which were now packed with food that was devoured at each meal. Even as food consumption declined relative to available income, it doubled in absolute terms from 1958 to 1975.

The distribution of family spending was a product of both family income and culture. In 1964, Spanish families spent 50.2 percent of their total income on food, by far the highest proportion among Western nations. The closest nation to this percentage was Italy at 46.9 percent, while the OECD average was approximately 40 percent. In 1972, Spaniards devoted 44 percent of their family budget to food, still higher than other Western countries, but the gap was closing. As the most substantial item in a family budget, the question of food, formerly dictated by survival, was now being diverted to buy previously unattainable products. This accounts, in part, for the increase in the diet of the amount of animal proteins, mostly meat.[57] While meat and fish consumption experienced the largest increases, "luxury" items such as coffee, tea, and alcoholic beverages saw significant increases as well. At the same time, bread consumption, the staple of the poor in the past, declined, along with other traditional foods including potatoes and legumes.[58] Lower-, middle- and upper-class families still maintained different consumer patterns in the early 1970s, a fact that can be explained in cultural and historical terms, not simply as a function of income. Poorer people still ate more bread and potatoes than rich ones; they ate almost the same proportion of fish and meat, but the poor frequented bars and restaurants less often. Certainly it was cheaper to eat at home, where people could be more confident of the quality and preparation of the food they ate, an aspect never overlooked by those who had suffered for decades from scarcity and food adulteration.

Ordinary Spaniards were tasting "prosperity" in the 1960s. Intellectuals, however, were asking themselves where Spanish society was going. In particular, they wondered how much of a consumer-driven, classically developed Western capitalist nation Spain had become. At the root of this question was not only a moral, left-wing concern about people's materialistic values, but also the depressing perspective that consumerism was buying people's consciousness and rendering the dictatorship unassailable and, even worse, popular. Frighteningly, all available data pointed to positive, if qualified, answers to these ultimately depressing questions. Yes, Spain was, or was about to become, a consumer society, and this revolution, because this is the word that was used to define what had happened, took place in the second half of the decade; and yes, Franco's prestige was running very high (though its decline would soon begin, as explained in chapter 5). And there were, for the first time in Spanish history, plenty of consumer goods in the streets and in people's homes. This expansion of consumerism had been possible because of the massive participation of the urban working class and the rural middle class, a fact that, as a left-wing intellectual generously conceded, was not "necessarily negative or something to fight against."[59]

Moral and ideological considerations aside, official data from the period confirm that the improvement had started to affect those who had, until then, been "less provided for," such as small and medium-sized farmers, and, particularly, workers.[60] There were three main keys to this consumer revolution among the poor. From 1964 until the severe recession that marked the end of the economic miracle in 1974, the average annual increase of private consumption was 5.7 percent, which was very similar to the 6 percent increase in per capita income for the same period. The second element was that the increase in income lagged behind that of productivity until the early 1970s. The third key, often neglected, was that workers worked their way out of poverty often by starting to toil while very young without having completed their education. Literally every consumer good in a humble house was paid for by years of education missed. Consumerism for the poor carried this invisible mortgage.

Any increases in the national economy rested in good measure on people's work (or, rather, exploitation), on the privations they accepted, and on their purchasing power; but not on the state's role. The state remained timid and unable to redistribute income and services across the social and regional chessboard. Private consumption as a proportion of GDP (or, if you prefer, state inhibition and tax relief for the rich) in that period was consistently higher in Spain than in all other Western nations. For example, in 1964 it was at 69.8 percent of GDP in Spain, while the United Kingdom was next with 64.7 percent and the lowest nation was Japan, traditionally an export- and savings-oriented economy, at only 52.1 percent. In 1969, private consumption in Spain still amounted to 68.6 percent of GDP; Italy was second at 63.5 percent, and Japan, predictably, remained last with 51.3 percent. Finally, in 1972, Spain still topped the list with 66.3 percent of GDP; Italy was second again with 64.6 percent and Japan last with 52 percent.[61] The pocketbooks, hard work, and missed opportunities of ordinary Spaniards, not the state or the taxes of the affluent, were once again footing the bill for change and modernity.

In the 1960s Spaniards were spending their money more and more on non-essential items. In this newborn consumer society, people first began to invest in their homes before having their "needs" heavily influenced by the nearly simultaneous introduction of television and visual advertising campaigns. Television was one of the star selling products: in 1960, only 1 percent of families owned a television set, six years later this had risen to 32 percent (in France the figure rose from 13 percent to 47 percent). People were also buying refrigerators for the first time: in 1960 only 19 percent of

Spanish homes had one, a figure that climbed to 36 percent in 1966 (while in France the figure rose from 24 to 42 percent). Washing machines, another large purchase for families, were increasingly in demand, and they could be found in 19 percent of Spanish homes in 1960 compared to 36 percent in 1966 (in France in the same period this figure rose from 24 to 42 percent of households).[62]

Another dramatic change was incorporated into the daily lives of ordinary Spaniards in the second half of the 1960s. It was called private transport, or, more specifically, scooters and cars. Workers began to travel to work on scooters, particularly the reliable Vespa, rather than bicycles. These were also the family vehicle. In the days when there was a more casual attitude to road safety, a Vespa could acrobatically accommodate up to five members of a family.[63] In spite of this, those who could afford them purchased automobiles. Car ownership in Spain went from 4 percent of all households in 1960 to 35 percent in 1971 (while France moved from 35 to 60 percent in the same period). The number of cars grew a staggering 290 percent between 1964 and 1971; in the same period, the number in France grew by 49 percent, in Italy by 30 percent, in Germany by 62 percent, and in the UK by 40 percent.[64] The mythical, uncomfortable, and underpowered Citröen 2CV, the Renault 4, and, of course, the incomparable Spanish-made Seat 600, launched in 1957, soon became the symbols of success for those who owned them. Though unsafe, unreliable and overcrowded, they were celebrated in songs and films as the symbols of the new-found happiness one experienced while living in sunny, smiling Spain.[65]

Consumerism came hand in hand with advertising. As had already happened in other European countries, large international advertising companies arrived in Spain in the mid-1960s, and they brought with them their capacity to inflame the consumer desires of increasingly better-off Spaniards.[66] By the end of the decade, the cost of advertising was equal to 1.3 percent of national income.[67] The most effective marketing tool available at the time was the state-run television monopoly that by 1968 had already made more than 1,400 million pesetas from broadcasting commercials. For advertising firms this was money well spent even if the number of television sets in Spain numbered just under 4 million at the time and there were several provinces where television ownership was barely at 20 percent of the total population. Television still offered better opportunities than the printed press because, before the late 1960s, not even a quarter of adults read a newspaper daily.

While reflecting the changing nature of Spanish consumer society, commercials still targeted a public with limited disposable income and promoted items they could afford: food products, drinks, appliances, and other household items. Advertisements for cars, vacations, and bank services, the staples of today's commercials, ware rare. What has not changed are the basic values and instincts of consumers, and their use in commercials, predictably focused – then and today, in Spain and elsewhere – on male versus female tensions, in which men impose control over others while seeking the conquest of women, while women behave with either submission or admiration toward men, or maternally toward their offspring and toward adult males.[68]

With advertising came the concept of "youth culture." While parents were busy eating more, buying new apartments or repairing them, and purchasing appliances, scooters, and cars, young people were developing their own consumer patterns and seemingly radical new habits, from what they drank to the music they listened to or the length of their hair. These tendencies were clearly influenced by publicity and were imitations of what they saw on television and in the movies: the trendy tastes of their Western counterparts. A 1971 study of the purchasing habits of young people demonstrated these new trends and, at the same time, the clear differences that existed between the genders.[69] Music, of course, was a sign of the changing times and in Spain, like everywhere in the Western world, this created a huge and noisy gap between parents and their children as 56 percent of youngsters now owned a record player and 82 percent owned a transistor radio. Young people were listening to records in English, a language that very few understood, almost no one spoke, and the aesthetics of the new pop music had little in common with the tastes of the post-war generation of Spaniards, who still preferred flamenco-inspired music (canción española). Another significant development was the increase in reading, especially by young people. Even if Spaniards read little in comparison with other Europeans, at least 49 percent of young people said in 1971 they had purchased a book, mostly novels, in the previous three months. Philosophy, psychology and sociology were collectively placed a distant second on the list.

Consumerism also affected gender values and interactions. The previously mentioned 1971 study revealed that, for example, 63 percent of men and 44 percent of women now smoked. For women, this was a new habit that very few of their mothers had engaged in. This was particularly true of women with peasant or working-class roots, since smoking among women had been considered to be a sign of either the preserve of the higher classes or a sign of vice. Modernity now demanded that women smoke. And men were now smoking more "blonde," American-style cigarettes than their fathers had, abandoning the strong taste of "dark" local tobacco. Young men, like their fathers, drank alcohol, mostly beer and wine, more often than women: 77 percent and 61 percent respectively. Moreover, it was now socially acceptable for young women to drink publicly, even in the previous bastions of male solitude, taverns and coffee shops. At the same time, young women embraced new hygienic habits and products more enthusiastically than their male counterparts: 99 percent of women said they used toothpaste, for example, a product not at all associated with traditional rural Spain; by comparison, toothpaste was used by 94 percent of Spanish men, or so they said. This difference did not escape advertising firms. A commercial ran for several years in the early 1970s portraying a young woman telling her fiancé: "Pepe, I love you, but if you use Colgate I shall love you more." Obviously, from that moment on, Pepe's breath was on the mend. The transforming effects of consumerism in this matter were laudable given that, in a rather warm country, only 65 percent of men deemed it necessary to use deodorant (while 91 percent of women interviewed for the 1971 said that they used it).

As the dictatorship entered its final years, Spain had become a consumer society where social disparities in terms of durable consumer goods had decreased but significant regional differences still existed. When analyzing income and household equipment in 1969, the Spanish Statistics Institute established rankings of regions by levels of well-being. The group ranked first, or best, included only the city of Madrid; the group ranked second was made up of the Basque provinces and Navarre; and in the third and fourth groups were all the Catalan provinces, Saragossa, and Huesca. The last four groups included most of the country: the south and the northwest (all of Andalusia, Extremadura, Galicia, and the provinces of southern Castile and Murcia). The have-not provinces had advanced at a faster rate than the privileged ones, but the regional differences were still stark.[70] Part of the explanation for this resides in the fact that unequal distribution of wealth was clearly more prevalent in the poorer provinces.[71] This phenomenon could also help to explain the fact that, in 1970, Spaniards ate approximately 300 calories less per capita than their counterparts in other Western countries. In any case, compared with the 1940s and 1950s Spaniards had "never had it so good," and some of the worst damage caused by autarky and lack of public investment had been repaired. The number of houses built, for example, had improved after decades of chronic underperformance, finally surpassing Germany, the United Kingdom, and Italy in 1971, though it was still well behind France and Holland.

The regime, of course, took credit for these improvements, appropriating the contribution of suffering and hard work of ordinary people and presenting it as a national achievement, brought about only because of Franco's Peace. It was a misrepresentation of reality that ignored the serious social shortcomings barely hidden behind this image of Spain's modern European consumer society. For example, the amount of newspaper consumed in kilos per capita in Spain – then a measure of culture rather than a sign of waste and pollution – remained abysmally lower than the amount recorded in all other European nations. This is not surprising for a country where more than 25 percent of children failed to graduate from elementary school, but what is disturbing is that the per capita newspaper consumption in 1971 was lower than it had been in 1968.[72]

On the whole, in the early 1970s the Spanish economy was still not able to feed, dress, house, or educate its citizens, particularly the poorer ones, to the same level as its European counterparts. This was a paradox for an economic model that was disproportionately based on private consumption, and a paradox with a nasty surprise in store. When the 1974 economic crisis hit Spain, it caused growing unemployment (worsened by the return of migrants from Europe) which led to drastic cuts in family spending, which further depressed the economy. The first and primary victims of the meltdown were the poorest and the least educated – unskilled laborers, women, and emigrants – who, after decades of extreme hardship, had ever so briefly glimpsed the prosperity the rest of Europe had known for more than 25 years. Consumerism was a just-tasted, sweet fruit that the hardworking and poor people of Spain watched vanishing in the last two years of the dictatorship.

Leisure

The post-war leisure habits of ordinary people continued in much the same way as they had in pre-war Spain.[73] Most activities were public in nature, and going to the movies was the first choice of most people (attendance was among the highest in the world, second only to the USA in 1947, and this pattern remained until the 1970s and the "triumph" of television).[74] Movies were the principal form of family diversion even if families did not necessarily attend the cinema together.[75] People flocked en masse to see American movies about cowboys, gangsters, and pirates, and the decision about what film to see was not based on who the director was (because almost no one knew what a director did), but on which stars were featured. Hollywood movies rather than nationally produced films were preferred, and Hollywood stars, their voices dubbed by local actors, were as famous in the smallest villages of Spain as they were on the streets of New York City.

There was also a small local film industry that featured a "Spanish" brand of movie and a star system of its own. The subjects were generally folkloric, often presenting supposedly Andalusian characters, music, and landscapes as part of their stories. Like Bollywood films, the themes and outcomes of these movies were entirely predictable: stories about star-crossed lovers who longed to be married, a circumstance that could only mean eternal happiness.[76] While the lovers waited to be married, the actors sang and sometimes danced while misguided villains attempted to wreck the party. The approach to plot was highly moralistic and conservative, portraying situations that were more often than not highly unrealistic. Politics and social conflict were avoided. A handful of political and historical films were produced, but their successes generally lagged far behind the appeal of comedies and dramas. Censorship helped frame the moral content of movies by erasing kisses and altering anything remotely "inappropriate." Equivocal situations or dialogue were manipulated – dubbing was an excellent tool for this – to conform to the strictest Catholic tenets. Later, in the 1970s, it was not uncommon for movies produced in Spain to have versions: one, spicier, for export, and a "decent" one for internal distribution.

Frequenting taverns and coffee shops was another public pastime, but this was primarily an adult and male activity. Decent women, especially if they were middle- or upper-class, could attend tearooms or special sections of cafeterias reserved for them, but they never went alone and never went with strangers. In taverns, men played cards or dominoes and talked while they drank. Different hours of the day had different drinks associated with them. Mornings featured coffee mixed with brandy, although workers often drank "eau de vie" (*aguardiente*) to start a hard day; for the rest of the day cheap wines and beers were the preference. If suppertime arrived and a man was not yet home, women would refrain from looking for him in a drinking establishment as this would shame the man in front of his peers by insinuating submission to his wife and her bad temper. Women either waited at home or sent a child with a message, an option deemed appropriate provided it was not repeated on a regular basis. Football matches, which became increasingly popular, and bullfights – which were more expensive and held less often than football events – were other examples of leisure activities that were a male stronghold where women were not generally welcome. When television arrived, it often came first to the neighborhood tavern, and men and children went there to watch their favorite teams and bullfighters in these noisy smoke-filled premises.

When young people wanted to mix with the opposite gender, options were few and often complex. A boy could try to take his girlfriend to the movies, but she would have to be chaperoned and in some cases she could go only if they were engaged.[77] If they were not engaged, it was not uncommon for a boy to invite a girl to the movies, pay for her and her friend's tickets, not enter the theater with them, and wait outside for the movie to end. If he did go into to see the show, he sat among his male friends but far away from the girl, because any young woman who sat next to a male who was not a relative would be considered "loose." If a man sat too close to a young woman, she was expected to stop him and denounce his advances. When married couples went to the movies they would seat themselves so that no male stranger was next to or even close to the wife.

It was imagined that many fearful things might happen in the darkness of the movie theater, and the cinema's employees were charged with monitoring it. It was not uncommon for notices to flash across the screen, alerting people to immoral behavior; sometimes these notices announced that people in row X were behaving improperly and warned that the next notice would point out their seat numbers. In exceptional cases men, full of indignation, had been known to stand up in the middle of a movie to denounce or even physically attack "immoral" people. If they were lucky the culprits would escape under the cover of darkness. All the same, in every neighborhood cinema such and such a corner was known to be better for physical contact than the rest of the theater, and it was widely assumed that people who were seated there had other things on their minds than simply watching the movie. This, of course, had moral implications for any woman who, for whatever reason, was seen there.

The two major exceptions to this limited gender interaction were throwing a party, which was bound to be supervised by older relatives and to feature morally acceptable types of dancing, or going for a walk, as long as the girl was not alone.[78] Since very few people had record players or records before the 1960s, post-war house parties required the hiring of a guitar and a good singer to enliven the evening. On these occasions young men drank alcohol while women were expected to abstain. Walking was the other, more intimate, option, but it also required prudence, for promenading in a secluded area or in the dark again had serious moral consequences for a young woman's reputation.

The greatest change in leisure-time activity in the post-war period was the transition from public-sphere activities to private ones as people moved from the streets to their living rooms. Radio was crucial in this transition because it helped to set new domestic patterns. Families would huddle together to listen to the same program, and as a result they would have common topics for conversation. The new "need" to listen to a specific show would lead people to change their daily habits, to cut some activities short and to withdraw to their homes more regularly. In many homes this led to the appearance of the living room, a special area in which people sat comfortably for long periods of time. This, of course, was only possible in larger homes. The majority of less well-off people continued to sit at their dining tables on stiff chairs, listening to the radio, often while eating, in the same way in which they would later watch television.

It could be argued that the spread of manufactured home entertainment in Spain started with the arrival of Latin American radio showmen in the late 1940s, who introduced an instant sensation: radio soap operas. Initially, the censors distrusted these convoluted stories where forbidden love and secret, even illegitimate, children, sometimes appeared. The regime, however, soon understood that soap operas offered an escape from reality and that their stories consistently ended with the triumph of traditional values; so, not by accident, the first serial ever produced in Spain had a strong Catholic theme: *La canción de Bernadette* (*The Song of Bernadette*).[79] This was the story of poor Bernadette Soubirous, a young girl tormented by an evil priest who was jealous because the Virgin appeared to her and not to him.[80] These things happen. Her terrible torment made millions cry (and not only in Spain – a filmed version, made by Henry King in 1943, won an Oscar). Bernadette's never-ending plight became astonishingly important to Spaniards. This series was such a success that it was broadcast three times.

Just as they had in nations across the Atlantic and in Europe, companies soon discovered that sponsoring these radio programs was an excellent way of promoting their products. Jingles praising consumer products at the beginning and end of broadcasts became standard fare. This was a new leap for mass consumerism: the simultaneous promotion of a single product across the country. Culturally, this meant unified tastes, attitudes, and expectations while reinforcing the tendency toward replacing local buyers with "national consumers." In fact, the addictive and ever-increasing habit of listening to the radio – in 1955 there were more than 2.7 million radios in Spain, giving it one of the highest per capita ratios in Europe – offered the dictatorship exciting new channels for propaganda: Radio Nacional de España, founded by the rebels during the war, and a number of local stations belonging to the Falange.

The Church also embraced broadcasting and created a number of its own small radio stations. They would eventually be unified in 1965 under the name COPE, a network that still exists today. A product of this ecclesiastic modernity was that post-war Spain had its own brand of radio preachers (the most famous of them probably being the 1950s far-right preacher Father Venancio Marcos) and several programs that advised women how to survive the challenges of combining family and the changing world.[81] Far and away the most famous of these domestic counseling programs was *Elena Francis*, which started in 1948 and survived until well after the return of democracy. Mrs. Francis did not exist; she had a woman's voice, but her advice to women was the creation of a predominantly male team that encouraged women to stand by their men, to suffer their faults and affairs in silence, and to pray to God.

This mix of modernity and leisure had further ramifications. It helped to develop in the Spanish people a new image of themselves as a group, and a new concept of their duties to each other. Radio brought cities and villages, poor and rich, Andalusians and Basques closer together, and most people enjoyed and accepted the experience. What it meant to be a Spaniard was being redefined and simplified. The events of a catastrophic flood in Valencia in 1957, for example, were transmitted by radio, and this helped jump-start a huge national campaign of solidarity to help those affected. Similarly, radio stations competed with each other's charity campaigns, especially at Christmas, in which broadcasters and artists "connected" with ordinary people to create a "feel-good," national and Catholic, identity. Another "everything is possible" sensation was produced when music and talent-spotting competitions were broadcast, and for the first time all Spaniards could listen to the same songs simultaneously, recognize voices, and follow the thrilling story of the more or less ephemeral fame of young artists and participants in variety shows. Next to music, perhaps no radio program reinforced the idea of a national community more than soccer matches, beginning with those broadcast in the 1940s for the national league and Franco's Cup and then, after international isolation had been eased in the 1950s, for international competitions. Since the national soccer team was a perennial under-achiever, Real Madrid's impressive string of victories in Europe, and particularly the five European Champions cups won between 1955 and 1960, broadcast on radio, became a symbol of Francoist Spain's international success.[82]

And then it happened. On February 15, 1959, Barcelona FC hosted its traditional, bitter rival, Real Madrid, and all of Spain held its breath. Passions were old but this time they brought a great novelty: this match was the first ever broadcast on television in Spain. At the time, it was said that television sets, an extremely scarce commodity, sold for the astronomical price of 2,000 pesetas, the equivalent of 130 euros. An exotic and expensive product, the sale of televisions had begun in Madrid in 1956. Five years later, the government abolished the luxury tax on televisions and their numbers started to rise, albeit modestly by international standards, from barely 600 sets in 1956 to 2,125,000 in 1966. Then, in the next four years their numbers doubled again. By 1970, 40 percent of all Spanish families owned a television set.[83]

Along with these televisions came the social impact this flood of them implied. From the mid-1960s on, people not only watched television, they talked about television and they started to shop based on what they saw and heard. In fact, to an even greater degree than the introduction of the radio two decades earlier, television helped change the way people interacted in both public and private spaces. Spain has a well-deserved, if somewhat exaggerated reputation for having a lively street life in its cities and villages. With the arrival of television, for the first time millions of people went home at the same time to watch their favorite programs. Children had their own treasured programs and, when they ended, the beginning of an adult show marked their bedtime.[84] Television now dictated to parents when their children should retire and when a couple was to enjoy private time, and, at this stage at least, it reinforced the concept and prescribed the practice of the nuclear family.

Watching television both reflected and changed the values and practices of society. According to a 1969 study, men watched more than women, younger people more than older ones, and better-educated Spaniards watched more than school dropouts and those who were illiterate.[85] The explanations for these trends are, of course, simple: the poor had less money to buy televisions, the values of older people didn't always match those of the programs they saw on the screen, and women worked longer hours, at home and at their day jobs (if they had one), than men, who, after work and at weekends, relaxed and watched television while their wives cooked, cleaned, and took care of the children. In any case, with television, men now had a greater motive to stay at home and less reason to patronize the neighborhood tavern, while women now paid fewer visits their friends and relatives. On Sundays, men watched the evening football match at home while enjoying a drink. Their wives may have watched as well, peaking at the screen while cooking supper, slowly breaking the convention that women and sport did not mix. Not long afterwards they too would go to watch football matches in person.

Television meant more: it guided people to behave in modern ways, presented new lifestyle possibilities and foreign and distant social landscapes and, at the same time, simplified the Spanish cultural heritage. Television was successful not just because it promoted escapism and fantasy. When they watched films or television, people saw their moral values reflected, if not the realities of their daily lives, as stories portrayed rigid familial morality, gender divisions regarding work, the prevalence of men in public and women in private spheres, and the asymmetry in the choice of roles and vocations available to parents and children.[86] Spanish television reinforced these values by producing programs for children and adults that adapted classic, but morally and politically screened, themes from novels and plays, with any disturbing ideas conveniently expunged, and with characters who expressed acceptable conservative values.[87]

Television became a socio-cultural phenomenon at a time when progress and modernity were still exciting. Owning a television and talking about it implied a sense of prestige. In the 1960s, when neighbors, friends, and relatives were invited to watch newly acquired sets, it immediately provoked a "me too" effect. When men at work talked about television, as did women at the market, and children in school, intentionally or not they taunted those without access to it. When richer Spaniards watched and knew about television, poorer citizens could not to wait to find a way to purchase this new symbol of comfort. This perhaps explains why, in 1966, 51 percent of homes in the larger towns had a television set while only 47 percent had a refrigerator.[88] Often, the solution was credit, obtained either directly from a store or through the efforts of a neighbor who, in many working-class areas, acted as a broker and matched reliable, honest people with appliance businesses. In a country where the majority still viewed such transactions from a distinctly Catholic, essentially anti-capitalist perspective, buying on credit now lost its previously dubious reputation not just because "everybody else was doing it" but also because a television set was "for the family," and everybody knew that, with the economy booming, repayment was more likely than default.

Television became part of a bid for a better life, made by people who had lived through very difficult times. It offered symbols of justice that promised better lives to those who watched. Perhaps, as intellectuals declared, it was opium, but for humble people it was optimism. The songs that rang in triumph across the screen, the serials featuring the good defeating the wicked, the talent contests that brought ephemeral fame to young stars, and the prize shows whose highlights were gifts, money, or fabulous new cars to the lucky winners all presented visions of hope. The new Spanish consumerism was best represented by the 1968 program *Un millón para el mejor* (*A Million for the Best One*). The show featured an ordinary person who appeared on television, gave all the right answers, and won the big prize: the mythical 1 million pesetas! Like many other programs, this was merely a copy of shows that were all the rage in Italy or France, themselves copies of American productions. Television also sent a message of security. Good to watch at home on winter nights, it brought viewers the warmth and color of summer beaches and exotic places. It also introduced tacky variety shows, song competitions, and festivals such as Eurovision and Benidorm (a bad copy of Italy's San Remo), and a simple sensation of the pleasure and happiness that, until now, had been the sole right of the elite.[89]

Television was also good for Franco's regime. The dictatorship invested in the consumer image of the New Spain's feel-good nature to promote escapism, and for direct or subtle political propaganda. In 1964 the state opened the large-scale Prado del Rey television studio just outside Madrid. From there it would broadcast both its distorted vision of current events through newscasts and a "brave new world" of material comforts through locally produced and imported American programming. That same year, the government started a network of tele-clubs that brought the illusions of television, and propaganda, to thousands of remote, until then semi-isolated, villages. By 1971, the number of tele-clubs was 4,414.[90]

Aware of its inherent political value, the government retained a monopoly over television by not licensing private channels while steadily injecting its propaganda into broadcast material. Other democratic governments, such as those of Italy and France, were not completely innocent in this regard, but there was no comparison.[91] The greatest concession the regime made to a different version of Spain was in 1964, when it authorized the

Barcelona branch of TVE to begin monthly broadcasts of televised theatrical productions spoken in Catalan.[92] This was as far toward social and cultural inclusiveness as Spanish television was allowed to lean, and was virtually the only reflection of a diversity that was otherwise being consistently suppressed.[93] Some small relief came with the partial lifting of censorship laws in 1966. The new legislation was the brainchild of the ambitious Manuel Fraga, Minister of Propaganda – officially known as the Ministry of Information and Tourism – and it primarily applied to books and, to a far lesser degree, newspapers, but it left television and radio tightly controlled. This was not accidental: most Spaniards rarely read books, and newspapers had very small readerships; only what was broadcast was considered to be important.[94]

In spite of all the controls, changing values and attitudes were slowly allowed to permeate Francoist television, but this never included anything that questioned either the political status quo or the core moral values of the regime. In that sense, television always lagged behind society's general trends. Finally, in 1972, as timid discussion of social matters began to permeate the country, Spaniards were given a weekly television slot with a semblance of political discussion. *Estudio abierto* (*Open Set*), mixed music with lengthy personal interviews that sometimes included carefully controlled debates that nevertheless went closer to the bone than ever before. Modernity and consumerism were also allowed to include a bare minimum of overt sexuality. The success of the program *Un, dos, tres, responda otra vez* (*One, Two, Three, Answer Again*) in 1972 relied not only on a brilliant combination of games, music, jokes, and prizes, but also featured several mini-skirted "secretaries" who helped the host keep the show rolling.[95] On the other hand, series such as *Crónicas de un pueblo* (*Chronicles from a Small Town*), produced in 1971, tapped into a different sort of craving. At a time when Francoism was faltering because the health of the dictator was deteriorating rapidly (television allowed people to see his hands trembling from Parkinson's disease as he delivered his annual Christmas message), as strikes mounted, and opposition to the dictatorship was on the rise, ordinary people watched the stories of an ideal community of peace and stability in a rural setting with nostalgia. Every week Spaniards could witness the comings and goings of a community that reminded them of their villages of origin; the striking difference was, of course, that this village was devoid of the bitter conflicts, misery, and suffering that they had left behind.

New Areas of Confusion

In the late 1960s change was relatively fast and it created social and cultural tensions. A 1972 study of ordinary people's attitudes and values showed that Spanish society was suffering a crisis of direction, and that traditional political and social patterns were faltering while new ones were not yet clearly acceptable to the majority.[96] This was particularly true of gender relations and moral values, but it also applied to the political expectations of the majority, as well as their faith in the capitalist economy, which almost half the population did not trust. The new attitudes were, of course, products of a faulty but expanding education system, greater wealth, and the influence of alternative images offered by tourism, media, and film, but they were also the result of daily experiences of exploitation and injustice. All of this led to a scrutiny of everyday social and family values, which was quite often linked to new political attitudes. The same people who criticized the dictatorship, for example, would notice and start to act on the fact that there was blatant gender discrimination or that moral values were far from being liberal.

Nevertheless, it would be a mistake to split society into two completely separate groups, the content majority and the critical minority. The social confusion of the final years of the dictatorship was difficult to discern because society as a whole, and not only the anti-Francoists, had been evolving, albeit to different degrees, and moving away from the narrow moral and social patterns that the dictatorship had been trying to impose since the end of the war. Foreign influences, television, movies, and material progress explained some of this evolution. There were, however, other reasons, such the growing distaste for injustice, or the influence of social and professional groups – from students to middle-class intellectuals, from progressive priests to opposition trade unionists – that advocated and fought actively for change (see chapter 5). In addition to all of the above, there were other powerful forces which created a socio-cultural dynamic that further eroded traditional morality. One, the influence of tourism, was external; the other, the progressive incorporation of women into paid employment, was internal. Both phenomena brought about or accelerated a wide range of changes in gender values and family relations.

Tourism in Spain was perceived both by the authorities and by ordinary people as a mixed blessing; because it brought wealth, no doubt, but also, for many, unwanted moral values and habits. In 1959, 2.8 million people visited the country as tourists; 10 years later, that number had leapt to 19 million. Tourism was officially hailed as progress. It brought more economic activity to the country, including to some very depressed areas along the Mediterranean coast, and much-needed hard currency, and it was hoped that it would make the dictatorship more acceptable abroad. The regime continually pointed out that Europeans adored Spain and saw how wonderful the country, its culture, its cuisine, and the public peace were.[97] But not everybody shared this rosy vision of the phenomenon, and deep reservations abounded. In particular, the Catholic Church and other traditionalists mistrusted the pernicious influence tourism had on society, seeing in it a selling out of the country's moral values in exchange for hard currency. As the bishop of the Canary Islands put it in 1964, "Just one of our children is worth more than all the indecent tourists of the world combined."[98] Many people agreed. As late as 1972, more than 40 percent of polled people saw the moral downside of so much exposed flesh and relaxed mores on Spanish beaches as something that was "ruining our youth."[99]

Not only were Spain's young people being "ruined" by this moral decay, older Spaniards were adversely affected by the evils of tourism as well. When priests polled tourist-sector workers on their religiosity in 1963 on the Costa Brava in Catalonia, they found to their dismay that many Spaniards were increasingly imitating foreigners' clothing, with women wearing bikinis and men wearing shorts. The priests were also appalled by these workers' lack of interest in religious matters (almost 70 percent of them failed to reply to their questionnaires). However important those concerns, there were no obvious ways to confront the effects of tourism on these people because the average attendance at mass among locals was low, 16 percent for men and 37 percent for women, and among immigrant workers it was even lower since they came, by and large, from the "pagan" regions of Andalusia and Extremadura.[100] Other priests conducted similar polls in 1963 on the Costa del Sol in Andalusia, and concluded that when people moved "to tourist areas [it] does not benefit their religious observance." Furthermore, they noted that former peasants, who used to go to mass in their villages, totally abandoned religious practice. This was certainly a sign that customs were changing in tourist areas more rapidly than in the interior of the country. The priest that conducted this study mentioned that the libertine phrase "everybody is free to do what pleases him" had not only become acceptable, but was now in common use.[101]

However, the controversy over the impact of tourism was not only about morality and it was most certainly not about the destruction of the environment, a question that was not yet being asked. The priests who conducted these polls noticed that while wealth had generally increased because of tourism, a very different reality was faced by those employed in the sector. Workers toiled longer hours and had inadequate housing, and their children were poorly schooled and neglected by their parents. To put it differently: the image of sunny and happy Spain hid the exploitation of the mostly seasonal workers who catered to the industry. A 1974 nation-wide study offers a glimpse into this grim reality.[102] As soon as children could work, they were taken out of school: 23 percent of those interviewed stated they had started working in the hospitality industry when they were between 7 and 13 years old, and 68 percent between the ages of 14 and 16.[103] Working conditions were harsh and far from secure. Two-thirds of employees had only temporary contracts; almost all contracts that did exist were verbal and subject to abuse; and only "docile" workers could expect to work the whole year or to have their contracts renewed. When they received their paycheck, most workers were asked to sign a blank form. Worker complaints, even those demanding the fulfillment of contract conditions or concerning unpaid work time, often led to unceremonious and uncompensated dismissals. Workers' representatives in the official unions were selected by management and were usually chosen from the ranks of foremen and submissive employees. The working day usually exceeded 10 hours, with only one day off each week. There was virtually no training and accidents were frequent, which was made worse by the fact that 60 percent of workers had no social security benefits.

If tourism, this new and key economic sector, brought with it serious cultural and social problems, another new socio-cultural phenomenon, the incorporation of women into the job market, was no less troubling. Women were not new to the working world. Like all peasant societies, Spanish women had always toiled in the fields while they cared for their families. But as the traditional socio-economic structure of the countryside changed so dramatically in the 1950s and 1960s, more poor women found employment in the industrial sector. In 1950 women made up only 15.8 percent of the official workforce, but by 1974, 29.6 percent of Spanish workers were female, though this was one of the lowest ratios in Europe.[104] New legal rights gained by women in the last years of the dictatorship did not immediately translate into an improvement in their lives, which were still hugely affected by traditional family roles and social prejudices. This was especially true for the least educated and the poor, who were still very much second-class citizens in both the private and public spheres. This was borne out by the fact that the new legislation did not carry stipulations for a hike in salaries to the level of those of men or for an improvement of their working conditions, which continued to lag far behind those of their male counterparts.

One of the sectors that saw its female workforce explode was the agro-food industry as both supply and demand for semi-processed, high-quality food products was expanding in an increasingly affluent Spain and Europe. Seafood processing and canning and fruit and vegetable packing were among the seasonal industries that demanded a low-skilled, low-paid workforce for several months a year to perform repetitive tasks for long hours. These jobs were primarily given to women, as they still are today, and featured low salaries, harsh working conditions – including searches and strict timing of visits to the washroom – and severe discipline enforced by mostly male foremen. Rights and benefits, if they existed, were minimal. Employers routinely escaped paying for social security and many forms of fraud were common. For anyone who wanted to keep her job, silence was the first rule, while a lack of solidarity was rule number two, though there were many reasons to speak up or to protest. A 1964 report on the working conditions of some 10,000 to 15,000 women in the fruit and vegetable industry in Murcia, prepared by the province's Catholic organizations, revealed that, during the high season, 12- to 18-hour working days were not unusual and extra hours were paid at ordinary rates. More than 71 percent of these women did not receive a signed or written paycheck. Complaints to the local labor inspectorate were highly unusual, however, as women were afraid to lose this relatively small but crucial source of income. Since many women brought their children with them to the packing plants, they too were often given minor tasks by employers. As a result, many schools in Murcia emptied during the high season. It was, of course, illegal for children to work before the age of 14, but the same study revealed that almost half of all employees surveyed had started before that age, and many before they were 10.[105]

Women were also in the majority in another low-paid sector: the textile industry. Like those in food packing, working conditions in the textile industry were unforgiving, often illegal, provided low salaries, and featured abusive treatment by managers. The industry experienced spectacular growth during the 1960s when several companies were created or expanded. In Madrid factories were located on the outskirts of the city, and by 1970 employed tens of thousands of women (female employment in the province in the textile industry rose sharply from about 32,000 in 1960 to about

83,000 10 years later). It was common for these women to have started working when they were 10 to 12 years of age. Their mothers would take them to learn how to sew in small shops known to be relatively safe (in moral terms, at least). Work in the textile industry was considered a "decent" profession for girls with no skills, and it provided a much-needed, albeit meager, income. By dropping out of school, girls were providing the income necessary for their families to prosper in the city. Given their vulnerable position in an industry with narrow profit margins, girls were exploited, and physical and verbal abuse was common. None of them was insured in any way until they reached the age of 14. As in other industries, men were paid more than women and were given the better jobs. In the early 1970s, some women textile workers began to organize because of these and other injustices, which led to affiliations with illegal unions.[106]

Access to greater opportunities in the labor market or to higher education was blocked for working women by the lack of affordable childcare. For most of them, the only options were to leave their children with relatives or neighbors or to stop working. Men did not usually take care of their children; that was considered an exclusively feminine job. Thus female paid work implied the beginning of another social debate about the duties of spouses and equality at home, which was to be problematic and at the same time a crucial element for change in people's values in matters of gender. If both spouses worked outside the home, the next move was to question why they did not both take on the same domestic responsibilities. And if both spouses were the de facto equals in duties, why not in rights? The same argument could be applied to the (up to then) different educational experiences of male and female children, their roles at home, and their future opportunities and expectations, both professional and personal. The transformation of gender roles had many sources, but the interaction of women's work and family duties was, no doubt a major one. Once democracy arrived, the debate about women's situation would accelerate and quickly open the way for full legal parity and an increasingly open discussion about real equality.[107]

If women did not have much support at home in the matter of childcare, the lack of interest in children's welfare on the part of both national and local authorities was notorious. A regime which willingly confused morality with social class, and meanness in social spending with fiscal probity, did not include spending on workers' children among its priorities. Politicians failed to act out of ideological prejudice, because they believed mothers should be caregivers and not make money outside the home: if people needed money, they should reduce their expenses, not increase their revenue while forfeiting their children's welfare and women's sacred mission. Furthermore, the regime's hierarchies, whose wives could easily and cheaply hire servants to take care of their family's needs, did not bother to understand that a working woman's salary was essential to her family's survival.

This reactionary, macho, and callous view of family duties resulted in a chronic and massive deficit of institutional childcare. The problem was particularly acute in immigrant neighborhoods and towns, where the population was young and fertile, and often both spouses had to work. In Manresa (Barcelona's industrial belt), for example, daycare centers had existed during the Second Republic and throughout the Civil War, but were summarily closed down by the dictatorship. As the local population grew spectacularly because of immigration (the town had 60,000 inhabitants in 1950 and 160,000 in 1970), the lack of social services became acute. In 1972 there were only two daycare centers serving the entire community: one belonged to a company and was reserved for its employees and the other had been founded in 1968 by a Catholic organization and catered mostly to widows, single mothers, and families in extreme difficulty. The result was that, of the close to 2,200 working families in Manresa with children between the ages of 0 and 4, only 170 had access to a daycare center.[108]

Migration, urbanization, higher levels of education, the advance of individualism and consumer values, tourism, and women going to work meant the progressive erosion of old patterns, creating a greater range of possibilities for gender relations, and for marriage. Local endogamy was eroded not only in the anonymity of cities but in the smallest of villages as well. People considering marriage were now less concerned with land or property and more interested in what possibilities the future had to offer as the suitability of partners came to be measured more and more by their level of education and capacity for entrepreneurship. This new openness, however, brought new risks and tensions along with it. While in the past, in rural societies, it had been easy to assess the character of a candidate for marriage among people who knew one another, in cities this became highly problematic and the risks associated with marrying became more individual and less conventional. More and more people made their decisions of their own free will and less and less through communal references. This made marriage more fulfilling but certainly less safe and more uncertain, as it navigated away from the traditional view of family where spouses were expected to endure failed marriages and women necessarily deferred to men's needs and desires.

Not by coincidence, in the early 1970s Spaniards openly talked about divorce for the first time since it had been banned at the end of the Civil War. The arguments used were not dissimilar to the polemics in Italy in the 1960s. Still, divorce was perceived by most people as a sign of foreign mores, something for Protestants and Hollywood stars. The debate over the matter was rather parochial and unfocused, often revolving around claims of widespread materialism and young women's lack of tolerance for their partners' failings. According to countless movies, popular songs, sensationalist reports in popular magazines, not to mention hot-headed clerics, foreign women (*extranjeras*) did not know how to treat their husbands. In fact, these *extranjeras* were presented as negligent wives and mothers, materialistic and sexually unrestrained. If we believed the dozens of films, mostly comedies, that poisoned people's minds in the early 1970s, what was bad for husbands and families in foreign countries presented great opportunities for Spanish men to chase or be chased by sex-hungry, scantily clad blonde tourists.[109] All of this because gender relations were, so Spaniards were told, only about sex: macho Spanish men needed it, and women, Spanish women at least, had to cope with this "fact" while keeping up their traditional roles. Countless mediocre movies presented the same story, which became "hotter" once a (female) tourist was involved: a repressed Spanish man yearns for sex, his fiancée will have none of it, he tries, often with success, to "engage" a beautiful tourist and then, having fulfilled his instincts, rediscovers his chaste Spanish wife-to-be and realizes she is the one he always wanted. Marriage and happiness ensue.[110]

These ludicrous arguments and debates took place against a background of widespread ignorance about sexuality and persistent whispering about birth control. To begin with, it was obvious to everybody without anyone having to check the statistics that Spanish women in the 1970s were having fewer, albeit not many fewer, babies than their mothers. The secret to this was, of course, birth control – the Francoist version. A 1973 study, very limited in scope because it was based on indirect questions to women, concluded that the most common methods used by women to avoid pregnancy were condoms and *coitus interruptus*.[111] For all its flaws, this study revealed a cultural change in reproductive patterns: younger couples used condoms more and *coitus interruptus* less than their parents. It also showed that more than 86 percent of the women who described themselves as practicing Catholics said that they did not regularly use any form of contraception, and half of those who did only did so occasionally.[112] Given the impoverished state of sexual knowledge among the general population, the lack of women's access to the pill, male reluctance to use condoms, and the practice of the unreliable Ogino system – the only method sanctioned by the Catholic Church – women in the 1970s still had only a limited ability to control pregnancy. A tragic consequence of this was that hundreds of thousands of women every year were forced to contemplate the daunting experience of abortion.

Abortion was, of course, illegal and harshly repressed (it had been made legal in republican Spain during the Civil War). It was also an option rejected by the majority of the country. Its legalization was not even discussed, and when it was talked about it was only to be condemned.[113] Little is known about its practice in the early decades of the dictatorship except that it was used often and that it was very dangerous, both legally and physically.[114] The most commonly used methods of abortion were very crude. They included inserting knitting needles into the vagina, mustard, parsley, large bars of soap, and hitting the 'bomb' (the pregnant stomach). Between 1965 and 1970 the regime prosecuted 741 cases of abortion and sentenced 1,067 people; between 1970 and 1975 these numbers declined to 505 cases prosecuted and 769 people sentenced in court. This was the tip of the iceberg, but again hypocrisy and repression hit the poor far harder than they did the powerful. Wealthy, better-connected people could more easily obtain the services of a doctor or, when abortion became legal in the United Kingdom in 1967, they could travel for a long weekend to "shop" in London. Repression did not stop abortion, but it killed thousands of women. How many is a matter of conjecture. According to a study in 1972, there were about 114,000 illegal abortions in Spain that year.[115] However, the 1974 Ministry of Justice annual report put the number at close to 300,000, though the methodology used to reach this conclusion was not explained. Since mortality due to abortion could easily reach 1 percent, this means that as many as 3,000 Spanish women may have died every year from unsafe, illegal abortions. Depending on which figures are used, this could represent the primary cause of mortality, between 17 percent and 30 percent, for Spanish women aged 17 to 35.[116]

∗∗∗

Social values and society's expectations at the end of the dictatorship were very different from those of the 1940s. Economic and cultural change also affected political perspectives. During the 1960s the fundamental moral and cultural values of Francoism had grown increasingly alienated from those of the younger and best-educated sectors of society; but this alienation was permeating the rest of the population. The regime's authoritarian discourse, unchanged since its birth, collided with the increasingly tolerant outlook of Spaniards, who were more interested in having a better life than in guarding the political essence of a system that seemed more and more a relic of a troubled past. In contrast to what happened when the Republic arrived in 1931, Spaniards did not care any more for land reform: the value and allure of the land had evaporated. Now they expected more from the state, from institutions, from businesses, from their families, and from their own lives. They wanted to satisfy new longings and cravings and forget about past necessities and outmoded solutions. Their values were urban and increasingly tolerant, and they started to consider themselves more European than ever before. They wanted to live in a normal European country in every respect: social, cultural, and, increasingly, political.[117] These contradictions, within society and between society and the dictatorship, created numerous tensions that threatened the future stability of the country. The final chapter will examine the political implications of those changes and contradictions.

5

ROADS TO CITIZENSHIP[1]

Life in the 1950s and early 1960s was predictable in the new agro-town of Llanos del Caudillo, a community in Ciudad Real province created by the dictatorship in the 1950s. Life for most people was primarily about working hard and trying to enjoy the few moments of leisure that remained at the end of the week. If anybody had cared to ask them, the inhabitants of Llanos del Caudillo would have said there were "no politics" in their town, but politics had not completely forgotten them. One day in 1957 the authorities announced that there would be a visit by the dictator to this town that carried his name. People were thrilled. Those who were there at the time later remembered that, as His Excellency approached Llanos del Caudillo, teachers made schoolchildren form lines to salute and the whole town was ready to wave; but, as the cars in Franco's motorcade approached, they "reduced speed, his bodyguards changed places and then the limousine sped up again down the road."[2] The visit was over. We don't know if the people of Llanos del Caudillo made jokes or bitter remarks over the incident. We do know that there was a near-consensus among the local population that there was peace and conformity. Consensus but for one person: someone had "ideas." This person voted "No" in the December 1966 referendum that prepared Franco's succession, and this lone vote caused a lot of head-scratching in the town. People asked themselves who had taken the risk. They never discovered who had dared. We know that, when democracy arrived in 1977 in the form of elections, many of these peasants were still deeply skeptical about party politics. They remembered what they had seen or heard about the years of the Republic and they said things like "All parties want to win and they do not accept defeat," or "We are going to go back to violence again."[3]

When democracy returned, elsewhere in Spain many other people had already gone down a very different road. Manuel Cortijo was one of these people. He was born in the early 1930s in the province of Guadalajara and moved to Catalonia in 1941 because his father, a peasant and a republican volunteer soldier, was deported there for political reasons. His father had also been condemned to forced labor, but the penury did not end there. During the war, local Francoists had taken most of Manuel's family's possessions for themselves, including their land. Manuel's grandfather had died in prison; the family suspected that he had been killed. The family had nowhere to go back to. In Catalonia, Manuel became a bricklayer and a communist. In the early 1960s he began to organize a banned Workers' Commissions union with fellow activists in his adopted city, Lleida (or Lerida). The Catholic HOAC helped them by, among other things, lending them space in a parish church for their meetings. Manuel remembers a trick they played on the police. Since "all policemen like football," they printed their subversive messages on the city walls when matches were being broadcast "because very few policemen were patrolling" during the games. Like other members of the Workers' Commissions before and afterwards, in 1967 Manuel infiltrated the official union as a representative of his fellow bricklayers. When his political leanings were discovered, he was quickly blacklisted and had to migrate to France to harvest grapes for several months a year to earn a living. After two years, the police withdrew his passport. According to Manuel, some employers tried to help by hiring members of the Workers' Commission and paying them a bit more to compensate them for benefits lost. They did all this without notifying social security. But most companies remained neutral and simply followed the law. He was arrested, along with other colleagues, for demonstrating on International Workers' Day, May 1, 1969.[4] When his father went to visit Manuel at the police station, he too was arrested.

As Spain entered the last years of the dictatorship, it was a complex society with an enormous amount of social, economic, political, and cultural diversity. There were many "Spains," and people expected or hoped for many different things. However, the most common hope and expectation among the majority of Spaniards was that they did not want a repeat of the carnage of the Civil War or a reiteration of the violence of the first years of the dictatorship. Yet, at the same time, dark clouds were gathering on the horizon. The darkest cloud hovered over the question of what was going to happen when the aging dictator died. Officially, the path was clear when in 1969 Juan Carlos de Borbón was appointed Prince of Spain and heir to Franco as the head of state.[5] That was only the theory, because everybody knew that Francoism without Franco was all but impossible, and so the future lay wide open. Politicians, intellectuals, industrialists, foreign diplomats, Francoist die-hards, opposition leaders, and ordinary people all made predictions, but, in their heart nobody felt confident when answering the big question: after Franco, what? Nothing was safe or predictable.

A Demobilized Society

After its initially strident fascist years, the dictatorship had settled into a pattern of "normalcy" that demanded both political demobilization and social conformism. Spaniards were encouraged to look to their personal lives and leave the rest to the regime. At public events, whether this involved a visit to a town by the dictator or simply attendance at an afternoon football match, people were expected to be spectators, not actors. Accordingly, the society that experienced an economic boom beginning in the 1960s was individualistic and politically apathetic; people were very concerned with the well-being of their families and fairly indifferent to the common good. These strategies helped poor people to survive the callousness of the state, but benefited a regime that counted on conservatism and widespread passivity to carry out projects that suited its interests. This passivity was deeply entrenched in the backward areas of the country, where poverty and accelerated migration had drained society of its energy. This was the case in the majority of provinces and in all of rural Spain. If any political problems were to arise for the regime, they would surface in the industrial areas, not there. Apathy was as easily found in the remote mountain regions of the north and in the central regions of the country as it was in the provinces of the south. All this was true of the Galician provinces in the northwest, Castile, Extremadura, most of Andalusia, portions of the Levant, Aragon, and the Canary Islands. The main characteristics of these areas were economic backwardness, the predominance of an agrarian economy and way of life, population loss or near-negative growth due to immigration, lack of industrialization, and a chronic paucity of educational and social services. There were, however, industrial centers and universities within these regions of lethargy that had a different dynamic. To the very end, the dictatorship never confronted the real challenges in these regions. Its only worries there were the activities of Catholic groups like HOAC and the work of progressive priests among workers and young people. These were irritants rather than real dangers.

For the dictatorship, apathy was desirable even if it affected its own Falangist institutions like the Frente de Juventudes (Youth Front) or the Sección Femenina (Women's Section). For example, in Segovia in 1962, after taking note of HOAC's activities and the mildly unsettling political behavior of some members of the clergy, the civil governor described the political climate as "calm and normal" and noted the "great disorientation among young people regarding political ideas since only a minority take part in the Frente de Juventudes."[6] The same year his colleague from Avila remarked on the "general apathy or lack of interest in political matters [...] Every day the lack of interest for the Falange [...] grows since the old militants had lost their will and strength to serve and the ranks of FET-JONS are not renewed and young people don't find a clear orientation that would lead it to enroll into the organization."[7] As the years went by, it became obvious that what was consistently important to the regime was the maintenance of public order, moderate progress and, first and foremost, the standing of the dictator. And so, when Franco's health began to fail, the big question surfaced again and again: who would replace him and what mechanisms could ensure the continuity of the values of the regime?[8]

Official politics had been reduced to El Caudillo's prestige. The Falange was clearly on the wane in the 1960s and the party became an empty shell in the 1970s. The Movimiento was nothing without Franco.[9] The party's problem was not only that it lacked real power within the structure of the regime, but also its inability to win the masses over to its side. Everyone knew that, when the dictator visited a town, people did not cheer for the men in the Falangist uniforms who surrounded him but for Franco alone. The Falangists still had state resources at their disposal, and they organized political events that were self-referential and which primarily attracted the converted, but their annual activities remained unchanged, and the same aging faces came to the same places year after year. In 1962 the governor of Logrono reported that

> Perhaps the most important event of the year, from which we can obtain the most substantial political benefit, is the act of renewal of the promise of loyalty to the national flag on July 18. On that occasion practically all the former combatants and their sons over 14 were mobilized.[10]

The same governor went on to outline the other important public activities of the year. They consisted of public lectures, the inauguration of new buildings, the annual homage to the founder of the Falange, José Antonio, and other "fallen ones" on November 20, and, finally, a competition for the prize of the most beautifully improved town in the province. These activities were hardly exciting, and not popular either.

The problem for the authorities was that, as the 1960s advanced and Spanish society became more complex and demanding, their attitudes and their same limited capacity to mobilize the population persisted, and this led to a justified sense of decline and irrelevance. Either they had no fear of the challenges the emerging society faced or they simply did not know how to respond to them; both of these were probably the case. In 1972, for example, after a decade of rapid socio-economic change in the country, the Falangists were still organizing the same kinds of public activities as 10 years earlier, but now they had an even more limited popular appeal. In Palencia, the governor's report for 1972 stated that the "really important political events" of the year were a meeting between mayors and local chiefs of the Falange in the House of Culture and the gathering of the IV Consejo Político-Social Sindical (Fourth Meeting of the Unions' Political and Social Council).[11] In Murcia, the most significant political events of the year were a mass for the first local Falangist who had died during the war, which some 3,000 people attended; another mass in the Valley of the Fallen for all local dead Falangists, with 200 people present; Youth Week activities – no attendance figures were provided in the report; other Catholic masses and small gatherings; and the usual competitions for the most improved town.[12] That year, the governor of Castellon de la Plana also reported the "great loyalty to the Caudillo," but then added how the majority of the population "ignores the political system of the country" and just asked for "peace and social justice."[13] From these reports it was obvious that, even in the most conservative areas of the country, economic development had not made Spaniards more *actively* supportive of the regime or increased the prestige of the country's only legal political party. Habit rather than fervor reigned here. What economic development did do was to create new needs, both social and cultural, that state organizations did not address and the Falange did not capitalize on. This social vacuum was partially filled by independent organizations, ranging from conservative groups of Catholic parents and other family associations to more progressive ones, such as neighborhood associations, that began to appear after a 1964 law allowed their creation. We shall see more on this below.

Despite the lack of public initiative and an almost complete absence of political activity, at the start of the 1970s the dictatorship still did not find itself seriously challenged by the majority of Spanish society. But political passivity did not mean that people lacked political opinions. The 1970

FOESSA (Fomento de Estudios Sociales y Sociología Aplicada) report, the main sociological study conducted in Spain at this time, pointed to a deep-rooted political conservatism, especially among the lower classes of society. According to this study, workers, particularly unskilled, older, and female employees, supported the maintenance of the political status quo while the most educated and younger people were more amenable to change. But it must be stressed, because it would be a crucial factor in the coming years, that the same impoverished people who, according to this report, appeared to be so politically conservative had deeply rooted social grievances and a sense of injustice that they ranked immediately after their desire for peace in the order of their socio-political priorities.[14] Regrettably, the FOESSA study, which has been a reference point for many academics, failed to extract further conclusions about the apparent contradiction that existed between supporting the "peace" of the status quo and, at the same time, being fully aware of, and angry about, the old and new social inequalities the regime had generated. The FOESSA study failed to project history into sociology and see how the weakest members of society had learned their political lessons well, and why they believed that Franco, not his regime or his henchmen, represented "peace."[15] The dynamics generated by both the crisis that battered the Spanish economy after 1973 and the death of Franco in 1975 would help to transform these ideas of social equality and fairness by linking them to concepts of political change and personal freedom. The death of the dictator meant the end of the equation of peace in exchange for political rights that had anchored the regime since the end of the war. And the same previously demobilized, poor people who had supported the status quo would start to support the movement towards political liberalization and begin learning how to be citizens of a democracy.[16]

Signs that this might be possible were already visible in the early 1960s in a minority of provinces where things had never been so easy for the dictatorship. There were conflicts and a growing focus of anti-Francoist activity in cities and towns that were homes to universities. This was the case of middle-sized university towns like Granada, Corunna, Valladolid, and Saragossa and even larger centers such as Seville and Valencia. These opposition activities were isolated in those places, but became more radical and more intense in areas with a strong industrial presence such as Madrid, Barcelona, Bilbao, and Asturias. All the latter areas possessed an increasingly confident working class whose pre-war memories of class-based unions had never been completely destroyed by the regime's repression. However, no community or province showed signs of heading towards violent confrontation between pro- and anti-Francoists. Even in the most complex regions, with the notorious exception of some groups in the Basque country, people with different attitudes, from the conformist majority to the subversive minority, coexisted comfortably and worked side by side. This was the case in Valencia. In June 1962, when Franco visited the province, "it wholly surrendered itself to him, with a unity of feeling, admiration and respect" that was both genuine and ebullient. It was a very different situation on the university campus the same year, where it transpired that there was "skepticism regarding the political situation" and where "the Falangist student organization barely holds on." Strikes had been staged in the province in the Sagunto steelworks a few weeks before Franco's visit. In spite of their differences, people lived in peace and the regime was safe, in Valencia and elsewhere.[17]

The largest, bitterest, and most internationally publicized strike under Francoism had taken place in the mining region of Asturias in the spring of 1962.[18] The strike soon spread to the Basque country, Navarre, Madrid, and Barcelona, and to isolated pockets all over Spain. Yet even this massive labor protest did not lead to public strife or to an immediate challenge to the regime's stability. Deeper threats were fermenting in different quarters, and would cause pain for decades to come. In some areas, labor protests teamed up with peripheral nationalism, another focus of political resistance within the country's recent historical memory. In 1962 in the conservative Basque province of Alava, formerly a part of the Carlist heartland, the governor reported "conformism [that] translates into positive loyalty to Franco, but also apathy regarding political problems and participation in public affairs." Nevertheless, there was a nascent nationalist feeling, which was being supported by sectors of the clergy, HOAC and Catholic Action's youth section, JOC, and was galvanized by the intermittent actions of the newly born ETA (Basque Fatherland and Freedom) terrorist group.[19] By 1968 public order in Alava had been severely compromised because of ETA. The governor asked for police reinforcements to deal with the problem.[20] By 1972, as economic difficulties mounted, workers' protests escalated, and this brought new levels of hostility, including an outbreak of violence during a long strike at the Michelin factory. Once again, the governor was forced to ask for reinforcements, including riot police.[21]

Even more threatening challenges to the dictatorship, and to public peace (and, although nobody suspected this, of course, to the future of democratic Spain), came from the two neighboring Basque provinces of Biscay and Guipuzcoa. In 1962 several strikes were staged in both provinces, but, as the governor of Biscay explained, the authorities were convinced that the strikes were the result of "high prices, insufficient salaries and lack of attention by the companies [...] plus the disillusionment of workers with the official unions."[22] The governor of Guipuzcoa reported that the Basque nationalist union (Basque Workers' Solidarity or STV), controlled "the vast majority of workers" and was behind most of the conflicts. By 1968 the situation had deteriorated to the point that ETA had killed for the first time, and the regime imposed martial law. Basque nationalist clerics were correctly pointed to as the source of the spreading discontent and as being apologists for ETA violence.[23]

It is telling that the two most important provinces in Spain, Barcelona and Madrid, were never as directly combative, or as murderous, as Biscay and Guipuzcoa. The regime was aware that Catalan national identity remained intact. In 1961 it was significant enough for the governor of Barcelona to remark that "[national identity] had changed little in the last forty years." However, this was peaceful nationalism.[24] Even in 1972 the climate had changed little. A report from Barcelona that year stated that illegal political parties and unions had been active, "even though they had not managed to politicize workers; [though] they had made them more sensitive to the spirit of [worker] solidarity."[25] That, however, was about to change.

Social and labor unrest under the dictatorship was bound to become overtly political. Political mobilization was not just the result of the protesters' initial intentions, but also of the fact that the dictatorship found itself with no response to the new social challenges. The absence of strategies for dialogue between the people and the regime created a condition of growing confusion and an atmosphere of political and cultural crisis. People of all persuasions were looking at models in Europe (some left-wing radicals still looked to east European and even Maoist models), and they found that the era of dictatorships, of fascist strong men and of middle classes terrorized by Bolshevism, were long gone. People saw that Europe was democratic and prosperous, and they liked what they saw, but they were realistic enough to realize that solutions for the future had to be found in Spain, not elsewhere, and take account of the country's realities, including its tragic past.

Old Memories, New Expectations

In the past few years Spain has witnessed a cascade of revelations about the elite's plans to transform the political system, to bring back democracy following the death of the dictator. According to these new insights, for many liberals within the regime, for highly placed bureaucrats, and for the prince himself, a political transition was deemed crucial. Of course, banned political parties and unions were also looking for a change of regime, but their plans differed from one another. Some of them still dreamed of reviving the Republic or of imposing their own brand of socialism. However, it would be a mistake to see the transition to democracy as merely the realization of the plans and wishes of the regime's powerbrokers and their dealings with the organized opposition. Democracy did not simply come to Spain as a gift proffered from the elite to the people. It was very a complex deal, in which nobody got exactly what they expected and nobody could foresee how the process or, rather, the experiment would turn out. Ordinary Spaniards had a lot to say about and to contribute to this "deal": their hard-learned political lessons. As crucially, they helped shape the birth of the New Spain in their daily routines at work, in their neighborhoods, with their families, and through the evolution of their values and hopes. It was a non-linear, uncharted process, but it can be defined as one in which Spaniards learned to negotiate, to demand more from the powerful, and to question tradition, both outside and inside their homes.

Change finally saw the removal of the dark shadow of the Civil War from the dreams of tomorrow. At first, this was especially true for young people and for those with a good education, but in time it came to be true for the majority of the population. Spaniards became citizens again and, when they did, it was with a more deeply rooted sense of civic duty and tolerance than they had had in 1931 when the Second Republic had been proclaimed. Paradoxically, while experiencing a dictatorship that doggedly protected the blatantly unequal distribution of wealth, shamelessly practiced cultural obscurantism, and ruthlessly maintained complete political control over the nation, Spaniards were now freer from poverty, ignorance, and political patronage than they had ever been. However, this did not mean that they had become oblivious to the past. On the contrary, the past continually resurfaced; only now, when it did, it was interpreted according to new realities and the expectations of a different society.

Perhaps the first year in which old memories and new expectations met face to face was 1962. In June, for the first time since 1936, representatives from all democratic political tendencies, from both inside and outside Spain, met in Munich. At this meeting of former enemies it was declared, rather optimistically, that "the Civil War has ended." Although the vicious attack by the regime's propaganda machine and the communists said otherwise, from now on the possibility of building a democracy in Spain could be founded on the support of the parties that, until the Civil War, had represented the overwhelming majority of the population. However, this possibility was still a very long way from becoming reality. Another event in 1962, the recovery of the economy from the bitter medicine of the 1959 Stabilization Plan, opened up a period of economic boom and optimism, which included the beginning of the massive migrations to Europe. Economic success, though painful and very late in arriving, might have made the regime complacent, except that that same year witnessed the biggest wave of strikes since the war. These strikes proved to the regime that old loyalties remained deeply entrenched in several working-class strong-holds. At the same time, it send a clear message that, after more than two decades of exploitation and suffering, workers wanted more and knew that now they could get it.

The meeting between old memories and new perceptions began in the coalmining region of Asturias. As the story goes, the founding of a new clandestine union that rejected the official unions, an informal group, was created by the miners in the La Camocha pit in 1957.[26] The model was expanded to other pits, but the Comisiones Obreras (Workers' Commissions), the name that this loose amalgamation of new and illegal unions eventually came to be known by, were very weak in their early years. They had barely any presence outside the Asturian mining valleys, even while the waves of the 1962–4 strikes were sweeping across the nation. Slowly, the commissions infiltrated and used official union channels, and by the end of the decade they were strongly affiliated to the Communist Party. A key moment came during the 1966 official unions' elections, when, because the economy was performing spectacularly well, the authorities became over-confident and showed relatively more tolerance than they had in past union elections. The commissions seized this opportunity to increase their ranks. As a result, their militants were elected and then controlled the officially allocated workers' representation in several of the Francoist unions' branches. These elections proved once again that, when offered a dose of freedom, workers would readily choose non-Falangist-approved candidates as their repre-sentatives.

Francoist tolerance was bound to be short-lived. At the end of any failed attempt by the regime to use the masses and gain legitimacy stood repression. In 1967 the Workers' Commissions were banned and harshly repressed by the police. This put a definitive end to a long-cherished Falangist fantasy and a permanent theme of the regime's propaganda: the pretense that workers were free to elect whom they wanted to positions in the official unions. As a result, any chance of worker support of a supposedly Falangist "third way" – a socio-economic and political model somewhere between democratic capitalism and socialism – was from then on as good as dead.

There was a legal angle to the phenomenon of the Workers' Commissions, for they had been, at least in part, a product of the regime's attempt to bring a new stability to labor relations. Up until 1958 there had been relatively few labor conflicts in Spain. The contraction of the economy in the year that followed the adoption of the Stabilization Plan only meant that, even with the increase in worker exploitation and a deterioration in living conditions, the "army or reserve" of the unemployed limited the possibility of strikes. The government approved the 1958 Law of Collective Agreements in response to the expanding industrial labor force and the increasing complexity of labor conflicts. This law cannot be separated from a wider process of making the economy less rigid and giving employers more latitude to manage their own companies. However, it was implemented slowly and, up until 1961, only 758 agreements were signed.[27] Although a salary freeze ended in 1961, it would not be until 1962 that this new way of bargaining would be extended across the country. That last year there was still only 2 million workers covered by collective agreements. Workers began to negotiate for higher salaries in exchange for higher productivity in the context of long-standing grievances and new expectations of improvement. Now, workers began to effectively use the strike as a negotiating strategy. Initially, most strikers had no political agenda. A study on the origins of strikes in the first half of the 1960s shows that at least 90 percent were strictly labor disputes, unconnected to any notion of solidarity with other workers or social issues outside the company; it also found that the strikes resulted in very little violence.[28]

The government knew that the 1962–4 waves of protest were spontaneous, even though some opposition groups, particularly the communists, tried to capitalize on them. It was also aware that the work stoppages were supported by a clear majority of the population, including Catholic sectors, and even some Francoists privately agreed that the workers' complaints were fair.[29] In spite of, or perhaps precisely because of, this support, the government decreed the introduction of martial law in 1962 in the striking provinces. Illegal detentions and torture then became commonplace.

Publicly, the dictatorship was united behind these hard-nosed measures. Behind the scenes there were important divisions between the Falangist leaders of the unions, who wanted to recognize a limited right to strike, and the regime's hardliners, led by the dictator himself. The official unions' top bureaucrats knew that workers viewed them, and rightly so, as merely a repressive tool of the government. They wanted to use these events to gain independence from the regime and prestige from the masses. Some Falangists even pointed out that many workers in factories and mills had not joined the protests even though they were located right next to striking labor centers because they were better treated by their employers. All of this was to no avail; the hardline approach was adopted. By choosing repression, the dictatorship made any present or future labor protests political and illegal, regardless of the protesters' intentions. Using article 222 of the Penal Code, strikes were now defined and punished as acts of sedition. A mixture of repressive measures and concessions in the context of the rapidly booming economy then restored a sense of calm.

The damage, however, had been done. The government's strong-arm tactics helped to make credible among workers the conviction that the best weapon for achieving material improvements was political solidarity. By repressing labor protests the dictatorship was not only creating political opposition, it was helping to shape it. Workers' commissions first became schools of protest and then political training grounds where future opposition party cadres would learn to negotiate tangible improvements and to undermine the regime at the same time.[30] The commissions' often spontaneous nature and flexibility meant that they were more difficult than traditional opposition groups for the police to dismantle, and they became the rallying and meeting places of old and new unionists, of Catholic groups, and of young labor lawyers. Here people learned to fight for their own rights and discovered the diversity of other people's interests, the differences within different cultural groups, and the rights of other genders and ideologies.

Antonio Cantano was one of the people who graduated from this form of labor and political education. He was born in Loja (Granada) in 1927 into a landless peasant family with socialist leanings that lost several relatives at the hands of the Francoists. Life was very hard for them and jobs were scarce and badly paid. They emigrated to Lerida, Catalonia, in 1956. One day in the early 1960s, Antonio met a fellow worker, a communist militant named Miguel Moreno, who told him about a group of people who gathered regularly to discuss the situation of the working class. "Those meetings caused me to feel something very strange. It was so different from what I could see in the street." Almost without noticing it, he found himself becoming a militant of the Workers' Commissions and then he became an activist with the Catalan Communist Party (PSUC). At meetings he talked and discussed, and afterwards he read and thought. He acquired a new language and was transformed by it as he came to describe with new words and concepts his emerging vision of the world. Antonio also learned diversity. He also met with Catholic militants of HOAC: "During the hard years of the dictatorship, they were always with us." They received help from the bishop, who many times mediated with the governor to have imprisoned workers freed and donated money to help the families of those detained. Through these interactions he also met individuals with liberal opinions who were from other social groups. The middle classes and the bourgeoisie ceased to be a feared, faceless, brutal class enemy allied to the regime and became real people with interesting and often illuminating ideas. Antonio was detained by the police several times. He was blacklisted, threatened, subjected to deceptions and betrayals, and physically abused.

Antonio did not change alone. His family and his neighborhood evolved too. Their new political vocabulary and analysis led to conclusions that would change the daily dynamics of many militants' families and of their own attitudes towards gender. Natividad, Antonio's wife, became a militant in her own right, with demands and expectations that did not depend on men's leadership. They demanded things from local authorities – and from their husbands.[31] These demands included things like improving the streets and obtaining new public services, but also gender equality. The family of Manuel Cortijo, whom we met at the beginning of this chapter, also experienced this wide-ranging change. In their case this included a growing identification with Catalan culture, thus making a connection between the labor movement and peripheral, yet socially inclusive, nationalism. Like the wives of other militants, Mercedes, Manuel's wife, discovered new possibilities for herself as she first started to help her husband and then became a militant in her own right. As Manuel described in his own words,

> My wife met me here and she knew what I was fighting for. She is a Catalan and we married here. She realized I was right and joined me wholeheartedly in the workers' movement and in the struggle. She distributed leaflets, put them in mailboxes and she had to be disguised when she went so as not to be recognized by the police. She took part in demonstrations as well and collected money for those detained.[32]

From a traditional husband–wife relationship they evolved towards equality, to become partners (*compañeros*).

Change was also felt beyond the shop floor. The politicization of labor soon led to the development of a reciprocal relationship with neighborhood associations, clubs, and women's groups. It became a collective experience. The growth of new political and social identities was far more rapid in the traditional industrial areas than it was in the new ones. It took longer in Madrid, Puertollano, and Cartagena than it did in Barcelona or the northern industrial regions, because old memories helped to shape and catalyze younger people and areas. This was the result, for example, of the interaction of experienced militant workers and the far less politicized new immigrants in the Baix Llobegrat in Barcelona's industrial belt. Post-war industrialization and the massive arrival of southerners had changed the area. The population of one of its main towns, Cornella, doubled between 1950 and 1960. Most workers were young, and they were being exploited.

The main employer in Cornella was the large Siemens factory. The relationship with the company went awry in 1958 when workers began to campaign for overtime by adopting the classic, relatively "safe" tactic of a work slowdown. Their legal representatives in the official unions, "honest people," suffered for this, and four of them were fired. One of them, Morilla, lived in a shack at the time and his wife was pregnant. His colleagues were furious because, "perhaps for the first time, they had men in a position to lead them" and they lost them to repression. In spite of the fact that the judge who heard their case found no legal reason for their dismissal, these men were de facto blacklisted. Morilla had to emigrate to Germany. Another colleague, Clemente, emigrated to France, while a third representative returned to working in the fields. Four years later, in May 1962, when the protest began again, the infamous Political-Social Brigade of the police called the workers' representatives to a "meeting" upstairs in the factory. They came back with bruises on their faces. One of the workers, González, recalled many years later how "They hit Padilla. He started working again, alone on the floor with 800 men – he was crying."[33]

However, 1962 was very different from 1958 and not just because workers' political learning curve had become steeper. By September most of the company's employees were on strike. Foremen started to take workers to their offices and told them to start toiling again or they would be fired immediately. Many returned to the floor; they had no option. However, their neighborhoods had changed: they were no longer the individualistic, amorphous conglomeration of immigrants of a few years earlier. When people from the town began to hear about what was happening they went en masse to the main gates to support the strikers, who now decided they would occupy the factory. Women and children entered the plant; food and drink arrived and was shared by all. The police arrived too and surrounded the premises. After a meeting with the captain in charge of the riot police, the workers struck a deal and everybody evacuated the building in peace. The next day, after finding out that the employers had closed the plant, the enraged workers demonstrated in the streets in their work clothes. This time the police attacked them and even beat their parish priest when he tried to protect the strikers by hiding them inside his church. The company then fired all the workers involved and demanded that they come back to the factory and sign new contracts. What followed was a symbolic act of disobedience, or liberation. The workers returned to the factory, received their new contracts and tore them up publicly in front of a cheering crowd. Not only had they torn a piece of paper with this act – they had also ripped away decades of fear and humiliation. In the end, the company agreed to the pay raise that was at the heart of the conflict. This was a hard-won victory as 42 workers were permanently dismissed and 12 of them were tried in a military court for sedition. They were not rehired, but they were not forgotten either. Fifteen years later, in May 1976, as democracy was being brought in and union activism was at its height, they were reinstated in their former jobs. For months their former colleagues supported these workers with donations collected at the factory and through the help of members of Catholic Action. This strike had a further significance. What started as a mere labor conflict became both a social and a political event. It brought together Christians and "reds," women and men, neighbors and families, union representatives and political activists, and from the struggle a local branch of the Workers' Commissions was born. Its first meetings were held in the parish church.[34]

The Risks of Peace

Cornella was a world apart from rural Spain. In Segovia, for example, in 1968, copywriters for sensationalist newspapers could not make a living. In this province just north of Madrid, there had not been that year "any homicides, murders or abortions" and crime had "continued to decrease" from the previous year; the only notable exceptions to this trend were a case of infanticide and four cases of physical assault. Theft had been the most common crime by far, with 39 convictions reported. The only other transgressions that had shown a significant increase were illegal and dangerous driving (in a province where there were only 13,000 registered motor vehicles). As a result, there were only three inmates in jail by the end of the year out of a total population of more than 160,000 people.[35] It was not much more interesting further south, in the poverty-stricken province of Badajoz. The number of crimes committed there in 1969 was very low for its population of 700,000. There were only 223 crimes against property and 461 against people, decency, and security that year. The star case was related to a nine-member gang of car thieves; they had been caught.[36] Criminal activity was also declining in Valladolid in 1969, a province of 400,000 inhabitants that was the site of several important industries. Once again, car theft was the exception. That year, 168 cars and 281 scooters were stolen. There were also 401 thefts not related to motor vehicles, 35 cases of fraud, 30 acts of aggression, and 44 crimes against morality.[37] None of these provinces recorded a single murder.

Compared to the demonstrations and barricades of the previous year in many parts of Europe, or the 1967 race riots in Detroit, there can be no doubt that Spain was a safe country in which to live. In fact, behind this image of calm, growing materialism and wealth stood political sclerosis and, 30 years after its formal end, the long shadow of the Civil War. This could loom anywhere and at any time. In remote, peaceful, picturesque Huesca, an agrarian, conservative province of Aragon, the impact of the government decree of March 1969 that amnestied political crimes committed before the end of the war was felt acutely and caused much discussion because, as the governor's report stated, there were "numerous exiles from this province, most of them with many relatives here and whose […] personal contacts have been maintained [and] reminiscences [are] difficult to extinguish."[38] The problem with this "peace" was that its main pillar, Franco, was part of the "reminiscences"; another way of describing the years of political killings and fear.[39]

However, the dictator was aging, and this created great anxiety. As the governor of Leon put it in his 1968 report: "Because of the age of His Excellency, people's natural concerns have [lately] become more acute." The governor also explained in that year's report that most people supported Franco and his policies because they believed that as long as he continued to be in charge they would enjoy the maximum amount of "trust and security."[40] The question of what would happen after Franco's death was always at the back of most people's minds, but it was rarely spoken aloud and only within the safety of circles of relatives or friends. In 1969, the governor of

Segovia said that people believed that "as long as Franco remains as Head of the State, we doubt that the political unity will be broken [even if there are] contradictory sentiments among the most intelligent minorities."[41]

Society could not get rid of the ghost of the past, the unspoken skeletons of Franco's "Peace." Now it seemed that, led by those "intelligent minorities," the apparent social consensus created by the economic boom was showing unexpected cracks, which nobody knew how to seal. These cracks included the growing split between the regime and young people, the increasing activities of ETA, and of course the labor world. There was nothing exclusively Spanish about these problems. The rebellion of youth, terrorism, and renewed worker militancy were happening in many other Western industrialized societies at this time. While those democratic societies adapted and solved the problem more or less successfully, the Francoist dictatorship could not count on the mediating mechanisms of a civil society to find solutions. Thus it became more aggressive towards those challenges and in so doing, ironically less able to solve them. In the process, its political survival became a matter of inertia, maintained only because the dictator was still alive.

The "youth" of Spain, of whom the authorities despaired – and they were not alone in their despair – were showing that the new generations were different, with their taste in clothes, their hairstyles, and their movies, theater, parties, music, and reading. They were also being influenced by "foreign" fashions and ideas, and by "progressive priests, who mixed with both young people and workers to help foment ideas and protests against the policies of the regime."[42] Even in the clearly conservative, pro-Franco province of Zamora in 1969, young people wanted "to transform the social environment," but were "confused" and found no venues for change. Accordingly, there was fear that local young people were evolving towards "extremely negative situations," social ills that "thank God, we are still in time to avoid." The local authorities hoped to be lucky when their new bishop arrived as the previous bishop had effectively controlled the minority of "progressive" priests that had been causing trouble.[43]

There was nothing new about youth being problematic at the end of the 1960s, except that the majority of young people were now showing signs of what had been going on among university students for years. The origins of student antagonism to the regime can be traced back to the end of the 1940s. A survey conducted in 1949 by their official union, Sindicato Español Universitario (SEU), demonstrated that a majority of students, including 90 percent at Madrid's Faculty of Humanities, professed an "incredible indifference towards political problems." Students were still in those years generally conservative, but, at the same time, they were idealists and they shared mixed feelings about politics (several Falangists, veterans of the Blue Division that fought alongside the Nazis on the eastern front, even expressed sympathy for the Soviet Union). Furthermore, other students were in "a period of evolution from indifference to the demagogic groups of opposition."[44]

Most students were primarily concerned about their own professional future. At the same time, they were skeptical about the regime's official line and began to divorce themselves from the Francoist vision. Students became critical after witnessing the regime's many failures to match rhetoric to achievement. They particularly resented the dictatorship's indifference regarding the inequalities in the country's economic development and the widespread social misery. Slums, a lack of agrarian reform and land distribution, corruption in government, the black market, poor funding for universities, the power of the Church and the army, and the growing power of Opus Dei, the reactionary Catholic organization, were all cited as sources of disillusionment on the 1949 student survey.[45]

During the 1940s and early 1950s, most students still used official terminology and reasoning to explain the state of things. However, Falangist language of equality and social justice, like Catholic rhetoric, was a double-edged sword for the authorities that so often provided glaring examples of hypocrisy.[46] Those who took this rhetoric seriously – those who, for example, read the fiery, poetic writings of José Antonio Primo de Rivera, the party's founder – often found themselves criticizing their own lives and, by extension, the regime when they looked around for evidence of the fulfillment of "National Syndicalist Doctrine."[47] The main peril of taking Francoism too seriously was that this most often led to a realization of how false its claims of justice were. Once this became clear it induced a process of disenchantment that often ended in open opposition or at least cynicism toward the dictatorship. For example, official propaganda claimed that Spain's peculiar political system was superior to others, but many students were noticing that this did not ring true. In a 1950 survey they said that, in countries like Germany and the United Kingdom, "in spite of all the strikes and party struggles, and all the difficulties, the truth is that [...] they have achieved an almost absolute normalcy in all aspects, especially in food supply."[48]

Up until 1952, the grievances of student protests were focused on purely professional issues such as asking for new courses, demanding improved instruction, and seeking an end to corruption and nepotism. What led to a shift to a position where many students viewed the regime as an oppressive dictatorship was not only that their grievances went unresolved or that the country's social problems were not being addressed; as important was the fact that, with the complicity of the SEU and the academic authorities, their protests were often met with senseless force by the police, as was witnessed in Madrid in November 1952. On that occasion, minor beatings and the formal detention of three people ended the matter, but the repression witnessed at these protests led many young people to think about politics for the first time, and they began to look for answers to the contradictions they saw around them.[49] It is surprising how rapidly some students, who often came from families connected to the regime, moved to positions of political opposition, and how quickly they made contact with other people with left-wing backgrounds. This was noted by the dictatorship, which realized that the vanguard of the student organizations no longer had a Falangist core. This was clearly demonstrated in February 1956 when a number of violent confrontations between protesting students and Falangist thugs in Madrid left a young Falangist gravely injured (since the students had no guns, the injury was likely inflicted by "friendly" fire). This incident caused a crisis in the government. The university was temporarily closed. There would be even more serious consequences for the regime than this. As a former Falangist university student leader explained, "After this, I had practically lost any hope that the Falange could carry out any revolutionary reform in Spain. The events of 1956 put an end to these hopes."[50] His conversion was far from unique.[51]

The truth is that only a minority of students moved in this direction at this time. The real divorce between the regime and students materialized later. In Madrid it happened between 1964 and 1965, when a number of protests and the overt repression that accompanied them served to radicalize students more than ever. It was then that pressure for democratization led to the dismantling of the SEU, the regime's official student union.[52] After this, the only tool the dictatorship felt it had at its disposal to deal with rebellious students was direct repression. Accordingly, from that time on the conflicts between students and authorities, and the riot police in particular, would increase in number and intensify in nature. This would fuel a dynamic of action–repression, until and beyond the end of the regime's tenure. The Madrid University protests became an example of how the official policy encouraging passivity had backfired, and in 1968, through a "cold and analytical assessment" of the situation, the authorities came up with the risible conclusion that "politicizing the youth" was the solution to their dilemma. But students were already politicized – in fact they had never been so politicized – it was just that they had different, often subversive, ideas.[53]

The presence of student centers rife with protest in a community created a markedly different political climate from those cities without a university, even if some university towns were relatively small, conservative, and lacked a sizable presence of mobilized workers. For example, in Valladolid in 1968, while worker activism remained calm and the "Marxist elements [...] did not undertake any public activities," students "promoted incidents in the streets, although on very few occasions and in small groups." No doubt, the improving trends in both employment and salaries had something to do with worker reticence.[54] The climate of restless student groups and calm workers was mirrored in Tenerife, where students from La Laguna University, "organized by a minority," engaged in political protests. By all indications, however, these actions were relatively small in scope. On the labor front in Tenerife, apart from one promptly solved minor conflict, the government was satisfied to see "the development of some sectors."[55] Similar reports were filed in the same year for Seville.[56] In the university town of Salamanca, disaffected youth made 1969 a "hot" year. Students boycotted classes and carried out numerous acts of protest, including the public reading of subversive poetry and music recitals. Authorities reported the singing of the Internationale. These protests were quelled only by the imposition of martial law. The student body, reported the authors of a confidential report, "previously indifferent," had started to take "notice of their rights," an inclination that even reached the local Pontifical University and its Faculty of Theology.[57] Even in Franco's relatively peaceful birth province of Corunna, students had joined Galician nationalist and Marxist groups and the Workers' Commissions, and they were making noises, often with the help of progressive priests and intellectuals.[58]

Student activism, and repression, now grew very quickly. In 1971, the police reported from Granada that the suspension of liberties that winter had helped them "to dismantle the subversive organizations related to student groups." They added that "the detention of students and other people foreign to the university, on the one hand, and, on the other, the flight [...] of the other activists mean an at least transitory, broken and disorganized" student mobilization.[59] Repression, however, did not achieve a reversal of the culture of change that had been cultivated among all young people – not only university students – who felt increasingly alienated from the political system and from what they perceived to be the outdated, negative values and expectations of the older generation. Local circumstances varied a great deal, but disgruntled high school teachers and poorly paid university professors, particularly those without permanent positions, also played a crucial role in mobilizing students and encouraging their rebellion. In 1971, in the relatively remote province of Caceres, for example, the police identified a number of temporary teachers as subversives, and the governor reported that "We have an agreement with the Ministry of Labor regarding their elimination [dismissal] as soon as the academic year is over." According to police, another source of the contamination of local youth was soldiers at local garrisons, usually young students themselves who had recently been drafted for their military service, but who flirted with "ideas." Caceres police denounced this influence, indicating the negative intoxicating impact that young priests, with their "Marxist," socialist leanings, and the soldiers, with their networks in larger centers like Madrid, had on the local youth.[60]

Certainly, the troublemakers and outright subversives were always in a minority. The quiet majority of young people remained passive. The gap between the contrarian minority and the politically conformist, pro-Francoist majority was real and could be seen on the streets. When the dictator visited the city of Cordoba in 1969 – a place that had strong left-wing traditions, and that later became a communist stronghold in the 1980s and 1990s – he received an "enthusiastic" reception from more than 100,000 people (out of a total population of 230,000).[61] December 1970 was a difficult month for the University of Salamanca, where protests against the Burgos trial (a famous military trial of ETA militants that handed down several death sentences, which the dictator later commuted), led to numerous incidents, including the use of Molotov cocktails by students. However, when Franco had visited the province on November 24 to inaugurate a dam, more than 50,000 people (in a city of 125,000) had gathered at the city's celebrated Plaza Mayor to greet the aging dictator. Again, on December 19, another 70,000 people demonstrated in support of the regime.[62]

This fervor for Franco was again massively manifest in December 1970 in Saragossa, where a huge "patriotic" demonstration took place in the city in support of the regime.[63] In Toledo, a city of 40,000, in 1970, the December 22 "patriotic" demonstration saw 30,000 people gather in support of the regime. This was reassuring given the fears that the installation of new factories and the creation of a university center were going to cause problems; "the infection by the politicized students from Madrid University" would be just a few kilometers away.[64] Although they were primarily protesting at "foreign interference" with the regime's policies against ETA, 1970's massive demonstrations in support of Franco illustrated that he still held a privileged position in the heart of Spaniards. He had become the semblance of an elderly, wise, and paternalistic martyr (Tío Paco, or Uncle Frank) who was suffering from international opprobrium for protecting his people from violence.[65]

An orchestrated television and print media propaganda campaign had a lot to do with this massive support in 1970, but the memory of civil strife from the war and the association of Franco with stability and order made the sentiments at these demonstrations genuine. He was more popular than his regime or his personally designated successor. When Prince Juan Carlos and his family visited the province of Valencia in February 1970, the most that local authorities could report about the event was the "enthusiastic" welcome by pupils at a local professional school. When Franco arrived in June, his welcoming was rather warmer and was described as an "apotheosis and a demonstration of homage by the whole province." This report may have been a bit exaggerated, but only a little, as photographs in newspapers attest. In December of the same year, when international condemnations rained down on the dictatorship because of the Burgos trial, a mass of "patriotic" people flooded Valencia's main square. This was very positive for the regime, given that this was a large city with a restive student population, "progressive priests," and active opposition unions in the area of Sagunto's port and steel mills.[66] In Granada, radicalized students were extremely active throughout the year in 1970 and, in July, construction workers had experienced a very nasty, violent strike that saw three of them shot dead by police. The civil government was still able to report that the December 25 "grandiose patriotic demonstration" gathered 80,000 people in the streets to show support for Franco. They sang and yelled in support of the regime as they passed by the gates of the civil government's headquarters, the provincial branch of the party and the "basilica of our Patron the Virgen de las Angustias, dissolving afterwards in perfect order."[67]

Most people knew they did not want violence, but, at the same time, they had very little knowledge of the problems the dictatorship and "peace" faced in the Basque country. Bombings and sabotage were not reported in the media, and neither was police brutality or torture. What was known about ETA then was that it was causing "trouble," and the majority of people adamantly rejected this. By 1970, Spaniards suspected that patriotic and pro-Franco fervor was far less evident in whole areas in the Basque country. Although it did exist, and remained strong, it had lost its supremacy on the streets. The days of the dictator's annual, wildly celebrated summer vacations in San Sebastian, which had included his participation in sailing and rowing competitions while thousands cheered, were over. Now his public appearances were rare when visiting the region, and he limited his stays to his summer palace (the Palacio de Ayete), or to sailing his yacht, the *Azor*. Security concerns for Franco were well justified. There was a lot of gloom and little to celebrate in the provincial governor's report for 1970.[68] That year, one person had been killed and several injured by police fire, 500 people had been detained, and 324, including several priests, fined. Several policemen were also injured. Apart from the deterioration of public order, bombings, attacks, and strikes, the worst part of this for the authorities was the "coldness of the population, its lack of reaction."[69]

The lack of public support for the regime in the Basque country was relatively new and, to an extent, it was the regime's own doing. Former left-wing guerrillas who returned in the 1940s knew that this region and Navarre had been hostile to them. The Basques had now lived in "peace" for two decades. ETA's first violent act was the derailment of a train full of veterans of the Francoist army who were on their way to San Sebastian to commemorate the July 18 holiday in 1961.[70] When ETA began to commit terrorist acts, Basque society was apolitical and nationalism was a distant memory for most people. As the founder of the organization's military branch remembered, "Young people of the 1960s generation knew nothing about our culture and traditions." Many of the early ETA militants came from Catholic circles, and priests were instrumental in "revealing" to these youngsters that they were different from Spaniards and that their Basque nation was being oppressed by Spain.[71] By the mid-1960s, the police began to feel frustrated with many prominent religious leaders, who were co-operating with subversive elements and using their privileged position to protect them.[72]

The ETA phenomenon cannot be separated from the rebellion of youth that most Western societies experienced in the 1960s, and from their idealization of the struggles of Third World countries. The terrorists first modeled themselves after Che Guevara and went to the countryside, as revolutionaries had done in Cuba, to look for the friendly, supportive peasantry who they thought would embrace their cause. They were disappointed. When, for example, on May 1, 1966, ETA members "liberated" the small village of Garay, Biscay, they had "to leave after failing to meet a single person. From time to time, someone looked from a window but, when approached, they closed them tightly."[73] Later their dreamed scenarios revolved around models such as good Catholic versus bad Protestant as in Ulster. Even more pathetically, some members of ETA dreamed of making a future independent Basque country a Western counterpart to Enver Hoxha's Albania.

Changing strategies after their failure to ignite a popular revolt, the young terrorists moved to actions of sabotage, assault, kidnapping, and ultimately murder. ETA first killed on June 7, 1968, when a young member of the Civil Guard from Galicia was murdered while on traffic patrol. A truck driver witnessed the incident and informed the police. One of the two terrorists involved died in the ensuing shootout; the other one was captured in a church the next day. He was condemned to life imprisonment. However, many people there already considered ETA militants as "freedom fighters" and "martyrs." The Civil Guard had to intervene several times to prevent the celebration of masses for the soul of the killer of the young member of the Civil Guard. The chain of events – of action–reaction – had begun; and a precedent had been set in which a local Basque killed by police was considered more a victim than a Spanish "foreigner."[74]

The Beginning of the End

The new decade promised to be crucial, even if nobody could predict accurately how events would develop. In 1970, the year of the Burgos trial, the regime was stable and the dictator popular, but problems ran deeper than anyone – either those within the hierarchy of the dictatorship or Spanish society at large – could see. Franco's plan of succession, in the person of Prince Juan Carlos, was problematic. It was met with far more loyalty than enthusiasm, "for being Franco's decision," by the regime's own supporters; and, of course, it was met with hostility from opposition groups. For many Francoists, the monarchy brought back memories of the hated liberal Spain, and they believed that Franco's plan ran the risk of ending up leading towards a political liberalization by the future Bourbon king. For opposition groups, Juan Carlos represented the continuity of the regime because he was Franco's choice. Most people perceived events with a mixture of indifference and concern.[75] Below these anxieties stood what escaped almost everybody – the government, the opposition, and the disoriented public – that the dictatorship had started to lose its grip on society. It is not that the regime had lost control of the streets or that a majority of Spaniards had become anti-Francoists (with the exception of parts of the Basque country and the universities). Both public order and the prestige of the aging dictator remained relatively constant. The regime, however, was now rapidly losing its hegemony over several key sectors of society such as organized labor, cultural circles, and community activists, who were vocally demanding change. In these spheres Francoism was seen as an annoying anomaly, an obstacle to a new, real normalcy. In addition to this, the economic model, a formula that had been so successful during the previous decade, was starting to show signs of serious wear.

The dictatorship had no alternatives available to address these challenges. Furthermore, this lack of perspective was starting to repel its own modern or civically minded sympathizers. This dearth of viable options to help resolve the new social and political demands of the 1960s and 1970s explains why the regime had to resort increasingly to repression. In 1968 the government imposed martial law in the Basque country, and in 1969 and 1970 this was extended to the whole of Spain. The dictatorship was firm on public order, but was increasingly adrift, in the grip of inertia. It even failed to understand the importance of the efforts of moderate or non-political groups and associations – neighborhood associations, parent groups, housewives' federations, professional colleges, cultural institutions, and a host of others – who worked within the political boundaries of the regime to reinvigorate society and to meet the challenges of a changing Spain. By ignoring the interests of these groups, it missed an opportunity to connect with its own society. In retrospect, it seems clear that Francoism could never have absorbed these changes from below because it ran against the regime's very nature to do so. While people were, to a greater or lesser degree, free to vote in their own associations, the dictatorship still held to its pretense that its fake elections represented the will of the Spanish people. And the most active sector of society was explicitly or implicitly rejecting this.

Repression had only a limited value. Following steps taken by the government the previous year, in 1968 the Supreme Court declared the Workers' Commissions "illegal and subversive." This opened a period of harsh repression that culminated in the detention of nine leaders of the organization's General Coordination Commission in 1972.[76] It was hoped that the group would disperse. It did not. In 1969, for example, the authorities detected an increase in the number of branches of the Workers' Commissions and other organizations in Madrid, especially in large companies in the metal sector such as Pegaso (trucks), Standard Eléctrica, Ericsson, Lanz Ibérica, Construcciones Aeronáuticas (planes), and others. The workers in these industries were the elite of Madrid's working class in terms of both job stability and wages. More worrisome for the regime was that the banned unions had begun to attract white-collar workers as well, and particularly in the larger banks – Banco Hispano-Americano, Banco Central, Banco Español de Crédito, and Banco Exterior de España. This sector had traditionally been very passive.

Rather than preventing the emergence of a new culture of protest, repression accelerated it, and it spread among groups that had previously been passive. This new culture transcended old class divisions and went well beyond unions merely seeking concessions from their employers. The word that best illustrates this new culture is solidarity, as organizations and groups began to challenge the regime and support the protests of other people or groups (both the role of the Church and the political use of solidarity between late Francoism in Spain and late Communism in Poland deserve a closer, comparative study). Although these new protests and the regime's response to them took place in a climate where a majority of Spaniards, particularly those who were older and socially weaker, still wanted next to nothing to do with politics, repression started to affect these same apolitical people. They may have gone on strike to protest for apolitical reasons. They believed they were only fighting for their rights, as many other people were doing, for what they *morally* deserved under the present political system. When these perceived rights were denied, and they or their relatives were beaten by the police, their moral values, and their indignation, became increasingly political. This development is consistent with the findings of the 1970 FOESSA study. There a majority of workers said that they preferred the present form of government, and only 30 percent preferred a republic (whereas, in stark contrast, only 1 percent of university students preferred the dictatorship while 76 percent wanted a republic). Yet the same people who wanted the system to continue also supported the right to strike (58 percent) and the freedom to organize that the government was so furiously fighting against.[77]

The tendency towards political change – or the conversion of social grievances and moral stances into demands for more freedom – moved slowly until the last two years of the regime, when it accelerated, but it only became dominant *after* the dictatorship's demise.[78] In another study, conducted in 1973, 54 percent of people said that they preferred Spain's present system of government and did not want to risk change; 33 percent stated that they thought the opposite. The minority advocating change was far more active than the politically inert, conservative majority even though, in the 1973 study, a clear majority of Spaniards thought that politics should imply more social responsibility for those in power (65 percent agreed with this statement while only 20 percent disagreed) and should be aimed at a more collective progress (62 percent agreed and 24 percent disagreed).[79] The majority's desire for peace first and foremost was evident, but the evolution of their political values showed them to be increasingly comfortable with the notion of plurality and tolerance as ways of resolving social disputes. In 1966, 68 percent of Spaniards polled chose the combination of peace, order, and stability as their first priority, while 20 percent chose the grouping of justice, freedom, and democracy. In 1975 the gap between these choices was reduced: 56 percent and 33 percent respectively. And in 1976 it shrank again: 44 percent chose peace, order, and stability while 40 percent chose justice, freedom, and democracy.[80]

What this pattern or evolution demonstrates is that the desire for peace shared by most ordinary people implied a rejection of violent confrontation but was not the same thing as carte blanche support for the regime. When political opposition groups demonstrating peacefully on the street or in the factory were met with violent measures by the dictatorship, these actions were counterproductive because they reminded people of the darkest past, of physical confrontation, what ordinary Spaniards feared and rejected most. When the regime's hardliners, who were never very popular, publicly called for even greater repressive tactics, ordinary people began to turn against them and, as the only available choice, towards democratic values that proposed tolerance and diversity as a solution. This may explain, on the other hand, why most Spaniards supported the government when ETA terrorists were put in prison and even when some were executed. People could distinguish fighting terrorists, a policy they agreed with, from the actions of the riot police when they beat and sometimes fired on striking workers or students, or detained neighbors when they were denouncing their *barrio*'s neglect. These repressive actions caused indignation. For the same reasons, people felt an increased distaste for the authorities' sanctioning of popular singers or writers who were expressing themselves and speaking for others. The yearning for peace was a part of a set of values that had given the dictatorship its political legitimacy in its early years. But now, in the increasingly diverse and demanding Spanish society of the late 1960s and early 1970s, these same values were undermining the regime's future.

These values also demanded that the language and positions of opposition groups conform to this desire for peace. No radical discourse, especially if it carried memories of violence along with it, was going to have significant popular support or electoral success. The "peaceful" attitudes of ordinary people encouraged moderation and tolerance and channeled the political options that were being offered on the path to democracy. The practical pessimism and pacifism of these same "pre-democrats," these ordinary Spaniards, set the parameters for the elite's repertoire of choices for a transition to democracy and defined the opposition's chances of achieving power in the future.[81]

The movement from passivity toward plurality in the late 1960s and early 1970s had its roots in the public's rejection of violence and repression, but was also connected to ordinary people's reactions to the absurd limits the regime imposed on people's cultural expression. Francoism had long since abandoned cultural leadership in the country, probably even before the 1950s, limiting itself from then on to the role of censor.[82] This passive-aggressive stance eventually took its toll on the regime. The desire to move beyond confrontation, to learn more about the past and the present, trans-formed into liberal and civic-minded values for the intellectual middle class and for young people from both right and left ends of the political spec-trum. Students and intellectuals read, often between the lines, the first mag-azines with reform agendas that the dictatorship allowed to be published: *Triunfo* (*Triumph*, first published in 1962), *Cuadernos Para el Diálogo* (*Notebooks for Dialogue*, which appeared in 1963), and *Cambio 16* (*Change 16*, first published in 1971) all offered fertile ground for the debate about peaceful change. The pursuit of these new values was helped along by the partial relaxation of censorship of the press that came in 1966. This new legislation brought an end to works being censored before publication but at the same time introduced several forms of punishment once openly critical opinions had been published. Nevertheless, this translated into a higher degree of transparency in regional newspapers, particularly Catholic dailies, which played a fundamental informational role for readers in the provinces. In the early 1970s, for example, the authorities constantly singled out Madrid's *Ya* and Seville's *Correo de Andalucía* for having a dissident voice, or, as it was put in the 1974 Seville civil governor's report, for pro-moting "subversion and manipulation."[83]

Most of the local incidents that caused such nervousness among the authorities were a direct result of the lack of civic representation within the political system and the absence of the regime's sense of responsibility toward the public. In this top-down, manipulative structure, the concerns and needs of ordinary people were far from the first priority. This strategy had worked well for the dictatorship when society was mostly rural, terror-ized, poorly educated, and had few expectations of government, but after the crucial social changes of the 1960s it was no longer an effective approach. As cities grew and the problems associated with this growth mounted, so did urban dwellers' demands on their chronically underfunded, barely responsive municipal councils. A minority response was to organize associations to protest. For example, in 1968, the until then quiet neighborhood of Barrio Yagüe in the city of Logrono (La Rioja) decided that they had had enough when the mayor asked them to contribute financially to the year's local holiday parade. Why would they do this? they asked. They wanted to know why money should be spent on this when their streets had gone unpaved for decades and they were recognized in other parts of the city by the mud on their shoes. Rather than monetary contributions they chose to paint critical messages on the neighborhood walls. The mayor was not amused, and neither were the political police (the Brigada), especially when they discovered that the parish priests were involved in this protest. Detentions followed, but with this action the regime's prestige sank a bit lower among the locals.[84]

This kind of expression of popular discontent had an added dimension, which was an expression of the dictatorship's political bankruptcy. Incompetence, and worse, delivered opportunities for local Francoist politicians to gain popularity by championing the issue at hand with cheap demagogy and by producing small scandals at city councils with explosive declarations in the local media. The conflicts within the city councils in the early 1970s, aired by a now freer press, represented, on the one hand, a growing dissidence inside the regime and, on the other, a desire by the local elites to capitalize on ordinary citizens' increasingly assertive discontent regarding the lack of services, mismanagement, growing signs of corruption, and general alienation from the system. The most active of these citizens were involved in neighborhood associations, cultural groups, and banned organizations, and in either moderate or increasingly subversive Catholic groups.[85] Catholic hegemony was more a product of the times than of genuine religious devotion. The only sphere that had escaped the regime's early attempts to monopolize public policy was that of the Church, and a number of alternative organizations sprang up from it. In fact, the only physical space that was safe belonged to the Church: parish houses, churches, and convents. This is why many labor and neighbors' associations started or had their headquarters in parish buildings.

Neighborhood associations were founded either in the late 1960s or, the majority, in the 1970s, and became part of this new civic movement.[86] The *barrios'* problems were growing exponentially because of the chaotic nature of their development. This shocked an increasingly affluent society. A logical approach to confronting these problems would have been to have frank, open debates and citizen participation in the decision-making process. This, however, went against the grain of the dictatorship and the interests of the local political elites, who did not wish to endure real public scrutiny. For this reason, official efforts to "solve" the social problems of cities were, by and large, pathetically self-referential and ineffective. They were full of trivial gestures and empty actions that reflected the power logic of the regime, but not the material needs of ordinary people, let alone their increasingly radicalized organizations. For example, the 1974–5 official plan to study Saragossa's neighborhood problems was conducted by the municipal government and city officials alone. No neighborhood associations were invited to participate and no public hearings took place. Popular representation was ignored and replaced by the regime's preferred Associations of Family Heads (Asociaciones de Cabezas de Familia), or, to put it bluntly, a group of pro-Francoist citizens who wanted to maintain the present system, not to challenge it. Those "moderate" citizens were often better off than those who lived in the *barrios*. Having "inspected" the city's neighborhoods in just one day and noting how much progress the city's periphery had made, Saragossa's authorities declared victory with satisfaction, patted one another on the back, and went home.[87]

Conservative yet civic-minded Spaniards, like the members of the Associations of Family Heads, had begun to mobilize in the mid-1970s, to voice their concerns about education and consumer issues. They were not alone. After a change in legislation in 1964, associations of Catholic parents, housewives, large families, domestic servants, people with disabilities, and a wide variety of others emerged in the last years of the dictatorship. In 1967 there were 1,672 such associations in Spain; in 1975 there were 4,074, including neighborhood associations. The people who participated in these new organizations were among the growing number of educated Spaniards, many of them political or social moderates, who in their role as professionals, employers, or civil servants despaired over the lack of responsiveness displayed by the Francoist system. They were deeply troubled by the anomaly that Spain's political system presented. They saw the mounting problems and the shortcomings of Spanish society, and looked to other European societies for solutions with an understanding that the answers were linked to a necessary but orderly political transition toward democracy. In principle, these groups were supposed to be apolitical, but most had internal democratic structures and many of their most intense debates revolved around how to vote for their leaders and how best to vet their actions, which made them, in practice, schools for the creation of a democratic civic culture. People could voice their opinions in their meetings, but they felt constrained and frustrated by the limited, if not non-existent, direct influence they had on politicians. People were free inside their association's walls, only to realize when the session was over and they stepped into the street that their country was still ruled by a dysfunctional, often aggressive dictatorship. Increasingly, like other far more radical organizations, they began to demand more accountability from those in power, which is to say democracy.[88]

On this same continuum of discontent of the educated were the growing ranks of limited-term and non-tenured university professors, *profesores no numerarios*. These intellectuals worked in precarious circumstances despite their education, and constituted a deeply dissatisfied and mobilized group.[89] They had similar values to their students, and quite often they protested alongside them (not unlike their counterparts in Paris or in Milan in 1968). They were among the people who read and cherished forbidden books of political theory or the banned or officially disavowed books of long since dead authors such as Federico García Lorca or Antonio Machado. When reading these works, they began asking about the fate of their authors – Lorca was executed by the Francoists shortly after the beginning of the war in his beloved Granada, while Machado died in exile in France shortly before the end of the war – and began asking why the country had gone so far down the road of violence in the 1930s. As they questioned the omissions in the stories of Spain's past, or rather the regime's version of it, they were examining Francoism itself. These same people who were reading these challenging poets and writers listened to the politically engaged music of singers such as Joan Manuel Serrat or Paco Ibañez, who mixed classic texts with openly subversive themes, both politically and morally.

The political culture of the growing minority was in constant conflict with the authorities. The regime and all other informed observers understood that in the early 1970s the majority of the creative elite – from painters to filmmakers, from writers to young singers – was firmly planted in the field of political opposition.[90] The world of culture operated in a climate of legal ambiguity, of tolerance without freedom, and artists often ended up with sanctions, fines, or some form of imprisonment for the scandals they caused or the supposed insults they leveled at the regime's personalities or institutions. As Manuel Andreu – a democratically elected leader of Barcelona's cultural institution Ateneo Colón – remembered about the years 1972 and 1973, when organizing an event they had to scratch their heads to find a way to avoid censorship or outright prohibition because, in those years, "you needed an official permit to even sneeze."[91] This repression had a profound effect on the country's cultural and artistic elites and created a collective sense of grievance among the increasing number of people with political and cultural interests. For example, even the most innocuous theatrical productions were interpreted politically by both the public and the regime, whether they were classical works or avant-garde plays and whether or not this was the intention of the artists. Every censored play (19 productions were closed for political reasons in 1970 and 48 in 1971) or banned song soon assumed celebrity status, and every artist who was a target of repression became a political champion of or national hero for freedom. This was particularly true of Catalan artists, who expressed themselves in their native language. In the early 1970s, to be educated increasingly meant being engaged in changing the country, and that was what was happening, to varying degrees, all over Spain.[92]

A key element of the regime's loss of cultural leadership was the internal divisions and transformation of the Catholic world, divisions and changes that became intensified after the Second Vatican Council and the promotion of progressive Spanish bishops by Pope Paul VI's nuncios. The culmination of this transformation came at the September, 1971 Joint Assembly of Bishops and Priests, which produced critical debates about the relationship between the regime and the Church. The dictatorship was alarmed, and spied on the bishops. However, while these developments were received with perplexity, "disorientation," and a sense of "a lack of authority or traditional discipline [within] the Church's hierarchical organization" by the conservative middle classes, the majority of the population met them with general indifference; most were more worried about material problems. What was most significant was that the assembly was the first public and critical reflection of any kind on the role of the Catholic Church during the Civil War.[93] This was the first time the dictatorship had received a clear signal that it could no longer count on the unconditional support of the bishops. More was to come. In a document from 1973 entitled "The Church and the Political Community," the bishops, for the first time, openly advocated a clear separation between church and state. An anxious and progressively adrift dictatorship knew that the Church's disengagement was backed by "the risk-taking and unclear attitude" of the prelates, 45 percent of whom – (35 out of 78) were identified as "progressives" and enemies of the regime.[94]

Facing the Future

Spaniards lived the end of the dictatorship under a darkening cloud of violence. ETA and the government were responsible for most of this. In 1969, in a relatively isolated act in Navarre, a provincial prison was attacked by ETA members who were trying to liberate their militant members.[95] The following year, as the Burgos trial progressed, there were incidents in Alava initiated by students, but these were primarily young people who were mimicking actions in other university towns across Spain. Alava was still a "safe" province for the regime, in spite of the contaminating influence of ETA that flowed from the other Basque provinces.[96] The environment was different in neighboring Biscay, where the level of active militancy by traditional left-wing groups, both parties and unions, was higher, and where nationalism and, in 1970 and more worryingly, ETA, already "had an important influence on a large sector of the population."[97] It must be stressed, however, that although it had already killed, this terrorist organization was primarily committing acts of sabotage and bank robberies, playing the role of a modern Robin Hood against both the state and local capitalism. The idealization of the terrorist was to have grave moral and political implications for the democratic future of Spain. After Franco's death ETA killed far more often, widely, and ruthlessly than it had during the dictatorship, and left-wing politicians would now be targeted as well. Of the roughly 800 victims of ETA terrorism in Spain, only 48 were killed under Franco while the rest were assassinated during the transition to democracy or once democracy had been restored.

Basque society was openly divided, but it retained important Francoist loyalties, which were made obvious in December 1970 by the heavy turnout at a "patriotic" demonstration in Bilbao in support of the dictator.[98] Spanish society as a whole was more pro-Franco, and certainly less sympathetic to political violence. These paths would diverge even further in the future, but these brewing contradictions literally exploded with the ETA killing of Admiral Luis Carrero Blanco on December 20, 1973. It was a stunning blow and a daring crime. Carrero had been the dictator's right-hand man since 1941. He was made deputy prime minister in 1967 and, as Franco's health deteriorated, was named prime minister in June 1973. It was widely understood that his mission was to guarantee the continuity of the regime after Franco's death and that he was to oversee the first years of his designated successor as head of state, the inexperienced, untested, and soon to be king,

Juan Carlos. Following the assassination, there was talk among the regime's diehards of striking back at all subversives.[99] Carrero's death could not have come at a worse moment for the regime, not only because Franco's health had noticeably deteriorated, but because it happened barely two months after the oil embargo that followed the Yom Kippur War and wreaked so much havoc on the world economy and on Spain.

Until Carrero's killing the regime had seemed to be in control of the situation. That year, for example, ETA, in spite of having "abundant means" to carry out its objectives, had failed to gain control of the "labor world, which is the objective of all organizations that confront the state" in Guipuzcoa, the province that along with Biscay shared the core of the terrorist organization's support. The clergy "took part [in] and showed solidarity" with ETA's actions; these included sermons in its support, collecting money for ETA members detained, and publicly denouncing their ill-treatment by police.[100] However, the province of Alava, another industrial region where ETA exerted some influence, had been practically incident-free in 1973, with the exception of a small number of strikes.[101]

Violence and confrontation marked the difference elsewhere too. Although it had far more industrial workers, in the province of Barcelona, in spite of the growing number of labor conflicts, the dictatorship felt that its challenges were manageable. In spite of this, in Tarrassa (Barcelona) in the first three months of 1973, there had been an "increase in actions by groups of workers, most of them young, and some fired from other companies [who] shamelessly opposed their official union representatives, calling them sell-outs, demanding their resignation through clandestine propaganda, and in some cases physically attacking managers, and proffering anonymous threats." Subversive activities in both "labor and student" spheres had been more intense between April and June, particularly around May 1, International Labor Day. In April, a worker had been killed when "the working mass confronted the police."[102] Also, in traditionally troubled Asturias, there were growing activities by communists and socialists, and even an openly political strike in the mines during the months of November and December, but workers' main concern that year was spiraling inflation.[103]

Prior to Carrero's death, the regime's officials in many parts of the country erroneously shared the notion that in 1973 tensions, and particularly labor conflicts, had been subdued. This impression came about largely because labor disputes had not increased as sharply as they had in the previous year and because, compared to Basque terrorism, other forms of protest were seen as minor offences. In the province of Corunna, the level of protest among workers and students had been rather "modest," in part because the leaders of a 1972 strike at the El Ferrol shipyard – where two workers had been killed – were still in prison. However the regime's attempt to launch an "institutional offensive" in Corunna to mobilize and reactivate its policies "did not go far among people."[104] Nothing particularly serious transpired in Seville that year.[105] In Saragossa there had been student protests, but fewer than in the previous year, while a number of worker strikes were reported.[106] In Granada there were "limited" subversive actions reported at the university, but attempts to commemorate May 1 and July 21, the anniversary of the 1970 killing of three workers by police, ended in failure as "the working mass did not at all follow the plans" of the subversive organizations. This was a province in which "political apathy [continued] to be the attitude of the majority" of a loyal population whose core concern was rising prices.[107] In nearby Malaga, the labor front had been quiet except for one strike at a textile factory that ended with 15 workers, including four union representatives, being fired. Their colleagues locked themselves into the cathedral for several days, but their demands were not met.[108]

In other parts of Spain the situation had been even less threatening in 1973. In the province of Alicante "the great majority [were] completely loyal to the organic structure of the country," but they had widespread concern about economic matters.[109] In Caceres no significant problems were reported, only "its peaceful social stability and its traditional political health."[110] In Gerona, the only troubling matter was that prices were rising faster than salaries.[111] The same was reported from the province of Cuenca.[112] In Orense, the situation was simply described as "good."[113] In the sometimes troubling province of Leon (where there were coalmines) there remained "unity and a firm attitude behind El Caudillo" and as long as he continued to be head of state "there will be no concern." It was further reported that the figure of the prince was becoming "more popular and accepted by people who initially did not sympathize with him."[114] Teruel reported an overwhelming "identification and loyalty towards the regime [...] and authentic veneration towards His Excellency head of state and generalissimo of the armies, Francisco Franco." As for the prince, it was stated that people "trust" him and "value his virtues." There was no significant political activity mentioned in the province.[115] However, this apparent calm would soon swirl into an open and definitive crisis.

In 1972 there were 853 labor disputes in Spain. In 1973 this number rose "modestly" to 931, but the very next year it exploded to 2,290, and in 1975 there were 3,156.[116] This mobilization of labor resulted in an increase in real salaries that was both significant – an average annual increase of over 8.5 percent between 1969 and 1975 – and slightly above increases in rates of productivity for the first time since the end of the Civil War. These income increases contributed to inflation, but paradoxically they led to a growing sense of frustration among workers. The process of salary negotiation took place once a year, at most. In practical terms, this meant that the percentage of income lost to inflation since the last wage revision went directly to the company's profit, and these profits were not passed on to employees. In other words, employees gained more in salaries, but, at the same time, as inflation spiraled, essentially worked for no pay for an increasing number of days.[117]

In the last two years of the regime there was a growing perception of the deterioration of both employers' and employees' material position. Inflation was hurting the economy, but mostly it was again denting poor people's incomes. The official rate of inflation from 1970 to 1974 was over 53 percent, and close to 17 percent in 1974 alone. Worse still was that the rate of inflation for essential family expenditure, items which ordinary people bought first, was even greater, surpassing 60 percent.[118] Inflation and the sensation of lost purchasing power despite rising salaries were closely linked, and this fueled more protests, which the widely discredited official unions and the regime were impotent to address.[119] The unelected and socially unaccountable authorities of the dictatorship were becoming irrelevant to both workers and employers. This led to an increasing degree of direct communication between employers and the representatives of the illegal unions – the Workers' Commissions, the resurgent Socialist Union, the UGT, and the smaller Catholic-Socialist Union, the USO. As the governor of Barcelona stated in 1974, "Workers, no doubt, are against the state institutions that affect them [the official unions]," and the companies were dealing directly with true worker representation, bypassing official channels.[120]

As the number of strikes mounted, the widespread impression was that, even though repression was as harsh as ever, the regime had all but lost its control over the most militant among the working class. In January and February 1974 alone, 24,814 workers were suspended without pay and 4,379 were fired outright.[121] Limited, targeted repression was not working and full-scale repression was no longer an option. Nobody wished to return to the horrors of the 1930s and 1940s. However, this loss of control was more a question of perception – so important to a repressive system – than of any real threat for, in spite of the huge impact the daily news of strikes and confrontations with the police had on the public, the total number of people striking in 1974 did not reach more than 650,000, and 70 percent of all strikes were concentrated in the Basque country, Barcelona, Madrid, and Asturias.[122]

Outside these difficult regions, the old mechanisms of control – apathy and threats of repression – were still effective. In 1974 in Granada, for example, the predictable "clear contrast between the capital and the rest of the province," primarily caused by the university, still existed. But the governor stated that most of the population identified with the regime, in spite of growing unemployment, communist penetration among workers, and the role of subversive priests.[123] In Seville, the "economic crisis" was causing "frustration" as problems mounted and were aggravated by rising unemployment as migrants returned from Europe. There were protests, but, again, nothing seriously threatened the regime.[124] In the province of Corunna, the most important political event of the year had been the "popular commotion caused by El Caudillo's illness this summer," even if there was an obvious "erosion" of order at the university (located nearby, in Santiago de Compostela), which was in part blamed on the academic authorities' tacit cooperation with those protesting. For most people, however, the main concerns were the year's price hikes, particularly those of gasoline and electricity, which created universal discontent that was augmented by the government's December 1973 decree that pay increases would be limited.[125] In other provinces such as Caceres,[126] Cuenca,[127] Gerona,[128] Teruel,[129] and Las Palmas,[130] the regime had the political situation under control and, in spite of a small number of labor conflicts, their climate remained relatively calm and "loyal."

This unraveling of control in 1974, or rather the public perception of unraveling, witnessed in the streets, in overtly confrontational protests at universities and through terrorism, was the most severe challenge that the dictatorship had ever faced. These events proved that the regime's tenets of "law and order" – its enemies called them terror and intimidation – were as good as dead. Public order and the economy, two of the three main tenets the dictatorship had upheld since the early 1960s, were foundering fast. The third and most important tenet, the dictator himself, was showing signs of grave physical decay. In 1974, Franco turned 82 and his health, already noticeably affected by Parkinson's disease, had faltered to the point where, that summer, he briefly relinquished power to Prince Juan Carlos. The regime's crisis intensified precisely at a time when the opposition was not only better organized than before but was actually coordinating its activities to plan for the future. Since 1973, opposition parties such as the socialist PSOE that was being protected by the International Socialist Organization, functioned openly with a semi-tolerated, although still illegal, status. Also, the reforming elites from outside and inside the dictatorship met frequently and more or less openly to discuss impending changes. This, of course, did not stop the political courts – the notorious Public Order Court – from prosecuting and sentencing political activists; of the 10,057 individuals brought to court between 1964 and 1976, 2,006 were people sentenced for subversive political activities. The Communist Party (PCE), the most active among the opposition parties, was particularly targeted for persecution. In the face of this, in July 1974 the PCE formed a coalition of parties to coordinate their anti-dictatorial struggle. The socialists founded their own platform in June 1975.

Then came the first shocks of the 1974 economic crisis, which was especially serious in Spain because of its acute dependence on oil imports and foreign investment, and because of the large number of emigrants, who began to return en masse. This phenomenon had two immediate negative consequences for the economy: a sharp increase in unemployment and the disappearance of currency remittances. Not least of all these factors was the government's inability to offer serious changes to its economic and social policies. By 1974 the dictatorship was reacting to these challenges in an increasingly erratic manner. Moreover, it had became incapable of imposing austerity policies on the highly mobilized workers. The Francoist government was becoming paralyzed, and at times lived in terror itself. A rude awakening came on April 25, 1974, when the sister dictatorship in Portugal was overthrown by a military coup. It did not escape the notice of the regime or of anybody else – everybody saw it on television – that the coup was enthusiastically received by the Portuguese population. However, despite some misplaced fears and hopes, depending on who was asked, there was no risk of a similar occurrence in Spain because the army, unlike the Portuguese military, was strongly in support of the dictatorship, a condition that would prove to be a major complication for the country when it began to move towards democracy.[131] Paralysis and fear were further increased because the regime's main international ally, the United States, proved that theirs was a calculated and limited friendship. In late 1975, following a diplomatic crisis with Morocco – which at one point seemed to point to war over the colony of Western Sahara – the United States clearly tilted towards its North African ally. Further international isolation followed, after five death sentences were passed against members of ETA and FRAP, a much smaller, Marxist terrorist organization, in September 1975. The huge protest demonstrations in Europe (the embassy in Lisbon was ransacked), the pressure of foreign governments, and even Pope Paul VI's call for clemency, went unheard. It was another sign of both the dictatorship's lack of direction and its intrinsically violent nature.

Francoism was not only adrift in world affairs. Its main pillar, Franco, was dying.

Anticipation of the end of the regime was full of fear and uncertainty, but when it arrived it was rather anticlimatic. On October 14, 1975, the dictator began to feel sick and he suffered a heart attack. From then on, his health deteriorated rapidly and, after a long and painful agony, he was officially declared dead early on the morning of November 20, 1975. In spite of all the socio-economic and political problems accumulated in the foregoing years, or perhaps precisely because of them, news of his death was met with a general calm and sadness. In his report for that year, written in 1976, the governor of Almeria explained that most people had supported the September executions, but that was secondary. The event of the year was "the emotional load, [of] his long and hard illness, that affected the majority of the Spanish people who witnessed with emotion the Calvary of such great Spaniard." He added that there had been several opposition demonstrations even there, in the deep and still very much impoverished south of Spain.[132] In the province of Cuenca, Franco's death caused "deep" pain among the population, and there was calm on the streets. A minority of people and some media reports were "pessimistic" or alarmist, the governor said, but most people had "trust" and supported "moderation."[133] In Las Palmas there was a "deep [show] of emotion, but serenity when confronting the long and painful illness" of Franco.[134] There was also "great pain" felt for Franco's death in Zamora.[135] Conversely, in Guipuzcoa, on the other side of the country both physically and mentally, it was ETA's activities and crimes, not the dictator's death, that seemed to matter most to people. ETA's crimes had increased during that year.[136]

For ordinary Spaniards, the anticlimatic "normalcy" of 1975 had been growing inflation, unemployment, and massive labor protests. In a nationwide poll conducted that year, 74 percent of respondents pointed to unemployment as their main concern, followed by inflation, social inequalities, strikes, and demonstrations. Only 24 percent of those polled seemed to be concerned with the lack of freedom.[137] And yet, in political terms, just around the time of the dictator's death strange things began to happen in places where next to nothing had occurred in decades. In the quiet province of Gerona, the governor stated that "Phrases and concepts were appearing, many of which were considered extinct. We witness the first signs of distress in the labor world and in some student circles."[138] In migration-bled, conservative Orense, some of the local newspapers were now making political life more "conflict-ridden." Suddenly, the governor began to remember and refer to guerrillas from the 1940s – which until now had been all but forgotten – the appearance of new political groups, the subversive activities of cultural organizations, and the resurgence of Galician separatist movements, while stating that the Movimiento had almost completely lost its influence.[139] From Seville, because of the increasing number of strikes, the governor denounced the "lack of a sense of responsibility of the working class," which was hindering the "democratic process" started by the government, "which the immense majority of Spaniards want."[140] This servant of the dictatorship, like so many other members of former Francoist elites, was in the process of becoming a spokesman for democracy and was trying desperately to put an inconvenient past behind him.

There has been plenty of debate about the degree to which Spanish society was democratic at the end of the regime's tenure. Evidently it had evolved rapidly towards democracy, and people who until the early 1970s had no political ideas, or so they said, had formed or were finding them to explain the new situation. For example, a study in 1971 revealed that only 12 percent of Spaniards believed that the existence of political parties was beneficial for the country; 23 percent declared the opposite, while 56 percent had nothing to say. In 1973, the numbers shifted to 37 percent in favor of political parties, 34 percent against, and 29 percent expressing no opinion. And then in April 1975, 56 percent were in favor of political parties, 22 percent were against, and 22 percent did not know if they were for or against the idea.[141] According to this study, in just four years Spanish, society had become "civic [and] democratic." However, this picture of a growing desire for pluralistic democracy must be questioned. In 1973, when people were asked a slightly different question, 61 percent of respondents declared their support for the existing system of political participation while only 23 percent wanted "representation through political parties." This means that, while most Spaniards in 1973 still wanted change, they were not, strictly speaking, in favor of democracy. However, they were aware that they had rights – including the right to choose their leaders – and that those rights stopped where other people's rights began. They were already citizens, and this would facilitate the ability of Spaniards to participate in democratic activity very soon, when political parties were legally formed and elections were held, for the first time since 1936, in 1977.[142]

The process of becoming a member of a democracy implied learning a new political language, but also remembering and speaking, bringing back the times witnessed, the stories suppressed during decades of repression, fear, silence, and lies. Perhaps there is no better summary of this process than the words of J.M.S., a woman and a social democratic voter from Alhama de Murcia: "I was happy with the transition to democracy. I lived for forty years with the regime and we were habituated to it, but I also missed the things that my father told me – he told me that socialism in democracy was participation."[143]

The year that Franco died, the balance had already tipped in favor of those who welcomed change over those who preferred the status quo.[144] And many would soon learn that what they had suffered for and what they had lost under the dictatorship could only be redeemed through democracy. The majority of ordinary people were beginning to "remember" what they had always known or suspected. This included revising their opinion of the man who ruled Spain with an iron fist and such a cold heart for close to 40 years. Finally, what people remembered of the terrible times of the dictatorship became his image.

NOTES

Introduction: Ordinary Spaniards in Extraordinary Times

1 See Paul Preston (1993), *Franco: A Biography*. HarperCollins, London.

2 For the "Golden Age" in perspective, see Mark Mazower (1998), *Dark Continent: Europe's Twentieth Century*. Alfred A. Knopf, New York, esp. chs. 6 and 9. For a more complete vision of the period see Tony Judt (2005), *Postwar: A History of Europe since 1945*. Penguin, New York, particularly from p. 241 on.

3 These accounts are derived from my experience growing up and the many stories I have heard from my family over the years. For a historical introduction to Almeria during the dictatorship see Óscar J. Rodríguez Barreira (2008), *Migas con miedo: prácticas de resistencia al primer franquismo. Almería 1939–1953*. Universidad de Almería, Almeria.

4 "The main causes of the present tension in prices are the ways economic development has taken place" and "the lack of elasticity in the offer to respond to demand." Food prices soared from a level 100 in 1955 to 138 by May 1958. As the unions from Saragossa stated, it was time that "workers living standards should truly rise, not just on paper, in cold statistics on consumption and in nice speeches." 1958. Consejo Económico Nacional Sindical (Gabinete Técnico). Informe sobre el problema de los precios. AGA-P 150.

5 This ludicrous project is best described by its protagonist in José Luis de Arrese (1982), *Una etapa constituyente*. Planeta, Barcelona.

6 For a critical view of Opus Dei see Joan Estruch (1995), *Saints and Schemers: Opus Dei and its Paradoxes*. Oxford University Press, New York.

7 The Falangists fought back hard with populist propaganda as, for example, they denounced the new policies by saying they were in line with big banks, "big hoarders of wealth," who were now restricting credit and "threatening ruin to small business[es]" owned by "thousands of Spaniards who, having only their honesty and work, launched themselves in the last years to develop small and medium industries." 27-6-1957. Falange Española Tradicionalista y de las JONS. Delegación Nacional de Información e Investigación. Nota

informativa n. 1342. AGA-P 145. The "oligopolies," they complained bitterly, considered that Opus Dei "had won the game." 27-6-1957. Falange Española Tradicionalista y de las JONS. Delegación Nacional de Información e Investigación. Nota informativa n. 1341. AGA-P 145.

8   See Enrique Moradiellos (2000), *La España de Franco (1939–1975): política y sociedad*. Síntesis, Madrid.

9   For an overview of the social development of Spain see Adrian Shubert (1990), *A Social History of Spain*. Unwin Hyman, London.

10   For an excellent local study see Roque Moreno Fonseret (1995), *La autarquía en Alicante (1932–1952)*. Instituto Gil-Albert, Alicante.

11   Jordi Catalán (1995), *La economía española y la Segunda Guerra Mundial*. Ariel, Barcelona, pp. 213–31.

12   For the evolution of the Spanish economy, see Keith Salmon (1995), *The Modern Spanish Economy: Transformation and Integration into Europe*. Pinter, London and New York. A brief study of the period can be found in Pablo Martin Aceña and Elena Martínez Ruiz (2007), "The Golden Age of Spanish Capitalism: Economic Growth without Political Freedom." In: Nigel Townson (ed.) (2007), *Spain Transformed: The Late Franco Dictatorship, 1959–75*. Palgrave, Houndmills, pp. 30–46. For the long view see Leandro Prados de la Escosura (2003), *El progreso económico de España*. Fundación BBVA, Madrid.

13   A classic, yet to be surpassed, study on Spanish peasantry is Eduardo Sevilla-Guzmán (1979), *La evolución del campesinado en España*. Península, Barcelona.

14   A complete sociological survey for the period may be found in Jesús Maria Vázquez (1967), *Realidades socio-religiosas de España*. Editora Nacional, Madrid. For an overview of the Catholic Church in Spain, see William Callahan (2000), *The Catholic Church in Spain, 1875–1998*. Catholic University of America Press, Washington.

15   An excellent local study is Javier Ugarte Tellería (1998), *La Nueva Covadonga Insurgente: orígenes sociales y culturales de la sublevación de 1936 en Navarra y el País Vasco*. Biblioteca Nueva, Madrid. A southern perspective can be found in Alfonso Lazo (1997), *Retrato de fascismo rural en Sevilla*. Universidad de Sevilla, Seville.

16   José Luis Leal et al. (1975), *La agricultura en el desarrollo capitalista español, 1940–1970*. Siglo XXI, Madrid.

17   Isaías Lafuente (1999), *Tiempos de hambre: viaje a la España de posguerra*. Temas de Hoy, Madrid. See also Miguel Ángel Almodóvar (2003), *El hambre en España: una historia de la alimentación*. Oberón, Madrid.

18   See Santos Juliá et al. (1999), *Víctimas de la Guerra Civil*. Temas de Hoy, Madrid.

19   Judt, *Postwar*, pp. 41–62.

20 Michael Richards (1998), *A Time of Silence: Civil War and the Culture of Repression in Franco's Spain, 1936–1945.* Cambridge University Press, New York, p. 7. See also Rafael Torres (2006), *Víctimas de la victoria.* Oberón, Madrid.

21 The number of victims of the Dutch famine has been estimated at between 18,000 and 30,000. Henri A. Van der Zee (1982), *The Hunger Winter: Occupied Holland 1944–1945.* J. Norman & Hobhouse, London, pp. 304–5.

22 1941. Resumé of report by the Medical Commission appointed by Dirección General de Sanidad to examine conditions in the provinces of Badajoz and Caceres. FO 371–26891.

23 More in Catalán, *La economía española.*

24 Juan Carlos Losada Málvarez (1990), *Ideología del ejercito franquista, 1939–1959.* Istmo, Madrid, pp. 157–61.

25 *Arriba* (1939), quoted in Rafael Abella (1984), *La vida cotidiana bajo el régimen de Franco.* Argos-Vergara, Barcelona, p. 21.

26 This was recognized in an official report that was quickly suppressed by the government. Ministerio de Agricultura. Servicio de Recuperación Agraria (1941?), *Memoria sobre la gestión realizada por este servicio desde su creación en mayo de 1938 hasta su extinción en diciembre de 1940.* Madrid.

27 Antonio Cazorla Sánchez (2000), *Las políticas de la victoria: la consolidación del nuevo estado franquista, 1938–1953.* Marcial Pons, Madrid, p. 87.

28 Ramón Garrabou et al. (1986), *Historia agraria de la España contemporánea,* vol. 3: *El fin de la agricultura tradicional (1900–1960).* Crítica, Barcelona, pp. 383–454.

29 Catalán, *La economía española,* p. 24.

30 Óscar Calvo-González (2006), "Neither a Carrot nor a Stick: American Foreign Aid and Economic Policymaking in Spain during the 1950s." *Diplomatic History* 30(3), 409–38.

31 See Sasha Pack (2006), *Tourism and Dictatorship: Europe's Peaceful Invasion of Franco's Spain.* Palgrave, Houndmills.

32 Quoted in Carme Molinero and Pere Ysás (1998), "Cambio socioeconómico y conflictividad social en España." In: José Manuel Trujillano and Pilar Díaz (eds.), *V Jornadas historia y fuentes orales: testimonios orales y escritos. España 1936–1996.* Fundación Cultural Santa Teresa, Avila, pp. 27–47.

33 The opinions of one of the fathers of the Francoist economy, in Higinio París Eguilaz (1981), *50 años de economía española.* H. París, Madrid.

34 Mar Cebrián Villar (2001), "Las fuentes del crecimiento económico español, 1964–1973." *Revista de Historia Económica* 19, 277–300.

35 Albert Carreras and Xavier Tafunell (2005), *Estadísticas históricas de España: siglos XIX y XX.* Nerea, Bilbao, vol. 2, p. 877.

1   The Politics of Fear

1   See Ian Gibson (1973), *The Death of Lorca.* J. P. O'Hara, Chicago.
2   The curious reader may google the words "Franco," "franquismo," and "cosas buenas" (good things), and will see that, from the leaders of Spain's main conservative party (Partido Popular) to ordinary people, this idea is rather frequent.
3   A very critical account of the left's role during the Republic in Stanley Payne (2006), *The Collapse of the Spanish Republic, 1933–1936: Origins of the Civil War.* Yale University Press, New Haven. For Asturias, see pp. 52–95.
4   See Helen Graham (2002), *The Spanish Republic at War, 1936–1939.* Cambridge University Press, Cambridge, 79–130.
5   For the long shadow of the Civil War in Spanish political life and its manipulation by Francoism, see Paloma Aguilar Fernández (2002), *Memory and Amnesia: The Role of the Spanish Civil War in the Transition.* Berghahn Books, New York.
6   To this day, national laws state that Spaniards will receive double pay cheques from their employers in the month of July, just as they do in December in celebration of Christmas.
7   For example, as early as February 1953 the secretary general of the party presented a confidential report on social housing and listed the "difficulties with materials, high cost of land [...] and lack of investment," among other difficulties, as the causes of the paltry offering for that year. In the whole country there were only 5,014 new apartments to be distributed in 37 provinces. 6-2-1953. Falange Española Tradicionalista y de las JONS. Secretaría Política, Sección Técnica. Resumen de las entregas de viviendas protegidas que se efectuaran con motivo del 18 de julio o en fechas próximas. AGA-P 92.
8   Perhaps the best example of this is Ronald Fraser (1979), *Blood of Spain: An Oral History of the Spanish Civil War.* Pantheon Books, New York.
9   Patrimonio Nacional (1950), *The National Monument of the Santa Cruz del Valle de los Caídos (Tourist Guidebook).* Patrimonio Nacional, Madrid, pp. 5–6.
10   Antonio Cazorla Sánchez (2007), "Patria Mártir: los españoles, la nación y la guerra civil en el discurso ideológico del primer franquismo." In: Javier Moreno Luzón (ed.), *Construir España: nacionalismo español y procesos de nacionalización.* Centro de Estudios Políticos y Constitucionales, Madrid, pp. 289–302.
11   Antonio Cobanelas Caamaño (1939), *Los cuatro meses de la modelo.* Gráf. Administrativa, Madrid, pp. 292–3.
12   Fernando Jansá (1956), *El encadenado por Cristo.* Manuel Sintes Rotger, Mahon, pp. 2–3.

13 23-2-1956. Falange Española Tradicionalista y de las JONS. Delegación Nacional de Información e Investigación. Movimiento y miembros del partido. AGA-P 56; 21-4-1956. Vicesecretaría General del Movimiento. AGA-P 56.

14 Antonio Cazorla Sánchez (2005), "Beyond They Shall Not Pass: How the Experience of Violence Re-Shaped Political Values in Early Franco Spain." *Journal of Contemporary History* 40, 503–20.

15 Antonio Cazorla Sánchez (2002), "Surviving Franco's Peace: Spanish Popular Opinion during World War II." *European History Quarterly* 32(3), 391–411.

16 Stanley Payne (2008), *Franco and Hitler: Spain, Germany, and World War II.* Yale University Press, New Haven.

17 Simona Colarizi (1991), *L'opinione degli italiani sotto il regime, 1929–1943.* Laterza, Bari.

18 Ian Kershaw (1985), *Popular Opinion and Political Dissent in the Third Reich: Bavaria 1933–1945.* Clarendon Press, Oxford.

19 Orlando Figes (2007), *The Whisperers: Private Life in Stalin's Russia.* Metropolitan Books, New York.

20 22-6-1949. The chargé d'affaires in Spain (Culbertson) to the Secretary of State. Reproduced in *Foreign Relations of the United States*, vol. 4: *Western Europe* (1975). United States Printing Office, Washington, DC, pp. 750–3.

21 November 1950. Falange Española Tradicionalista de las JONS. Jefatura Provincial de Málaga. Parte mensual de información correspondiente a noviembre de 1950. AGA-P 268.

22 November 1950. Falange Española Tradicionalista y de las JONS. Jefatura Provincial de Valencia. Informe que emite el Jefe Provincial del Movimiento de Valencia ante el Delegado Nacional de Provincias para conocimiento del Secretario General, en resumen del ambiente político y de las actividades desarrolladas a lo largo del mes de noviembre de 1950. AGA-P 268.

23 Vicente Fernández Benítez (1993), "Los lugares comunes en la memoria colectiva." In: José Manuel Trujillano Sánchez (ed.), *III Jornadas historia y fuentes orales: memoria y sociedad en la España contemporánea.* Fundación Cultural Santa Teresa, Avila, pp. 71–91.

24 Ministerio de Justicia (1946), *The Red Domination in Spain: The General Causa.* Afrodisio Aguado, Madrid.

25 Fernández Benítez, "Los lugares comunes en la memoria colectiva."

26 Ibid.

27 A very critical account of the Church's role during the war in Julián Casanova (2005), *La Iglesia de Franco.* Crítica, Barcelona.

28 Raúl Soutelo Vázquez and Alfredo Varela Sabas (1993), "Variaciones en las formas de represión y resistencia popular en el medio rural ourensano. 1936–1946." In: Trujillano Sánchez (ed.), *III Jornadas historia y fuentes orales*, pp. 217–33.

29 Ibid.

30   Julio de la Cueva Merino (1998), "Religious Persecution, Anticlerical Tradition, and Revolution." *Journal of Contemporary History* 33(3), 355–69.

31   Begoña Serrano Ortega (1993), "La represión franquista en Asturias a través de las fuentes orales." In: Trujillano Sánchez (ed.), *III Jornadas historia y fuentes orales*, pp. 239–49.

32   In August 1950 the authorities of the province of Seville were happy to report the "absolute normality and tranquility" that month (despite some "difficulties" among poor people because of the lack of basic staples) as the Civil Guard had killed two "bandits" and the police detained several left-wing militants, most of them anarchists. 21-8-1950. FET y de las JONS. Jefatura Provincial de Sevilla. AGA-P 267.

33   Ricard Vinyes, Montserrat Armengol, and Ricard Belis (2003), *Los niños perdidos del franquismo*. De Bolsillo, Barcelona.

34   Jesús J. Alonso Carballes (1993), "La integración de los niños vascos exiliados durante la guerra civil en la sociedad franquista de posguerra." In: Trujillano Sánchez (ed.), *III Jornadas historia y fuentes orales*, pp. 173–84.

35   Saturnino Rodríguez (1999), *NO-DO: catecismo social de una época*. Editorial Complutense, Madrid.

36   28-3-1953. Informe del compañero Antonio Morales Belmonte, recién llegado de España. Maestro nacional. AFPI–635–32.

37   Fuensanta Escudero Andújar (2000), *Lo cuentan como lo han vivido (republica, guerra y represión en Murcia)*. Universidad de Murcia, Murcia, p. 139.

38   For more on women militants see Fernanda Romeu Alfaro (1994), *Mujeres contra el franquismo*. SF Alfaro, no place given.

39   Carmen González Martínez (1997), "Sobrevivir a la represión franquista: condiciones de vida y trabajo de los represaliados murcianos." In: José Manuel Trujillano and José María Gago (eds.), *IV Jornadas historia y fuentes orales: historia y memoria del franquismo*. Fundación Cultural Santa Teresa, Avila, pp. 425–37.

40   His case was far from unique. See Antonio Castillo and Feliciano Montero (coord.) (2003), *Franquismo y memoria popular: escrituras, voces y representaciones*. Siete Mares, Madrid.

41   José Aldomar Gutiérrez (2006), *Condenado a muerte (1939–1941)*. Historia Social, Valencia.

42   Ibid., p. 76.

43   Serrano Ortega, "La represión franquista en Asturias."

44   Encarna Nicolás Marín and Alicia Alted Vigil (1999), *Disidencias en el franquismo (1939–1975)*. Diego Marín, Murcia.

45   Francisco Moreno Gómez (1985), *La Guerra Civil en Córdoba (1936–1985)*. Alpuerto, Madrid.

46   Dolors Marín Silvestre (2002), *Clandestinos: el Maquis contra el franquismo, 1934–1975*. Plaza y Janés, Barcelona.

47 Juan Martínez Alier (1968), *La estabilidad del latifundismo: análisis de la interdependencia entre las relaciones de producción y la conciencia social en agricultura latifundista en la Campiña de Córdoba*. Ruedo Ibérico, Paris.

48 An exhaustive analysis of the issue in George Collier (1987), *Socialists of Rural Andalusia: Unacknowledged Revolutionaries of the Second Republic*. Stanford University Press, Stanford.

49 Political activists would make up the majority of those detained and persecuted during strikes and periods of socio-political tension of the Franco years. In the whole country 3,899 people were detained in 1947, 1,698 in 1956, and 1,442 (plus 996 strikers) in 1962[0]. They were also to be the ones who passed on ideas, methods, and inspiration to the new generation of labor and opposition groups of the 1960s. Abdón Mateos (2003), "Vieja y nueva oposición obrera contra Franco." *Historia Contemporánea* 26, 77–89.

50 For the pre-war period see Rafael Cruz (2006), *En el nombre del pueblo: república, rebelión y guerra en la España de 1936*. Siglo XXI, Madrid. For the war on the republican side see Michael Seidman (2002), *Republic of Egos: A Social History of the Spanish Civil War*. University of Wisconsin Press, Madison.

51 Fraser, *Blood of Spain*.

52 A good local study is Javier Cervera Gil (2000), *Madrid en guerra: la ciudad clandestina, 1936–1939*. Alianza, Madrid.

53 Javier Rodrigo (2005), *Cautivos: campos de concentración en la España franquista, 1936–1947*. Crítica, Barcelona, p. 71.

54 Escudero, *Lo cuentan como lo han vivido*, p. 108.

55 Carlos Gil Andrés (2006), "Vecinos contra vecinos: la violencia en la retaguardia riojana durante la Guerra Civil." *Historia y Política* 16, 109–30.

56 Susana Narotzky and Gavin Smith (2002), "'Being Político' in Spain: An Ethnographic Account of Memories, Silences and Public Politics." *History and Memory* 14(1/2), 189–228.

57 Julius Ruiz (2005), "A Spanish Genocide? Reflections on the Francoist Repression after the Spanish Civil War." *Contemporary European History* 14(2), 171–91.

58 José Manuel Sabín (1996), *Prisión y muerte en la España de postguerra*. Anaya-Mario Muchnik, Madrid.

59 1943. Informe sobre la Moralidad en España del patronato de Protección de la Mujer. APG 40–1 and 2.

60 Edward Malefakis (1970), *Agrarian Reform and Peasant Revolution in Spain: Origins of the Civil War*. Yale University Press, New Haven.

61 1938. Memoria del Gobierno Civil de Asturias, AGA-G 2796; 1938. Memoria del Gobierno Civil de Vizcaya. AGA-G 3175.

62 See Cazorla Sánchez, *Las políticas de la victoria*, pp. 98–110.

63 Antonio Cazorla Sánchez (1999), *Desarrollo sin reformistas: dictadura y campesinado en el nacimiento de una nueva sociedad en Almería, 1939–1975*. Instituto de Estudios Almerienses, Almería, p. 100.

64 15-5-1957. Jefatura Provincial de Cáceres. Síntesis informativa para el Excmo. Sr. Ministro Secretario General del Movimiento. AGA-P 1937.

65 Antonio Soriano (1989), *Éxodos: historia oral del exilio republicano en Francia, 1939–1945*. Crítica, Barcelona, pp. 77–88.

66 Ibid., pp. 123–30.

67 Dolores Pla Brugat (1997), "La experiencia del regreso: el caso de los exiliados republicanos catalanes." In: Trujillano and Gago (eds.), *IV Jornadas historia y fuentes orales*, pp. 71–92.

68 Ibid.

69 Ibid.

70 27-3-1957. Presidencia del Gobierno. Secretaría Política. Informe personal y reservado sobre españoles recientemente repatriados de Rusia. AGA-P 147 sp.

71 Juan Marsal (1979), *Pensar bajo el franquismo*. Península, Barcelona.

72 Francisco Sevillano Calero (1998), *Propaganda y medios de comunicación en el franquismo*. Universidad de Alicante, Alicante, pp. 78–95.

73 Juan Sáez Marín (1988), *El Frente Juventudes: política de juventud en la España de postguerra (1937–1960)*. Siglo XXI, Madrid. Rosario Sánchez López (1990), *Mujer española: una sombra de destino en lo universal*. Universidad de Murcia, Murcia.

74 Vázquez, *Realidades socio-religiosas de España*, pp. 92–119.

75 Losada, *Ideología del ejercito franquista*, pp. 270–9.

76 See Carme Molinero (2005), *La captación de las masas: política social y propaganda en el régimen franquista*. Cátedra, Madrid.

77 José Babiano Mora (1998), *Paternalismo industrial y disciplina fabril en España (1938–1958)*. Consejo Económico y Social, Madrid.

78 A local example can be found in Abdón Mateos (2005), *La contrarrevolución franquista: una aproximación a la represión contra UGT y al nacionalsindicalismo desde Cantabria rural, 1937–1953*. Historia del Presente, Madrid, and an international example in Abdón Mateos (1997), *La denuncia del Sindicato Vertical: las relaciones entre España y la Organización Internacional del Trabajo*. Consejo Económico y Social, Madrid.

79 27-12-1954. Delegación Nacional de Sindicatos. Servicio de Organización. AGA-S 4805.

80 26-9-1958. Peticiones de la Delegación Sindical del Puerto de Sagunto al Secretario General de la Organización Sindical. AGA-S 4848.

81 1954. Sindicatos. Secretaría Política. Informe sobre Sindicatos de Barcelona. AGA-P 100 sp.

82 23-5-1951. Falange Española Tradicionalista y de las JONS. Jefatura Provincial. Madrid. AGA-P 89.

83 Carmen Benito del Pozo (1993), *La clase obrera asturiana bajo el franquismo*. Siglo XXI, Madrid.

84 1949. Peticiones que elevan al Camarada Raimundo Fernández Cuesta, como Ministro y Secretario General del Movimiento, las Secciones Sociales y Económicas de los Sindicatos provinciales de Huesca. AGA-P 49 sp.

85 5-11-1953. El Gobernador Civil de Vizcaya y Jefe Provincial del Movimiento. Consejero Nacional. AGA-P 91 sp.

86 September, 1953. Delegación Provincial de Sindicatos. Salamanca. Informe general sobre la Organización Sindical de la Provincia. AGA-S 4805.

87 15-12-1955. Delegación Nacional de Sindicatos. Reservado. AGA-S 4748.

88 c.1950. Tomas de Allende y García-Baxter. Notas sobre sindicalismo agrario. AGA-S 4763.

89 A local study in Manuel Ortiz Heras (1992), *Las Hermandades de labradores en el franquismo. Albacete 1943–1977*. Diputación de Albacete, Albacete.

90 16-11-1954. Delegación Nacional de Sindicatos. Servicio de Organización. AGA-S 4805.

91 Cazorla Sánchez, *Las políticas de la victoria*, pp. 183–91.

92 14-1-1958. Del Ministro de Trabajo al Sr. D. José Solís Ruiz. Ministro-Secretario General del Movimiento. AGA-S 4353.

93 28-10-1960. Secretario General del Movimiento. El Secretario Técnico. AGA-S 4353.

94 15-12-1960. El Secretario General de la Organización Sindical. AGA-S 4354.

95 15-2-1961. Excmo. Sr. D. Camilo Alonso Vega. Ministro de la Gobernación. Madrid. AGA-S 4353.

96 These data are taken from the *Repertorio biográfico de procuradores en Cortes* (Madrid, 1971), quoted in José Félix Tezanos (1975), *Estructura de clases en la España actual*. Cuadernos Para el Diálogo, Madrid, p. 131.

97 Between 1949 and 1952 the Catholic missions were concentrated in the following mining and industrial areas: Almeria, Asturias, Barcelona, Cuenca, Ciudad Real, Leon, Murcia, Gerona, Santander, Teruel, Palencia, Biscay, and Saragossa. 1-8-1955. Campaña misionales organizadas y desarrolladas por la Dirección General de Apostolado (Subsección de Misiones) en las zonas mineras e industriales. AGA-S 4358.

98 [1958]. Delegación Nacional de Sindicatos. Lista de los pueblos mineros-industriales y ganaderos misionados por la Asesoría Eclesiástica Nacional. AGA-P 150.

99 In 1958 the missionaries working in the mining regions of Palencia made a curious distinction between souls (30,000) and workers (10,000) cured, demonstrating pride in the fact that they had attended to so many of the latter, more difficult, group. At the same time, it was noted that technicians and managers did not attend the different activities because they considered the missions to strictly be "for working elements." It was the only black spot on an otherwise successful campaign of the impressive army of 16 Capuchins, 11 Franciscans, eight priests from the Holy Heart of Mary, six Dominicans, two Passionists, one Jesuit, and seven parish priests. Ibid.

100 7–16-4-1961. Misión General de Puertollano. Folleto informativo dirigido a los Padres Misioneros por el P. Villalobos, Director de la Misión. AGA-S 4358.

101 The best study in Joan Maria Thomàs (1999), *Lo que fue de la Falange*. Plaza y Janés, Barcelona.

102 September 1942. Falange Española Tradicionalista y de las JONS. Delegación Nacional de Información e Investigación. Resumen del ambiente político general de la segunda quincena del mes de setiembre. AGA-P 240.

103 A local study in Manuel Ortiz Heras (1996), *Violencia política en el II República y el primer franquismo*. Siglo XXI, Madrid.

104 Cazorla Sánchez (1999), "Dictatorship from Below: Local Politics in the Making of the Francoist State, 1937–1948." *Journal of Modern History* 71(4), 882–901.

105 A good local study is Damián González Madrid (2007), *Los hombres de la dictadura: personal político franquista en Castilla-La Mancha, 1939–1945*. Ediciones de Almud, Ciudad Real.

106 Escudero, *Lo cuentan como lo han vivido*, p. 131.

107 See Mercedes Vázquez de Prada (2003), "La oposición al régimen franquista en Barcelona. Algunas muestras entre 1948 y 1951." *Hispania* 63(3), 215, 1057–78.

108 "Indifference among the population" was the description many governors used as they prepared for the 1948 municipal elections. 15-11-1948. Falange Española Tradicionalista y de las JONS. Secretaría. Jefatura Provincial de Guadalajara. AGA-P 197.

109 17-11-1948. Jefatura Provincial Falange Española Tradicionalista de las JONS de Pontevedra. Informe. Apreciaciones de orden político que sugiere esta Jefatura Provincial la convocatoria a elecciones municipales y, especialmente, el desarrollo de estas en lo relacionado con la proclamación de candidatos por el tercio de representación familiar. AGA-P 197.

110 16-11-1948. Gobierno Civil de la Provincia de Valladolid. Secretaría Política. AGA-P 197.

111 18-11-1948. Falange Española Tradicionalista de las JONS. Jefatura Provincial de valencia. Personal y reservado. Informe que eleva el jefe Provincial del Movimiento de Valencia al Secretario General, en contestación al telegrama oficial de fecha 15 de noviembre de 1948. AGA-P 197.

112 16-11-1948. Gobierno Civil de la Provincia de Cuenca. Secretaría General. AGA-P 197.

113 18-11-1948. Falange Española Tradicionalista de las JONS. Jefatura Provincial de Sevilla. AGA-P 197.

114 19-11-1948. Jefatura Provincial de FET de las JONS de Ciudad Real. Reservado. AGA-P 197.

115 15-11-1948. Falange Española Tradicionalista de las JONS. Secretaría. Jefatura Provincial de Orense. AGA-P 197.

116 There were also 1,062 former leftists and republican councilors elected, but the authorities confirmed that in 100 percent of these cases these people were now diligent followers of the regime. 1952. Secretaría General del Movimiento. Delegación Nacional de Provincias. Resumen estadístico de los ayuntamientos de España, totalizados a raíz de las elecciones municipales de noviembre de 1951, según datos facilitados por las jefaturas provinciales del Movimiento. AGA-P 317.

117 A local study in Francisco Cobo Romero and Maria Teresa Ortega López (2005), "No sólo Franco: la heterogeneidad de los apoyos sociales al régimen franquista y la composición de los poderes locales. Andalucía, 1936–1948." *Historia Social* 51, 49–72.

118 1950. Falange Española Tradicionalista y de las JONS. Jefatura Provincial de Guipúzcoa. Parte mensual de actividades, correspondiente al mes de junio de 1950. AGA-P 266.

119 1950. Falange Española Tradicionalista y de las JONS. Jefatura Provincial de Barcelona. Parte mensual de actividades, correspondiente al mes de junio de 1950. AGA-P 266.

120 December 1954. Falange Española Tradicionalista y de las JONS. Jefatura Provincial de Baleares. Informe sobre campaña electoral de 1954. AGA-P 266.

121 3-3-1957. Albacete. Informe de la Jefatura provincial del Movimiento sobre elecciones municipales de 1957. AGA-P 318.

122 4-11-1957. Falange Española Tradicionalista y de las JONS. Informe sobre las próximas elecciones municipales a celebrar en la plaza de Ceuta. AGA-P 318.

123 21-10-1957. FET y de las JONS. Jefatura Provincial de Soria. Urgente y Reservado. Orden de Servicio para todos los jefes locales del Movimiento. Circular 4/57. AGA-P 318.

124 1971. Memoria de gestión del Gobierno Civil de Huesca. AGA-I 507.

125 1971. Memoria de gestión del Gobierno Civil de Vizcaya. AGA-I 504.

126 1971. Memoria de gestión del Gobierno Civil de Las Palmas. AGA-I 503.

2   The Social Cost of the Dictatorship

1 In the regions of the sierras of Cazorla, Segura, and Magina in Andalusia and in all of Jaen province, more than three-quarters of those shot by the Francoists up to 1950 were landless peasants. Francisco Cobo Romero and Teresa María Ortega López (2003), "La protesta de sólo unos pocos: el débil y tardío surgimiento de la protesta laboral y la oposición democrática franquista en Andalucía Oriental, 1951–1976." *Historia Contemporánea* 26, 113–60.

2 Jesús J. Alonso Carballes (1997), "La integración de los niños vascos exiliados durante la guerra civil en la sociedad franquista de posguerra." In: Trujillano and Gago (eds.), *IV Jornadas historia y fuentes orales*, pp. 173–84.

3 Luis Enrique Alonso and Fernando Conde (1994), *Historia del consumo en España: una aproximación a sus orígenes y primer desarrollo*. Debate, Madrid, p. 131.

4 David Ginard i Feron (2002), "Las condiciones de vida durante el primer franquismo: el caso de las Islas Baleares." *Hispania* 62(3), 212, 1099–1128.

5 Ibid.

6 Abella, *La vida cotidiana bajo el régimen de Franco*, pp. 49–52.

7 19-8-1941. British Embassy, Madrid. FO 371–26891.

8 Manuel Pérez Urruti (1942), *España en números: síntesis de la producción, consumo y comercio nacionales, 1940–1941*. M. Aguilar, Madrid, p. 8.

9 4-3-1941. Distribution B; Spain. FO 371–26890.

10 1941, Résumé of report by medical commissions appointed by the Dirección General de Sanidad to examine conditions in the provinces of Badajoz and Caceres, FO 371–26891.

11 Alonso and Conde, *Historia del consumo en España*, pp. 124–5, 133.

12 Richards, *A Time of Silence*, p. 7.

13 Juliet Gardiner (2004), *Wartime Britain*. Headline, London, pp. 160–89. For Germany see Götz Aly (2005), *Hitler's Beneficiaries: Plunder, Racial War, and the Nazi Welfare State*. Metropolitan Books, New York.

14 Conxita Mir Cucó (2000), *Vivir es sobrevivir: justicia, orden y marginación en la Cataluña rural de posguerra*. Milenio, Lerida, pp. 134–9.

15 Cámara de Comercio de Bilbao (1945), *La economía vizcaína en 1944: principales estadísticas de producción, consumo y tráfico*. Cámara de Comercio, Bilbao, p. 74.

16 1950. Memoria-informe que eleva al Excmo. Sr. Ministro de la Gobernación el Gobernador Civil de Almería. AGA-G 3310.

17 This was suggested in a comparative study with Italy in Leandro Prados de la Escosura and Vera Zamagni (eds.) (1995), *El desarrollo económico de la Europa del sur: España e Italia en perspectiva histórica*. Alianza, Madrid.

18 1953. Consejo de Economía Nacional. Resultado de una encuesta sobre los salarios en la industria española. AGA-P 95 sp.

19 Vázquez de Prada, "La oposición al régimen franquista."

20 8-2-1950. Delegación Nacional de Sindicatos. Secretaría Nacional. AGA-P 61.

21 Jesús A. Martínez (coord.) (1999), *Historia de España siglo XX, 1939–1996*. Cátedra, Madrid, p. 58.

22 10-1-1956. Sindicato Vertical de Industria Químicas. Acuerdos de la Sección Social Central del Sindicato Vertical de Industrias Químicas. AGA-P 56.

23 1958. Secretaría General del Movimiento. Secretaría Técnica. Comisión Delegada de Sanidad y Asuntos Sociales. Ambiente Social. Precios y Salarios. AGA-P 150.

24 20-8-1949. Delegación Nacional de Sindicatos. Delegación. AGA-P 52.

25 1952. Informe sobre paro estacional agrícola en la provincial de Jaén y posible remedios del mismo. AGA-P 130 sp.

26 27-3-1951. Secretaría General de Falange Española Tradicionalista y de las JONS. Informe sobre situación obrera en Jaén y su provincia. AGA-P 72.

27 Brothels were not always just somewhere for quick sex; in places, they were a source of family and community sustenance. It was not uncommon for several generations of the same family to work or live in brothels, including children and husbands. Andrés Moreno Mengíbar and Francisco Vázquez García (2004), *Historia de la prostitución en Andalucía*. Fundación José Manuel Lara, Seville, pp. 243, 246–9.

28 An overview in Mirta Núñez Díaz-Balart (2003), *Mujeres caídas: prostitutas legales y clandestinas en el franquismo*. Oberón, Madrid.

29 14-3-1951. Falange Española Tradicionalista y de las JONS. Jefatura Provincial. Ciudad Real. Acta del Consejo Provincial de FET de las JONS celebrado el 14 de marzo de 1951. AGA-P 278. 27-3-1951. Falange Española Tradicionalista y de las JONS. Jefatura Provincial. Almería. Copia del acta numero veintidós de la reunión del Consejo Provincial de FET de las JONS celebrado el día veintisiete de marzo de 1951. AGA-P 278.

30 AGA-P 278. 27-3-1951. Falange Española Tradicionalista y de las JONS. Jefatura Provincial. Almería. Copia del acta numero veintidós de la reunión del Consejo Provincial de FET de las JONS celebrado el día veintisiete de marzo de 1951. AGA-P 278.

31 See Mónica Orduño Prada (1996), *El auxilio social (1936–1940)*. ONCE, Madrid.

32 31-1-1953. Informe y datos estadísticos sobre el Seguro Obligatorio de Enfermedad. AGA-P 298.

33 Esteban Rodríguez Ocaña (1998), "La construcción de la salud infantil: ciencia, medicina y educación en la transición sanitaria en España." *Historia Contemporánea* 18, 19–52.

34 A description of this phenomenon can be found in José Martí Gómez (1995), *La España del estraperlo*. Planeta, Barcelona.

35 Margaret Van Epp Salazar (1998), *"Si yo te dijera…": una historia oral de la Sierra de Huelva*. Fundación Machado, Seville, pp. 218–25.

36 Escudero, *Lo cuentan como lo han vivido*, p. 193.

37 Julio Prada and Raúl Soutelo (1998), "La resistencia económica en el primer franquismo. Una aproximación al estraperlo desde la memoria oral: Orense, 1939–1952." In: Trujillano and Díaz (eds.), *V Jornadas historia y fuentes orales*, pp. 77–93.

38 Ricardo A. Guerra Palmero (2001), "El mercado negro en Canarias durante el periodo del Mando Económico: una primera aproximación." *Revista de Historia Canaria* 183, 175–89.

39 April 1950. Gobernador Civil. Presidente de la Junta Asesora de Comercio. Notas sobre asuntos económicos de Santa Cruz de Tenerife. AGA-P 60.

40 José Maria Gago González (1997), "El pequeño comercio en el periodo autárquico, 1939–1950." In: Trujillano and Gago (eds.), *IV Jornadas historia y fuentes orales*, pp. 289–313.

41 París Eguilaz, *50 años de economía española*, p. 57.

42 April 1955. Delegación Provincial de Sindicatos de FET y de las JONS. Córdoba. Informe sobre paro en la provincia de Córdoba. AGA-P 120.

43 In Cordoba, for example, unemployment among journeymen was never below the 5,000 mark in the best months of the year. In 1949 their number reached more than 20,000. April 1953. Delegación Provincial de Sindicatos de FET y de las JONS. Córdoba. Informe sobre paro en la provincia de Córdoba. AGA-S 4756.

44 14-10-1954. Del Secretario Nacional de Sindicatos a Vicesecretario n. Ordenación Social. AGA-S 4750. September 1954. Problema del paro obrero en la provincia de Córdoba. AGA-S 4750.

45 September 1954. Grave problema de paro obrero en la provincia de Jaén. AGA-S 481.

46 13-2-1956. Delegación Nacional de Sindicatos. Servicio de Organización. Reservado. AGA-S 481.

47 Acción Católica (1953), *Los problemas sociales del campo andaluz*. Acción Católica, Madrid, pp. 204–7.

48 Ibid.

49 Ibid., pp. 232–42.

50 November 1950. Falange Española Tradicionalista de las JONS. Jefatura Provincial de Málaga. Parte mensual de información correspondiente a noviembre de 1950. AGA-P 268.

51 24-9-1955. Informe que eleva el Delegado Provincial de Sindicatos de Granada, sobre la Finca "Moreda," al Delegado Nacional. AGA-S 4762.

52 8-6-1961. Delegado Provincial de la Organización Sindical de FET de las JONS. Cádiz. Nota informativa reservada del pueblo Castellar de la Frontera. AGA-S 4746.

53 14-3-1961. Delegado Provincial de la Organización Sindical de FET de las JONS. Cádiz. Nota informativa sobre problema paro de los trabajadores viticultores de Sanlúcar de Barrameda. AGA-S 4746.

54 9-12-1954. Delegación Nacional de Sindicatos. Servicio de Organización. AGA-S 4815.

55 8-4-1957. El Jefe del Sindicato Nacional Textil. Nota informativa para el Excmo. Sr. Ministro de Trabajo. AGA-S 4796.

56 17-9-1960. Delegación Provincial de la Organización Sindical. Málaga. Informe sobre el gravísimo problema del paro en esta provincia. AGA-S 4798.

57 Consejo Económico Sindical Provincial (1962), *Estructura y posibilidades del desarrollo económico de Almería*. Hispalense Industrial, Madrid., p. 31.

58 Cazorla Sánchez, *Las políticas de la victoria*, pp. 124–5.
59 Pilar Folguera et al. (2003), *El mundo del trabajo en RENFE: historia oral de la infraestructura*. Fundación de los Ferrocarriles Españoles, Madrid, pp. 120–3, 156.
60 21-2-1950. Gobierno Civil de Valladolid. Secretaría Política. Nota informativa sobre situación económica del personal de RENFE, resumiendo datos proporcionados por la Junta de la Sección Social-Sector Caminos de Hierro- y otros obtenidos directamente del personal obrero de confianza. AGA-P 73.
61 28-5-1954. Delegación Nacional de Sindicatos. Servicio de Organización. AGA-S 4807.
62 Isaías Lafuente (2002), *Esclavos por la patria: la explotación de los presos bajo el franquismo*. Temas de Hoy, Madrid.
63 [March 1955]. Sindicato del Metal. Linares. Necesidades de urgente solución. AGA-S 481.
64 26-5-1955. Informe sobre la actual situación de la zona minera de Huelva. AGA-S 4766.
65 24-10-1958. Delegación Provincial de Sindicatos Organización Sindical de FET de las JONS. Ciudad Real. AGA-S 4748.
66 8-7-1955. Delegación Provincial de Sindicatos Organización Sindical de FET de las JONS. Ciudad Real. Informe de la Delegación Provincial de Sindicatos de Ciudad Real sobre Almadén y sus minas de mercurio. AGA-S 4748.
67 2-4-1950. Falange Española Tradicionalista y de las JONS. Secretaría. Jefatura Provincial de Orense. Informe Situación Política, Social y Económica de la Provincia. AGA-P 265.
68 May 1950. FET de las JONS. Jefatura Provincial de Sevilla. Parte mensual. AGA-P 265.
69 October 1950. Falange Española Tradicionalista y de las JONS. Parte de Actividades. Mes de octubre. AGA-P 267.
70 3-6-1950. Falange Española Tradicionalista y de las JONS. Jefatura Provincial de Santa Cruz de Tenerife. Parte Mensual de Actividades. Mayo de 1950. AGA-P 265.
71 This information comes from government reports written between 1949 and 1951 in Barcelona, Biscay, Madrid, Seville, Pontevedra, Almeria, Lugo, and Orense. AGA-P 264.
72 23-4-1951. Comisión que actuó en el Gobierno Civil de Vizcaya sobre el problema del abaratamiento de la vida. AGA-P 73.
73 26-7-1949. Sindicato Nacional del Textil. Jefe Nacional. Particular. Informe. AGA-P 66.
74 May 1950. Informe mensual reservado correspondiente al mes de mayo de 1950 del Sindicato Nacional Textil. AGA-P 66.
75 October 1950. Falange Española Tradicionalista y de las JONS. Jefatura Provincial de Barcelona. Parte mensual del mes de octubre. AGA-P 267.

76 22-12-1954. Delegación Nacional de Sindicatos. Servicio de Organización. AGA-S 4759.

77 11-1-1950. Informe que rinde el Lugarteniente Provincial de la Guardia de Franco de la Provincia de Tenerife Camarada Manuel Guerrero Padrón al Consejero Nacional Camarada Sancho Dávila Fernández de Celis de los hechos ocurridos en la citada provincia y que han sido la causa de la destitución del citado Lugarteniente Provincial. AGA-P 66.

78 Cazorla Sánchez, *Las políticas de la victoria*, pp. 183–91.

79 In the Basque province of Biscay the local union had reported in December 1953 that workers suffered not only from frozen salaries and rampant inflation, but from an increase of two hours a day in their working hours, from eight to 10 hours. This resulted in a further deterioration in the union's prestige which was manifested in the workers' increased use of the Church-sponsored HOAC (the workers' branch of Catholic Action) to express their anger at both their impoverished situation and the denial of their right to free association and their right to strike. 11-12-1953. Delegación Provincial de Sindicatos de FET de las JONS. Vizcaya. AGA-S 4851.

80 5-12-1953. Delegación Provincial de Sindicatos de FET de las JONS. Vizcaya. AGA-S 4851.

81 20-3-1954. Informe sobre algaradas estudiantiles con motivo de la reciente elevación de tarifas en "Tranvías de Sevilla S.A.." AGA-P 101.

82 1957. [Ministerio de Trabajo]. Contestación a la Organización Internacional del Trabajo sobre supuestas violaciones a la libertad sindical. AGA-P 140.

83 9-10-1957. Delegación Sindical provincial. Santander. Informe sobre desarrollo de las elecciones para mandos de las entidades sindicales provinciales de la CNS de Santander. AGA-P 141.

84 2-10-1957. [Falange Española Tradicionalista y de las JONS]. Delegación Nacional de Información e Investigación. Nota Informativa. AGA-P 141.

85 14-5-1957. Falange Española Tradicionalista y de las JONS Nota de la Secretaría Política. Elecciones. AGA-P 141.

86 26-3-1956. Delegación Nacional de Sindicatos. Servicio de Organización. AGA-S 4805.

87 28-3-1956. Delegación Nacional de Sindicatos. Servicio de Organización. AGA-S 4763.

88 20-6-1956. Delegación Nacional de Sindicatos. Servicio de Organización. AGA-S 4763.

89 10-10-1956. Delegación Nacional de Sindicatos. Servicio de Organización. Reservado. AGA-S 4760.

90 22-6-1956. Delegación Nacional de Sindicatos. Servicio de Organización. Reservado. AGA-S 4760.

91 3-9-1956 and 18-10-1956. Delegación Nacional de Sindicatos. Servicio de Organización. AGA-S 4805.

92   28-6-1956. Delegación Nacional de Sindicatos. Servicio de Organización. AGA-S 4807.

93   12-2-1954. Delegación Nacional de Sindicatos. Servicio de Organización. AGA-S 4799; 20-2-1956. Delegación Nacional de Sindicatos. Servicio de Organización. AGA-S 4799.

94   5-6-1957. Delegación Provincial de Sindicatos de FET de las JONS. Vizcaya. Informe. AGA-S 4853.

95   21-1-1961. Carta a Francisco Jiménez Torres, Secretario General de la Organización Sindical, de Carlos Iglesias Selgas. AGA-S 4796.

96   5-5-1958. Informe que eleva a la consideración de las autoridades superiores la Delegación Provincial de Sindicatos, de acuerdo con los informes recibidos en los distintos sindicatos afectados por las incidencias ocurridas en el día de hoy. AGA-S 4790.

97   [March 1958]. Información sobre conflictos laborales en Asturias, desde el día 15 de febrero. AGA-S 4529.

98   25-6-1958. Información sobre la reciente visita a Asturias del Excmo. Sr. Ministro de Trabajo. AGA-S 4529. Also, 23-6-1958. Nota informativa recibida en la mañana de hoy y referida a la impresión recogida en los sectores obreros después de la vista del Excmo. Sr. Ministro de Trabajo a Asturias. AGA-S 2529.

99   Cazorla Sánchez, *Las políticas de la victoria*, pp. 171–90.

100 This was noted by the Francoist authorities. When reporting from Asturias in 1958 where miners were again showing signs of unrest, the Falangists reported that, "We can observe how workers, in both their conversations and written petitions, use the expression *minimum vital salary*, a sentence used by both communists and HOAC." 1958 [CNS Asturias]. Información sobre conflictos laborales en Asturias, desde el día 15 de febrero. AGA-S 4529.

101 2-10-1957. [CNS] Informe sobre situación política social actual. AGA-S 4353.

102 5-10-1959. CNS de Zaragoza. Breve resumen de la situación económico-social de Zaragoza y su provincia. AGA-S 4855; 14-9-1961. Delegación Provincial de la Organización Sindical. Vizcaya. Confidencial. Informe sobre la situación económica actual. AGA-S 4853.

103 The result of this added oppression was that, in 1960, Spanish workers, in both fields and factories, consumed an average of 2,730 calories per day while the middle class consumed 2,950 and major landowners 3,500. Demetrio Casado (1967), *Perfiles del hambre*. Cuadernos Para el Diálogo, Madrid, pp. 72, 167.

104 A study on this, practically ignored by the public, is Ramón Navarro Sandalinas (1990), *La enseñanza primaria durante el franquismo (1936–1975)*. PPU, Barcelona.

105 In other areas it was worse. In 1955 the Spanish state spent only 0.015 percent of its national budget on research while France spent 0.5 percent, the United

Kingdom 0.7 percent, and Germany 1 percent. June 1955. El Ministro de Educación. Memoria sobre el adjunto proyecto de presupuesto de gastos del Ministerio de Educación Nacional para el bienio 1956–7. AGA-P 117.

106 Antonio Guzmán et al. (1955), *Causas y remedios del analfabetismo en España*. S.N., Madrid, pp. 15–20, 31–49.

107 Gregorio Cámara Villar (1984), *Nacional-catolicismo y escuela: la socialización política del franquismo (1936–1951)*. Hesperia, Jaén, pp. 258, 255.

108 June 1955. El Ministro de Educación. Memoria sobre el adjunto proyecto de presupuesto de gastos del Ministerio de Educación Nacional para el bienio 1956–7. AGA-P 117.

109 Ibid.

110 Maria del Carmen Agulló Díaz (1997), "Transmisión y evolución de los modelos de mujer durante el franquismo (1951–1970)." In: Trujillano and Gago (eds.), *IV Jornadas historia y fuentes orales*, pp. 491–502.

111 José Felix Tezanos et al. (1968), *El bachillerato ¿para qué? Encuesta-informe sobre problemas de la enseñanza media*. Cuadernos Para el Diálogo, Madrid, pp. 15–17.

112 Cámara Villar, *Nacional-catolicismo y escuela, passim*.

113 For the post-war purging of teachers, see Francisco Morente Valero (1997), *La depuración del magisterio nacional*. Ámbito, Valladolid.

114 See Carolyn P. Boyd (1997), *Historia Patria: Politics, History and National Identity in Spain, 1875–1975*. Princeton University Press, Princeton.

115 Alfredo Jiménez Núñez (1987), *Biografía de un campesino andaluz: la historia oral como etnografía*. Publicaciones de la Universidad de Sevilla, Seville, pp. 165–6.

116 Ibíd., pp. 174–5.

117 Ministerio de Educación y Ciencia (1972), *Informe sobre la escolarización en enseñanza general básica*. Ministerio de Educación y Ciencia, Madrid. More data in Alfonso García Barbancho (1982), *Población, empleo y paro*. Pirámide, Madrid, p. 72.

118 As negative a picture as these figures paint, the real situation was actually worse because, of the provinces the ministry had recorded as "fully" enrolled, only the three underpopulated provinces of Soria, Zamora, and Guadalajara had more than 90 percent of their school-age children attending classes regularly. And even here these statistics hid problems of quality. According to the governor of "lucky" Soria, in 1968 the province had a "great number of schools with more than 50 percent of its school positions vacant, but the quality of our education is far from good." 1968. Memoria de gestión del Gobierno Civil de Soria, AGA-I 52-487.

119 Ministerio de Educación y Ciencia, *Informe sobre la escolarización en Enseñanza General Básica*, pp. 6–26.

120 Carreras and Tafunell, *Estadísticas históricas de España*, pp. 213–28.

121 José Luis Abellán (1975), *La industria cultural en España*. Cuadernos Para el Diálogo, Madrid, pp. 50–62. See Carlos Paris (1974), *La universidad española actual: posibilidades y frustraciones*. Cuadernos Para el Diálogo, Madrid, pp. 117–77.

3 Migration

1 Alfonso García Barbancho (1979), *Disparidades regionales y ordenación del territorio*. Ariel, Barcelona, pp. 55–73.

2 The depopulation of southern and central Spain (with the exception of Madrid) continued into the 1970s as the impact of the oil crisis played havoc with the weak Spanish economy, unemployment skyrocketed, and tens of thousands of Spanish immigrants returned to their home towns from Europe. In that decade, Leon lost more than 200,000 people, Extremadura 241,000, La Mancha 236,000, and Andalusia 621,000. García Barbancho, *Población, empleo y paro*, p. 92.

3 Eric Hobsbawm (1994), *Age of Extremes: The Short Twentieth Century 1914–1991*. Penguin, London, pp. 289–90.

4 Judt, *Postwar*, pp. 324–37.

5 Vincent J. Knapp (1976), *Europe in the Era of Social Transformation 1700–Present*. Prentice Hall, Upper Saddle River, NJ, p. 220.

6 Xavier Doménech Sampere (2003), "La otra cara del milagro español: clase obrera y movimiento obrero en los años del desarrollismo." *Historia Contemporánea* 26, 91–112.

7 Víctor Pérez Díaz (1974), *Pueblos y clases sociales en el campo español*. Siglo XXI, Madrid, pp. 138–49.

8 A classic account is Malefakis, *Agrarian Reform and Peasant Revolution in Spain*.

9 Cobo Romero and Ortega López, "La protesta de sólo unos pocos."

10 Victoriano Camas Baena (1993), "Trabajo y reconstrucción de la realidad." In: Trujillano Sánchez (ed.), *III Jornadas historia y fuentes orales*, pp. 331–51.

11 Ibid.

12 Antonio López Ontiveros (1974), *Emigración, propiedad y paisaje agrario en la Campiña de Córdoba*. Ariel, Barcelona, pp. 119–27.

13 Juan Seisdedos Robles (1968), *Dos problemas graves de la economía de Zamora: la emigración y el paro encubierto*. Gabinete Técnico, Zamora, p. 12. Ignacio Prieto Sarro (1996), *Despoblación y despoblamiento en la provincia de León: 1950–1991*. Universidad de León, Leon, pp. 49–57.

Peasants and small farms were traditionally entrenched in mountain regions all over Spain. Accordingly, mountains became deserted. The Sierra of Huelva, which is a successful area of added-value pork products today, suffered severe depopulation during the 1960s. The areas of Aracena and Valverde alone lost close to 42,000 people.

People either moved to the capital of the province, nearby Seville, or to Barcelona, or temporarily emigrated to Germany, France, Belgium, or Switzerland. Manuel Moreno Alonso (1979), *Despoblamiento y emigración en la Sierra de Huelva*. Ayuntamiento de Aracena, Aracena, pp. 11–18. The end of traditional agriculture also meant the disappearance of another aspect of the mountain economy: the last transhumant shepherds, a fixture in Spain since the Middle Ages. Joaquín Bandera and José Miguel Marinas (1996), *Palabra de pastor: historia oral de la transhumancia*. Universidad de León, Leon, pp. 52–62.

14 The following accounts are drawn from oral accounts reproduced in Marcelino Fernández Santiago (1993), "Estudio de las migraciones estacionales: Los segadores gallegos en Castilla." In: Trujillano Sánchez (ed.), *III Jornadas historia y fuentes orales*, pp. 261–74.

15 Pérez Díaz, *Pueblos y clases sociales*, pp. 215–26.

16 See Víctor Pérez Díaz (1991), *Structure and Change of Castilian Peasant Communities: A Sociological Inquiry into Rural Castile, 1550–1990*. Garland, New York and London, pp. 106–14.

17 Ibid., pp. 124–204.

18 Joseph Acevedes (1971), *Social Change in a Spanish Village*. Schekman, Cambridge and London, pp. 62–4.

19 In the 1940s there was an average of up to 22,000 shacks in the city of Barcelona alone. Francisco Candel (1986), *Los otros catalanes veinte años después*. Plaza i Janés, Barcelona, p. 113.

20 Francisco Candel (1965), *Los otros catalanes*. Península, Madrid, pp. 128–31.

21 The only children from the village that went on to university were, paradoxically, from one of the very few families that stayed behind. José Ramón Valero Escandell (1993), "De Matián a Ibi: el éxodo masivo de una aldea del norte de Granada." In: Trujillano Sánchez (ed.), *III Jornadas historia y fuentes orales*, pp. 345–61.

22 Antonio Cazorla Sánchez (2006), "At Peace with the Past: Explaining the Spanish Civil War in the Basque Country, Catalonia and Galicia." In: Noel Valis (ed.), *Teaching Representations of the Spanish Civil War*. Modern Languages Association, New York, pp. 63–72.

23 Candel, *Los otros catalanes*, pp. 153–62.

24 José Manuel López de Juan (1970), *Llodio: crisis y crecimiento. Aportación para un conocimiento sociológico y planificación de los servicios sociales*. Cáritas Diocesanas, Vitoria.

25 The "only" was justified by the rate of population growth of other towns in the area in the 1960s: Lejona 310 percent, Echevarri 171 percent, Santurce 150 percent. Antonio F. Canales Serrano (2003), "Desarrollismo, inmigración y poder político local: el problema escolar en Barakaldo." *Historia Contemporánea* 26, 57–76.

26 The situation was so critical in 1965 that the local press reported a group of university students were looking for a basement to teach some of the town's 2,000 unschooled children. Even those who went to school had to endure buildings with no heating, electricity, or cleaning services.

27 Both before and after the war, people from the island primarily emigrated to seek their fortune in the New World; this would still be the favored destination of a trickle of local immigrants until the early 1970s. In the early 1950s islanders, most of them agrarian laborers, began to move from rural areas to the capital, Palma, and to the first of the tourist developments, rather than off the island. Sebastiá Busquets Serra et al. (1993), "Mallorca: de la emigración a la inmigración." In: Trujillano Sánchez (ed.), *III Jornadas historia y fuentes orales*, pp. 285–310.

28 This movement created moral and social concerns. Catholic women's associations edited books about how to treat domestics and how to "help" them find the right way in life. The lady of the house had more responsibilities in her relationships with the family's domestics than those of a simple employer. Leonor Meléndez (1962), *El servicio doméstico en España*. Consejo Nacional de Mujeres de la Acción Católica, Madrid.

29 Nicolás Ortega Cantero (1979), *Política agraria y colonización del espacio.* Ayuso, Madrid.

30 Maria José Romano Serrano (2005), *Llanos del Caudillo: memoria e historia oral de un pueblo de colonización agraria.* Ayuntamiento de Llanos del Caudillo, Ciudad Real, pp. 26–34.

31 Cazorla Sánchez, *Desarrollo sin reformistas*, pp. 237–67.

32 Mariano González-Rothvoss (1949), *Los problemas actuales de la emigración española.* Instituto de Estudios Politicos, Madrid, pp. 133–5.

33 José Babiano Mora and Ana Fernández Asperilla (2002), *El fenómeno de la irregularidad en la emigración española de los años sesenta. Documentos de Trabajo. 3.* Fundación 1 de Mayo, Madrid.

34 Instituto Español de Emigración (1966), *Emigración a Suiza.* S.N., Madrid.

35 José Babiano Mora and Ana Fernández Asperilla (2003), "En las manos de los tratantes de seres humanos (notas sobre la emigración irregular durante el franquismo)." *Historia Contemporánea* 26, 35–56.

36 Babiano Mora and Fernández Asperilla, *El fenómeno de la irregularidad en la emigración española.*

37 For example, when the Socialist Youth Organization of Westfalen made a study of living conditions for immigrant workers in the late 1960s it discovered that more than 50 percent of families lived in one or two rooms, only 40 percent had a kitchen, and only 32 percent had a toilet. And, to an extent, these were the lucky people. On the outskirts of the very posh city of Geneva there were numerous shacks in 1971; 64 percent of their inhabitants were Spanish immigrants. Moisés Cayetano Rosado (1977), *Maletas humanas (obreros emigrantes).* D.L., Badajoz, pp. 49–56.

38   Ibid., pp. 11–35.
39   Quoted in Víctor Canicio (1972), *¿Contamos contigo! (Krónicas de la emigración)*. Laia, Barcelona, p. 10.
40   Juan Anllo Vázquez (1966), *Estructura y problemas del campo español.* Cuadernos Para el Diálogo, Madrid, pp. 173–5.
41   Julio Prada Rodríguez (1993), "Conflicto y consenso: la emigración como instrumento de cambio ideológico y transformación social." In: Trujillano Sánchez (ed.), *III Jornadas historia y fuentes orales*, pp. 315–37.
42   Jaime Muñoz Anatol (1972), *La familia española migrante en Francia.* CSIC, Madrid, pp. 177–8.
43   Ibid., p. 160.
44   Ronald Fraser (1985), *Mijas: república, guerra, franquismo en un pueblo andaluz.* Antoni Bosch, Barcelona, pp. 208–11.
45   Ibid.
46   It is easy to understand the satisfaction expressed by Spain's Labor Attaché in Brussels when, in the context of the Franco regime's diplomatic victory that resulted from President Eisenhower's visit to Madrid, he stated, "The political problem of Spanish workers in Belgium has had a change of direction." 23-5-1960. Agregaduría Laboral. Bélgica. Nota informativa. AGA-S 4885.
47   When trying to tighten the hold the official unions had on these immigrants, the Falangists had to recognize the "pernicious influences of left-wing organizations" among workers. 5-10-1958. Organización Sindical de Guipúzcoa. Agrupación Sindical de Trabajadores Españoles en Francia. Informe. AGA-S 4765. See also José Babiano Mora (2002), "Emigración, identidad y vida asociativa: Los españoles en Francia de los años sesenta." *Hispania* 62(2), 211, 561–76. Also Rose Duroux (2002), "La emigración a Francia (segunda mitad del siglo XX): unas reflexiones sobre retornos y reintegraciones." *Hispania* 62(2), 211, 577–96.
48   30-8-1959–15-7-1960. Embajada de España en Paris. El Agregado de A.S. Informe extraordinario (Ejemplar actualizado a junio de 1960). Características de la acción político-social-asistencial, realizada, en desarrollo y a realizar respecto a dicha emigración por esta agregaduría a nuestra embajada en París. Beneficios y costo ponderado de esta acción. AGA-S 4885.
49   Guillermo Díaz-Plaja (1974), *La condición del emigrante: los trabajadores españoles en Europa.* Cuadernos Para el Diálogo, Madrid, pp. 341–4.
50   Quoted in Babiano Mora and Fernández Asperilla, *El fenómeno de la irregularidad en la emigración.*
51   14-8-1957. [FET-JONS] Nota sobre el proyecto de decreto que restringe el nuevo establecimiento de trabajadores en Madrid. See also 1-4-1957. Delegación Provincial de Sindicatos de FET-JONS. Madrid. Delegación. Algunas consideraciones acerca del problema de la vivienda en Madrid. AGA-S 4789.

52   2-10-1952. Delegación Nacional de Sindicatos. FET de las JONS. Particular. Notas sacadas del informe verbal dado al Excmo. Sr. Ministro Secretario General del Movimiento por el Delegado Nacional de Sindicatos sobre su visita a Santander. AGA-P 81.

53   25-1-1952. Deligación Provincial de Sindicatos de FET y de las JONS. Madrid. Informe. AGA-P 81.

54   1953. Secretaría General de Falange Española Tradicionalista y de las JONS. Secretaría Política. Sección Técnica. Resumen de las entregas de viviendas protegidas que se efectuaran con motivo del 18 de julio o en fechas próximas. AGA-P 92.

55   [1954]. Resumen de la inspección de grupos de viviendas protegidas en Córdoba. AGA-S 4750.

56   The poor quality of the houses themselves was compounded by a mediocre water-supply system, the lack of public spaces for parks, and, especially lack of public services. For example, see 2-5-1958. Obra Sindical del Hogar y Arquitectura. Inspección Nacional. Informe reservado sobre el grupo "Francisco Franco" de Avilés redactado como consecuencia de la visita de inspección realizada los días 24 a 26 de abril de 1958. AGA-S 4529.

57   For an overview see David Kynaston (2007), *Austerity Britain: 1945–1951.* Bloomsbury, London.

58   The unions' branch in charge of social housing, the Obra Sindical Hogar y Arquitectura, was said to have built 138,686 houses between 1939 and 1960. [1961] Organización Sindical Española. AGA-S 4886.

59   José Fonseca (1945), *El problema de la vivienda.* Gráficas Barragán, Madrid, pp. 9–12.

60   Semanas Sociales de España (1954), *La crisis de la vivienda.* Secretariado de la Junta Nacional de Semanas Sociales, Madrid, pp. 40–1, 45–6.

61   Miguel Royo Martínez (1953), *La crisis de la vivienda.* EDELCE, Seville.

62   Ministerio de la Vivienda (1958), *Plan de urgencia social.* Gráfica Expres, Madrid, pp. 28–9.

63   Pilar Folguera (1995), "La construcción de los cotidiano durante los primeros años del franquismo." *Ayer* 19, 165–87.

64   Vicesecretaría de Obras Sindicales (1968), *El problema social de la vivienda.* Organización Sindical, Madrid, p. 7.

65   Colegio Oficial de Agentes de la Propiedad Inmobiliaria (1968), *El problema de la vivienda.* El Colegio, Barcelona.

66   Curiously, the same reasoning was used by the authorities in an official report in 1960 when they declared that "there are many uninhabited old and new buildings." José Luis González Santander (1960), *El problema de la vivienda.* Cabal, Madrid, pp. 25, 27.

67   Maria del Carmen García-Nieto (ed.) (1991), *La palabra de las mujeres: una propuesta didáctica para hacer historia (1931–1990).* Editorial Popular, Madrid, pp. 65–83.

68 Ibid.
69 Ibid.
70 Ibid.
71 Ibid.
72 Cáritas Diocesanas de Madrid (1967), *Informe sociológico sobre la situación de Madrid*. Cáritas Diocesanas de Madrid, Madrid, pp. 235, 256, 323–4.
73 Ministerio de la Vivienda (1969), *Absorción del chabolismo: teoría general y actuaciones españolas*. Ministerio de la Vivienda, Madrid, pp. 6, 10.
74 Cáritas Diocesanas de Madrid, *Informe sociológico sobre la situación de Madrid*, pp. 223–4.
75 Ibid., pp. 36–41.
76 See Juventud Obrera Cristiana (1983), *Identidad de la JOC: documentos básicos para la identidad de la JOC (Juventud Obrera Cristiana) en España*. Ediciones de ACE, Madrid.
77 This information was taken from the Cáritas report by Pedro Bordes Roca et al. (1965), *Parroquia de Nuestra Señora de Fátima: estudio sociológico y planificación social*. Parroquia de Nuestra Señora de Fátima, Granollers.
78 Ibid.
79 From Joaquim Clusa i Oriach (1967), *Estudio-informe de los barrios Can de Oriach, Plana del Pintor, Torrent del Capella*. Serracanta Copisteria, Sabadell.
80 Ibid.
81 Ibid.
82 Ibid.
83 García-Nieto, *La palabra de las mujeres*, pp. 23–63.
84 Ibid.
85 Ibid.
86 Ibid.
87 The link between recent immigration and criminality has been well documented. The Bishops' Commission for Migrations explains the connection in a 1969 report that discusses immigrant difficulties when integrating. Also, in a study published in 1970, official experts explained this link when analyzing the situation in Barcelona. The report states, "in general, the trajectory of young people towards delinquency originates in the suburbs of the cities" (meaning the poor marginal neighborhoods on a city's periphery). The reasons for this delinquency are listed as the "lack of communication" between family members, their lack of effectiveness, broken families, truancy, and lack of attention paid to children by their overworked parents. Instituto de Reinserción Social (1970), *La problemática de la marginalidad social en Barcelona*. Instituto de Reinserción Social, Barcelona, pp. 20–1.
88 That prisons were places where the poor paid dearly for their own misery was made painfully obvious in a report from a study of Madrid's main prison in the late 1960s. This report showed that at least 40 percent of the inmates were

illiterate, while a further 45 percent had only attended school for a few years. Of 500 inmates, 269 came from extremely poor families, 132 from a working-class background, 87 were middle-class and only 12 came from advantaged backgrounds. Ibid., p. 18.

89   Ibid., pp. 77–8.
90   Demetrio Casado (1976), *La pobreza en la estructura social de España*. Ayuso, Madrid, pp. 67–144.
91   Unskilled workers, especially in agriculture and those in the south, in rural Castile, the Canary Islands, and in Galicia, formed the core of the bottom tier of Spain's active working population in terms of income and access to services and education. In the early 1970s the impoverished in these regions constituted more than two-thirds of all the poor in Spain. An unskilled, agrarian, landless peasant, for example, had an average annual income in 1970 of barely 75,000 pesetas per family, an income lower than that of any other category of worker in Spain, including those who were unemployed. They lived in a poverty that deepened (and never fully recovered) as the result of the Civil War and Franco's agrarian counter-revolution first and autarky next. For a view of how poverty was geographically distributed in Spain, see Antonio Bosch Doménech (ed.) (1998), *La desigualdad y la pobreza en España, 1973–1981*. Instituto Ortega y Gasset, Madrid.
92   Tezanos, *Estructura de clases en la España actual*, pp. 177–9.
93   For the next decade, as unemployment rose at times to 20 percent of the population, poor Spaniards still had to resort to family solidarity and minimum consumption to survive. Once again, in poor, urban neighborhoods, young married couples stayed in crammed houses with their parents because, among other things, it was never certain who was going to have a salary the following month. When the last Francoist politicians and the first democratic ones talked of "tightening the belt" to face the crisis, they chose to ignore the fact that some people had never had a belt in their lives and, if they had one now, it was old, cheap, and out of fashion. The politicians' view of reality had little to do with the realities of the poor, whose numbers included around a quarter to a third of the country's total population and who had sacrificed so much to help make Spain a successful "first world" country. Unfortunately, the poor would have to wait yet again to enjoy the privileges that this label implies. See Demetrio Casado (1994), *Sobre la pobreza en España, 1965–1994*. Hacer, Barcelona, pp. 223–40.
94   Antonio Taboada Arceo (1969), *Galicia dormida ante el II Plan de Desarrollo Económico y Social: proposición abierta a quienes pueden y deben redimir a Galicia de su pobreza*. Cámara Oficial de Comercio, La Coruña.
95   People were poor, especially agricultural workers. They also wanted a better future. Sixty-one percent wanted a better education for their children and only 22 percent wanted them to become farmers, preferring that they work in factories or offices; two-thirds wanted better homes; one in five landless peasants

was planning to emigrate soon to Germany or to Madrid, Barcelona, or Bilbao; 92 percent of those who emigrated were 34 years old or younger. Comisaría del Plan de Desarrollo (1969), *Estudio económico y social de Extremadura*. Ministerio de Agricultura, Madrid.

96 See José Cazorla Pérez (1973), *Estratificación social de España*. Cuadernos Para el Diálogo, Madrid, pp. 102–43.

97 Barbancho, *Disparidades regionales*, pp. 76–127.

98 Antonio Burgos (1972), *Andalucia, ¿tercer mundo?* Círculo de Lectores, Madrid, pp. 118–25, 178.

99 Demetrio Casado (1970), *Plan Social Baza: una experiencia de desarrollo social*. Cáritas Española, Madrid.

100 Alfonso Carlos Comín (1970), *Noticia de Andalucía*. Divulgación Universitaria, Madrid, pp. 115–24.

101 Juan Goytisolo (1962), *La Chanca*. Librería Española, Paris.

102 1974. Organización Sindical Almería. Encuesta informe referido a aspectos sociológicos de las barriadas de trabajadores. Archivo Histórico Provincial de Almería. I am indebted to my colleague Óscar J. Rodríguez Barreira for making this document available to me.

103 Similar neighborhoods of extreme misery around social housing appeared in all the big cities and major towns of Andalusia and Extremadura: Tres Mil Viviendas in Seville and el Polígono in Granada are just two of many. From their creation to this day they are notorious for their poverty and their high levels of crime, lack of basic educational facilities, and appalling social and living conditions that are frequently referred to in the media.

4   A Changing Society

1 1971. Memoria de gestión del Gobierno Civil de Huesca. AGA-I 507.

2 See Adrian Shubert (1987), *The Road to Revolution in Spain: The Coalminers of Asturias*. University of Illinois Press, Urbana.

3 Acción Católica (1943), *Jornadas de caridad*. Acción Católica, Saragossa, pp. 60–1.

4 Curiously, the author of this book concluded that, despite their meager salaries, the police force should be included in the middle class. Acción Católica (1951), *Problemas de la clase media*. Acción Católica, Madrid, pp. 72, 77–8.

5 Ibid., p. 167.

6 See Casanova, *La iglesia de Franco*.

7 José Hurtado Sánchez (1997) "Las cofradías de Sevilla y la política (1940–1991)." *Demófilo* 23, 77–91.

8 Quoted in Belén Solé i Mauri (1997), "El discurso moral de la Iglesia y su vivencia popular." In: Trujillano and Gago (eds.), *IV Jornadas historia y fuentes orales*, pp. 457–67.

9 Basilia López García (1995), *Aproximación a la historia de la HOAC, 1946– 1981*. HOAC, Madrid.

10 In 1959 in Valladolid, one of the heartlands of the original Falange, the party's information service, Falangist spies, disclosed that in local Catholic circles there was a constant "discrediting" of those who collaborated with the official unions. It was also worrying for a regime that had counted on the demobiliza- tion of labor that there was an increasing presence of workers at the meetings. 27-6-1959. Servicio de Información del Movimiento. Nota informativa. AGA-S 4850.

11 7-5-1957. Delegación Nacional de Sindicatos de Falange Española Tradicionalista y de las JONS. Vicesecretaría Nacional de Ordenación Social. Servicio Nacional de Inspección de Vicesecretarías Provinciales. Actividades realizadas por las HOAC durante el día 1 de mayo de 1957. AGA-P 145.

12 Some bishops eventually started speaking up against the dire social conditions and the regime's pretension of having a monopoly over workers' lives. In January 1955 the bishop of Las Palmas de Gran Canaria, the otherwise very conservative and prudish Monsignor Pildain, drafted a public letter that clearly stated that the official unions were not in accordance with Catholic doctrine and that workers rejected them at heart; he also stated his desire to withdraw the priest who was acting as the union's ecclesiastical adviser. 15-1-1955. El Gobernador Civil de las Palmas a Excmo. Sr. D. Raimundo Fernández-Cuesta y Merelo. Ministro Secretario General del Movimiento. AGA-P 105.

13 Callahan,, *The Catholic Church in Spain*, pp. 509–26.

14 Salvador Blanco Piñán (1964), *Los obreros ¿Son los culpables?* ZYX, Madrid, pp. 10–19.

15 Juan Arias (1965), *Las cosas claras: los obreros*, 2 vols. El Perpetuo Socorro, Madrid, vol. 1: p. 37, vol. 2: pp. 23–5, 68–70.

16 Ramir Pampols et al. (1987), *Curas obreros: entre la Iglesia y el Reino. Evaluación, perspectivas*. Cristianisme i Justicia, Barcelona, pp. 12–19.

17 One of the consequences (and causes) was that the number of vocations shrank drastically from an average of 8,000 males studying in seminaries in the 1950s to barely 1,800 in the 1972/3 academic year.

18 The following life stories are drawn from a series of interviews collected in Ángel Castro and Margarita Serrano (1977), *La gran desbandada (curas secu- larizados)*. Cuadernos Para el Diálogo, Madrid.

19 Many parishes became known as havens for meetings and activism and for striking workers. In 1971, when the striking bakers of Cadiz were harassed by police and violently expelled from the factory they had been occupying, they took refuge in the parish of the Divine Shepherd, which was administered by a

Capuchin monk "who frequently attacks the regime." 1971. Memoria de gestión del Gobierno Civil de Cádiz. AGA-I 506.

20 Audrey Brassloff (1998), *Religion and Politics in Spain: The Spanish Church in Transition, 1962–96.* Macmillan, Houndmills, pp. 42–78.

21 Acción Católica (1943), *¿Quieres ser buena?* Acción Católica, Madrid, p. 1.

22 Rufino Villalobos Bote (1948), *¿Es pecado bailar? ¿No es pecado bailar? Respuesta serena y objetiva a estas apasionantes preguntas de la juventud de hoy.* Secretariado de Propaganda de la Juventud Masculina de Acción Católica, Don Benito, *passim.*

23 Carlos Salicrú Puigvert (1944), *Cuestiones candentes acerca de la moralidad pública.* La Hormiga de Oro, Barcelona, *passim.*

24 Congreso de la Familia Española (1959), *Síntesis de ponencias provinciales en torno a la familia y la moralidad publica.* Ediciones del Congreso de la Familia Española, Madrid.

25 Teresa Rodríguez de Lecea (1995), "Mujer y pensamiento religioso en el franquismo." *Ayer* 17, 173–200.

26 See e.g. Acción Católica (1958), *Cultivemos nuestra juventud.* Acción Católica, Barcelona.

27 For a complete overview of these issues see Aurora G. Morcillo (2000), *True Catholic Womanhood: Gender and Ideology in Franco's Spain.* Northern Illinois University Press, DeKalb.

28 Esperanza Luca de Tena (1961), *Educación de hijos.* Nuevas Gráficas, Madrid, pp. 5–7.

29 Esperanza Luca de Tena (1961), *Deberes conyugales.* Nuevas Gráficas, Madrid, pp. 9–11.

30 A short study of rural values and morality in transition can be found in Acevedes, *Social Change in a Spanish Village*, pp. 118–31.

31 Maria Isabel Diez Gil and Dolores García Sainz (1993), "Alimentación y sociedad. Testimonios orales (Camargo)." In: Trujillano Sánchez (ed.), *III Jornadas historia y fuentes orales*, pp. 149–59.

32 Cristina Borderías et al. (2003), "Los eslabones perdidos del sindicalismo democrático: la militancia femenina en las CCOO de Catalunya durante el franquismo." *Historia Contemporánea* 26, 161–206.

33 Pilar Díaz Sánchez (1993), "Familia y cambio social en la II República española." In: Trujillano Sánchez (ed.), *III Jornadas historia y fuentes orales*, pp. 139–47.

34 Juan Frigolé Reixach (1982), "Estrategias matrimoniales e identidad sociocultural en la sociedad rural: llevarse a la novia y casarse en un pueblo de la Vega Alta del Segura." *Agricultura y Sociedad* 25, 71–109.

35 Adela Alfonsi (1999), "La recatolización de la moralidad sexual en la Málaga de posguerra." *Arenal* 6(2), 365–85. This normalization of marriage happened elsewhere too.

36 Jane Lewis (1992), *Women in Britain since 1945: Women, Work and the State in the Post-War Years*. Basil Blackwell, Oxford, p. 43.

37 Pérez Díaz, *Pueblos y clases sociales*, pp. 191–7.

38 Jesús Maria Vázquez (1958), *Así viven y mueren: problemas religiosos de un sector de Madrid*. Ope, Madrid., pp. 196–203.

39 Ibid., pp. 208–24.

40 Manuela Cantón Delgado (1994), "Género, lenguaje y metáforas cotidianas en Triana (Sevilla)." In: Congreso de Historia de Andalucía, *Actas del III Congreso de Historia de Andalucía*. Cajasur, Córdoba, pp. 365–75.

41 See a moving account of a popular working-class neighborhood of Seville in the 1940s and early 1950s in Alfonso Guerra (2004), *Cuando el tiempo nos alcanza: memorias (1940–1982)*. Espasa-Calpe, Madrid, pp. 17–63.

42 There were also at least two places where "pornographic" literature – French and made-in-Spain editions – and other immoral products, such as banned and much-sought-after condoms, were sold; another grievance against these sinful establishments was that they also sold comic books to children. Vázquez, *Así viven y mueren*, pp. 270–6.

43 Ibid., pp. 150–77.

44 Carmen Martín Gaite (1994), *Los usos amorosos de la posguerra española*. Anagrama, Barcelona.

45 José Antonio Pérez Pérez (2004), *Los espejos de la memoria: historia oral de las mujeres de Basauri, 1937–2003*. Área de Igualdad, Basauri, p. 30.

46 Rafael Torres (2002), *El amor en tiempo de Franco*. Oberón, Madrid.

47 Francisco Muñoz Roldán (1995), *Mujeres públicas: historia de la prostitución en España*. Temas de Hoy, Madrid.

48 Jean-Louis Guereña (2003), *La prostitución en la España contemporánea*. Marcial Pons, Madrid, pp. 399–449.

49 Núñez Díaz-Balart, *Mujeres caídas*.

50 José Maria Cañas (1974), *Prostitución y sociedad*. Publicaciones Editoriales, Barcelona, pp. 9–14, 48–9, 122–3.

51 Enrique Gómez Arboleda and Salustiano del Campo (1959), *Para una sociología de la familia española*. Congreso de la Familia Española, Madrid.

52 Folguera, "La construcción de los cotidiano."

53 This process of change, especially for women, has been summed up by an anthropologist as a process moving "from duty to desire." Jane C. Collier (1997), *From Duty to Desire. Remaking Families in a Spanish Village*. Princeton University Press, Princeton.

54 Maria del Rosario Ruiz Franco (2007), *¿Eternas menores? Las mujeres en el franquismo*. Biblioteca Nueva, Madrid.

55 Maria del Pilar de la Peña (1974), *La condición jurídica y social de la mujer*. Cuadernos Para el Diálogo, Madrid, pp. 35–7.

56 See Maria Luisa Peinado Gracia (1985), *El consumo y la industria alimenta-ria en España: evolución, problemática y penetración del capital extranjero a partir de 1960.* Instituto de Estudios Agrarios, Pesqueros y Alimentarios, Madrid.

57 Subsecretaría de Planificación, Presidencia del Gobierno (1976), *Consumo.* Presidencia del Gobierno, Madrid, pp. 14–42.

58 Ibid., pp. 161–6.

59 Alberto Miguez et al. (1970), *España: ¿Una sociedad de consumo?* Guadiana de Publicaciones, Madrid, pp. 79–81.

60 In the 1966 FOESSA report quoted in DATA S.A. (1969), *Comportamiento y actitud de las economías domésticas hacia el ahorro y el consumo.* Confederación Española de Cajas de Ahorros, Madrid, p. 127.

61 Subsecretaría de Planificación, *Consumo.*

62 Alonso and Conde, *Historia del consumo en España*, pp. 170–5.

63 The trick was to place the eldest child in front of the driver, who was always the father, holding on to the handle bar, with a second child clinging to the father, while the mother, always seated sideways and always wearing a skirt, held the smallest child in her arms.

64 Alonso and Conde, *Historia del consumo en España*, p. 220.

65 Long before the Guinness book, this writer made a memorable four-hour trip with seven people, three of them vomiting, in a miniscule Seat 600.

66 See Victoria de Grazia (2005), *Irresistible Empire: America's Advance through Twentieth-Century Europe.* Harvard University Press, Cambridge, MA.

67 Manuel Martín Serrano (1970), *Publicidad y sociedad de consumo en España.* Cuadernos Para el Diálogo, Madrid, pp. 22–3.

68 Ibid., p. 30.

69 All the following data have been obtained from Metra Seis (1971), *Estudio sobre hábitos de compra y consumo de la juventud española: penetración de los distintos medios publicitarios.* Movierecord Cine, Avila.

70 Instituto Nacional de Estadística (1970), *Encuesta sobre bienes de consumo duradero en las familias.* INE, Madrid, pp. 20–31.

71 DATA S.A., *Comportamiento y actitud de las economías domésticas.* p. 132.

72 Ibid.

73 See Jorge Uría (ed.) (2003), *La cultura popular en la España contemporánea.* Biblioteca Nueva, Madrid.

74 Valeria Camporesi (1993), *Para grandes y chicos: un cine para los españoles.* Turfán, Madrid, p. 72.

75 Josep Estivill Pérez (1999), "La industria española del cine y el impacto de la obligatoriedad del doblaje en 1941." *Hispania* 59(2), 202, 677–91.

76 Uría, *La cultura popular*, p. 215. See also Camporesi, *Para grandes y chicos*, pp. 67–87.

77 Martín Gaite, *Los usos amorosos de la posguerra española.*

78 Normally, young people in working-class neighborhoods reserved Sunday evenings for leisure and spent this time in different ways depending on the season. According to a study carried out in the 1950s, in the winter young people would go to the cinema 51 percent of the time, engage in dancing 42 percent of the time, and go walking 13 percent of the time, but in the summer movie-going almost entirely disappeared as an activity while excursions became popular (31 percent), walking increased (35 per cent), and dancing declined to 27 per cent of leisure-time activities. Vázquez, *Así viven y mueren*, pp. 290–1.

79 Here are more details for those less well versed in Catholic culture: the story of Bernadette was about a poor nineteenth-century French girl who, perhaps because her country was being taken over by republicans and atheists, began to see visions of the Virgin Mary in a cave in Lourdes. The Bernadette series featured all the troubles that this blessing caused the poor, chosen girl until the miracle was finally authenticated.

80 Juana Ginzo (2004), *Mis días de radio: la España de los cincuenta a través de las ondas*. Temas de Hoy, Madrid, pp. 219–20.

81 Armand Balsebre (2002), *Historia de la radio en España*, vol. 2: *1939–1985*. Cátedra, Madrid, pp. 118–22.

82 See Duncan Shaw (1987), *Fútbol y franquismo*. Alianza Editorial, Madrid.

83 Manuel Palacio (2005), *Historia de la televisión en España*. Gedisa, Barcelona, pp. 53–61.

84 The effects of television in Spaniards' daily lives were no different from those described for Italians by John Foot (1999), "Television and the City: The Impact of Television in Milan, 1954–1960." *Contemporary European History* 9(3), 379–94.

85 Ministerio de Información y Turismo (1969), *La audiencia de televisión en España*. Ministerio de Información y Turismo, Madrid.

86 Jorge Grau Rebollo (2002), *La familia en la pantalla: percepción social y representación audiovisual de etnomodelos procreativos en el cine y la televisión en España*. Septem, Oviedo, pp. 193–4.

87 Mario García de Castro (2002), *La ficción televisiva popular: una evolución de las series de televisión en España*. Gedisa, Barcelona, pp. 23–63.

88 Palacio, *Historia de la televisión en España*, p. 64.

89 Although everybody knows that "Eurovision" is a showcase for cheap nationalism, Franco went a step further: it has recently been revealed that his regime bought Spain's victory in 1969.

90 22-3-1971. [Ministerio de Información y Turismo]. Los teleclubs en España. AGA-C 586.

91 See Richard Vinen (2000), *A History in Fragments: Europe in the Twentieth Century*. Little, Brown, London, pp. 373–5.

92 Josep Maria Baget Herms (1993), *Historia de la televisión en España, 1956–1975*. Feed-Back, Barcelona, pp. 135–6.

93 A detailed account of the repression of Catalan language and culture is Josep Solé i Sabaté and Joan Villarroya (1994), *Cronologia de la repressió de la llengua i la cultura catalanes, 1936–1975*. Curial, Barcelona.

94 Manuel Vázquez Montalbán (1970), "Los medios de comunicación de masas y el consumo." In: Miguez et al., *España: ¿Una sociedad de consumo?*, pp. 145–68.

95 An analysis of late 1960s and early 1970s television programs can be found in Fausto Fernández (1998), *Telebasura española*. Glènat, Barcelona, pp. 41–78.

96 Rafael López Pintor (1975), *Los españoles de los años 70: una versión sociológica*. Tecnos, Madrid, pp. 46–101.

97 Sasha D. Pack (2007), "Tourism and Political Change in Franco's Spain." In: Townson (ed.), *Spain Transformed*, pp. 47–66.

98 Antonio Pildain Zapiain (1964), *El turismo y las playas, las divisas y otros escándalos*. Gráf. Torres, San Sebastian, pp. 6, 9.

99 López Pintor, *Los españoles de los años 70*, p. 59.

100 Ángel Herrera Oria (1964), *Sacerdotes y seglares ante el turismo en España*. Secretariado Nacional de Pastoral, Madrid, pp. 74–87.

101 Ibid., pp. 122–45.

102 They labored at olive-picking in Spain from December to February, traveled to France from March to June for either construction work or to service tourist areas, and, after working at home in the summer, they returned to France in September and October for the grape harvest.

103 The report showed that the motivation to work in tourism pointed to two main factors: poverty and communal links at origin. Workers went to work in the tourist sector for the following reasons, in descending order: a "suggestion" from friends and relatives, lack of work in their towns, to make money, to escape from poverty and because all the family had moved. Before they left, 65 percent had a job waiting for them thanks to the help of friends and relatives. Mario Gaviria (1974), *España a Go-Go: turismo charter y neocolonialismo del espacio*. Turner, Madrid.

104 In general, post-war southern Europe lagged behind northern and eastern Europe in female employment, and Europe behind North America. See Hartmut Kaelble (ed.) (2004), *The European Way: European Societies in the 19th and 20th Centuries*. Berghahn Books, New York, p. 281.

105 Gloria Bayona Fernández (1997), "Utilización del documento escrito-administrativo como marco metodológico de la fuente oral: reconstrucción de la memoria histórica de la industria conservera en Murcia en los años 60." In: Trujillano and Gago (eds.), *IV Jornadas historia y fuentes orales*, pp. 259–74.

106 Pilar Díaz Sánchez (2001), *El trabajo de las mujeres en el textil madrileño: racionalización industrial y experiencias de género (1959–1986)*. Universidad de Málaga, Malaga.

107 An American female anthropologist saw a change in women's perception of their won situation between 1962 and the early 1980s. They declared that "wives who have once been subordinated to their husbands had become their husbands' equals." The anthropologist, a feminist, did not agree. Collier, *From Duty to Desire*, p. 129.

108 Cáritas-Manresa (1972), *Les guarderies infantils a Manresa: informe sobre la seva necesítate*. Cáritas, Manresa.

109 This opinion was shared by many ordinary people. "Young people only think about sex. They think that any foreign girl will sleep with them," said a bar-owner in the Costa del Sol to his interviewer in the early 1970s. Fraser, *Mijas*, pp. 188–95.

110 While there are dozens of this kind of film, just the title of one made in 1973 is revealing: *The Hot Stuff Starts at the Pyrenees* (*Lo verde empieza en los Pirineos*). More on this in Equipo Cartelera Turia (1974), *Cine español, cine de subgéneros*. Fernando Torres, Valencia.

111 Juan Diez Nicolás (1973), "La mujer española y la planificación familiar." *Tauta* 8, 86–97.

112 Salustiano del Campo and Manuel Navarro (1985), *Análisis sociológico de la familia española*. Ariel, Barcelona, pp. 124–5.

113 There were a number of movies that denounced the "crime" of abortion. A very influential anti-abortion film was one made in Mexico in 1951: *The Right to Be Born* (*El derecho de nacer*). The first Spanish film to address the topic was made in 1973; its title is highly illustrative: *Criminal Abortion* (*Aborto criminal*).

114 A 1943 semi-official study argued that for every three births in Spain there was one abortion. This meant about 125,000 every year. A law adopted in 1941 declared abortion a crime against the state; practitioners suffered severe punishment if caught, with a minimum sentence of six years in prison. A local study of Saragossa in the 1940s showed that those most often prosecuted were single women, widows, and some married women. Frequently the "single women and widows" prosecuted were linked to prostitution. Inmaculada Blasco Herranz (1999), "Actitudes de las mujeres bajo el primer franquismo: la práctica del aborto en Zaragoza durante los años 40." *Arenal* 6(1), 165–80. A local study is Rodríguez Barreira, *Migas con miedo*, pp. 357–63.

115 J. M. Deleyto (1972), "El aborto en España." *Tribuna abierta* (1 diciembre), 20–3.

116 Julio Iglesias de Ussel (1979), *El aborto: un estudio sociológico sobre el caso español*. CIS, Madrid, p. 49.

117 Alonso and Conde, *Historia del consumo en España*, pp. 194–5.

5 Roads to Citizenship

1 The word "citizenship" is used here to describe the level of political development and self-perception of most Spaniards at the end of the dictatorship. As used here, the concept goes back to its origins, both in theory and in practice, during the first years of the French Revolution (*citoyen*). It means that, although political parties did not exist, and most people did not have a clear idea of how to channel their opinions and interests, they agreed that society had to be based on equal rights and duties for all. An important difference is that during the French Revolution those rights were not extended to women, whereas Spanish society in the 1970s was ready to concede this. Among the rights that everybody was entitled to, personal freedoms were essential; so too was the right to hold government accountable to the people, and not, as Franco claimed, to "God and History."

2 Romano Serrano, *Llanos del Caudillo*, pp. 84–8.

3 Ibid.

4 Ibid., pp. 119–39.

5 Álvaro Soto Carmona (2005), *¿Atado y bien atado? Institucionalización y crisis del franquismo*. Biblioteca Nueva, Madrid.

6 1962. Memoria de gestión del Gobierno Civil de Segovia. AGA-G 11330.

7 1962. Memoria de gestión del Gobierno Civil de Ávila. AGA-G 11324. According to the governor of Cadiz, the National Movement was composed of "a militant minority, and a large contingent with no enthusiasm" while the majority of the population lived in "complete inhibition from political matters." 1962. Memoria de gestión del Gobierno Civil de Cádiz. AGA-G 11326.

8 The report from Salamanca in 1962 discussed the real "importance of social matters over political ones" among the public, and how "workers do not show political interest, being interested only in what helps them to resolve their problems," resorting to the official unions only to gain "fair salaries." 1962. Memoria de gestión del Gobierno Civil de Salamanca. AGA-G 11330. In Gerona it was also noted that political matters were "secondary" because attention was "focused on economic matters, so present today." 1962. Memoria de gestión del Gobierno Civil de Gerona. AGA-G 11326.

9 Cazorla Sánchez, *Las políticas de la victoria*, pp. 25–43.

10 1962. Memoria de gestión del Gobierno Civil de Logroño. AGA-G 11328.

11 1972. Memoria de gestión del Gobierno Civil de Palencia. AGA-G 447.

12 1972. Memoria de gestión del Gobierno Civil de Murcia. AGA-G 476.

13 1972. Memoria de gestión del Gobierno Civil de Castellón de la Plana. AGA-G 474.

14 Amando de Miguel (2003), *El final del franquismo: testimonio personal*. Marcial Pons, Madrid, pp. 358–9.

15 In this vein, one governor gave a very perceptive reading of the country's temperament when he wrote his 1972 report from Cadiz, where he explained: "The silent majority clearly tends towards modern Socialism which would balance social progress with a fair distribution of wealth [...]. This ideological tendency is easily adaptable to any regime or political system that could implement it." 1972. Memoria de gestión del Gobierno Civil de Cádiz. AGA-G 474. This opinion was not very far from the one expressed by the civil government of Huesca: "The mass of the population is mainly concerned with economic development and the consequent improvement of their living standards, an acceleration of the diminution of social inequalities [...] peace and order in the country [...] and the desired political evolution of the established order." 1962. Memoria de gestión del Gobierno Civil de Huesca. AGA-G 475.

16 For this process, see Víctor Pérez Díaz (1983), *The Return of Civic Society: The Emergence of Democratic Spain.* Cambridge University Press, Cambridge.

17 1962. Memoria de gestión del Gobierno Civil de Valencia. AGA-G 11331.

18 The coal produced here was becoming uncompetitive and was extracted only because of the protectionist nature of the Spanish economy. These structural problems were made worse by the recession caused by the 1959 Stabilization Plan and the steep increase in prices that followed, which was not paired with a hike in salaries. For an overview, see Ramón García Piñeiro (1990), *Los mineros asturianos bajo el franquismo, 1937–1962.* Fundación Primero de Mayo, Madrid.

19 1962. Memoria de gestión del Gobierno Civil de Álava. AGA-G 11324.

20 1968. Memoria de gestión del Gobierno Civil de Álava. AGA-G 480.

21 1972. Memoria de gestión del Gobierno Civil de Álava. AGA-G 473.

22 1962. Memoria de gestión del Gobierno Civil de Vizcaya. AGA-G 11331.

23 1968. Memoria de gestión del Gobierno Civil de Guipúzcoa. AGA-G 483.

24 1961. Memoria de gestión del Gobierno Civil de Barcelona. AGA-G 11323.

25 1972. Memoria de gestión del Gobierno Civil de Barcelona. AGA-G 473.

26 Rubén Vega García (1997), "Orígenes y desarrollo de Comisiones Obreras en Gijón: de La Camocha a la transición democrática." In: Trujillano and Gago (eds.) (1997), *IV Jornadas historia y fuentes orales,* pp. 207–15.

27 José Maria Maravall (1970), *El desarrollo económico de la clase obrera (un estudio de los conflictos obreros en España).* Ariel, Caracas and Barcelona, pp. 91–3.

28 Ibid., pp. 100–6.

29 For numerous examples of police reports on the population's attitudes, see Rubén Vega García (coord.) (2002), *Hay una luz en Asturias: las huelgas de 1962.* Fundación Juan Muñiz Zapico, Gijón, pp. 17–29.

30 David Ruiz (ed.), *Historia de las Comisiones Obreras (1958–1988).* Siglo XXI, Madrid.

31 Gregori Gallego i Marin (1996), *Els anònims de la transició: historia oral del moviment obrer a Lleida i a Balaguer (1960–1970).* Pagés, Lerida, pp. 21–53.

32 Ignasi Riera and José Botella (1976), *El Baix Llobregat: 15 años de luchas obreras*. Blume, Barcelona, p. 127.

33 Riera and Botella, *El Baix Llobregat*, pp. 21–35.

34 Ibid., pp. 37–56.

35 1968. Memoria de gestión del Gobierno Civil de Segovia. AGA-I 52-486.

36 1969. Memoria de gestión del Gobierno Civil de Badajoz. AGA-I 494.

37 1969. Memoria de gestión del Gobierno Civil de Valladolid. AGA-I 496.

38 1969. Memoria de gestión del Gobierno Civil de Huesca. AGA-I 52-491.

39 Political passivity was just not a Spanish phenomenon, particularly among women. According to Maurice Duverger, in the 1950s only 15 percent of women in France declared themselves to be interested in politics. Ruth Henig and Simon Henig (2000), *Women and Political Power: Europe since 1945*. Routledge, London and New York, pp. 14–15.

40 1968. Memoria de gestión del Gobierno Civil de León. AGA-I 52-485.

41 1969. Memoria de gestión del Gobierno Civil de Segovia. AGA-I 494.

42 1969. Memoria de gestión del Gobierno Civil de León. AGA-I 490.

43 1969. Memoria de gestión del Gobierno Civil de Zamora. AGA-I 495.

44 13-3-1949. Contestación al cuestionario presentado a la Delegación del SEU. AGA-P 240.

45 Both Falangists and others shared a common disdain for the growing power of Opus Dei in the universities. In 1950, after learning that the new professor of the history of law at Madrid University was a member of the order and suspecting foul play, a group of students caused a noisy scandal at his induction ceremony, where it was announced. "It seems that today, in order to be full professor you have to become a member of Opus Dei," reported a local chief of the Falangist student union. 10-1-1950. Sindicato Español Universitario. Jefatura Nacional. AGA-P 60.

46 For a personal account of this time, see Pablo Lizcano (1981), *La generación del 56: la universidad contra Franco*. Grilabo, Barcelona.

47 For many people this contradiction between discourse and practice appears to be at the root of their disenchantment with Falangism. See Marsal, *Pensar bajo el franquismo*.

48 10-1-1950. Sindicato Español Universitario. Jefatura Nacional. AGA-P 60.

49 26-11-1952. Secretaría General de Falange Española Tradicionalista y de las JONS. Secretaría Política. Secretaría Técnica. AGA-P 80.

50 José Maria Maravall (1978), *Dictadura y disentimiento político: obreros y estudiantes bajo el franquismo*. Alfaguara, Madrid, p. 166.

51 Many realized that "[the students'] symbols are no longer those of the National Movement" – this was the sentiment expressed in 1957, for example, in a confidential report by an official government think-tank on the universities of Madrid and Barcelona. Many knew that, on the contrary, student concerns had shifted to a focus on social issues and to the contrast between official

discourse and reality. "Their orientation is today toward rejection and existentialism, to the point of reaching occasionally real heterodoxies or an active declaration of Marxist faith." 19-6-1957. Instituto de Estudios Políticos. Nota sobre una acción coordinada para recuperar el ambiente de la Universidad. AGA-P 147 sp.

52 Miguel A. Ruiz Carnicer (1996), *El Sindicato Español Universitario (SEU): la socialización política de la juventud universitaria en el franquismo*. Siglo XXI, Madrid.

53 Aside from its own anemic student groups, the dictatorship's police had identi-fied at least 56 different independent groups that were active at the university that year, ranging from neo-Nazis to anarchists, but with a clear predominance of left-wing, Marxist organizations. This situation was a time-bomb waiting to go off, the police claimed, and was made even more dangerous by an impor-tant concentration of increasingly restive workers in the nation's capital. 1968. Memoria de gestión del Gobierno Civil de Madrid. AGA-I 52-485.

54 1968. Memoria de gestión del Gobierno Civil de Valladolid. AGA-I 52-487.

55 1968. Memoria de gestión del Gobierno Civil de Tenerife. AGA-I 52-488.

56 1968. Memoria de gestión del Gobierno Civil de Sevilla. AGA-I 52-487. In Murcia, a poor province of Spain at the time that had a university, not even students showed any sign of unrest. Furthermore, the authorities reported how, in 1968, the most important political event was "the homage to the three branches of the army." 1968. Memoria de gestión del Gobierno Civil de Murcia. AGA-I 52-488. For a detailed analysis of why and how 1968 was the key year for the University of Seville, see Juan Luis Rubio Mayoral (2005), *Disciplina y rebeldía: los estudiantes de la Universidad de Sevilla (1939–1970)*. Universidad de Sevilla, Seville, pp. 157–227.

57 1969. Memoria de gestión del Gobierno Civil de Salamanca. AGA-I 495.

58 1970. Memoria de gestión del Gobierno Civil de La Coruña. AGA-I 498.

59 1971. Memoria de gestión del Gobierno Civil de Granada. AGA-I 509.

60 1971. Memoria de gestión del Gobierno Civil de Cáceres. AGA-I 506.

61 1969. Memoria de gestión del Gobierno Civil de Córdoba. AGA-I 52-492.

62 1970. Memoria de gestión del Gobierno Civil de Salamanca. AGA-I 502.

63 1970. Memoria de gestión del Gobierno Civil de Zaragoza. AGA-I 498.

64 1970. Memoria de gestión del Gobierno Civil de Toledo. AGA-I 499.

65 "We must highlight that next to the support of Franco's person, the passivity and lack of interest in politics were the main aspect of the political situa-tion." 1970. Memoria de gestión del Gobierno Civil de Almería. AGA-I 487.

66 1970. Memoria de gestión del Gobierno Civil de Valencia. AGA-I 52-493.

67 1970. Memoria de gestión del Gobierno Civil de Granada. AGA-I 52-479.

68 For insight into the perspective of the riot police see Julián Delgado Aguado (1996), *Prietas las filas: recuerdos de un capitán de los grises*. Editorial Libros PM, Barcelona.

69   1970. Memoria de gestión del Gobierno Civil de Guipúzcoa. AGA-I 52-497.

70   Xavier Zumadle Romero (2004), *Mi lucha clandestina en ETA*. Status, Arrigorriaga, p. 69.

71   For this process, see Gregorio Morán Morán (1982), *Los españoles que dejaron de serlo*. Península, Barcelona.

72   See some examples in Julián Delgado Aguado (2005), *Los Grises: víctimas y verdugos del franquismo*. Temas de Hoy, Madrid, pp. 180–206.

73   Ibid., p. 200.

74   1968. Memoria de gestión del Gobierno Civil de Vizcaya. AGA-I 52-489.

75   These sets of opinions are exposed in the regime's internal reports. 23-8-1969. [Ministerio de Información y Turismo. Oficina de Enlace]. Impresiones obtenidas por la resignación de su Alteza Real Don Juan Carlos de Borbón como sucesor del Caudillo. AGA-C 673.

76   This, in turn, was the first step of what would become the infamous Trial 1001, in which sentences ranging from six to 20 years were handed down. Maravall, *Dictadura y disentimiento político*, pp. 62–3.

77   Antonio López Pina and Eduardo López Aranguren (1976), *La cultura política de la España de Franco*. Taurus, Madrid, p. 85.

78   For a more detailed analysis see Rafael López Pintor (1982), *La opinión publica española del franquismo a la democracia*. CIS, Madrid.

79   Ibid., p. 66.

80   Santos Juliá (1994), "Orígenes sociales de la democracia en España." *Ayer* 15, 165–88.

81   For the role of the elites, and in particular the reformers from within the regime, see Cristina Palomares (2007), "New Political Mentalities in the Tardofranquismo." In: Townson (ed.), *Spain Transformed*, pp. 118–39. For an international comparative perspective, see John Higley and Richard Gunther (eds.) (1992), *Elites and Democratic Consolidation in Latin America and Southern Europe*. Cambridge University Press, New York. For the process of democratization of the population after 1975, see Mariano Torcal (2007), "The Origins of Democratic Support in Post-Franco Spain: Learning to be a Democrat under Authoritarian Rule?" In: Townson (ed.), *Spain Transformed*, pp. 195–226. For a different perspective, see Pere Ysàs (2007), "¿Una sociedad pasiva? Actitudes, activismo y conflictividad social en el franquismo tardío." *Ayer* 68, 31–57.

82   For an account of how the cultural elites moved away from the regime to a clear opposition, see Shirley Mangini (1987), *Rojos y rebeldes: la cultura de la disidencia durante el franquismo*. Anthropos, Barcelona.

83   1974. Memoria de gestión del Gobierno Civil de Sevilla. AGA-I 11446.

84   Roberto Germán Fandiño Pérez (2003), *Historia del movimiento ciudadano e historia local: el ejemplo del barrio Yagüe en Logroño (1948–1975)*. Instituto de Estudios Riojanos, Logroño, pp. 101–14.

85   For a good local example, see Oscar José Martín García (2006), *Albacete en transición: el ayuntamiento y el cambio político, 1970–1979.* Instituto de Estudios Albacetense, Albacete, pp. 29–83.

86   I am indebted to Professor Pamela B. Radcliff for letting me use both her published and unpublished material for this part of the book. For more on the role of urban movements in transforming societies, see Manuel Castells (1986), *La ciudad y las masas: sociología de los movimientos urbanos.* Alianza, Madrid.

87   *Problemática de los barrios de Zaragoza.* Ayuntamiento de Zaragoza, Saragossa (1975).

88   Pamela Radcliff (2007), "Associations and the Social Origins of the Transition during the Late Franco Regime." In: Townson (ed.), *Spain Transformed*, pp. 140–62.

89   Francisco Morente Valero (2001), "Las luchas de los enseñantes públicos en la crisis del franquismo y la transición a al democracia (1970–83)." *Cuadernos republicanos* 46, 101–24.

90   1972. Ministerio de Información y Turismo. Tendencias conflictivas en cultura popular. AGA-C 580. This document includes a list of about 500 subversive artists which reads like a who's who of everybody who mattered in Spanish culture at the time.

91   Eduard Molner Closas (1997), "La crisis del Ateneo Colón del Poblenou. 1972–1973." In: Trujillano and Gago (eds.), *IV Jornadas historia y fuentes orales*, pp. 430–55.

92   In 1973 the governor of Segovia reported: "Examining the situation with objectivity, we understand that there are groups of people appearing who, pretending that their activities are religious, cultural or sporting, have an underlying political intention." These groups included protesting priests, the bishop, HOAC, and a small group of lawyers, teachers, and some industrialists, "brilliant individuals who [generated] opinions that are non-favorable for the regime." He might well have added, people who could read and who had lost their fear. 1973. Memoria de gestión del Gobierno Civil de Segovia. AGA-I 11440.

93   This meeting was received with perplexity and "disorientation" – "a lack of authority, discipline to the traditional discipline of the Church hierarchical organization" – by the conservative middle classes, but was met with only general indifference by most of the population. The latter were more worried about rising prices and lack of schools than about semi-public reflections on the role of the Church and the Civil War. Ministerio de Información y Turismo. Reservado. Informe provincial del 22 al 28 de septiembre. AGA-C 605.

94   June 1973. [Ministerio de Información y Turismo]. Reservado. Radiografía urgente del Episcopado español actual. AGA-C 560.

95   1969. Memoria de gestión del Gobierno Civil de Navarra. AGA-I 488.

96   1970. Memoria de gestión del Gobierno Civil de Álava. AGA-I 500.
97   1970. Memoria de gestión del Gobierno Civil de Vizcaya. AGA-I 500.
98   Ibid.
99   Javier Tusell (1993), *Carrero: la eminencia gris del régimen de Franco*. Temas de Hoy, Madrid. The day Carrero was killed, a macro-trial – known as Trial 1001 – of 10 leaders of the Workers' Commissions was due to begin. Although these leaders had absolutely no relationship to events, there were well-founded fears that they could be lynched by extremists. For a study of the killing of Carrero and its repercussions, see Equipo de Investigación de El País (1983), *Golpe mortal: asesinato de Carrero y agonía del franquismo*. El País, Madrid. A brief yet insightful introduction to ETA is Patxo Unzueta (1997), *El terrorismo: ETA y el problema vasco*. Destino, Barcelona.
100 1973. Memoria de gestión del Gobierno Civil de Guipúzcoa. AGA-I 11438.
101 1973. Memoria de gestión del Gobierno Civil de Álava. AGA-I 11436.
102 1973. Memoria de gestión del Gobierno Civil de Barcelona. AGA-I 11436.
103 1973. Memoria de gestión del Gobierno Civil de Oviedo. AGA-I 11439.
104 1973. Memoria de gestión del Gobierno Civil de La Coruña. AGA-I 11437.
105 1973. Memoria de gestión del Gobierno Civil de Sevilla. AGA-I 11440.
106 1973. Memoria de gestión del Gobierno Civil de Zaragoza. AGA-I 11440.
107 1973. Memoria de gestión del Gobierno Civil de Granada. AGA-I 11438.
108 1973. Memoria de gestión del Gobierno Civil de Málaga. AGA-I 11439.
109 1973. Memoria de gestión del Gobierno Civil de Alicante. AGA-I 11436.
110 1973. Memoria de gestión del Gobierno Civil de Cáceres. AGA-I 11437.
111 1973. Memoria de gestión del Gobierno Civil de Gerona. AGA-I 11438.
112 1973. Memoria de gestión del Gobierno Civil de Cuenca. AGA-I 11438.
113 1973. Memoria de gestión del Gobierno Civil de Orense. AGA-I 11439.
114 1973. Memoria de gestión del Gobierno Civil de León. AGA-I 11439.
115 1973. Memoria de gestión del Gobierno Civil de Teruel. AGA-I 11440.
116 For an analysis of the dynamic of this acceleration, see Álvaro Soto Carmona (dir.) (1994), *Clase obrera, conflicto laboral y representación sindical (evolución socio-laboral de Madrid 1939–1991)*. GPS, Madrid.
117 On the basis of the difference between the inflation rate and the delayed salary increases, from the period April 1970 to February 1975 the average worker gave to her or his company about 25,000 pesetas. At the time this amount represented approximately four months' pay for a specialized worker in the metal sector. José Iglesias Fernández (1975), *Precios, salarios e inflación en España*. Cuadernos Para el Diálogo, Madrid, pp. 15, 16, 24.
118 Ibid.
119 When put in terms of 'millions of hours lost' there had been a growing trend since 1968 that became massive after 1973 – 11 million in 1973, 18 million in 1974, 10 million in 1975, and 110 million in 1976! Workers had become convinced that striking was their best weapon. Most of the strikes were in older

industrial areas and in sectors such as metal, mining, textiles, construction, and chemistry, but they were also in service sectors such as education, banking, and health.

120   1974. Memoria de gestión del Gobierno Civil de Barcelona. AGA-I 11442.

121   Maravall, *Dictadura y disentimiento político*, p. 71.

122   1974. Memoria de gestión del Gobierno Civil de Madrid. AGA-I 11445.

123   1974. Memoria de gestión del Gobierno Civil de Granada. AGA-I 11444.

124   1974. Memoria de gestión del Gobierno Civil de Sevilla. AGA-I 11446.

125   1974. Memoria de gestión del Gobierno Civil de La Coruña. AGA-I 11443.

126   1974. Memoria de gestión del Gobierno Civil de Cáceres. AGA-I 11443.

127   1974. Memoria de gestión del Gobierno Civil de Cuenca. AGA-I 11444.

128   1974. Memoria de gestión del Gobierno Civil de Gerona. AGA-I 11444.

129   1974. Memoria de gestión del Gobierno Civil de Teruel. AGA-I 11446.

130   1974. Memoria de gestión del Gobierno Civil de Las Palmas. AGA-I 11445.

131   For the composition and psychology of the army, see Julio Busquets (1984), *El militar de carrera en España*. Ariel, Barcelona. See also José Antonio Olmeda Gómez (1988), *Las fuerzas armadas en el estado franquista*. El Arquero, Madrid.

132   1975. Memoria de gestión del Gobierno Civil de Almería. AGA-I 11447.

133   1975. Memoria de gestión del Gobierno Civil de Cuenca. AGA-I 11449.

134   1975. Memoria de gestión del Gobierno Civil de Las Palmas. AGA-I 11451.

135   1975. Memoria de gestión del Gobierno Civil de Zamora. AGA-I 11453.

136   1975. Memoria de gestión del Gobierno Civil de Guipúzcoa. AGA-I 11450.

137   López Pintor, *La opinión publica española*, p. 20.

138   1975. Memoria de gestión del Gobierno Civil de Gerona. AGA-I 11449.

139   1975. Memoria de gestión del Gobierno Civil de Orense. AGA-I 11451.

140   1975. Memoria de gestión del Gobierno Civil de Sevilla. AGA-I 11452.

141   López Pina and López Aranguren, *La cultura política de la España de Franco*, p. 109.

142   See Howard Penman and Eusebio Mujal-León (1985), *Spain at the Polls, 1977, 1979, and 1982: A Study of National Elections*. Duke University Press, Durham, NC. See also Richard Gunther et al. (1988), *Spain after Franco: the Making of a Competitive Party System*. University of California Press, Berkeley.

143   Encarna Nicolás Marín et al. (1998), "Actitudes de la sociedad murciana en la etapa 1936–1978." In: Trujillano and Domínguez (eds.), *V Jornadas historia y fuentes orales*, pp. 113–30.

144   Francisco Sevillano Calero (2000), *Ecos de papel: la opinión de los españoles en la época de Franco*. Biblioteca Nueva, Madrid, p. 206.

BIBLIOGRAPHY

Abella, Rafael (1985) *La vida cotidiana bajo el régimen de Franco*. Argos-Vergara, Barcelona.

Acción Católica (1943) *Jornadas de caridad*. Acción Católica, Saragossa.

Acción Católica (1943) *¿Quieres ser buena?* Acción Católica, Madrid.

Acción Católica (1951) *Problemas de la clase media*. Acción Católica, Madrid.

Acción Católica (1953) *Los problemas sociales del campo andaluz*. Acción Católica, Madrid.

Acción Católica (1958) *Cultivemos nuestra juventud*. Acción Católica, Barcelona.

Acevedes, Joseph (1971) *Social Change in a Spanish Village*. Schekman, Cambridge and London.

Aguilar Fernández, Paloma (2002) *Memory and Amnesia: The Role of the Spanish Civil War in the Transition*. Berghahn Books, New York.

Aldomar Gutiérrez, José (2006) *Condenado a muerte (1939–1941)*. Historia Social, Valencia.

Alfonsi, Adela (1999) "La recatolización de la moralidad sexual en la Málaga de posguerra." *Arenal* 6(2), 365–85.

Almodóvar, Miguel Ángel (2003) *El hambre en España: una historia de la alimentación*. Oberón, Madrid.

Alonso, Luis Enrique, and Conde, Fernando (1994) *Historia del consumo en España: una aproximación a sus orígenes y primer desarrollo*. Debate, Madrid.

Aly, Götz (2005) *Hitler's Beneficiaries: Plunder, Racial War, and the Nazi Welfare State*. Metropolitan Books, New York.

Anllo Vázquez, Juan (1966) *Estructura y problemas del campo español*. Cuadernos Para el Diálogo, Madrid.

Arias, Juan (1965) *Las cosas claras: los obreros*, 2 vols. El Perpetuo Socorro, Madrid.

Arrese, José Luis de (1982) *Una etapa constituyente*. Planeta, Barcelona.

Babiano Mora, José (1998) *Paternalismo industrial y disciplina fabril en España (1938–1958)*. Consejo Económico y Social, Madrid.

Babiano Mora, José (2002) "Emigración, identidad y vida asociativa: los Españoles en Francia de los años sesenta." *Hispania* 62(2), 211, 561–76.

Babiano Mora, José, and Fernández Asperilla, Ana (2002) *El fenómeno de la irregularidad en la emigración española de los años sesenta. Documentos de Trabajo. 3.* Fundación 1 de Mayo, Madrid.

Babiano Mora, José, and Fernández Asperilla, Ana (2003) "En las manos de los tratantes de seres humanos (notas sobre la emigración irregular durante el franquismo)." *Historia Contemporánea* 26, 35–56.

Bade, Klaus (2003) *Migration in European History.* Blackwell, Oxford.

Baget Herms, Josep Maria (1993) *Historia de la televisión en España, 1956–1975.* Feed-Back, Barcelona.

Balsebre, Armand (2002) *Historia de la radio en España*, vol. 2: *1939–1985.* Cátedra, Madrid.

Bandera, Joaquín, and Marinas, José Miguel (1996) *Palabra de pastor: historia oral de la trashumancia.* Universidad de León, Leon.

Benito del Pozo, Carmen (1993) *La clase obrera asturiana bajo el franquismo.* Siglo XXI, Madrid.

Blanco Piñán, Salvador (1964) *Los obreros ¿Son los culpables?* ZYX, Madrid.

Blasco Herranz, Inmaculada (1999) "Actitudes de las mujeres bajo el primer franquismo: la práctica del aborto en Zaragoza durante los años 40." *Arenal* 6(1), 165–80.

Borderías, Cristina, et al. (2003) "Los eslabones perdidos del sindicalismo democrático: la militancia femenina en las CCOO de Catalunya durante el franquismo." *Historia Contemporánea* 26, 161–206.

Bordes Roca, Pedro, et al. (1965) *Parroquia de Nuestra Señora de Fátima: estudio sociológico y planificación social.* Parroquia de Nuestra Señora de Fátima, Granollers.

Bosch Doménech, Antonio (ed.) (1998) *La desigualdad y la pobreza en España.* Instituto Ortega y Gasset, Madrid.

Boyd, Carolyn P. (1997) *Historia Patria: Politics, History and National Identity in Spain, 1875–1975.* Princeton University Press, Princeton.

Brassloff, Audrey (1998) *Religion and Politics in Spain: The Spanish Church in Transition, 1962–96.* Macmillan, Houndmills.

Burgos, Antonio (1972) *Andalucía, ¿tercer mundo?* Círculo de Lectores, Madrid.

Busquets, Juan (1998) *Veinte años de prisión: los anarquistas en las cárceles de Franco.* Fundación Anselmo Lorenzo, Madrid.

Busquets, Julio (1984) *El militar de carrera en España.* Ariel, Barcelona.

Callahan, William (2000) *The Catholic Church in Spain, 1875–1998.* Catholic University of America Press, Washington, DC.

Calvo-González, Óscar (2006) "Neither a Carrot nor a Stick: American Foreign Aid and Economic Policymaking in Spain during the 1950s." *Diplomatic History* 30(3), 409–38.

Cámara de Comercio de Bilbao (1945) *La economía vizcaína en 1944: principales estadísticas de producción, consumo y tráfico.* Cámara de Comercio, Bilbao.

Cámara Villar, Gregorio (1984) *Nacional-catolicismo y escuela: la socialización política del franquismo (1936–1951)*. Hesperia, Jaen.

Campo, Salustiano del, and Navarro, Manuel (1985) *Análisis sociológico de la familia española*. Ariel, Barcelona.

Camporesi, Valeria (1993) *Para grandes y chicos: un cine para los españoles*. Turfán, Madrid.

Canales Serrano, Antonio F. (2003) "Desarrollismo, inmigración y poder político local: el problema escolar en Barakaldo." *Historia Contemporánea* 26, 57–76.

Cañas, José Maria (1974) *Prostitución y sociedad*. Publicaciones Editoriales, Barcelona.

Candel, Francisco (1965) *Los otros catalanes*. Península, Madrid.

Candel, Francisco (1986) *Los otros catalanes veinte años después*. Plaza i Janés, Barcelona.

Canicio, Víctor (1972) *¡Contamos contigo! (Krónicas de la emigración)*. Laia, Barcelona.

Cáritas Diocesanas de Madrid (1967) *Informe sociológico sobre la situación de Madrid*. Cáritas Diocesanas de Madrid, Madrid.

Carreras, Albert, and Tafunell, Xavier (coord.) (2005) *Estadísticas históricas de España: siglos XIX y XX*. Fundación BBVA, Bilbao.

Casado, Demetrio (1967) *Perfiles del hambre*. Cuadernos Para el Diálogo, Madrid.

Casado, Demetrio (1970) *Plan Social Baza: una experiencia de desarrollo social*. Cáritas Española, Madrid.

Casado, Demetrio (1976) *La pobreza en la estructura social de España*. Ayuso, Madrid.

Casado, Demetrio (1994) *Sobre la pobreza en España, 1965–1994*. Hacer, Barcelona.

Casanova, Julián (2005) *La Iglesia de Franco*. Crítica, Barcelona.

Castells, Manuel (1986) *La ciudad y las masas: sociología de los movimientos urbanos*. Alianza, Madrid.

Castillo, Antonio, and Montero, Feliciano (coord.) (2003) *Franquismo y memoria popular: escrituras, voces y representaciones*. Siete Mares, Madrid.

Castro, Ángel, and Serrano, Margarita (1977) *La gran desbandada (curas secularizados)*. Cuadernos Para el Diálogo, Madrid.

Catalán, Jordi (1995) *La economía española y la Segunda Guerra Mundial*. Ariel, Barcelona.

Cayetano Rosado, Moisés (1977) *Maletas humanas (obreros emigrantes)*. D.L., Badajoz.

Cazorla Pérez, José (1973) *Estratificación social de España*. Cuadernos Para el Diálogo, Madrid.

Cazorla Sánchez, Antonio (1999) *Desarrollo sin reformistas: dictadura y campesinado en el nacimiento de una nueva sociedad en Almería, 1939–1975*. Instituto de Estudios Almerienses, Almeria.

Cazorla Sánchez, Antonio (1999) "Dictatorship from Below: Local Politics in the Making of the Francoist State, 1937–1948." *Journal of Modern History* 71(4), 882–901.

Cazorla Sánchez, Antonio (2000) *Las políticas de la victoria: la consolidación del Nuevo Estado Franquista, 1938–1953.* Marcial Pons, Madrid.

Cazorla Sánchez, Antonio (2002) "Surviving Franco's Peace: Spanish Popular Opinion during World War II." *European History Quarterly* 32(3), 391–411.

Cazorla Sánchez, Antonio (2005) "Beyond They Shall Not Pass: How the Experience of Violence Re-Shaped Political Values in Early Franco Spain." *Journal of Contemporary History* 40, 503–20.

Cazorla Sánchez, Antonio (2006) "At Peace with the Past: Explaining the Spanish Civil War in the Basque Country, Catalonia and Galicia." In: Noel Valis (ed.), *Teaching Representations of the Spanish Civil War.* Modern Languages Association, New York, 63–72.

Cazorla Sánchez, Antonio (2007) "Patria Mártir: los españoles, la nación y la guerra civil en el discurso ideológico del primer franquismo." In: Javier Moreno Luzón (ed.), *Construir España: nacionalismo español y procesos de nacionalización.* Centro de Estudios Políticos y Constitucionales, Madrid, 289–302.

Cebrián Villar, Mar (2001) "Las fuentes del crecimiento económico español, 1964–1973." *Revista de Historia Económica* 19, 277–300.

Cervera Gil, Javier (2000) *Madrid en guerra: la ciudad clandestina, 1936–1939.* Alianza, Madrid.

Clusa i Oriach, Joaquim (1967) *Estudio-informe de los barrios Can de Oriach, Plana del Pintor, Torrent del Capella.* Serracanta Copisteria, Sabadell.

Cobanelas Caamaño, Antonio (1939) *Los cuatro meses de la modelo.* Gráf. Administrativa, Madrid.

Cobo Romero, Francisco, and Ortega López, Teresa Maria (2003) "La protesta de sólo unos pocos: el débil y tardío surgimiento de la protesta laboral y la oposición democrática franquista en Andalucía Oriental, 1951–1976." *Historia Contemporánea* 26, 113–60.

Cobo Romero, Francisco, and Ortega López, Teresa Maria (2005) "No sólo Franco: la heterogeneidad de los apoyos sociales al régimen franquista y la composición de los poderes locales. Andalucía, 1936–1948." *Historia Social* 51, 49–72.

Colarizzi, Simona (1991) *L'opinione degli italiani sotto il regime, 1929–1943.* Laterza, Bari.

Colegio Oficial de Agentes de la Propiedad Inmobiliaria (1968) *El problema de la vivienda.* El Colegio, Barcelona.

Collier, George (1987) *Socialists of Rural Andalusia: Unacknowledged Revolutionaries of the Second Republic.* Stanford University Press, Stanford.

Collier, Jane C. (1997) *From Duty to Desire: Remaking Families in a Spanish Village.* Princeton University Press, Princeton.

Comín, Alfonso Carlos (1970) *Noticia de Andalucía.* Divulgación Universitaria, Madrid.

Comisaría del Plan de Desarrollo (1969) *Estudio económico y social de Extremadura.* Ministerio de Agricultura, Madrid.

Congreso de la Familia Española (1959) *Síntesis de ponencias provinciales en torno a la familia y la moralidad publica.* Ediciones del Congreso de la Familia Española, Madrid.

Congreso de Historia de Andalucía (1994) *Actas del III Congreso de Historia de Andalucía.* Cajasur, Cordoba.

Consejo Económico Sindical Provincial (1962) *Estructura y posibilidades del desarrollo económico de Almería.* Hispalense Industrial, Madrid.

Cruz, Rafael (2006) *En el nombre del pueblo: república, rebelión y guerra en la España de 1936.* Siglo XXI, Madrid.

Cueva Merino, Julio de la (1998) "Religious Persecution, Anticlerical Tradition, and Revolution." *Journal of Contemporary History* 33(3), 355–69.

Delgado Aguado, Julián (1996) *Prietas las filas: recuerdos de un capitán de los grises.* Editorial Libros PM, Barcelona.

Delgado Aguado, Julián (2005) *Los Grises: víctimas y verdugos del franquismo.* Temas de Hoy, Madrid.

Díaz-Plaja, Guillermo (1974), *La condición del emigrante: los trabajadores españoles en Europa.* Cuadernos Para el Diálogo, Madrid.

Díaz Sánchez, Pilar (2001) *El trabajo de las mujeres en el textil madrileño: racionalización industrial y experiencias de género (1959–1986).* Universidad de Málaga, Malaga.

Diez Nicolás, Juan (1973) "La mujer española y la planificación familiar." *Tauta* 8, 86–97.

Doménech Sampere, Xavier (2003) "La otra cara del milagro español: clase obrera y movimiento obrero en los años del desarrollismo." *Historia Contemporánea* 26, 91–112.

Duroux, Rose (2002) "La emigración a Francia (segunda mitad del siglo XX): unas reflexiones sobre retornos y reintegraciones." *Hispania* 62(2), 211, 577–96.

Equipo de Investigación de El País (1983) *Golpe mortal: asesinato de Carrero y agonía del franquismo.* El País, Madrid.

Escobar, Carlos Javier, and Herradón, Cesar (2003) *La herencia de la palabra: historia oral de El Carpio de Tajo.* Asociación Amigos de El Carpio, Toledo.

Escudero Andújar, Fuensanta (2000) *Lo cuentan como lo han vivido (república, guerra y represión en Murcia).* Universidad de Murcia, Murcia.

Estivill Pérez, Josep (1999) "La industria española del cine y el impacto de la obligatoriedad del doblaje en 1941." *Hispania* 59(2), 202, 677–91.

Estruch, Joan (1995) *Saints and Schemers: Opus Dei and its Paradoxes.* Oxford University Press, New York.

Fandiño Pérez, Roberto Germán (2003) *Historia del movimiento ciudadano e historia local: el ejemplo del barrio Yagüe en Logroño (1948–1975).* Instituto de Estudios Riojanos, Logroño.

Fernández, Fausto (1998) *Telebasura española*. Glènat, Barcelona.

Figes, Orlando (2007) *The Whisperers: Private Life in Stalin's Russia*. Metropolitan Books, New York.

Folguera, Pilar (1995) "La construcción de los cotidiano durante los primeros años del franquismo." *Ayer* 19, 165–87.

Folguera, Pilar, et al. (2003) *El mundo del trabajo en RENFE: historia oral de la infraestructura*. Fundación de los Ferrocarriles Españoles, Madrid.

Fonseca, José (1945) *El problema de la vivienda*. Gráficas Barragán, Madrid.

Foot, John (1999) "Television and the City: The Impact of Television in Milan, 1954–1960." *Contemporary European History* 9(3), 379–94.

Foreign Relations of the United States, vol. 4: *Western Europe* (1975). United States Printing Office, Washington, DC.

Fraser, Ronald (1979) *Blood of Spain: An Oral History of the Spanish Civil War*. Pantheon Books, New York.

Fraser, Ronald (1985) *Mijas: república, guerra, franquismo en un pueblo andaluz*. Antoni Bosch, Barcelona.

Frigolé Reixach, Juan (1982) "Estrategias matrimoniales e identidad sociocultural en la sociedad rural: llevarse a la novia y casarse en un pueblo de la Vega Alta del Segura." *Agricultura y Sociedad* 25, 71–109.

Gallego i Marin, Gregori (1996) *Els anònims de la transició: historia oral del moviment obrer a Lleida i a Balaguer (1960–1970)*. Pagés, Lerida.

García Barbancho, Alfonso (1979) *Disparidades regionales y ordenación del territorio*. Ariel, Barcelona.

García Barbancho, Alfonso (1982) *Población, empleo y paro*. Pirámide, Madrid.

García de Castro, Mario (2002) *La ficción televisiva popular: una evolución de las series de televisión en España*. Gedisa, Barcelona.

García-Nieto, Maria del Carmen (ed.) (1991) *La palabra de las mujeres: una propuesta didáctica para hacer historia (1931–1990)*. Editorial Popular, Madrid.

García Piñeiro, Ramón (1990) *Los mineros asturianos bajo el franquismo, 1937–1962*. Fundación Primero de Mayo, Madrid.

Gardiner, Juliet (2004) *Wartime Britain*. Headline, London.

Garrabou, Ramón, et al. (1986) *Historia agraria de la España contemporánea*, 3 vols. Crítica, Barcelona.

Gaviria, Mario (1974) *España a Go-Go: turismo charter y neocolonialismo del espacio*. Turner, Madrid.

Gibson, Ian (1973) *The Death of Lorca*. J. P. O'Hara, Chicago.

Gil Andrés, Carlos (2006) "Vecinos contra vecinos: la violencia en la retaguardia riojana durante la Guerra Civil." *Historia y Política* 16, 109–30.

Ginard i Feron, David (2002) "Las condiciones de vida durante el primer franquismo: el caso de las Islas Baleares." *Hispania* 62(3), 212, 1099–1128.

Ginzo, Juana (2004) *Mis días de radio: la España de los cincuenta a través de las ondas*. Temas de Hoy, Madrid.

Gómez Arboleda, Enrique, and del Campo, Salustiano (1959) *Para una sociología de la familia española*. Congreso de la Familia Española, Madrid.

González Madrid, Damián (2007) *Los hombres de la dictadura: personal político franquista en Castilla-La Mancha, 1939–1945*. Almud, Ciudad Real.

González-Rothvoss, Mariano (1949) *Los problemas actuales de la emigración española*. Instituto de Estudios Politicos, Madrid.

Goytisolo, Juan (1962) *La Chanca*. Librería Española, Paris.

Graham, Helen (2002) *The Spanish Republic at War, 1936–1939*. Cambridge University Press, Cambridge.

Grau Rebollo, Jorge (2002) *La familia en la pantalla: percepción social y representación audiovisual de etnomodelos procreativos en el cine y la televisión en España*. Septem, Oviedo.

Grazia, Victoria de (2005) *Irresistible Empire: America's Advance through Twentieth-Century Europe*. Harvard University Press, Cambridge, MA.

Guereña, Jean-Louis (2003) *La prostitución en la España contemporánea*. Marcial Pons, Madrid.

Guerra, Alfonso (2004) *Cuando el tiempo nos alcanza: memorias (1940–1982)*. Espasa-Calpe, Madrid.

Guerra Palmero, Ricardo A. (2001) "El mercado negro en Canarias durante el periodo del Mando Económico: una primera aproximación." *Revista de Historia Canaria* 183, 175–89.

Gunther, Richard, et al. (1988) *Spain after Franco: The Making of a Competitive Party System*. University of California Press, Berkeley.

Guzmán, Antonio, et al. (1955) *Causas y remedios del analfabetismo en España*. S.N., Madrid.

Henig, Ruth, and Henig, Simon (2000) *Women and Political Power: Europe since 1945*. Routledge, London and New York.

Higley, John, and Gunther, Richard (eds.) (1992) *Elites and Democratic Consolidation in Latin America and Southern Europe*. Cambridge University Press, New York.

Hobsbawm, Eric J. (1994) *Age of Extremes: The Short Twentieth Century, 1914–1991*. Penguin, London.

Hurtado Sánchez, José (1997) "Las cofradías de Sevilla y la política (1940–1991)." *Demófilo* 23, 77–91.

Iglesias Fernández, José (1975) *Precios, salarios e inflación en España*. Cuadernos Para el Diálogo, Madrid.

Iglesias de Ussel, Julio (1979) *El aborto: un estudio sociológico sobre el caso español*. CIS, Madrid.

Instituto Español de Emigración (1966) *Emigración a Suiza*. S.N., Madrid.

Instituto de Reinserción Social (1970) *La problemática de la marginalidad social en Barcelona*. Instituto de Reinserción Social, Barcelona.

Jansá, Fernando (1956) *El encadenado por Cristo*. Manuel Sintes Rotger, Mahon.

Jiménez Núñez, Alfredo (1987) *Biografía de un campesino andaluz: la historia oral como etnografía.* Universidad de Sevilla, Seville.

Judt, Tony (2005) *Postwar: A History of Europe since 1945.* Penguin, New York.

Juliá, Santos (1994) "Orígenes sociales de la democracia en España." *Ayer* 15, 165–88.

Juliá, Santos, et al. (1999) *Víctimas de la Guerra Civil.* Temas de Hoy, Madrid.

Juventud Obrera Cristiana (1983) *Identidad de la JOC: documentos básicos para la identidad de la JOC (Juventud Obrera Cristiana) en España.* Ediciones de ACE, Madrid.

Kaelble, Hartmut (ed.) (2004) *The European Way: European Societies in the 19th and 20th Centuries.* Berghahn Books, New York.

Kershaw, Ian (1985) *Popular Opinion and Political Dissent in the Third Reich: Bavaria 1933–1945.* Clarendon Press, Oxford.

Knapp, Vincent J. (1976) *Europe in the Era of Social Transformation 1700–Present.* Prentice Hall, Upper Saddle River, NJ.

Kynaston, David (2007) *Austerity Britain: 1945–1951.* Bloomsbury, London.

Lafuente, Isaías (1999) *Tiempos de hambre: viaje a la España de posguerra.* Temas de Hoy, Madrid.

Lafuente, Isaías (2002) *Esclavos por la patria: la explotación de los presos bajo el franquismo.* Temas de Hoy, Madrid.

Lazo, Alfonso (1997) *Retrato de fascismo rural en Sevilla.* Universidad de Sevilla, Seville.

Leal, José Luis, et al. (1975) *La agricultura en el desarrollo capitalista español, 1940–1970.* Siglo XXI, Madrid.

Lewis, Jane (1992) *Women in Britain since 1945: Women, Work and the State in the Post-War Years.* Basil Blackwell, Oxford.

Lizcano, Pablo (1981) *La generación del 56: la universidad contra Franco.* Grijalbo, Barcelona.

López García, Basilia (1995) *Aproximación a la historia de la HOAC, 1946–1981.* HOAC, Madrid.

López Ontiveros, Antonio (1974) *Emigración, propiedad y paisaje agrario en la Campiña de Córdoba.* Ariel, Barcelona.

López Pina, Antonio, and López Aranguren, Eduardo (1976) *La cultura política de la España de Franco.* Taurus, Madrid.

López Pintor, Rafael (1975) *Los españoles de los años 70: una versión sociológica.* Tecnos, Madrid.

López Pintor, Rafael (1982) *La opinión publica española del franquismo a la democracia.* CIS, Madrid.

Losada Málvarez, Juan Carlos (1990) *Ideología del ejercito franquista, 1939–1959.* Istmo, Madrid.

Luca de Tena, Esperanza (1961) *Deberes conyugales.* Nuevas Gráficas, Madrid.

Luca de Tena, Esperanza (1961) *Educación de hijos.* Nuevas Gráficas, Madrid.

Malefakis, Edward (1970) *Agrarian Reform and Peasant Revolution in Spain: Origins of the Civil War*. Yale University Press, New Haven.

Mangini, Shirley (1987) *Rojos y rebeldes: la cultura de la disidencia durante el franquismo*. Anthropos, Barcelona.

Maravall, José Maria (1970) *El desarrollo económico de la clase obrera (un estudio de los conflictos obreros en España)*. Ariel, Caracas and Barcelona.

Maravall, José Maria (1978) *Dictadura y disentimiento político: obreros y estudiantes bajo el franquismo*. Alfaguara, Madrid.

Marín Silvestre, Dolors (2002) *Clandestinos: el Maquis contra el franquismo, 1934–1975*. Plaza y Janés, Barcelona.

Marsal, Juan (1979) *Pensar bajo el franquismo*. Península, Barcelona.

Martí Gómez, José (1995) *La España del estraperlo*. Planeta, Barcelona.

Martín Gaite, Carmen (1994) *Los usos amorosos de la posguerra española*. Anagrama, Barcelona.

Martín García, Oscar José (2006) *Albacete en transición: el ayuntamiento y el cambio político, 1970–1979*. Instituto de Estudios Albacetenses, Albacete.

Martín Serrano, Manuel (1970) *Publicidad y sociedad de consumo en España*. Cuadernos para el Diálogo, Madrid.

Martínez, Jesús A. (coord.) (1999) *Historia de España siglo XX, 1939–1996*. Cátedra, Madrid.

Martínez Alier, Juan (1968) *La estabilidad del latifundismo: análisis de la interdependencia entre las relaciones de producción y la conciencia social en agricultura latifundista en la Campiña de Córdoba*. Ruedo Ibérico, Paris.

Mateos, Abdón (1997) *La denuncia del Sindicato Vertical: las relaciones entre España y la Organización Internacional del Trabajo*. Consejo Económico y Social, Madrid.

Mateos, Abdón (2003) "Vieja y nueva oposición obrera contra Franco." *Historia Contemporánea* 26, 77–89.

Mateos, Abdón (2005) *La contrarrevolución franquista: una aproximación a la represión contra UGT y al nacionalsindicalismo desde Cantabria rural, 1937–1953*. Historia del Presente, Madrid.

Mazower, Mark (1998) *Dark Continent: Europe's Twentieth Century*. Alfred A. Knopf, New York.

Miguel, Amando de (2003) *El final del franquismo: testimonio personal*. Marcial Pons, Madrid.

Miguez, Alberto, et al. (1970) *España: ¿Una sociedad de consumo?* Guadiana de Publicaciones, Madrid.

Ministerio de Agricultura. Servicio de Recuperación Agraria (1941?), *Memoria sobre la gestión realizada por este servicio desde su creación en mayo de 1938 hasta su extinción en diciembre de 1940*. Madrid.

Ministerio de Educación y Ciencia (1972) *Informe sobre la escolarización en enseñanza general básica*. Ministerio de Educación y Ciencia, Madrid.

Ministerio de Información y Turismo (1969) *La audiencia de televisión en España.* Ministerio de Información y Turismo, Madrid.

Ministerio de Justicia (1946) *The Red Domination in Spain: The General Causa.* Afrodisio Aguado, Madrid.

Ministerio de la Vivienda (1958) *Plan de urgencia social.* Gráfica Expres, Madrid.

Ministerio de la Vivienda (1969) *Absorción del chabolismo: teoría general y actuaciones españolas.* Ministerio de la Vivienda, Madrid.

Mir Cucó, Conxita (2000) *Vivir es sobrevivir: justicia, orden y marginación en la Cataluña rural de posguerra.* Milenio, Lerida.

Molinero, Carme (2005) *La captación de las masas: política social y propaganda en el régimen franquista.* Cátedra, Madrid.

Molinero, Carme, and Ysás, Pere (1998) *Productores disciplinados y minorías subversivas: clase obrera y conflictividad laboral en la España franquista.* Siglo XXI, Madrid.

Moradiellos, Enrique (2000) *La España de Franco (1939–1975): política y sociedad.* Síntesis, Madrid.

Morán Morán, Gregorio (1982) *Los españoles que dejaron de serlo.* Península, Barcelona.

Morcillo, Aurora G. (2000) *True Catholic Womanhood: Gender and Ideology in Franco's Spain.* Northern Illinois University Press, DeKalb.

Moreno Alonso, Manuel (1979) *Despoblamiento y emigración en la Sierra de Huelva.* Ayuntamiento de Aracena, Aracena.

Moreno Fonseret, Roque (1995) *La autarquía en Alicante (1939–1952): escasez de recursos y acumulación de beneficios.* Instituto Gil-Albert, Alicante.

Moreno Gómez, Francisco (1985) *La Guerra Civil en Córdoba (1936–1985).* Alpuerto, Madrid.

Moreno Mengíbar, Andrés, and Vázquez García, Francisco (2004) *Historia de la prostitución en Andalucía.* Fundación José Manuel Lara, Seville.

Morente Valero, Francisco (1997) *La depuración del magisterio nacional.* Ámbito, Valladolid.

Morente Valero, Francisco (2001) "Las luchas de los enseñantes públicos en la crisis del franquismo y la transición a al democracia (1970–1983)." *Cuadernos republicanos* 46, 101–24.

Muñoz Anatol, Jaime (1972) *La familia española migrante en Francia.* CSIC, Madrid.

Muñoz Roldán, Francisco (1995) *Mujeres públicas: historia de la prostitución en España.* Temas de Hoy, Madrid.

Narotzky, Susana, and Smith, Gavin (2002) "'Being Político' in Spain: An Ethnographic Account of Memories, Silences and Public Politics." *History and Memory* 14(1/2), 189–228.

Navarro Sandalinas, Ramón (1990) *La enseñanza primaria durante el franquismo (1936–1975).* PPU, Barcelona.

Nicolás Marín, Encarna, and Alted Vigil, Alicia (1999) *Disidencias en el franquismo (1939–1975)*. Diego Marín, Murcia.

Núñez Díaz-Balart, Mirta (2003) *Mujeres caídas: prostitutas legales y clandestinas en el franquismo*. Oberón, Madrid.

Olmeda Gómez, José Antonio (1988) *Las fuerzas armadas en el estado franquista*. El Arquero, Madrid.

Orduño Prada, Mónica (1996) *El auxilio social (1936–1940)*. ONCE, Madrid.

Ortega Cantero, Nicolás (1979) *Política agraria y colonización del espacio*. Ayuso, Madrid.

Ortiz Heras, Manuel (1992) *Las hermandades de labradores en el franquismo: Albacete 1943–1977*. Diputación de Albacete, Albacete.

Ortiz Heras, Manuel (1996) *Violencia política en el II República y el primer franquismo*. Siglo XXI, Madrid.

Pack, Sasha (2006) *Tourism and Dictatorship: Europe's Peaceful Invasion of Franco's Spain*. Palgrave, Houndmills.

Palacio, Manuel (2005) *Historia de la televisión en España*. Gedisa, Barcelona.

Pampols, Ramir, et al. (1987) *Curas obreros: entre la Iglesia y el Reino. Evaluación, perspectivas*. Cristianismo i Justicia, Barcelona.

Paris, Carlos (1974) *La universidad española actual: posibilidades y frustraciones*. Cuadernos Para el Diálogo, Madrid.

París Eguilaz, Higinio (1981) *50 años de economía española*. H. París, Madrid.

Patrimonio Nacional (1950) *The National Monument of the Santa Cruz del Valle de los Caídos (Tourist Guidebook)*. Patrimonio Nacional, Madrid.

Payne, Stanley (2006) *The Collapse of the Spanish Republic, 1933–1936: Origins of the Civil War*. Yale University Press, New Haven.

Payne, Stanley (2008) *Franco and Hitler: Spain, Germany, and World War II*. Yale University Press, New Haven.

Peinado Gracia, Maria Luisa (1985) *El consumo y la industria alimentaria en España: evolución, problemática y penetración del capital extranjero a partir de 1960*. Instituto de Estudios Agrarios, Pesqueros y Alimentarios, Madrid.

Peña, Maria del Pilar de la (1974) *La condición jurídica y social de la mujer*. Cuadernos Para el Diálogo, Madrid.

Penman, Howard, and Mujal-León, Eusebio (1985) *Spain at the Polls, 1977, 1979, and 1982: A Study of National Elections*. Duke University Press, Durham, NC.

Pérez Díaz, Víctor (1974) *Pueblos y clases sociales en el campo español*. Siglo XXI, Madrid.

Pérez Díaz, Víctor (1983) *The Return of Civic Society: The Emergence of Democratic Spain*. Cambridge University Press, Cambridge.

Pérez Díaz, Víctor (1991) *Structure and Change of Castilian Peasant Communities: A Sociological Inquiry into Rural Castile, 1550–1990*. Garland, New York and London.

Pérez Pérez, José Antonio (2004) *Los espejos de la memoria: historia oral de las mujeres de Basauri, 1937–2003*. Área de Igualdad, Basauri.

Pérez Urruti, Manuel (1942) *España en números: síntesis de la producción, consumo y comercio nacionales, 1940–1941*. M. Aguilar, Madrid.

Pildain Zapiain, Antonio (1964) *El turismo y las playas, las divisas y otros escándalos*. Gráf. Torres, San Sebastian.

Prados de la Escosura, Leandro (2003) *El progreso económico de España*. Fundación BBVA, Madrid.

Prados de la Escosura, Leandro, and Zamagni, Vera (eds.) (1995) *El desarrollo económico de la Europa del sur: España e Italia en perspectiva histórica*. Alianza, Madrid.

Preston, Paul (1993) *Franco: A Biography*. HarperCollins, London.

Prieto Sarro, Ignacio (1996) *Despoblación y despoblamiento en la provincia de León: 1950–1991*. Universidad de León, Leon.

Problemática de los barrios de Zaragoza (1975). Ayuntamiento de Zaragoza, Saragossa.

Richards, Michael (1998) *A Time of Silence: Civil War and the Culture of Repression in Franco's Spain, 1936–1945*. Cambridge University Press, New York.

Riera, Ignasi, and Botella, José (1976) *El Baix Llobregat: 15 años de luchas obreras*. Blume, Barcelona.

Rodrigo, Javier (2005) *Cautivos: campos de concentración en la España franquista, 1936–1947*. Crítica, Barcelona.

Rodríguez, Saturnino (1999) *NO-DO: catecismo social de una época*. Editorial Complutense, Madrid.

Rodríguez Barreira, Óscar J. (2008) *Migas con miedo: prácticas de resistencia al primer franquismo. Almería 1939–1953*. Universidad de Almería, Almeria.

Rodríguez de Lecea, Teresa (1995) "Mujer y pensamiento religioso en el franquismo." *Ayer* 17, 173–200.

Rodríguez Ocaña, Esteban (1998) "La construcción de la salud infantil: ciencia, medicina y educación en la transición sanitaria en España." *Historia Contemporánea* 18, 19–52.

Romano Serrano, Maria José (2005) *Llanos del Caudillo: memoria e historia oral de un pueblo de colonización agraria*. Ayuntamiento de Llanos del Caudillo, Ciudad Real.

Romeu Alfaro, Fernanda (1994) *Mujeres contra el franquismo*. SF Alfaro, no place given.

Royo Martínez, Miguel (1953) *La crisis de la vivienda*. EDELCE, Seville.

Rubio Mayoral, Juan Luis (2005) *Disciplina y rebeldía: los estudiantes de la Universidad de Sevilla (1939–1970)*. Universidad de Sevilla, Seville.

Ruiz, David (ed.) (1994) *Historia de las Comisiones Obreras (1958–1988)*. Siglo XXI, Madrid.

Ruiz, Julius (2005) "A Spanish Genocide? Reflections on the Francoist Repression after the Spanish Civil War." *Contemporary European History* 14(2), 171–91.

Ruiz Carnicer, Miguel A. (1996) *El Sindicato Español Universitario (SEU): la socialización política de la juventud universitaria en el franquismo*. Siglo XXI, Madrid.

Ruiz Franco, Maria del Rosario (2007) *¿Eternas menores? Las mujeres en el franquismo*. Biblioteca Nueva, Madrid.

Sabín, José Manuel (1996) *Prisión y muerte en la España de postguerra*. Anaya-Mario Muchnik, Madrid.

Sáez Marín, Juan (1988) *El Frente Juventudes: política de juventud en la España de postguerra (1937–1960)*. Siglo XXI, Madrid.

Salicrú Puigvert, Carlos (1944) *Cuestiones candentes acerca de la moralidad pública*. La Hormiga de Oro, Barcelona.

Salmon, Keith (1995) *The Modern Spanish Economy: Transformation and Integration into Europe*. Pinter, London and New York.

Sánchez Agustí, Ferrán (2003) *Espías, contrabando, maquis y evasión: la II Guerra Mundial en los Pirineos*. Milenio, Lerida.

Sánchez López, Rosario (1990) *Mujer española: una sombra de destino en lo universal*. Universidad de Murcia, Murcia.

Saz, Ismael, and Gómez Roda, Alberto (eds.) (1999) *El franquismo en Valencia: formas de vida y actitudes sociales en la posguerra*. Episteme, Valencia.

Seidman, Michael (2002) *Republic of Egos: A Social History of the Spanish Civil War*. University of Wisconsin Press, Madison.

Seisdedos Robles, Juan (1968) *Dos problemas graves de la economía de Zamora: la emigración y el paro encubierto*. Gabinete Técnico, Zamora.

Semanas Sociales de España (1954) *La crisis de la vivienda*. Secretariado de la Junta Nacional de Semanas Sociales, Madrid.

Sevilla-Guzmán, Eduardo (1979) *La evolución del campesinado en España*. Península, Barcelona.

Sevillano Calero, Francisco (1998) *Propaganda y medios de comunicación en el franquismo*. Universidad de Alicante, Alicante.

Sevillano Calero, Francisco (2000) *Ecos de papel: la opinión de los españoles en la época de Franco*. Biblioteca Nueva, Madrid.

Shaw, Duncan (1987) *Fútbol y franquismo*. Alianza Editorial, Madrid.

Shubert, Adrian (1987) *The Road to Revolution in Spain: The Coalminers of Asturias*. University of Illinois Press, Urbana.

Shubert, Adrian (1990) *A Social History of Spain*. Unwin Hyman, London.

Solé i Sabaté, Josep, and Villarroya, Joan (1994) *Cronologia de la repressió de la llengua i la cultura catalanes, 1936–1975*. Curial, Barcelona.

Soriano, Antonio (1989) *Éxodos: historia oral del exilio republicano en Francia, 1939–1945*. Crítica, Barcelona.

Soto Carmona, Álvaro (dir.) (1994) *Clase obrera, conflicto laboral y representación sindical (Evolución Socio-laboral de Madrid 1939–1991)*. GPS, Madrid.

Soto Carmona, Álvaro (2005) *¿Atado y bien atado? Institucionalización y crisis del franquismo*. Biblioteca Nueva, Madrid.

Taboada Arceo, Antonio (1969) *Galicia dormida ante el II Plan de Desarrollo Económico y Social: proposición abierta a quienes pueden y deben redimir a Galicia de su pobreza*. Cámara Oficial de Comercio, Corunna.

Tezanos, José Félix (1975) *Estructura de clases en la España actual*. Cuadernos Para el Diálogo, Madrid.

Tezanos, José Felix, et al. (1968) *El bachillerato ¿para qué? Encuesta-informe sobre problemas de la enseñanza media*. Cuadernos Para el Diálogo, Madrid.

Thomàs, Joan Maria (1999) *Lo que fue de la Falange*. Plaza y Janés, Barcelona.

Torres, Rafael (2002) *El amor en tiempos de Franco*. Oberón, Madrid.

Torres, Rafael (2006) *Víctimas de la victoria*. Oberón, Madrid.

Townson, Nigel (2000) *The Crisis of Democracy in Spain: Centrist Politics under the Second Republic*. Sussex Academic Press, Brighton.

Townson, Nigel (ed.) (2007) *Spain Transformed: The Late Franco Dictatorship, 1959–75*. Palgrave, Houndmills.

Trujillano, José Manuel, and Díaz Sánchez, Pilar (eds.) (1998) *V Jornadas historia y fuentes orales: testimonios orales y escritos. España 1936–1996*. Fundación Cultural Santa Teresa, Avila.

Trujillano, José Manuel, and Gago, José María (eds.) (1997) *IV Jornadas historia y fuentes orales: historia y memoria del franquismo*. Fundación Cultural Santa Teresa, Avila.

Trujillano Sánchez, José Manuel (ed.) (1993) *III Jornadas historia y fuentes orales: memoria y sociedad en la España contemporánea*. Fundación Cultural Santa Teresa, Avila.

Tusell, Javier (1993) *Carrero: la eminencia gris del régimen de Franco*. Temas de Hoy, Madrid.

Ugarte Tellería, Javier (1998) *La Nueva Covadonga Insurgente: orígenes sociales y culturales de la sublevación de 1936 en Navarra y el País Vasco*. Biblioteca Nueva, Madrid.

Unzueta, Patxo (1997) *El terrorismo: ETA y el problema vasco*. Destino, Barcelona.

Uría, Jorge (ed.) (2003) *La cultura popular en la España contemporánea*. Biblioteca Nueva, Madrid.

Van Epp Salazar, Margaret (1998) *"Si yo te dijera…": una historia oral de la Sierra de Huelva*. Fundación Machado, Seville.

Van der Zee, Henri A. (1982) *The Hunger Winter: Occupied Holland 1944–1945*. J. Norman & Hobhouse, London.

Vázquez, Jesús Maria (1958) *Así viven y mueren: problemas religiosos de un sector de Madrid*. Ope, Madrid.

Vázquez, Jesús Maria (1967) *Realidades socio-religiosas de España*. Editora Nacional, Madrid.

Vázquez de Prada, Mercedes (2003) "La oposición al régimen franquista en Barcelona: algunas muestras entre 1948 y 1951." *Hispania* 63(3), 215, 1057–78.

Vega García, Rubén (coord.) (2002) *Hay una luz en Asturias: las huelgas de 1962*. Fundación Juan Muñiz Zapico, Gijon.

Vicesecretaria de Obras Sindicales (1968) *El problema social de la vivienda*. Organización Sindical, Madrid.

Vinen, Richard (2000) *A History in Fragments: Europe in the Twentieth Century*. Little, Brown, London.

Vinyes, Ricard, Armengol, Montserrat, and Belis, Ricard (2003) *Los niños perdidos del franquismo*. De Bolsillo, Barcelona.

Ysàs, Pere (2007) "¿Una sociedad pasiva? Actitudes, activismo y conflictividad social en el franquismo tardío." *Ayer* 68, 31–57.

Zumadle Romero, Xavier (2004) *Mi lucha clandestina en ETA*. Status, Arrigorriaga.

INDEX